DR JESAIAH BEN-AHARON was born in Is his Ph.D. on the phenomenology of Edmur Haifa University. He is the co-founder of Gl folding (GN3: www.globenet3.org), Activists ιοr ιsraeιι Civil Society (ICS: www.civilsociety.co.il), and of a School for Spiritual Science (www.ybaschool.co.il). He is also a co-founder of Kibbutz Harduf (1980) where he lives with his wife Adira and their daughter and son.

By the same author:

The Spiritual Event of the Twentieth Century, An Imagination,
 The Occult Significance of the 12 Years 1933–45 in the Light of
 Spiritual Science
America's Global Responsibility, Individuation, Initiation and
 Threefolding

The New Experience of the Supersensible

The Anthroposophical Knowledge Drama of Our Time

Jesaiah Ben-Aharon

TEMPLE LODGE

Temple Lodge Publishing
Hillside House, The Square
Forest Row, East Sussex
RH18 5ES

www.templelodge.com

Published by Temple Lodge 1995
Second edition 2007
Reprinted 2014

A catalogue record for this book is available from the British Library

ISBN 978 1902636 84 9

Cover by Andrew Morgan. Inset: Rudolf Steiner's plasticine model for his sculpture 'The Representative of Humanity'. (Photograph by John Wilkes, reproduced by kind permission of Rudolf Steiner Press.)

Typeset by DP Photosetting, Aylesbury, Bucks.
Printed and bound by 4Edge Ltd., Essex

'Being held out into the nothing, as *Dasein* is ...
makes man a lieutenant of the nothing. We are so
finite that we cannot even bring ourselves originally
before the nothing through our own decision and
will. So profoundly does finitude entrench itself in
existence that our most proper and deepest
limitation refuses to yield to our freedom.'

(Martin Heidegger, 1929)

'It is comforting, however, and a source of profound
relief to think that man is only a recent invention, a
figure not yet two centuries old, a new wrinkle in our
knowledge, and that he will disappear again as soon
as that knowledge has discovered a new form. [...]
Then one can certainly wager that man would be
erased, like a face drawn in sand at the edge of the
sea.'

(Michel Foucault, 1966)

'*If this were all*, freedom would light up in the human
being for a single cosmic moment, but in the very
same moment the human being would dissolve
away ... We are here pointing to the abyss of
nothingness in human evolution which man must
cross when he becomes a free being. It is the working
of Michael and the Christ-impulse which makes it
possible for him to leap across the gulf.'

(Rudolf Steiner, January 1925)

Contents

Author's Note

This book assumes a basic knowledge of the modern spiritual science of Anthroposophy, as founded by Rudolf Steiner (1861–1925). This should be especially emphasized where use is made of concepts, names and expressions taken from the Christian heritage. These are used here strictly in the sense given them by Anthroposophy, according to the modern experience and research of the free spirit of the present times, i.e. as universal-human values belonging to humanity as a whole. Aside from any religious traditions, dogmas and differences, they spring from the spirit that strives to unite all religions and world-conceptions around the living core of the true being of free and spiritual humanity. The name 'Christ' is used here strictly in the sense of the spiritual, essential being of humanity as such, its 'Higher Self', uniting all human beings spiritually. This being is known by various names in different religions and cultures, but is not the possession of any of them.

Turning to the Living Spirit

(Modified translation of the original German interview of Dr Jesaiah Ben-Aharon by Thomas Stöckli at Christmas 2000, published in *Das Goetheanum* no. 7/2001, Dornach, Switzerland.)

Experiencing life together with the Other

Dr Jesaiah Ben-Aharon, in 1993 and 1995 you came out with two unique publications about supersensible research. As founder of the Harduf Anthroposophical Community in Israel in 1980, you are deeply engaged in social questions. What moves you at present?

In the summer of 2000 I returned from a two-year sabbatical in the USA. Since returning to Israel I have continued to be active in the main fields of activity in which I have been engaged now for some 30 years. On the one hand, I am working on a constant transformation and updating of anthroposophical work; on the other, I am trying again and again to deepen and expand my engagement with Israeli and global social reality. As always, I am constantly moving back and forth between the two.

In the anthroposophical work I shape my way of working in such a manner that it allows me to practise and experience what is thought, said and done in a living way. I do not want to add to the otherwise rather widespread intellectualism or traditionalism, but rather I wish to encourage other people and myself to find and realize our spiritual and human freedom and independence. This means that in meeting one another we strive together to take responsibility for shaping our coming together in a fully human way, be it in spiritual study and practice, in the arts, esoteric work or, above all, in any social context. I take seriously the fact that anthroposophy is a hundred years old and aging fast. The problem of how to make it young again, without compromising its seriousness and depth, is a very challenging one. People who have joined our work through the years are mostly pioneers seeking fresh ways of renewal, the resurrection and transformation of old to new, and the realization of wholly new impulses.

xi

This process of becoming young again is based on developing experience, knowledge and practices that support individual and institutional becoming. This means understanding and practising the events of initiation in the daily, cultural, social and historical life of the present time. Our task today is to deepen, enlarge, and transform anthroposophy through this human-becoming of initiation, an initiation that is in full swing in contemporary daily human life. The events and processes of everyday life are already an unconscious initiation, and anthroposophy can become a worthy part of this stream of becoming. Of course, you can only offer your living experience of this initiation if you dare consciously to undertake it in your own daily life.

I am truly enthusiastic about shaping each meeting as an experiment and experience in which it is possible to enter fully into what I call 'the event'. Any fixed and dead situation can be opened up and can become a place of resurrection and transformation of the individual, group and institution. In the other person I want to experience the real 'other' — the really unknown — and I want to enjoy what is fresh and unrecognized in her, the untraditional and unintellectualized meeting with the real world, its beings and events.

How do you experience the current situation in Israel?

The current situation here is the same as the general human situation, only more visible than in Europe. While Middle Europe is only slowly beginning to awaken from the post-traumatic coma of the Second World War, here everything is very awake and alive. Here too, if we want to live a truly human, social and spiritual life, we must consciously practise the awakening experience of meeting the other in yourself and dis-covering yourself through the other person. Confrontation with the other provokes deeper and more truthful self-knowledge of ourselves, and thus brings to light the highest and the lowest in us. This can work miracles. To ever again and again only reflect yourself and what you already know is not only the most boring and uncreative thing in the world, it also blocks the way to meeting the living present as an event, recognizing the future potential in the event and actualizing it. The future flows from the yet unknown world. Only in my 'wholly other' that becomes through me can I become anew, be resurrected and redeemed from my sleepiness, forgetfulness, and — socially speaking — irresponsibility.

What I do not yet know, let alone love, is my only salvation! Here too it is necessary, at least as a first step, to plunge courageously into real life. As long as the Israelis cannot bring themselves to meet the Palestinians as their real others, as long as they want to continue to play the modern western, highly unsocial and tragic game, they are destroying and will continue to destroy Israel and Palestine. They will meet only their doubles in endless conflict, because this is what happens if you avoid meeting your true self through the true other — you see only your double and you fight him, believing you are fighting 'the enemy'. Truly you are fighting only your lower, unrecognized self. This is called suicide, and this is what Europe committed itself to in the twentieth century. Can Israel avoid this fate? Can the Palestinians avoid it? Both will certainly not avoid it if they continue to meet in the way they have done to this day, through mutual destruction and suffering. In the end, after all the bloodshed, the other will still be there, waiting for acceptance, integration and appreciation.

The third spiritual-cultural sector: spiritual and social engagement in everyday life

Can you say something about yourself and your activities in Israel?

In 1980 I founded the anthroposophical community of Kibbutz Harduf as an integrated part of the Kibbutz movement. This was done because I wanted Anthroposophy to become a living stream inside Israeli society, not an exported, foreign element. The Kibbutz movement was then the best portal of entry, because it has been — and still is, though in a different way — an important social and spiritual movement in Israel since the beginning of the twentieth century. In Harduf we have prepared fertile human and spiritual soil that harbours all anthroposophical initiatives and institutions. It has become a true microcosm of all the various achievements of the anthroposophical movements in the course of the twentieth century.

It was, however, also clear to me in the 1980s and 1990s that both movements were getting old and tired: the Kibbutz movement *socially* and Anthroposophy *spiritually*. Both have to a certain extent at least lost much of their original significance for Israel and the world, because they neglected to update themselves socially and spiritually, and haven't sufficiently transformed themselves in the course of the last hundred years. I realized early on that we lack both an updated social as well as spiritual vision and strategy to offer the twenty-first century.

The most important social task for me today is to engage Anthroposophy not as a separated faction or sector but rather as part of our general society as a whole in living dialogue with everything else that is of real value. Therefore today I strive to develop what we call 'tri-sector' relationships and cooperation, as a new societal strategy. This means, for example, to try to engage the so-called third social sector in such tri-sector processes. This third sector is the cultural-spiritual sector, and it is the one in which Anthroposophy and its various institutions are rooted. I believe that a new anthroposophical movement will come to life in this manner, renewing itself in the process, while also renewing society as a whole. Anthroposophy can become socially relevant only if it is participating in such threefold social processes as part of a new global and local 'trialogue' between the economic, political and cultural-spiritual sectors. I am convinced that this is the only way through which new Michaelic impulses can flow into society in the twenty-first century.

Alongside my other duties I constantly work to support these initiatives by helping to create an effective network both globally and in Israel itself.*

For me this seems crucial for the future of the State of Israel no less than for the anthroposophical movement. The State of Israel has 'run out' morally and ideologically, and increasingly people in Israel awaken and seek new spiritual and social inspiration. Generating this power of inspiration, however, is much more difficult than organizing conferences, talking and writing books on social issues. In order to achieve even a modest beginning in the social field, Anthroposophy must become an active, powerful force for human-social transformation.

Could you say something about your family?

My parents immigrated to Palestine in the 1920s. My father, Yitzhak, was born near Chernivtsi, Bukovina (part of Romania between the World Wars, now in the Ukraine) and my mother, Miriam, came from Russia. Both were pioneers in the Israeli Kibbutz, Workers' and Labour movements. They co-founded Kibbutz Giva't H'aim (meaning 'Hill of Life') in 1933. I was born there in 1955 and so I grew up in this idealistically motivated socialist-humanistic-Zionist community of immigrants and refugees from almost all countries of the world, a true microcosm of Israeli society then and today. Its social, cultural and educational life was based on an atheist and socialist ideology. My mother was a teacher of art and literature, working all her life with youth and adult education. Both of my parents lived lives committed to the survival of the Jewish people and the State of Israel. My father's biography is an exemplary individual picture of the Jewish and human history of Europe and Israel in the course of the twentieth century as a whole (he lived from 1906 until 2006). He was the leader of the

---

* In this context a global social network for threefolding was created in 2000 together with Nicanor Perlas and many friends in various countries. This impulse found expression in a watershed conference in Gothenburg (Sweden) at the turn of the millennium 1999/2000. This 'Global Network for Threefolding', which went public on the occasion of the UN Millennium Summit in New York in September 2000, has grown since then and has groups and affiliations in many countries (see: www.globenet3.org).

'Histadrut', the Israeli head organization of the Workers' movement and unions, the Minister of Transportation in Ben-Gurion's last government, and a life-long member of the Knesset, the Israeli parliament. He was well known and appreciated in Israel by people with very different political and ideological views. Through my upbringing, therefore, I was always strongly connected to Israel's social and political life, to the destiny and vocation of this land and this country. Though he was far from being (in his conscious mind!) even close to anthroposophy, my father was always eager to hear as many lectures of mine as he could attend, and he supported the founding and development of Harduf and my engagement in Israeli social life with all his heart forces and energy!

The experience of the birth of a Spiritual Self

How did it happen that you put the experience of the Higher Self of Humanity (called Christ in Christian traditions) at the centre of your spiritual path, as you presented in your book The New Experience of the Supersensible*?*
  Can you describe how these spiritual experiences came about?

At the beginning of my twenty-first year of life I had a supersensible experience that transformed my entire life. In the years before, especially between 17 and 20, I was struggling to find meaning in life. I was, on the one hand, half-consciously certain that there must be a different dimension to life but, on the other hand, nothing in my surroundings seemed to suggest such a possibility. Though as a child I had been an eager and fast learning boy, I left school during the tenth grade because I had lost all interest in conventional, high school learning. In the course of these rather rich and adventurous years, I was gradually experiencing an existential youth crisis. At a certain point I actually remember telling myself: if there's no other meaning to life than this conventional and meaningless routine, I would rather die than grow up to be like that!

Can you describe this experience in some detail?

After some remarkable but unconscious preparatory soul- and life-experiences and processes, I felt one early evening during the spring of 1975 that the inner and outer walls surrounding and blocking my soul were beginning to crumble down. I felt that my entire soul was opening up and that a stream of unknown life of great beauty and intensity was flowing in and through me. It was a true revelation that continued off and on for a whole week. Even if I were to write dozens of books, I would not be able to describe what went on in and through me at this time. So I decided to write only one book ... But the central and continuous event can be described rather abstractly thus. I found myself living together in the company of a spiritual being and presence through which I was actually becoming my true Self. I was at one and the same time becoming myself, witnessing my becoming and participating consciously — though in a wholly different state of consciousness — in my own supersensible, spiritual becoming process. I became increasingly aware that this being was actually 'teaching' me something, a kind of special way of self-transformation and becoming. This becoming was at the same time cosmic, human, historical, and part of an infinite stream of life. He/she showed me what life was all about in this sense. It was the birth process of an identity as a Spiritual Self.

Many years of study and research were required in order to understand this mystery. He/she demonstrated it by taking my normal self into its living stream of infinite becoming. I experienced how my Self was being born out of supersensible, spiritual reality, how it is constantly transforming itself in this reality, and how it grows and changes in this stream of becoming.

It was my most real 'birthday' (actually 'birthweek') ever, because my real 'I' was born there. During this birth and becoming process I learned that the 'I' is a being of becoming, of transformation, of the mystery of 'die and become'. In this regard I feel myself today, as then, a newborn beginner, ever ready to start again to experience and research this mystery. And I know this will always be so, as long as I don't forget 'myself'.

And how would you characterize this Higher Self being?

It is a being of becoming and transformation. It can transform, resurrect, redeem everything and 'make everything new' — death into life, evil into good. The experience inspires the direct evidence and conviction that there is absolutely nothing outside of this becoming, healing, transforming stream and that if human life is indeed part of it — as in reality it is — it is able to transform human, social and even political reality. This transformation process must, however, also be understood as operating within time and history, maturing in us only gradually and through many difficulties, because it is such a new and unknown process.

And why did you later call this supersensible experience 'the knowledge drama of the Second Coming'?

Kindly consider that I experienced what I have just described without any previous concepts. I had no preconceived mental images to think in the normal way what I went through. The only texts that supported me during this week was a first-time reading from the Old and the New

Testaments, especially certain passages from the Prophets and Chapters 13–17 from the Gospel of St John. I was led to read these passages by the Being referred to in them. I could recognize the same Presence coming to meet me out of them as the One I experienced. This gave me the only mental hold and grounding that I had in order to grasp the otherwise purely supersensible experiences. The biblical passages and the purely spiritual experiences supported and complemented each other. Kindly consider also that before this event I never got to know these passages at all, because as I told you, I had been raised in a secular Israeli Kibbutz where all Jewish religious (as well as Christian) traditions had been omitted.

After the spiritual 'I'-birth described above, I lived in two separate realities: in the physical and in the spiritual. It was like living in one house on both of its two storeys at the same time, between which self-conscious bridges were not yet built. While being on the one floor, the memory of my identity on the other was indistinct. I had to build 'stairs' or a 'bridge' of consciousness and cognition in order to link my two 'Selves' together.

This bridge-building process was and is for me the knowledge drama as such, of Anthroposophy as such. And Anthroposophy is alive today if it also becomes a path of knowledge that creates real spiritual-scientific foundations for understanding the becoming process and deepening identification of humanity with its Higher Self. This is the true reality behind the often misunderstood and misused concept of the 'Second Coming' among Christians, the 'Messiah' among Jews, and the 'Imam Mahdi' among Muslims.

The actual knowledge drama process in my life began a year later, when, as part of my anthroposophical studies, I read Rudolf Steiner's book *The Philosophy of Freedom* for the first time. This was the second decisive life-transforming event for me. What was so striking was the fact that, for the first time, I could experience the same spiritual light, known to me until then only as the spirit light illuminating my spiritual experience, as part and parcel of my thinking activity. Then I knew what my spiritual task would be from that point on: to create a bridge from this thinking spiritual activity to the supersensible Higher Self experience. Obviously at that time I did not know that this would require more than 15 years of daily anthroposophical labour, research, obstacles, struggles and hard trials on so many levels of my life.

Through the intuitive activity of my thoughts that lit up in my soul I could for the first time in normal, daily consciousness develop, by means of my own spiritual activity, the same spiritual light that up to that point I had known only as supersensible light in another, supersensible state of consciousness. Now I was able to kindle it through my self-conscious activity in the physical world. From that point on, I could work alternately from each floor to the other, from both sides of the 'tunnel' towards each other, until I could bring the two ever closer. Finally, when I was 35 or 36, the supersensible bridge or tunnel construction work 'met in the middle' and the working parties from both sides could meet and celebrate the completion of the bridge. Only then could I think it through to the end and begin to write it down in physical words on physical paper.

This 'bridge-building work' is described in this book. This spiritual-scientific work enabled me to enter the supersensible realm independently and 'recapitulate' consciously what I experienced as a young man. This research work led me also to investigate some central supersensible problems of the history of the twentieth century that enabled me to show the power of transformation within the history of humanity as a whole. This is what I put down in my first little published book, *The Spiritual Event of the Twentieth Century* (Temple Lodge, London 1993, second edition 1997).

From spiritual experience to the path of knowledge

Can you characterize the method of your spiritual research?

It is important to abolish positivistic and materialistic notions of spiritual experience and spiritual research. One can never 'possess' them. A true spiritual experience is only present in its full actuality: in its living process of incarnating, becoming realized spirit presence in the living present, excarnating and disappearing. Otherwise, it is merely a shadowy and dead concept, an empty shell, a corpse of its true being. Also, one cannot wilfully 'command' the comings and goings of such experiences. It is always a grace and a gift, offered by the supersensible being that one meets. Such a being comes to meet one if *this being* so wishes, if this is part of the will of the spiritual worlds. The earthly-human participant can only strive to prepare a suitable, potential meeting place, to which he or she can humbly and joyfully invite the other, and then await the advent of the real spirit event.

I developed in the course of my research various ways to do this, differentiated according to the specific needs of my investigation or practical social work. For the moment it will suffice to indicate that only in the purity of actively created nothingness and in the purposefully established state of 'un-knowing' could I expect a renewal and recapitulation of true supersensible experience. I have to be very active and precise in order to create the 'immaculate' virginity that is the uncontaminated, non-intellectual place to which I may humbly invite the supersensible other. This is a strict scientific requirement if we are to be able to approach the spiritual.

Supersensible beings cannot be grasped by our brain-bound intellect because it is simply too coarse, too hardened, too proud and loveless. Of course we should strive to learn, to think, and to understand the world as deeply as we can. For the purpose of conducting spiritual research, however, we must, in freedom, free ourselves from this acquired knowledge. What is essential in learning is not the remembered sum of concepts preserved in memory, but rather the creative soul forces and faculties developed *through* the activity of study. The creative faculties developed through study cannot be retained in memory, but can be reactivated if memory is intentionally suppressed. No true supersensible event, process or being would come to meet me as long as I block its way by means of my already existing concepts and mental pictures, habits and routines.

If we develop our thinking in a living, creative way, giving up and forgetting its results, thinking will come back to us from *our spirit* outside. Because we freed it from our possession, because we have demonstrated our loyalty and love to its true being, selflessly releasing it from its bondage—in us—to Ahriman, the spirit being of thinking shows its thankfulness in a remarkable manner. While we lose it intentionally, it comes back from the world and finds us! That is to say, if we learn to hold back the finished, formed results contained in the intellect, we discover that we are richly rewarded: the supersensible may reappear fresh and alive, and at the same time fully irradiated and transparent with an inner light of cosmic thinking. This thinking that shines through our imaginations is 'our' cosmic thinking or, better, the revelation of the thinking of the Higher Self. In other words, the giving up of intellectualism allows true thinking to be resurrected as a supersensible cosmic-human, human-cosmic process. Truly modern and spiritually scientific imaginative perceptions and pictures are always 'thoughtful'. We don't have to supply them with external interpretations in order to understand them as living processes. They explain themselves much better than we would ever be able to do, and yet the light of thinking that illuminates them is our own freed and redeemed thinking. We feel our true Self active therein; it is a living immanence free from any transcendental residues of external spiritual or metaphysical elements.

For me this method became the foundation for developing research and creativity in spiritual science, art, and in social life, as I pointed out above. Anthroposophy may become in this manner a path and a method, in order to actualize the spiritual. No actualization of a real event is possible unless we learn to practise spirit-*remembering*, spirit-*faithfulness* (called spirit-*awareness* in the second verse of the Foundation Stone Meditation), and spirit-*beholding*, as stages of actualizing the etheric meeting with the Higher Self of humanity.

Through the moment of death to the powers of resurrection in thinking

Can you elaborate further on the 'die and become' process that you describe at length in your book?

In the short space of this interview it is hardly possible to give more than a couple of characteristic indications. First, I have to bring my soul-condition into a kind of 'threshold condition'. This happens through the transformation of thinking indicated above. I have to start at that point at which I actively experience how thinking dies in my everyday cognition. I actively seek and actualize *the time and place where thinking dies*. This sought-after 'cross' and 'tomb' of thought is a pictorial expression for this process of bringing to consciousness the sacrificial death process that the living being of thinking undergoes in order to become available for our daily, normal, modern cognition. Any so-called 'living thinking' that does not originate in this stage is but a luciferic self-enjoyment of sorts. For me, this is a sacred place of the knowledge drama of true spiritual science. I really have to learn how to 'put myself in this grave', in order to become inwardly identified with thinking's passion. In so doing, I gradually learn to love death as I would love a good teacher and helpful friend of the path — as paradoxically as this may sound. Death is my helper and teacher because it teaches me how to free myself from the unconscious — and hence given — thinking, feeling and will. For only out of death comes the resurrection of the spiritual soul, cognition, higher consciousness and new social capacities. Therefore not only do I avoid 'overcoming' death by any wilful act on my part, but I actually invite its presence and action. I experience death within the region of my own soul and life forces and learn to actualize it within myself and on myself. I learn to be active there, at the grave of cognition, wide awake, alert, and poised; I gratefully acknowledge and accept the death process of my soul and the tired, old, used, habitual self that it harbours. Death then is my helping master teacher and it shows me a way to the threshold that only it knows. Only there does the true, lucid, supersensible life begin to emerge.

And now one has to imagine that one awakens gradually at dusk, into the twilight between worlds, and increasingly draws near to one's 'night-being'. This being is indeed a being that dwells in another dimension of reality. This reality, in comparison with ours, is 'super-real', so intense and full of life and substance that our daily conscious-ness immediately fades away, sinking into deep unconscious sleep, when we encounter it. (This happens, after all, each night.) The living being of death is the only power that can transform the power of cog-nition and can awaken far deeper forces of awareness than we possess in ordinary consciousness. Now, because one has befriended death, one can intensify one's powers of wakefulness, while at the same time lowering somewhat the intensity of this 'super-reality' of the spiritual, and thereby consciously wake up *within* the abysmal depth of super-sensible reality. There one experiences a birth of one's Spiritual Self that, as Steiner put it, 'comes to meet you from the grey abyss of the spirit'. Yes, this place is indeed grey-black to begin with, if thought, discovered and explored consciously. Later it lights up and the great celebrations can begin. But the way there is difficult and somewhat hazardous.

Obviously, like in the earthly world, a newborn spirit baby needs grown-ups to tend for it, feed it, and serve as living examples of the faculties it has to develop as its matures. This is also the case in the supersensible realm. Thus, in the spiritual world we find the Higher Self, in its etheric (living, radiant) garment, as mother-father-midwife and teacher. As the 'firstborn' of all humans to achieve the ultimate goal of earthly evolution, this Higher Self being is the one who can best teach us what we are going to become. He/she is the great teacher of future becoming, and an expert master of the mysteries of the 'die and become' processes. In and through him/her, our newborn baby Spirit Self can safely learn to stand up and walk, talk, think and learn to experience and gradually come to regard itself as an independent 'I' in the midst of supersensible reality.

Now it will be our no less difficult task to learn how to bring together and bridge both sides of our two selves—the 'day-self' and the 'night-self'—to coordinate and link them into relations of mutual recognition, help and cooperation, because we want to realize a new cultural life, new communities, and a tri-sector social order on the earth as humans in the age of the consciousness soul. The Higher Self is the model of all true future community, and the centre around which already in the course of this age human beings will learn to come together in the spirit of true cooperation, love and freedom.

In search of the appropriate language of the spiritual

How can spiritual experiences and results of spiritual research be adequately communicated?

You touch here on one of the most painful wounds of a spiritual scientist! Spiritual research is a living, most dynamic, initiatory process. But then it must be communicated. If communication is done via living talk—dialogue—in a suitable soul atmosphere of true love and trust between humans, it is still possible to convey something of the true experience and reality involved. When it comes to the written text, however, things become difficult indeed. Texts, as Paul and Steiner said, kill the spirit. This is, of course, necessary, as I indicated above, because transforming death in our age is a prerequisite of wide-awake spiritual cognition. And, of course, writing is still necessary as a means of keeping records in memory. However, the written, dead word must be constantly resurrected, and this can only occur if social life becomes actualized as living event, in the intimate sharing of life experiences in dialogue. That which is most important can only be communicated from one human heart to another, and what is written should only function as a reminder: 'There, see, there's a new possibility for experience, dialogue, event. Now forget the book and begin to live the true life ...'

We are ripe enough today to be able to experience how inter-human dialogue in itself is already a spiritual reality. But we are still afraid to go to the place of uncovering our true voice, because we know that if this develops we may enter into true initiation processes and events. Many still fear this, although they may write or speak a great deal about it! I am actively engaged in the problem of how dialogue can become an essential life-giving element of spiritual research and the various applications of Anthroposophy in social and cultural life. In particular, my endeavours in the field of creating appropriate forms for the School of Spiritual Science have shown me again and again how far we are from the true community-building practices of the near future.

With what hopes are you looking to the future?

It became clear to me that since the beginning of the twenty-first century the new impulse of Michael relies on our being able consciously to unite the earthly form of Anthroposophy, as inherited physically from the last century, with the supersensible stream of Michael, which has gone through great transformations in the course of history since Steiner's death in early 1925. First of all, Anthroposophy will only become relevant for this wholly new century if and only if we learn to actualize living human and spiritual experience and research of the truly living event of becoming. Secondly, the new work can only spring to life via the periphery. Centralized organization is today absolutely ahrimanic. In smaller and greater connections, the updated, currently developing Michaelic spirituality of the time spirit Michael has sown the seeds of the future on the whole planet during the course of the twentieth century. As long as the 'centre' — all centres, starting from my small dictatorial ego — dominates social and spiritual life, Ahriman will continue to be satisfied with us, as he was so tragically during the course of the twentieth century. Resurrection forces, the harvest of the twenty-first, will grow and mature only through selfless, decentralized, global, 'peripheral', cosmopolitan and all-encompassing human capacities and institutions. This will be worthy of the second century of the Michaelic age.

This means, therefore, that many important ideas and many personalities from all corners of the earth and from unexpected cultural, social, national and economic peripheries will become 'central' bearers of true future impulses, and that we, the western-centrists, will have to listen to our own decentred selves if the calamity of western, Euro-American civilization of the twentieth century would not be repeated on a global scale in the twenty-first.

Let us be open, quick, humble, networked, very flexible and prompt with our esoteric faculties and our social and cultural institutions, because 'He comes as a thief in the night', and we are still fast asleep. Then we will have our hands full to integrate the re-enlivened Anthroposophy with the many strong, new social and spiritual forces that we can already meet in ourselves everywhere.

Preface

In the Preface to my first book, *The Spiritual Event of the Twentieth Century*, I indicated that its contents were a result of general research work made in connection with the theme of the modern Christ experience of the 'time picture' of the twentieth century as a whole. For the present book, I originally intended that this research work should be included in the eighth, and last, chapter, entitled: 'The Imaginative Life-Time Picture of the Twentieth Century'. Subsequently, I decided to omit Chapter 8 and devote to it a separate study to be published later.

This was done because I became increasingly aware of the fact that such a picture, though it seemed to be in its main outlines complete for the whole living time-flow of the twentieth century, contains at its highest, flowering time formation a still developing time-seed that indicates the new possibilities for the *next* century. This new seed was formed in the etheric world at the second third of the twentieth century through the Michaelic participation in the culmination of the second Mystery of Golgotha, described in the *The Spiritual Event of the Twentieth Century*. This seed has been gaining strength and vitality through the universal-human work done on the Earth by the Michael School in the last third of the century. And if it is understood and nourished in the right way in the human soul from the beginning of the next century, it might be ready for the new season of growth and spiritual maturity in the twenty-first century — the second, middle century of the present Michael age as a whole. This means that in order to investigate the *whole* time picture of this century, including its direct continuation into the next century, one must *wait* for the proper time conditions, available maybe only just at the threshold of the new millennium. These conditions might enable us to complete the spiritual-scientific research done hitherto in connection with the supersensible development of the Time Spirit of the twentieth century, in a way that will link organically the time picture of this century with the beginning and goals of the next.

Regarding the composition of the present book, the following should be pointed out. The reader will find an extensive and detailed 'Notes and References' section attached to the main body of the text. This part fulfils a fourfold function:

1

1 To show that the spiritual-scientific results presented in the book are all rooted in, and carried by, Rudolf Steiner's life-work *as a whole*. This is done for purely anthroposophical as well as scientific reasons: anthroposophically, because it must be demonstrated that Anthroposophy as such is the source of both the modern Christ experience and of its knowledge drama; scientifically, because the reader has the right to ask for concrete indications in the researches of Rudolf Steiner and his pupils that are relevant to the study presented.

2 To point out, at least provisionally, the general spiritual situation of humanity in the twentieth century, and some of its main knowledge-dramatic moments that run parallel with, and underline, the knowledge drama of the Second Coming. This is done especially in Chapter 5.

3 To 'open up' and 'break down' the 'margins' of the text and suggest diverse, manifold, 'unsystematic' and also contrary possibilities of interpretation, in order to preserve the potential and unformed substance of text in its original living flow, as far as writing allows that at all. Writing is the great (unavoidable, beneficial) enemy of supersensible experience and living spiritual-scientific research. The third aspect of the 'Notes and References' section of the book presents, therefore, a self-conscious, ironical (in the Goethean sense) effort to erase naive pretensions to completion and self-enclosure, and demonstrate the infinite diversity and unconquered plurality of the living spirit also in the bounds of the killing, written flesh.

4 This book was written in a way that tries to remain true to the experiential and experimental reality at its basis. Therefore, I believe it can be read without taking any note of the 'Notes' and without referring to the 'References' and, eventually, the reader might experience the whole as a self-sustaining reality existing outside of any text, including the one in which it is 'written'.

J. Ben-Aharon
Harduf, Israel
Summer 1994

Introduction

I — Methodological Approach

Rudolf Steiner repeatedly pointed out that the greatest spiritual event of this century is the etheric appearance of the Christ, whose experience and perception will be the outcome of the natural development of new, conscious, supersensible faculties of perception. The modern 'Damascus Experience' will be, for the first time in the evolution of human consciousness, *a naturally given initiation*. Those human beings who undergo this initiation 'will not require documentary evidence in order to recognize Christ, but they will have direct knowledge as is today possessed only by the initiates'. This development is a result of the inner law that underlies the spiritual evolution of human consciousness. This law states that 'all the faculties that today can be acquired only by means of initiation will in the future be universal faculties of humanity. This condition of soul, this experiencing of soul, is called in esotericism the "Second Coming of Christ".'[1]

We hear today from many sides about true and significant Christ experiences. When we study these experiences we might be deeply impressed by their truth and beauty, and we can share — if we open ourselves honestly to them — their healing, refreshing, graceful Life Spirit. In a real sense we become true anthroposophical participants in the spirit of our time only if we find our way to a deep understanding and appreciation of such experiences. In the last years there is growing evidence for an increased anthroposophical interest in this field. Valuable materials and diverse points of view concerning the different questions that arise through the anthroposophical study of such experiences are to be found in the volumes of the 'Das Ätherische Christus-Wirken' series.[2] Our own methical approach will be *described* in Part I of this Introduction and will be *demonstrated* in Part II which follows.

Since the Mystery of Golgotha, the Christ has lived inside the earthly sphere and is unceasingly active therein. But during the greater part of this period humanity was still in the epoch of the mind (or intellectual) soul, or in its after-effects. Its approach to the Christ was conditioned by this fact, and was based mainly on the religious and mystical paths of the

3

Middle Ages. Thinking, as well as self-conscious supersensible experience and research, had to humbly retire before such direct knowledge, and in the age of the mind soul this was done for entirely necessary and justified reasons. However, in the age of the consciousness soul, and especially since the beginning of the new Michael age and the new age of light, Christ's being and activity can for the first time become the goal of fully individualized human experience and research. Anthroposophy is precisely this: the fully free human knowledge of a thoroughly Christ-permeated and transformed universe, nature, and human evolution and history.[3]

The more the epoch of the consciousness soul develops and the more it emerges out of the intellectual residues of its immediate past, the more this soul will be recognized in its true nature. And its *true* nature is indeed already highly spiritual. But *spiritual* means sovereign, creative and active, inwardly aflame with the fire of love and enthusiasm for the mysteries of the world and of man, and thoroughly irradiated and penetrated with the forces of clear, precise and living thinking and Imagination.[4] It experiences any passivity, givenness and obscurity only as the resistance on which it can unfold and strengthen its independent cognitive and moral forces. These characteristics of the consciousness soul, if they are truly developed, are those that enable it to come to grips with the new, naturally developing faculties of supersensible perception, which bring about the modern Christ experience as a natural initiation event, because it finds in this event an infinite source of possibilities for the future strengthening and spiritualizing of its innate spirit forces.

The meeting with the Christ described in Chapter 4 combines in *one* event two aspects of human reality that are separated from each other in ordinary consciousness: the usually unconscious reality of the spiritual world and the experience of awakened self-consciousness. *Supersensible self-consciousness is the new self-situation and self-reality constituted in this experience.* That is, in this meeting, an objective supersensible reality is experienced as the formative force of human self-consciousness that, until now, was capable of individualizing itself in the physical world alone. Therefore, this meeting can become, by means of the spiritual-scientific method, an object of an independent, ongoing development and conscious spiritual research. We can conceive the essence of this meeting as an initiation process in the following way.

In the perceived world a Being appears — the only one of its kind in our world — through whose etheric appearance process the totality of the Idea, the divine archetype of man, can be directly experienced. Man, who participated actively in this world-forming process, knows this form of the Idea to be his own human-cosmic Self. What otherwise is possible only in the sphere of intuitive thinking — the self-transforming

4

self-meeting through self-perception, in the self-realization process of the simultaneous inner creation and perceiving of pure ideas—is experienced here in an objective-supersensible way, in the consciousness soul's self-conscious participation in Christ's etheric appearance. This means that through self-conscious imaginative perception man sees and experiences in this initiatory meeting his *own* ideal spirit, being and becoming as it comes to meet him from without. In this naturally given initiation, man receives his deepest inwardness as it flows towards him from the objective reaches of the world periphery; his truest and most intimate Self comes to meet him from the farthest, infinite horizon of his world existence, in and through the cosmic-human being of the etheric Christ.

This event can become the greatest possible call for free development of the inner spiritual activity of the consciousness soul, because man learns in the experience to recognize *himself* ever more in his true nature. The profoundest impulses of will and knowledge are ignited, spurring him to ever-deepening self-knowledge, because he realizes that this meeting is in truth the beginning of an infinite *self*-meeting, revealing the heights and depths of the forming process of human nature from the remotest past to the farthest future.

From an anthroposophical, spiritual-scientific point of view, every experience, be it sensible or supersensible, is a *given* and therefore, as such, an *external* fact. So long as it is not thoroughly penetrated and transformed by the active and independent cognitive thinking and imagining forces of the consciousness soul, it remains a personal, subjective event that, notwithstanding its personal value, cannot become *in this form* a matter of scientific study. For spiritual science, therefore, such an experience must first become an object of anthroposophical research. This means that a mutual relation must be established between the spiritual-scientific activity and the Christ experience it investigates. This constitutes the life-question and task of the knowledge drama of the Second Coming. On the one hand, it has to ever again re-present and so re-member this experience in reflective and discursive thinking. That is, it has to despiritualize it in order to bring it down to ordinary consciousness. On the other hand, it has to use the inner forces of this experience in order to continually spiritualize the spiritual-scientific activity and so transform it into a fully modern and living path of anthroposophical initiation. The weaving together of the opposite, mutually complementary and enhancing movements of the despiritualizing of the modern Christ experience and the spiritualizing of spiritual scientific activity is the centre of the Michael-Christ event of the present Michael age in the beginning of the new cosmic age of light.

It is, therefore, the nature of the unique spiritual situation of the human soul itself at the threshold of the twentieth and twenty-first centuries that determines not only the content of the present book but, above all, its form. The nature of the common Christ experiences consists in the personal salvation of the single human soul. Such an event is a fully justified end in and for itself. As was mentioned above, Rudolf Steiner characterized this experience also as a natural initiation through which man will have a direct knowledge of what until today only the initiate knew. But from the anthroposophical point of view this natural initiation *fact* can have a further significance, namely, by becoming a starting point for anthroposophical initiation *science*. This requires the development of a suitable method, the aim of which will be to transform the naturally given initiation experience into a fully individualized spiritual-scientific experience and knowledge.

Rudolf Steiner's spiritual-scientific investigations have shown that in St Paul's experience at the gates of Damascus these two aspects came together for the first time in human evolution. Paul's experience was a naturally given Christ event, but he was also an 'initiate of the old Cabala'[5] prior to this experience. In his case a naturally given initiation experience merged with old initiation knowledge, and his life task was to form out of the two the higher and new synthesis of the Christian path of initiation. This synthesis was his new spiritual creation. That is, the Pauline, consciously investigated Christ experience is the *Ur**-example of the self-conscious and free, active mutual reversal of the naturally given Christ initiation and the knowledge of Christ by means of modern anthroposophical initiation science.

In the twenty-first century Anthroposophy will increasingly become, in the course of its natural evolution, an expression of the flowing together of a growing number of individualized spiritual-scientific paths. Accordingly, the aim of the research presented here is to offer an *intrinsically and essentially incomplete, purposefully experiential and experimentally open example* of such an individual anthroposophical path. In order to prepare its presentation, however, I will first describe the spiritual-scientific method of research which underlies it. This description can be introduced through the following consideration.

Our problem is obviously not that the Christ Being and the being of Anthroposophia are separated in the realm of eternal being. In the macrocosmic connections the two stand in the closest, deepest connection with each other.[6] Our first problem is the limitation of *our* conscious understanding of this connection. But the first step on the way that leads to the lofty realms of their eternal union is taken only if we begin ever anew our anthroposophical spiritual-scientific work with the living experience of the fact that *for us* they are *not* yet at all united. That is, our immediate task cannot be to discover an already existing spiritual reality

* Editor's note: The German word *Ur*, meaning 'primordial', is used throughout the text.

6

that exists independently of us. Rather, we have to *create*, in the world-corner that depends exclusively on our cognitive and moral creativity, a new, *humanly* established mutual relationship between them — in man's being and in the being of the world that man creates out of his transformed being.[7]

The primordial world-connection between the being of Anthroposophia and the being of the Christ must indeed be eventually discovered. But this discovery is made possible through the realization that, as far as the man-world creation is concerned, this connection must first be *originally* created.[8]

The realm where the being of both is primordially interwoven — where they are, were and always shall be mutually interpenetrated — is not *given* to us, neither in Anthroposophy as such (that is, in the form that it assumes through our intellectual understanding on the physical plane) nor in the Christ experience as such (in its given, supersensible form). In the case of the first we have, to begin with, only its despiritualized mental representation in ordinary earthly consciousness. In the second we have a given supersensible experience, that occurs above the earthly faculty of ordinary remembered representation. Both must, therefore, undergo a mutually reversed transformation before their unity can be created anew as the foundation of the *future* universe.[9]

Now the question concerning our method must naturally arise: how is this mutual reversal to be carried through? Conceptually expressed, the answer is: we must transform the highest intensity of thought and knowledge experienced in the practice of *The Philosophy of Freedom* into the form of a *living inner archetype* of this method. What is freely created in the intuitive act of knowledge as the process of self-realization of man's true Spirit Self can become a living, knowledge-creating organ, through which the two opposite spirit movements can reverse each other in — and into — each other interchangeably. The creative activity of pure thinking *spiritualizes* the spiritual-scientific knowledge-process and *condenses* the naturally given imaginative perception and thus brings about a mutually transforming perception and knowledge of the supersensible through thinking and thinking through the supersensible. It weaves dynamically the doubled, two-way etheric bridge of consciousness's continuation and remembrance over the abyss of spirit forgetfulness, in the darkness of which the living spirit reality of our age is obscured and forgotten by humanity.

Pictorially expressed, the answer to the question of method is: the given appearances of Anthroposophy and the Etheric Christ are transformed by means of the crossing and the mutual penetration of the two appearances by means of the growing knowledge of the essence of the other. The goal is to achieve a systematically increased intensification and acceleration of the rhythmic sway between the poles of their given appearances, so that an active and cognitive spiritual heart organ is formed through their mutually reversed breathing movement. In this dynamically cognizing heart organ their enhanced life in each other reveals, through its inner conscious pulsation, the secret of their being and becoming in man: the living Christ in and through the Being of Anthroposophia, and the living Being of Anthroposophia in and through the Christ. Behind both appearances we have to unveil the veiled secret: *the reality of world-man in the man-created, Christ-permeated world – man as the Christ-permeated, consciousness soul's child of Anthropos-Sophia, bearing and nourishing the future earthly-human Sun in his heart.*[10]

As was indicated above, this method already exists. In its earliest form, it was first developed by St Paul from his Christ experience at the gates of Damascus. And it was brought to its greatest perfection for the age of the consciousness soul in the anthroposophical spiritual-scientific research of Rudolf Steiner. We shall bring before us now the origin and essence of the 'Pauline method'[11] as described by Rudolf Steiner's anthroposophical investigations.

The first problem encountered by Paul as a result of his natural Christ initiation was the question about the true nature of human thinking:

> So Paul came to realize that an enemy attacked human evolution, and that this enemy is the source of error on the Earth ... Only in a world in which the human being could be influenced by the ahrimanic forces – so Paul now felt – could the error occur that led to the death on the cross. And now, when he understood this, he realized for the first time the truth of esoteric Christianity. *The assimilation of death into life: this is the secret of Golgotha.* Previously man knew life without death; now he learned to know death as part of life, as an experience that strengthens life ... Humanity must strengthen its life, if it wants to pass through death and yet live. And death means, in this connection ... the intellect ... the intellect makes us inwardly cold, makes us inwardly dead. The intellect paralyses us. Man must truly feel it, that man lives not when man thinks; that man wastes his life in dead mental pictures, and that man must have strong life in himself in order to feel creative life in the dead mental pictures ... This I tried to do in my *Philosophy of Freedom*. This *Philosophy of Freedom* is in reality a moral conception that should be a preparation for the vitalization of dead thinking through moral impulse, in order to bring it to resurrection.[12]

And further:

> What Paul meant by the resurrected Christ was that the Christ experienced death, but that he overcame death, that he as spiritual-living triumphant being came forth out of death in the resurrection and that He lives since then with humanity, that without Christ man

8

would have had only dead thinking ... Whereas before, in former times, thinking still carried its living essence into earthly life, since the third and fourth centuries ... the earthly human soul can awaken its thinking through the direct beholding of the Mystery of Golgotha.[13]

Paul faced the same problem not only in connection with the riddle of thinking but also in connection with the riddle of sense-perception. This was described by Rudolf Steiner as follows:

The oriental religious doctrine blames the 'gods' for the fact that man sees the world as maya. 'Beat your breast' — says Paul. 'You came down [to the Earth through the fall from Paradise] and corrupted your senses to such an extent that colour and sound do not really appear as spiritual to you. Thou believest that colour and sound are there as something material. This is maya! You yourself made it into maya. You, man, you must first release yourself again from this ... And you can do this if you take the power of Christ into you, which will show you the outer world in its reality!'
    In my two books *Truth and Knowledge* and *The Philosophy of Freedom* it was my purpose to base the theory of knowledge on this Pauline foundation. These two books are focused on what is the great achievement of the Pauline conception of man in the western world. That is why these books are so little understood ... because they presuppose the whole impulse that found its expression in the movement of spiritual science. *In the smallest must be seen the greatest!*[14]

The same was summarized again by Rudolf Steiner as follows:

I must call these thoughts on epistemology Pauline for the following reason: that the world in the first form of its appearance to the senses seems to us unreal, and that our subjective activity converts it into reality. The Pauline theory of knowledge, when taken into the philosophical realm, is nothing else than that man, on entering the world as the first Adam, experienced it only partially and, through Christ, experienced the whole of reality. Christianity can afford to wait for philosophy and the theory of knowledge to deal with it.[15]

So we see: the Pauline, first modern Christ experience leads from the direct Imagination of the etheric Christ to the quest for a method by means of which the spiritualization of objective, fallen, earthly thinking and sense-perception can be carried out. And vice versa, this spiritualization of earthly consciousness, if successfully practised, strives to condense the conscious exploration of the etheric appearance of the Christ. *A free life cycle, a conscious breathing in spiritual-soul rhythm is thus created*, oscillating between the given etheric sight of the Christ and the conscious cognitive anthroposophical activity. The more man 'breathes in', individualizes

9

and despiritualizes the modern Christ experience, the stronger and farther expands the 'outbreathing' to the anthroposophically illuminated spiritual worlds. The two life-streams flow parallel with each other until they increasingly cross each other the nearer they draw to their common infinite horizon: the one stream in which, with the help of the forces of the etheric Christ, man spiritualizes thinking and sense-perception inwardly and lifts them into higher states of consciousness; and the other in which his free anthroposophical activity transforms his original Christ experience and brings it down to the state of full human knowledge. So that increasingly 'having an experience of the Christ' and 'developing free anthroposophical activity' become an expression of the *one* pulse of life of individual man in the age of the consciousness soul.

We can now describe the Pauline method with its new name: it is the thorough spiritualization of the consciousness soul by means of *the new Michaelic yoga practice* described by Rudolf Steiner for the first time in the 1919 lecture cycle on the mission of Michael, exactly 40 years after the beginning of the new Michael age.[16] A year later it was developed further as an elaborated Goetheanistic and spiritual-scientific method in the first lecture cycle of the School of Spiritual Science at the not yet completed First Goetheanum. There we find the following description of the new Michaelic yoga method:

> Pure thinking is related to exhalation just as perception is related to inhalation ... by bringing mobility into the life of the soul, one experiences the pendulum, the rhythm, the continual interpenetrating vibration of perception and thinking ... the Westerner achieves a kind of breathing of the soul-spirit in place of the physical breathing of the yogi ... And gradually, by means of this rhythmic pulse, by means of this rhythmic breathing process in perception and thinking, he struggles to rise up to spiritual reality in Imagination, Inspiration and Intuition ... The Oriental says: systole, diastole; inhalation, exhalation. In place of these the Westerner must put perception and thinking. Where the Oriental speaks of the development of physical breathing, we in the West say development of a breathing of the soul-spirit within the cognitional process through perception and thinking.[17]

The difference between this method and the more traditional occult training methods offered in the books *Knowledge of the Higher Worlds* and *Occult Science* is that it allows a direct spiritualization of the main forces of the consciousness soul: free thinking and sense-perception, as Goethe and Rudolf Steiner practised them.[18] Through the transformation of sense-perception, this method can bring about a resurrection of Goetheanism in Anthroposophy. And when the result of the transformation of thinking according to *The Philosophy of Freedom* crosses and fertilizes the Goetheanistic transformation of sense-perception, man is enabled 'to understand through the *earthly* forces the coming Christ impulse; this is the connection between the world of thoughts in *The Philosophy of Freedom* and the higher forces of knowledge that evolve in our soul'.[19] In Chapter 5 of our present study, entitled 'The Knowledge Drama of the Second Coming', the aim of which is to recapitulate the modern Christ experience through an elaborated spiritual-scientific research, we shall explore this new yoga practice in some detail. For now, it suffices to add the following historical remarks.

The inner link between the Pauline method and the first Michaelic-Christian yoga practice originated in the first supersensible Christ experience itself. Its source is to be found in the light-radiating, life-giving spiritual aura of the Christ, the Nathanic-Krishna Being.[20] Then it found its historical continuation through the esoteric school that Paul established in Athens, under the guidance of his pupil, Dionysius the Areopagite[21] who became the founder of the neo-Platonic Christianity that spiritualized Christianity up to the late Middle Ages and, indeed, right into the dawn of the age of the consciousness soul, as the life and writings of Nicolaus Cusanus show.[22] Both major streams of thought in the West, in their highest medieval expression in the Platonic-Christian teachings of Bernardus Sylvestris and Alanus ab Insulis, in the twelfth century, and in the Aristotelian-Christian Scolasticism of Albertus Magnus and Thomas Aquinas, in the thirteenth century, were deeply enlivened and animated by the still powerful spiritual element of esoteric Christianity that survived in the Pauline tradition of Dionysius. Here the true esoteric method used by Paul lights up again and is preserved, through its union with Platonism and Aristotelianism, in order to rescue the last vestiges of the original etheric Christ experience.

In his lecture cycle on Thomas Aquinas, Rudolf Steiner described the Pauline method of Dionysius in the following way:

> Dionysius is described as having two paths to the Divine, and so indeed he had ... How can one deal with a personality who gives not one theology, but two; one positive and one negative, one rationalistic and one mystical? ... For Dionysius, the Divinity was a Being who had to be approached by a rational path, by the finding and giving of names. But he saw that to travel by this path only is to lose the way ... Therefore, in conjunction with it, another way must also be taken, namely, the way that strives towards 'The Nameless'. If a man takes either path alone he will never find the Divine, but if he takes both paths, then he will find the way to the Divine *at that point at which the two paths cross* ... when the human soul finds itself *at their crossing-point*, then both roads together lead to the desired goal.[23]

Here, then, we have the required indications. The method was pointed out by means of which the appropriate language can be created, in order to articulate, in a vocabulary suited to the consciousness soul, the new anthroposophical experience of the etheric Christ. A bridge can be constructed, fashioned from the modern, given Christ experience, and the Pauline-Michaelic yoga method, bridging the abyss that still exists between the earthly form of Anthroposophy and the Christ in His new appearance. The seed for this lies, as we saw above, in Rudolf Steiner's philosophical and scientific creations: 'I must say, in the books *Truth and Knowledge* and *The Philosophy of Freedom* ... there lives the Pauline spirit. *It is possible to find the bridge from this philosophy to the Christ spirit.*'[24] And the results of our anthroposophical endeavours in this respect can be true if they illuminate, and in illuminating create, the new sphere of creative human freedom; the place in which, in the free being of man in the age of the consciousness soul, world knowing and world creating merge in and through the new anthroposophical knowledge drama of the new Christian initiation. Then we can bring our highest anthroposophical freedom as a loving offering to the Christ. This was expressed by Rudolf Steiner in the following words:

> The thought of freedom should not lay hold of men without the thought of redemption through Christ. Only then is the thought of freedom justified. If we will to be free, we must bring this offering of thanks to Christ for our freedom! Only then can we truly grasp it.[25]

II — The Threshold Situation of the Abyss

The second part of this Introduction aims to demonstrate the indispensable condition for the knowledge drama of the Second Coming: the new Michaelic yoga practice, put in the service of the Pauline method described in Part I above. The writer is convinced that a construction of a fully conscious spiritual-scientific bridge between the twentieth and twenty-first centuries is possible if it is based on thoroughly individualized spiritual experience and knowledge. Such a bridge can only result from the individuation of the three great spiritual events of the twentieth century: 1) the founding of anthroposophical spiritual science, 2) the awakening of the new supersensible soul-and-spirit faculties and 3) mutual transformation and enhancement. The first event took place in the first third of the century, and the second began in the middle third. The third is their synthesis that begins at the end of the last third, on the threshold of the twentieth and twenty-first centuries. This part of the Introduction aims to demonstrate a certain aspect of this synthesis, developed in order to form the cognitive Michaelic-Pauline tools for the spiritual-scientific investigation of the modern Christ experience.

We can find a valuable indication concerning the required individuation of spiritual science if we bring before us Rudolf Steiner's experience of thinking at the end of the *last* century, out of which he wrote *The Philosophy of Freedom*. We need only change the word 'Philosophy' to 'Anthroposophy' in his letter to Rosa Meyreder a hundred years ago (4 November, 1894) to have an example of the soul mood which, at the end of *this* century, is the foundation of the individuation of spiritual science itself:

> I do not teach; I tell what I experienced inwardly. I tell it so, as I experienced it. Everything in my book is meant in a personal way. Also the thought-formation ... I wanted to show the biography of a soul that fights its way to freedom ... in my own, entirely individual way I scaled many cliffs and battled in my own unique manner through many thickets. Man only knows that he has reached his goal when he arrives. But perhaps the time for teaching in such matters is already past. *Philosophy* [today we can also say: Anthroposophy] *interests me only as experience of the individual person.*[1]

The Philosophy of Freedom, if experienced in the way its originator experienced it, as the fully individual biography of the soul's struggle for its freedom, leads man, to begin with in *thinking*, to a thorough overcoming of the intellect. This overcoming is an essential precondition for the individuation of Anthroposophy in our time, because such an overcoming contains the seed-potential for genuine supersensible research. Supersensible experience and research is the great liberator of the soul forces from their enslavement to the brain-bound intellect, which achieved in the twentieth century an almost total victory over human consciousness and life on the Earth. Therefore, when man has transformed his thinking to such an extent that he can live and weave freely in its intuitive force dynamics alone, regardless of its positive representational content, he will always be able to participate in full self-consciousness in the process of inwardly reactivating and reformulating the offered results of supersensible research because he has, in thinking, followed the very same path.[2] Taken in *this* sense, the experience of intuitive thinking developed by means of *The Philosophy of Freedom* becomes in itself supersensible experience and, as such, the most suitable soil for the growth of the new supersensible faculties and their transformation in the knowledge drama of the Second Coming.

The modern Christ experience described in this book is a real supersensible experience. This means, therefore, that its conscious anthroposophical investigation must come to terms with *the threshold* situation of the abyss, because this situation is the place of its occurrence. Now at the threshold of the spiritual world man learns to experience his stored conceptual knowledge not only as something completely external to his real being but also as an obstacle and threat to his wakeful spirit existence. Man knows himself in the abyss of existence. He knows that he must struggle to reach the point where he can actively recreate and thus individualize the nothingness of this world and make it into the deliberately actualized nothingness of his *own* being. Everything belonging to the soul life on Earth is experienced here as an unbearable burden, fettering the dormant wings of the soul and hindering their enfoldment. In this situation, when the excarnation from the physical and etheric bodies is already accomplished, but the rebirth of the soul-spirit has not yet been realized in full self-consciousness, man does not truly exist so long as he carries anything in him which is not the result of the active annihilation of all earthly contents.

In earthly existence man gains and maintains a sustainable and substantial state of mind when he fills his consciousness with the *abiding, remembered contents* of his past soul activity. Because he is positively focused on this content, which gives him his solid and endurable earthly identity, he usually forgets the living soul activity and spiritual movement that brought it about.[3] His personal identity crystallizes around this memorized, devitalized soul content. By means of the sum-total of the mental pictures that he has engraved in himself, he *is*. Exactly the reverse is true at the threshold. Here, all existing contents become a heavy burden. This burden must *die* away, if man is to truly *live* in his new situation; the ordinary identity must die together with it. Here, in this situation, earthly reality must first disappear entirely before a new spiritual man-and-world activity and movement can be born into it. Only then can man be rejuvenated from the widths of his world-periphery and be resurrected out of the nothingness of the abyss. Then he can be granted the modern Pauline Christ experience: 'Not I [in so far as this "I" is centred in the contents of earthly memory], but my Self is active, therefore I AM.'[4] This experience constitutes the ground of selfless self-identity in truly conscious excarnation. But only through the repeated practice of the living creation of absolute annihilation does man develop the power that gradually cracks the hardened shell of his enclosing mental egg. And it is out of this hardened enclosure that the 'wings of passage' will be released in due course, carrying him over the abyss into spirit existence in the midst of which the etheric Christ appears.

An important concept concerning the relation between the spiritual path of *The Philosophy of Freedom* and the modern Christ experience is gained if we realize that if Rudolf Steiner's theory of knowledge is individualized and assimilated in ordinary consciousness by means of the practice of intuitive thinking it is transformed near the abyss into the essential inner foundation of the higher spiritual faculties of cognition. The study of this phenomenon shows that, near the threshold, it is metamorphosed into a light-radiating faculty capable of clearly illuminating and condensing the naturally given imaginative perceptions. The indispensable contribution of *The Philosophy of Freedom* to the developing Time Spirit here becomes especially evident, because for many people born after the middle of the twentieth century this abyss situation is not uncommon; the experience belongs to their 'ordinary' daily existence.[5] Through the newly-developing supersensible faculties and experiences, in the centre of which stands the modern Christ experience, man already lives and weaves in the abyss opened through a greater or lesser separation of the soul forces. This separation may express itself, to begin with, in the loosening of the unconscious, instinctive connection between sense-perception and thinking. This means that there is a certain disintegration of the objective world picture and the normal self-identity, which must, therefore, be brought to full consciousness if it is to become a source of blessing to man's development and not of illness. In such a case, man might feel the inner necessity to place before his soul again and again Rudolf Steiner's exactly delimited point of departure of all free and fully conscious human knowledge, namely, the intuitive, boundary thought-experience of the 'world' as it would appear before a being that confronts it without combining his sense-perceptions with the results of his reflective mental activity:

'This "directly given" picture is what 1) flits past us, 2) disconnected, but 3) undifferentiated. In it 4) nothing appears distinguished from, related to, or determined by, anything else.'[6]

In the physical world these four levels are integrated unconsciously, and together create a solid and memorizable world picture:

1) the physical body is responsible, by means of its natural physical-mineral inertia, for the fact that the world picture *does not* at all constantly 'flit past us' but remains rather static and fixed;
2) the etheric body, united with the physical, brings it about that all sense-perceptions, as well as the inner events of the soul life, are experienced as basically *connected* with one another in *one* picture;
3) the astral body brings into this pre-established unity the consciousness of individual *differentiation* of details;
4) the ego distinguishes, relates and determines this manifold but thoroughly united world picture and carries it as its own inwardly sustained and condensed experience of beingness and identity.

The nearer we draw to the threshold, 'the grey spirit abyss' out of which the etheric Christ appears, this coherent and solid 'I'-and-world picture increasingly disintegrates and falls apart. The seed-centre of the soul and spirit strives to be experienced wholly free from everything that in one way or another was gathered externally in the world of ordinary sense-and-thought life. And in the age of the consciousness soul, when man is naturally strongly intellectualized, this means, as was indicated above, the release from all physically gained elements of knowledge:

abstract concepts, mental pictures, memories and above all the deeply ingrained thought habits of our rationalistic-materialistic age.[7] Before man draws near to the abyss, he must, therefore, overcome the two great 'knowledge enemies' of our age: first, the belief in a physical or spiritually given and objective Reality that is directly accessible to us without our creative cognitive efforts and can be passively perceived and acquired; and second, the belief that Truth can be represented as a mental picture, and be taken hold of and privatized as an enduring mental possession in the personal collection of 'my own truths'. Also for the pupil of anthroposophical spiritual science this might become a great challenge, because he carries in his mental pictures and memories a rich treasure of spiritual knowledge which he finds objectively given in books and institutions of spiritual science. But though the given objectivity of this content and the possibility to memorize it are necessary for its practical existence on the Earth, it becomes a burden the more man approaches the threshold of true spiritual reality; man is continuously tempted in this regard, and might refuse to give it up, clinging to what he knows through his earthly intellect *about* the spiritual worlds, at the moment when he has to create actively the annihilation of all objective and reflected contents of earthly existence.[8] So that a properly developing spiritual-scientific training, though it necessarily begins with the study *material* as such, must from the very beginning also make clear the difference between the interest invested in the finished contents of knowledge and the dynamic schooling in the active *creative movement* of knowledge. That is, it must transform the passive assimilation of represented anthroposophical contents into the experiential and experimental *experience* of the ways in which true supersensible knowledge comes about.[9] Such an experiential study is the necessary preparation for the knowledge drama of anthroposophical knowledge, and it alone can bring to full consciousness the modern Christ experience in its complex and multi-levelled form.

One suitable place from which the study of the knowledge process can begin is created if we bring together two aspects of Rudolf Steiner's spiritual-scientific work that, though separated from each other in time, spring from the same deeper life source of Anthroposophy as a whole. These two are his *first* philosophical and scientific works (1886–93) and the *last* ones (1917–24). From this point of view the greatest importance must be given to the spiritualized form of the specifically Aristotelian approach to science and knowledge developed for the first time by Rudolf Steiner in his book *Von Seelenrätseln* ('Riddles of the Soul') (1917) that served as the spiritual-scientific foundation for the whole edifice of the fertile third seven-year period in the development of Anthroposophy.

The uniting of the beginning and end of Rudolf Steiner's knowledge endeavours[10] creates a foundation for the transformation of the consciousness soul into the imaginative soul,[11] which is the main cognitive power by means of which the modern Christ experience can be investigated. According to *Von Seelenrätseln*, if the imaginative faculty is to be developed, 'the soul must be familiar with the inner *process* that combines psychic representation with sense-impression; so familiar that *it can hold at arms length the influx of the sense-impressions themselves (or of their echoes in after-experience) into the act of representing*. This keeping at bay of post-sense-experiences can only be achieved if one has detected the way in which the *activity* of representing is pre-empted by these after-experiences. Not until then is one in a position to combine one's spiritual organs with the act itself and thereby to receive impressions of spiritual reality. Thus the act of representing is impregnated from quite another side than in the case of sense-perception. And thus the mental experiences are positively different from those evoked by sense-perception.'[12]

In what follows we shall try to demonstrate briefly how the intuitive thought experience of the 'directly given' picture described in *Truth and Knowledge* (see above) is transformed into the fundamental structure of conscious supersensible knowledge by means of the path indicated in *Von Seelenrätseln*. For ordinary consciousness this situation of the 'directly given' picture is an archetypal 'boundary representation'[13] which, because it annihilates itself in its very coming-into-being in ordinary consciousness, can be transformed into a unique cognitive faculty that can lift to full self-consciousness the situation of the abyss without becoming a burden and obstacle. Because it is a negative and reversed, that is, an actively produced non-relation between perception and thinking, it delimits and therefore gives-up the ground structure of ordinary consciousness. It lifts the formative forces of this ground structure up and transforms them into the forces that serve as the source of imaginative consciousness.

Ordinary consciousness comes into existence when the 'I' realizes, by means of inner activity, the structure of earthly cognition through the synthesis of sense-perception and thinking. This synthesis results in the production of memorizable mental pictures, or representations. The giving-up and transforming of this synthetic activity is the etheric foundation of the anthroposophical knowledge drama of the Second Coming, which is described in Chapter 5.

The individuation of the 'I' in the physical world occurs in the synthetic activity of the act of knowledge. When man reflects *after* and *about* this living activity, this activity itself is long *past*. He has then within his waking consciousness only the dying, devitalized picture-shadow of its end result.[14] Spiritually seen, every coming to rest of soul-and-spirit activity creates a fixed and permanent mental sedimentation, which can *later* be remembered in consciousness as an event of past time. A closer look at this coming to rest of spiritual activity reveals a threefold devitalizing structure. It 1) contracts and thereby 2) *condenses*, and finally 3) *suppresses* the living future life-stream, creating in its vacant, negative shadow-place of time an abiding, reversed and isolated past-picture of external or internal reality. On this opaque resistance of the synthesized *products* of its living knowledge activity the thinking 'I' reflects and so also pictures *itself* and thus makes itself into a self-conscious being.[15] In this way it stamps a preservable imprint of its unseen being and, together with the growing treasures of imprinted individualized world-pictures, gains a stronger hold of itself as a self-centered being.

However, the real 'I', while it busily multiplies the contents of ordinary consciousness through external sense-perception and intellectual reflection, is in reality not interested in increasing the memorizable quantity of the intellectual results of its past acts of knowledge, but rather in enhancing the inner quality of the power of living spiritual *action*.[16] This hidden 'I' activity can be lifted to consciousness through practising a reversal of the synthetic activity of ordinary knowledge. This practice shows that beneath the threshold of ordinary consciousness, that is, in supersensible reality, the 'I' unceasingly reverses and thereby enlivens the threefold devitalizing process described above. It 1) unblocks, '*up-presses*' the suppressed, living future time and life-stream, and thereby 2) *dissolves* its dead past condensations, and finally 3) *releases* its original blocking congestion. When it annihilates, enlivens and transfigures in this manner the ground-structure of its representation-forming faculty (or memory), it goes unhindered *backwards* through the mental pictures that resulted from its brain-bound acts of knowledge. It makes them transparent through this hidden, invisible reversing activity, and so strengthens and increases its real power. The more active the 'I' is, the more it makes its thinking into pure will, into self-accelerating movement, and the more it gains the ability to raise this hidden work into consciousness.

When this happens, man can observe how the 'I', as a real active *force-being*, unites itself increasingly, by means of its ability to annihilate, enliven and transfigure its own mental-picture creations, with the world-essence that flows *towards* it *through* every freed and transparent sense-perception. It is a new, future-orientated, will-like remembrance of the 'I'. So it comes to meet itself, reversed, as a universal, expanded world-self.[17] Let us study this process in greater detail.

A closer observation of the act of knowledge in its *totality* reveals the fact that, whenever the 'I' transfigures and so passes backwards through a mental picture, it lights up and radiates an intense illumination it did not have before. Why does the 'I', as a real spirit being, light up in this passing-through? Because *this passing through is a self-gathering – or self-*

remembering – of the 'I' to itself from the vast periphery of its scattered and dismembered universal existence. While in ordinary consciousness the results of the acts of knowledge crystallize into finished mental forms, *below* the threshold of this consciousness the 'I' meets and unites itself with its world-self, which, unhindered by man's representations, comes to meet it through every sense-perception. But every representation leaves an enduring dead and darkening *trace* in the living light-being of man and of the world. It is this opaque shadowy trace-residue that originally divides the real human-world being of the 'I' into seemingly two wholly disconnected, unrecognized halves: into an inner (thinking) 'self' and an externally (perceived) 'world'.[18]

Now this primordial world-self wholeness would remain unconscious if it could not come to itself first as a divided world-self, which ignites its separate self-consciousness in the forming of every devitalized mental picture. But the self-conscious cognitive forces generated in the *earthly* act of knowledge, which overcome this duality, can become an eternal power of the 'I'. This happens when they are consciously reversed and are redirected to dissolve and enliven the dying darkening residue of ordinary consciousness *that enabled their coming into being in the first place.*[19] Then these reversed cognitive forces allow the wholeness of the 'I' to come together re-collected and re-membered, in an enhanced, rhythmical self-world/world-self movement of supersensible knowledge.

This, therefore, is the reason why, when the 'I' transforms a dying-darkening mental picture into a livingly shining, world-dialogue (speaking, inspired) Imagination, it lights up in itself stronger than before. As with Goethe's *Green Snake and the Beautiful Lily*, its inner transparent brilliance grows with every assimilated and transfigured representation, and its dynamic unrepresented force-nature warms up the more it gathers in its scattered universal being from the periphery of sense-perception. The act of knowledge, perceived thus from *both* sides of the threshold, means the liberation and transfiguration of the sense- and brain-bound, dead and frozen elements of ordinary cognition. But in these elements the true human-world 'I' is primordially torn to pieces, scattered and buried; therefore, when these are spiritualized and gathered to their new living wholeness, it is the 'I' itself that experiences itself resurrected into the full future consciousness of its world-man nature.

Now the observation studied above can be investigated from yet another perspective. When the 'I' carries out this work on the forces of ordinary consciousness that create the mental picture, it actually penetrates and transforms the mirror and veil of memory which is embedded in the devitalized part of the etheric body. In this work it vivifies and enlivens, on the one hand, this dying part of the etheric body, which is continuously deadened by the consolidation of every new memorized representation. Weaving further in this enlivened part, the 'I' achieves conscious *intuitive thinking*.[20] Through this act, on the other hand – by means of the assimilation of the death forces inherent in the mental picture – the 'I' also kills an originally living part of the etheric body; and it is through this part that it achieves conscious *imaginative perception*.[21] Yet this happens in one and the same act. The enlivening of the originally dying part deadens the originally living part, and vice versa; the deadening of the originally living enlivens the originally dying part. This is the self-conscious double process of 'the assimilation of death into life' that was mentioned in Part I of this Introduction as the foundation of esoteric Christianity and the 'Pauline Method' (see pp. 7–8).

The originally dead part of the etheric body is unconsciously killed in each new act of earthly cognition; so it serves the consolidation of daily waking consciousness. It is now *consciously enlivened*. The originally living part of the etheric body remains unconscious during ordinary life. It becomes conscious through the enlivening of the dying part, and thus it can be *consciously killed*. At the 'place of time' where the enlivened dying life and the dying living life meet, cross and reverse themselves in and through each other, something wholly new is created in human self-consciousness: a fully conscious *and* living mental-picturing faculty comes into being, that is, a fully thought-permeated (inspired) Imagination. It is begotten out of the living annihilation of the annihilation forces of the consciousness soul. This is the birth of the imaginative soul out of the consciousness soul. So the conscious spiritualization of the death forces that create the mental picture in ordinary consciousness is, in reality, a spiritualized soul birth – the birth of an undying state of consciousness inside the grey abyss of the brain-grave of modern intellectuality and materialism, out of which 'supersensible knowledge must be resurrected because with it the knowledge of Christ Jesus will be resurrected out of this grave.'[22]

This birth occurs in a unique space of time which is, at the 'same' – ever self-dividing, ever self-uniting – time, a birth and death place of cognition, each *inside* and *through* the other. And in this mutual inter-crossing and reversing of death into life and life into death 'as a chemical combination',[23] *in this living death process of Death*, the foundation is created for the interweaving of intuitive thinking and imaginative perception each-into-the-other, which constitutes the true nature of the imaginative soul and at the same time also the seed-potential for the still higher faculties of inspired and intuited consciousness.

For ordinary consciousness this delicate and subtle cognitive process remains unconscious; through the spiritual-scientific knowledge drama of the Second Coming it can be lifted to full consciousness. In ordinary cognition this moment is hidden and suppressed precisely *behind* the formation and crystallization process of every mental picture. That this picture *rises up* and becomes fully conscious in ordinary cognition is due to the fact that the process described above simultaneously *sinks down* below the threshold of daily consciousness at the same *split moment* of time. The conscious individuation of the act of knowledge, described here, brings the *whole* event before the inner eye: the simultaneous rising up of the reality-drained mental picture, and the sinking down of the reality-saturated life element, and the moment of the mutual crossing and reversing of their paths.[24]

This process is described in the book *Von Seelenrätseln* ('Riddles of the Soul') as follows: 'Now the conceptual life does not really get lost but carries on its existence, separated from the region of consciousness, in the unconscious spheres of the soul. And then it will be found again by spiritual organs.'[25]

The first living place of time where the suppressed life of the mental pictures is found by the spiritual activity of the imaginative soul is the above-indicated moment of the twilight: the sinking down of the inner night Sun of the 'I' and the rising of the external day Sun of the 'I' on the mental horizon of consciousness. The holding fast of this difference between the worlds at the living moment of their twilight split can enable us to reverse this process and study it backwards as shown above. This means to liberate man's flowing life-time organization from its bondage to reflection, and open wide the time difference between night and day, sleeping and awakening. Instead of letting thinking and sense-perception devitalize each other in the forming of the brain-and sense-bound mental picture, we let them flow freely *through* each other and be reversed *into* each other. Living thought thus reaches to the living origin of sense-perception, and pure sense-perception reaches as far as the original source of thinking. Beyond their midway cross point they are both gradually reversed into each other, at once keeping, trans-forming and giving up their original identity in the reversal process inside each other's opposite stream. When thinking grasps the origin of perception it becomes, as thought, perception, and when perception penetrates to the source of thinking it becomes, as perception, thinking. In this living, mutual exchange of thinking in and through perception, and perception in and through thinking, thinking is perceived through living sense-perception, and sense-perception is thought through living thinking. The first, the livingly perceived thinking, *inspires* the second, and the second, the thought-penetrated sense-perception, *imagines* the first. A fully saturated, inspired imaginative faculty is thus created, on the basis of which the next necessary cognitive step can be taken.

During this transformation of the ordinary act of knowledge and its mental-picture creations, the forces are prepared that can then lead to the full evacuation of the soul. As we pointed out above, such an evacuation is a necessary precondition for self-conscious existence at the threshold's abyss. The deeper levels of the modern Christ experience are discovered only when we realize that His etheric form crystallizes in reality not in the etheric world but in the 'grey spirit abyss' of the *astral* world.[26] This means that if we seek to penetrate to the deeper nature of His appearance *process*, we must be able to study the *becoming* process of this appearance and not only its finished outward etheric form. In order to study properly the living process of this etheric appearance with the research methods of anthroposophical spiritual science, we have first to spiritualize our initial etheric perception and purify it from its external as well as internal, personal and accidental characteristics. This is achieved to a large extent by means of the transformation of the act of knowledge described above and the developing of inspired imaginative perception through it. But this faculty itself must be brought one step further if we wish to be able to study in detail the actual process through which this etheric appearance in the astral world is taking place. We must, therefore, evolve the force that is able to experience and comprehend the real nature of the world in which this appearance takes place.

This cognitive force is developed in the knowledge process if, after we have brought it to the point in which pure thinking and sense-perception meet and cross each other as described above, instead of allowing them to flow in and through each other and so complete each other in the fully self-transparent and self-supporting wholeness of intuitive thinking and imaginative perception, *we hold them fast at the point of their crossing*. We stop their accelerated inner time movement and arbitrarily suppress their reversal into each other. We hold them at the moment when both cancel each other, before they let each other be born again imaginatively in and through each other on the other side of themselves. Here we have the tiny time space, the needle's eye, that we have to gradually enlarge through the continuous inward emptying of its past time substance. We have to bring to a standstill and thus separate the living flow of the two time streams at the point of their mutual reversal, in which they always momentarily annihilate and immediately enliven themselves again. We have to make this ever-present, unconscious annihilation activity into our own fully self-conscious self-annihilation process, *in order to overcome inwardly the substantial etheric reality of the stream of time-past*. In this way we reverse, open and penetrate into the inner structure of the destruction process of time and individualize it. This means to enact and realize time's inner nullity through our own soul forces and then, carrying its evacuation further beyond its null point, to reach its infinite negativity within in absolute soul emptiness.

As will be shown in detail in Chapter 5, this means to individuate and cross the stream of time's annihilation entirely and reach the astral soul-shore on the other side of time. *The central aim of the knowledge drama of the*

22

Second Coming is to make this exit out of, and back into, time, into an ever wakeful, secure and remembered bridgeway. It aims to make possible fully self-conscious spiritual-scientific research of the living becoming and appearance processes of the visible etheric body of the Christ in the soul world. Christ's body of appearance is a life-time body that appears in, through and across man's own ever-recurrent process of etheric death and rebirth that continually takes place in man's life-time body. And the place of this appearance is the soul's nullity experience in the astral world, into which man enters the moment he crosses the river of time's annihilation.

When the bridge that can make possible the free entry into the appearance realm of the Christ in His Second Coming is firmly established, empirical supersensible research can investigate the different aspects of Christ's etheric becoming and appearance in a way that, both methodically and experientially, fulfils the justified cognitive and scientific requirements of our age. That is, it can be anchored safely in the ground structure forces of the consciousness soul that are systematically transformed into the intuited and inspired imaginative soul.[27] When this soul transformation is achieved, not only further differentiated and detailed knowledge of Christ's etheric appearance is possible to supersensible research, but, through the manifold methodical ramifications and applications of anthroposophical spiritual science, it can also serve other areas of spiritual investigation in nature and in history.

Chapter 1

The *Ur*-Mystery of Remembrance

Through the *Ur*-Mystery of Golgotha, the Sun Being began His way of reunion with the Earth — an actual transference of the Sun centre from the aging Sun to a new Sun centre.[1] For the Earth and for humanity, it marked the beginning of their active, collaborative remembrance of their Christ nature in preparation for their future cosmic communion as new Sun, complementing and supporting the evolution of the dying old Sun.[2] When the two Suns are combined — at the planetary evolutionary stage of 'Venus' — they will constitute together, as one body, the starting point of a whole new cosmic system.[3]

But what did the cosmic Sun Being, the Christ, bring with Him to the Earth? He brought back to the Earth its forgotten, because exhausted, living time, and with it the foundation of living spirit remembrance — that is, the possibility of consciously regulating the present connections to the Christ-permeated cosmic whole.[4] Since the *Ur*-Mystery of Golgotha, the historical evolution of the Earth has a meaning only through this fact. Its Sun-becoming process is the central meaning of all future evolution. Whatever happened, happens and shall happen, in the past, present and future time of the Earth, can be rightly understood and judged only in relation to this retiming of its being with the living, Christ-permeated cosmos. More concretely expressed, this means that historical time, i.e. the stream of time that passes through human self-consciousness, has been, since Golgotha, necessarily divided into two streams: one stream that penetrates man by the spiritual power that flows from Golgotha, and a second stream that bypasses this event.

Both streams exist side by side, interwoven, in the life-body of every human being. The first is the living, and hence unconscious, Christ-filled life-stream; the second is the stream of life's annihilation, and hence the basis of man's awakened consciousness. In the first stream, man sleeps in the being of the Christ within him; in the second man awakens to his physical, daily consciousness. Usually, in normal daily life, these streams — the unconscious and the conscious — are strictly separated. In the new, Christian initiation, they are first brought to mutual interpenetration and transformation.[5]

In the three years of His earthly, bodily life — up to the moment of His death on Good Friday afternoon — the Christ could only work on His

24

disciples through these two separated levels: either supersensibly, but unconsciously, during their sleep, or during the waking hours, physically and externally, but without their being able to recognize His true spiritual being.[6] Christ's purpose was to carry His incarnation process so far that He could pour His whole cosmic, supersensible being directly into the earthly life-stream of His pupils, in order to enable them consciously to remember, be aware and see Him. To achieve this, however, meant to die into their life, or, which is the same thing, to live their death. And in doing so He went through the Mystery of Golgotha, planting in the dead cross the living seed of the *Ur*-Mystery of remembrance. Step by step, gradually sacrificing His cosmic power and splendour, the Christ worked His way to this goal.

In bringing the three years to their fulfilment, the Christ dramatically impressed on His pupils His whole physical being in the sacred event of the last supper. This means that into man's released, emancipated and shrivelled bodily sheaths there was poured the finest essence of Christ's earthly life. Here only the thinnest veil still remained. At one moment it was actually momentarily pierced,[7] in order, however, to be revealed soon after in its consciousness-subduing and darkening form. We can point to the exact moment when Christ began the final pouring of His life into His disciples' death. It was the moment when Judas, the personification of the disciples' collective death forces, ate his share of Christ's bread of life. Here, Christ's nearness to the being of Death causes its dramatic externalization and provokes him to the last confrontation. Christ forces him, through Judas partaking of His freely offered life, to take Him into himself and — in the coming three nights — to merge with Him completely.[8]

From that Gethsemane night, through the holy Friday of the passion and crucifixion, the sojourn in Kamaloka in the great Passover Sabbath, up to the visitation of the empty tomb and the first resurrection experiences of the women on Sunday morning, the Christ was livingly and consciously entering the dying life-stream of humanity and the Earth. He thus planted the seed of His newly created death in life and life in death in the souls of His pupils: a conscious, life-preserving, life-giving death![9] Through His life in human death, and His death in human life, He gained the power to teach His disciples and impart to them, for the first time in human evolution, this secret: the secret of the 'bridge'.

In the coming 40 days He could teach them the most modern of all arts of consciousness: the art of preserving, consolidating and resurrecting self-conscious spirit remembrance, awareness and seeing, over the abyss of death and spirit forgetfulness. This abyss stands mightily before us when we look, together with the bewildered and shocked disciples, into the empty tomb of Sunday morning. It signifies the deepest abyss of consciousness in the whole evolution of humanity and the Earth. On the earthly side we have the physical, external Christ memory of humanity, as preserved in the Gospels. On the other side of the tomb we have the mysterious pentecostal event and the Pauline transformation on the way to Damascus. In between, however, we have only unclear, disjointed reminiscences and rumours of resurrection and ascension. A virtual abyss, a tumultuous stream of life's annihilation and spirit forgetfulness, separates everything that went before Easter from everything that came after Pentecost.[10] And ever since then, the Death being of our Earth threatens to widen this abyss up to the point where no memory of the bridge will be possible at all.[11]

Only when, through Rudolf Steiner's research, we enter into the souls of those who experienced this abyss as their own do we begin to recreate in our own soul the anthroposophical gospel of knowledge, which is the foundation stone of the bridge of spirit remembrance over humanity's abyss of consciousness, past, present and future. In the events from Easter to Pentecost we have the archetypal model on which alone we can mould our own anthroposophical foundation of spirit remembrance. For in the twentieth century this abyss must be vividly and freely experienced.[12]

Let us, then, place before us in the liveliest way possible the experiences of the close disciples of Christ as described by Rudolf Steiner in his lectures on the Fifth Gospel.[13] Awakening as they did in the event of Pentecost from their special sleeplike state of consciousness to which they had succumbed more and more since Gethsemane night, they had the following remarkable experience. Looking backwards in the stream of time, they saw themselves as they were during the last 50 days since the events of Golgotha. They said to themselves: during these days we were spiritually in another, dreamlike state of consciousness, in the company of a spiritual Being who taught us something out of the spiritual world. But we could neither recognize Him, nor clearly understand His teaching. On the other hand — so they said to themselves at the moment of their pentecostal awakening — we have those dream-like, earthly memory pictures of our physical life with Him and, as the summation of our physical life with the Christ — gathered and, as it were, condensed — there appears to us the memory picture of the last supper. But only when the two come together — when the purely spiritual Imaginations are fused with the background of the most spiritually potent physical memory picture of the last supper — do we remember and recognize Him as the same one who was with us both before, physically, and after, spiritually, the Mystery of Golgotha.

Anthroposophically understood, this means: through the teachings of the Christ during the 40 days — and in His mysterious acts during the next 10 days of His ascension — a special transformation took place in the organization of the disciples. The two life-streams, that of life without memory and that of memory without life, began to cross and impregnate each other. The death-stream that received the life element of the physical Christ and the life-stream that received His spiritual death element of Golgotha were woven into one coherent stream. We can also say: the dead memory (intellectual) stream was so powerfully penetrated by the lifeblood stream of the Christ that it could begin to illuminate — that is, awaken — the consciousness of the purely spiritual being and essence of the Christ. The dead stream was enlivened while the living stream was deadened. Where they crossed each other — on the inner cross of the disciples' own being — there was born the living, spirit-consciousness, awakening the Holy Spirit of Pentecost.[14]

According to Rudolf Steiner, the pentecostal awakening had the following stages: first, the realization that the body on the cross was the body of Jesus of Nazareth, with whom they were together in the last short three years; second, that the crucifixion was in reality no ordinary death but a birth, the birth of the cosmic spirit of love into the Earth; and third, that a ray of this spirit was now the consciousness-awakening power of their souls. This threefold recognition is, as Rudolf Steiner pointed out, the first knowledge gained through the Fifth Gospel. Now 'day after day' the whole time between Golgotha and ascension became visible, and with it the ultimate question concerning the identity of the Christ Being could be positively answered — their bridge of consciousness-continuation was complete.[15] 'It was a complete streaming together of the memories from that consciousness that was in a state of sleep with the memories of that which had happened before. They experienced it as two pictures that were superimposed on one another: one picture of the experiences after the Mystery of Golgotha, and one from before it, as if shining from the time before their consciousness was clouded. So they knew that these two Beings belong together: the Risen One and He with whom, a relatively short time before, they had wandered about physically ... This is what causes amazement: the invariable coincidence of one picture of an experience of the Apostles with the Christ *after* the Mystery of Golgotha with a picture of a happening they had actually lived through in their normal consciousness while together physically with Christ Jesus'.[16]

We are now in a position to understand better the meaning of the 50 days between Easter and Pentecost. During this time the Christ completed an initiation of his disciples by not only metamorphosing their higher members but also their etheric life bodies. This means that — after the work of ascension was completed — these specially prepared etheric bodies could reflect back the purely spiritual events into living spirit-consciousness; in the inner light of their etherically reflected, purified egos and astral bodies, they received consciously, for the first time in

27

human evolution, the living picture of the risen Christ and the content of His supersensible teaching. And what is more, they brought it into harmony with the physical world, that is, with the memories of Christ's physical life with them. And this conscious linking of the purely supersensible with the earthly physical is the achievement of the new Christian (today anthroposophical) initiation.[17]

Macrocosmically, the new Holy Spirit was born at the moment of death on Golgotha; microcosmically, in the being of humanity, it was born at Pentecost, as described above. The promise of the last supper[18] was fulfilled: the Holy Spirit — the spirit of consciously gained and freely remembered knowledge of the spirit — was created (in death), was 'sent' (that is, taught in the 40 days), and was received (at Pentecost). The first archetypal, macrocosmic-microcosmic birth, growth, maturation and ripening process of free spirit knowledge was consummated; the first seed of Anthroposophia was planted in humanity and in the Earth.

In order to deepen our study at this point, our exploration must differentiate itself into three main routes that run their course parallel with each other and are intertwined in the most complicated ways. The one is the evolution of the Christ Being Himself, especially from His earthly birth at the Mystery of Golgotha up to Pentecost. The second is the evolution of the Apostles as a result of His teachings and acts at this time, enabling them, eventually, as we saw, to receive the pentecostal illumination and remembrance. And the third is the evolution of the being of the Earth, in and through the other two. In the Christ Being we have the active, sacrificing, earthly-becoming Sun-centre, that had worked from the moment of His earthly birth on Golgotha directly into the being of His disciples and also into the being of the Earth as a whole. In the disciples we see that which is prepared, in the aforesaid time, to begin to reflect consciously — from Pentecost on — the Sun power of Christ in a direct, human way. And in the Earth we see the objective planetary results of this interaction between the Christ and humanity; every enhancement and deepening of this process becomes an objective world foundation, transforming the Earth into a new cosmic earthly-human Sun-sphere.

What, then, was the sacred, sacrificial evolution of the Christ Being? *The Fifth Gospel* shows us the following. The baptism by John in the Jordan was the moment of His earthly *conception*. He only began to touch — through the emptied bodily sheaths of Jesus of Nazareth — the earthly sphere, being still a cosmic Sun Being, expanded over and above the Earth. The three years were, in successive stages, an earthly *embryology* of the Christ. He became ever more human-like as He contracted and condensed His cosmic form, undergoing unimaginable suffering, so that He could finally assume the likeness of a human form. The Mystery of Golgotha itself was the event of the earthly *birth* of the Christ, and the

40 days were his real — and only — *earthly life*, when He supersensibly taught the disciples in their special state of consciousness. The so-called Ascension to Heaven is His earthly *death* — the pouring of His being far deeper still into the spiritual part of the Earth, establishing His Heaven — or Devachan — upon the Earth, and thereby rejuvenating its physical, etheric and astral life-streams. The pentecostal event is, therefore, the revelation of the fact that Christ accomplished His goal, namely, 'to assume such a form that is necessary for Him in order to live in community with human souls from now on'. This is the form (*Gestalt*) 'that He needed in order to live in communion with human souls on the Earth', in such a way that they will know, in their daily, self-conscious life, that He lives among them.[19] Bearing all this in mind, we can turn now to the development of the disciples on their way to becoming apostles.

Now the question here must be: what actually took place during Christ's teachings in the 40 days of His true earthly-spirit life, and during the 10 days of his earthly-spirit death (ascension)? In order to answer this question we must briefly recall some of the basic results of Rudolf Steiner's investigations concerning the essence of Christian initiation. All initiation culminates eventually — after the due preparation has been accomplished — in extending the inner transformation of the soul by imprinting it into man's subtle lower bodies, and first and foremost into the etheric body. The soul must first develop its organs of supersensible perception; it then has to imprint the result of its work into the etheric body. And this imprinting is deepened in three stages. The first impression gives the first conscious Imaginations; the impressions engraved deeper still bring about inspirational consciousness; and the deepest engravings are those that transform the etheric body to such an extent[20] that intuitive consciousness is produced.[21] Now in all old initiations the final impression, or engraving, of the soul and spirit processes into the etheric body took place magically, through external initiatory influences, directed to the disciple who for three days was brought into a condition of deathlike sleep, in which one part of his etheric body was released from the physical. When the neophyte was subsequently awakened, he was illuminated; in his carefully prepared etheric body there was reflected all that he had experienced unconsciously in his spiritual sojourn during the three days of deathlike sleep, and also in all the stages of his long preparation beforehand.

The initiatory period of the disciples — the 50 days between the Mystery of Golgotha and Pentecost — is divided clearly into two. The 40 days of Christ's teaching took place while they were half awake and half asleep. They were as 'sleep walkers',[22] running their daily life as usual but given up, unconsciously, to a continuous initiatory process. In this stage a certain separation of the astral and ego from the physical and etheric bodies was experienced. In the 10 days of Christ's ascension they lost Him altogether and entered their deepest and darkest state of sleep, experiencing thereby the greatest loneliness, desolation and despair.[23] This state meant, however, that a certain loosening gradually took place also in their etheric bodies, so that, as in the old initiations, they could consciously receive on coming back to themselves at Pentecost the imprint of all that they had experienced since Golgotha and before.[24] They could inwardly perceive, looking into the prepared mirror of their life, the conscious reflection of all that had taken place. This they felt to be as an outpouring of the most concentrated, fiery illumination of the spirit of Christ's resurrection, teaching and ascension, but now completely individualized, i.e. felt to be part and parcel of their own conscious selves.

From the point of view of the modern Christ experience and the event of the Second Coming, which it is our task to investigate here, this special preparation and transformation of the etheric bodies of the disciples is especially significant. For reasons that will become clear in Chapters 4 and 5, we must say that this specially prepared etheric body, through which the great illumination and outpouring of the Holy Spirit of Pentecost was made possible, contains the purest archetypal life element of Christ's human lifetime. It serves humanity as the body of spirit memory, the vehicle of the *Ur*-remembrance of Christ for all ages to come. Today we strive to build and maintain our own bridge of supersensible consciousness over the abyss of death and forgetfulness out of the forces of the Christ in His purely etheric appearance. The penetration into this *Ur*-body of Christ remembrance, as it might be termed, through the souls of the disciples, as described in Rudolf Steiner's lectures on *The Fifth Gospel*, is an essential, most powerful practical help on our way. Let us, therefore, present another aspect of the supersensible process by means of which the Christ, in the 40 days of His active teaching, brought about a spiritualization of the forces of memory in the etheric bodies of His pupils.

According to Rudolf Steiner, the reason why man does not normally perceive the light streams, movements and radiations of his etheric body, which contains in a supersensible, imaginative way the powers of memory, lies in the fact that the ahrimanic beings bind it too strongly to the physical body. If it had been possible for the human soul 'out of light to observe the processes in its own light-body, it could have freed itself from the forces of Ahriman that otherwise darken the processes in the light-body'.[25] But then man would be able to perceive in living, streaming light the living etheric world and, in this world, the etheric being of the Christ. This means, therefore: *the redemption of the etheric body from the ahrimanic bondage through the setting free of the forces of the light ether* is the essence of Christ's teaching and acts in the 50 days, the preparation of the first human etheric bodies capable of imaginative remembrance of the supersensible being of the Christ. Rudolf Steiner also offers in the above-quoted lecture the content of the prayer that was taught by the risen Etheric Christ to His disciples in order to enable them to dispel, through His redeemed etheric forces, the ahrimanically-bound light forces of their etheric bodies.

This process was only possible at that time in an unconscious way, namely, the transformation of the human etheric body through the direct supersensible meeting with the Christ after the Mystery of Golgotha, which can be developed consciously today through the natural course of human evolution. But this faculty is also capable of a thorough spiritualization by means of a further, voluntary and free anthroposophical esoteric schooling. In this way shall the developing natural endowment — the growing ability of human beings to see and remember the Etheric Christ through the released light-ether forces of their etheric bodies — be transformed ever more through Anthroposophy, so that, in overcoming the darkening ahrimanic influences, human beings will be able to see imaginatively 'in the light and through the light' the etheric, light figure of the Christ in His full, majestic radiance.[26]

The overcoming of death through Christ's thoroughly transformed soul, life and body, preserved in death by means of the death that became the earthly source of a new Sun life: this essence of His active 'teaching' and 'ascension' became a member of the disciples' Sun-imbued life organism — a vehicle of preserved, resurrected spirit memory of the spiritual-earthly form, words and acts of the risen Christ. In this preserved life-organism of the Apostles we have the key both to the *Ur*-Mystery of spirit remembrance and to the awakening power of the Holy Spirit which is, up to our own days, the archetypal example of the construction of a conscious link between objective and supersensible states of consciousness.

Now in order to understand this Mystery, we will have to observe more closely the origin of the new, pentecostal Holy Spirit in connection with the preserved bridge of remembrance. This, however, leads us to consider the role of the Earth in this process. Seen from outside, from the surrounding cosmic spaces, the moment of death on Golgotha was perceived as a sudden appearance of new light in the Earth's otherwise long since darkened planetary aura.[27] The birth of the cosmic Spirit of Love into the Earth sphere began to illuminate and inwardly regenerate her wasted old planetary sheaths. It was in the astral-soul atmosphere of the old Earth that the first light shone most clearly, penetrating, however slightly, also its etheric as well as physical bodies. To begin with, this was to be seen only at the actual place of the crucifixion, that is, Golgotha, Jerusalem. It is still specially marked there today.[28] But in order to carry this change further, the Earth depends on the spiritual work of human beings, especially with regard to the etherization building process of her new planetary astral, etheric and physical bodies.[29] And this work, the beginning of which was undertaken by the early true esoteric Christians, can be described as follows.

The old and darkened, wounded Mother Earth was beginning to regain her lost vitality and virginity through the Christ-impulse.[30] Since Golgotha, beginning with the Apostles and then, in the last 2,000 years, spreading through the whole world, whenever incarnated human beings have made their Christ-permeated spirit and soul strong enough, so that their inner religious experiences could become a real, permanent part of their life-organism — whenever, in other words, the Christ's life, death and resurrection truly worked among people, so that they began truly to live his form, words and acts, i.e. eating his spirit flesh and drinking his lifeblood[31] — there was produced, sheltered and nourished in the newly reborn virgin sheaths of Mother Earth, a preserved, condensed and redeemed planetary life-stream of etheric Christ-permeated human forces. Into the wasted and empty life-bodies of thousands of human beings the Christ poured His living forces through the ages. And when these human beings passed through the gate of death, they left behind them their transformed and Christ-permeated life-forces, held fast by the renewed earthly mother soul sphere. These forces rained upwards, streaming together into a growing life ocean of the Earth. And slowly a whole Christ-permeated planetary, rhythmical, breathing cycle of universal, humanly produced life was developed as a new earthly 'Heaven'.[32] This Heaven, when sufficiently saturated with new earthly Christ life, could begin to rain back down to the Earth from its abundance, incorporating and reflecting the cosmic Holy Spirit of the Christ. Now the very first revelation of this new rhythm of the Christ-permeated planetary life was the pentecostal outpouring of the Holy Spirit and, later, the Christ experience of Paul at the gates of Damascus. The Holy Spirit is, then, the universally gathered, Christ-permeated fruits of earthly-human Sun life, received into the soul womb of virgin Mother Earth and reflected back, overflowing with earthly-heavenly life, awakening human souls to their conscious community with the Christ on Earth itself.[33]

The Christ, condensing His cosmic Sun form into a narrow earthly human shape, took His spirit residence in community with human beings on the Earth. Through the offering of His bodies to the Earth, His new light and life restored her primordial virginity. And those human souls who transformed their etheric bodies through Christ's presence fertilized her Christ-permeated being with a new etheric, human-earthly Sun seed, in order to receive it back from her as an illumination of their individual, eternal, spirit-consciousness. In that sacred life-cycle is to be found the true nature of all Christian initiation. From the Christ it flows

32

to humanity, where it is assimilated, preserved and radiated forth into the earthly soul atmosphere. The Earth receives and nourishes these human life-seeds in her chaste womb, reflecting their matured, Holy Spirit radiance back into human consciousness, which knows itself then in its full, self-conscious spirit identity.

It is our task today, as pupils of modern anthroposophical spiritual science in the age of the consciousness soul, to raise this whole process into fully awakened consciousness. What the early Christians up to the Middle Ages and then the pupils of Christian Rosenkreutz produced, still only half-consciously, we must strive today to create consciously, that is, anthroposophically. So that not only the final stage of the pentecostal illumination but also the whole eternal way from Golgotha through the 40 + 10 days to Pentecost will become our conscious spiritual practice. Then shall stream into our awakened consciousness the mighty spirit-fire illumination of the end of the twentieth century, revealing and recalling the unseen workings of the modern Christ among us, in the same way that in the *Ur*-Pentecost the unconscious and forgotten deeds of the Christ were remembered by the *Ur*-disciples. As Anthroposophia in the form adapted to the mind soul was born for the first time at Pentecost, so is Anthroposophy today — as the creation of the age of the consciousness-soul — being continually reborn out of the modern Christ experiences and initiation, inspired and directed by the eternally preserved, living, initiatory example of Rudolf Steiner's life among us.

As mentioned above (see the Introduction), the central meaning of the modern, anthroposophically illumined Christ experience to be described in this book, is this: that the experiences which have been a reality in our world for more than half a century will be consciously assimilated into its own (anthroposophical) spirit by means of the new 'Pauline method' of anthroposophical spiritual science. Anthroposophy will then become what, indeed, it always has been: the living, conscious, ever-present and active illumination and remembrance of the past, present and future Christ evolution of humanity and the Earth.

In order to prepare rightly for our study of the modern Christ experience of the twentieth century, we must impress into our life the experience of St Paul at the gates of Damascus — because here, for the first time in human history, an event took place that anticipated far in advance our own times. The fruits of what the disciples achieved still only half-consciously during the three years and 50 days was offered to St Paul in a condensed, fully-conscious twinkling of an eye — that lasted three days — owing to the appearance of the etheric Christ in the radiating new soul sphere of the Earth. Instead of the cosmic Midnight Sun of the old initiations, an earthly Midday Sun was revealed, openly shining and pouring its living radiance into an awakened, self-conscious and free human soul.

Chapter 2

St Paul at the Gates of Damascus

The contemplation of St Paul's Christ experience at the gates of Damascus, as communicated in the Acts of the Apostles and in his Epistles to the first Christian communities, offers a most important help in creating the right spiritual awareness in order to decipher the riddles of the modern Christ experience. In that sense it is, and always will be, a modern event: an archetype of a radical transformation in man's relationship to the Christ. Before embarking on our study in greater detail, let us emphasize again the nature of this change. Before Damascus — and, as we saw above, this pertains also to the experiences of Christ's disciples — man's relationship with the Christ was unconscious; it was regulated either generally through Jehovah, as a 'night god',[1] or through the old temple initiation of the eastern cultures. The reason for this was based first and foremost on the fact that humanity, as an earthly ego creation, was still in the making, and the Christ was its creative source. For humanity as a whole He was always the sacrificial divine Being, through whom everything that was made was actually realized in earthly evolution. In great, epochal acts of cosmic-earthly sacrifices, He shaped humanity from the very first steps of its earthly evolution, forming it in the process more and more in His likeness[2] and, as we saw above, increasingly forming Himself also in the likeness of man[3] until the time came when both sides were ripe enough to allow a mutual 'face to face' penetration to take place.[4] The first was Jesus of Nazareth's complete merging in spirit, soul and body with the cosmic Christ. This event is the eternal cornerstone of the whole temple of Christ-permeated humanity, the archetypal form of all future meetings of Christ with humanity up to the end of earthly evolution.[5] As Rudolf Steiner repeatedly pointed out, in the transformation of Saul to Paul at the gates of Damascus — though taking place before the middle of the fourth post-Atlantean epoch — we can see the first form of an experience of the Christ which belongs essentially to the *fifth* cultural epoch and beyond. The reason for this modernity can be explained in the following way.

Though St Paul was an initiate in the old Hebrew Mysteries,[6] his actual meeting with the Christ was, on the other hand, a natural, midday experience, taking place in full self-consciousness for the first time in human evolution. It was the first naturally 'bridged' spiritual experience ever, welding together all those opposites that up to our own time divide and separate our true soul-and-spirit life from our physical, external life. The spirit shone *through and inside* the physical world without suppressing it entirely, as was the case in the old initiation. It was at once a delicately sensible and supersensible experience, a day and a night experience, a fully incarnated as well as a mighty excarnated experience, a most personal and yet absolutely universal event, and so forth. In other words, St Paul's experience shows, at least as a first indication, in the form of the supersensible experience itself, the beginning of the modern knowledge drama of the Second Coming, which the modern Christ experience brings to full expression. But as a matter of fact this also means that Christ assumes His new and future-orientated creative role in regard to humanity. He appears as educator and initiator of the human ego towards freedom and love, establishing man's future mysteries of self-consciously acquired spirit knowledge.[7] And this revealing of Himself openly as an initiator of modern man, transforming man directly out of the spiritual world without impairing in the least his self-consciousness but rather strongly consolidating it in supersensible reality, teaching, as it were, publicly the most intimate secrets of His community and communion with humanity — this is the true nature of His etheric Second Coming, which begins in the twentieth century.[8] We can now look more closely at some of the basic elements of St Paul's experience at the gates of Damascus.

The first stage of the Pauline experience results directly from the spirit radiance that emanates from the figure of the Etheric Christ. It is what might be termed *the powerful illumination of self-knowledge*, by means of which man learns directly to see the true nature of his death forces. The second element is the experience of *the transformation and remoulding* of the human soul, as a result of Christ's demonstration of his real soul being in the soul world. The third and most difficult element to grasp is that process in which *the Christ confers on man the future seeds of spirit, soul and bodily evolution*, actually transferring into his self-conscious spirit hands the responsibility for the future evolution of humanity and the Earth. Let us, therefore, observe in St Paul's own words these three elements: self-knowledge, transformation of the soul, sowing the seeds of all future human evolution.

From the most external description of the events at the gates of Damascus, it is immediately evident that Christ's appearance illuminates man's being in such a way that it becomes the source of a most true and exact self-knowledge. Saul is immediately confronted with his inner Death being, with that part of the soul that continuously persecutes the Christ in us. Those shattering words, 'Saul, Saul, why persecutest thou me?'[9] have resounded esoterically ever since in each true, fully-conscious meeting with the Christ—and in the twentieth century with an even greater devastating force. Especially for the anthroposophically motivated modern Christ experience—as I shall endeavour to show in Chapter 4—this is of the utmost significance. Through Christ's light, man begins to see to what an overwhelming extent the forces of illness and death (the luciferic-ahrimanic forces) penetrate and corrupt his soul and bodily sheaths. Man is actually convinced, beyond any possible doubt or self-delusion (because of the absolute clarity of his sight at this moment) that he, Saul, his daily self, is woven and formed almost entirely out of these forces; that, when compared with the sublime light being that emerges mysteriously out of the still completely unknown province of his soul life, it must be admitted, with no escape, that man's daily personality is constituted of those forces that cause evil, sickness and death in the world and in man—that is, out of those forces that are necessary in order to transform man into an independent, self-conscious, separated being in the cosmos.[10]

For St Paul the presence of this 'Saul' being within himself, and the basic, ever-present, duality of Saul-Paul, became the positive ground on which he based his whole life and teaching. Wherever we open his Epistles and come upon his descriptions of man, Christ, and man's transformation through Christ, we always find first of all this basic motif.[11] The fruits of this self-knowledge are twofold: firstly, a moral one; secondly, a cognitive one. The first finds its expression in the realization that love is the highest soul reality of Christ-permeated man. The second is the conscious striving towards clear knowledge of the Christ and man's transformation through Christ. So for St Paul, true self-knowledge—gained on the path of death and freedom to Damascus, immediately after his participation in the stoning to death of St Stephen and, striving mightily further to persecute all Christians wherever they happened to be—became the resurrected power of a new cognitive and moral life. We can also formulate it thus. *Over and above his Saul-Paul duality, St Paul continuously endeavours to construct a bridge of free knowledge and moral love on which he could firmly stand, holding himself upright in the sight of the Christ and justifying his upright soul position.* He must transform his self-knowledge, so we feel, into such a motivating moral and cognitive power that will enable him to freely develop his conscious knowledge capacities, in order to achieve an ever deeper penetration into the mysteries of Christ's being and activity. We can therefore say: the Christ experience, as St Paul experienced it, is not a momentary and passing 'lightning' event; the actual revelation is, in reality, the sowing of a seed of permanent, ongoing transformation in the human soul, effective for all subsequent development of the whole man. What one achieves in the Christ experience continues to take place on all levels if one understands it so. It is gradually transformed from an historical event in a specific time and place into an ever-present process of the evolving drama of spirit knowledge.

St Paul's Christ experience became the starting point of a true initiation into the deepest mysteries of human existence, borne in the full self-consciousness and freedom of the individual. As we pointed out above, when we investigate St Paul's experience carefully we discover that he refers, esoterically, to three basic levels in his experience and knowledge of the Christ. The first stage is described in the following way: 'for now I know in part, but then shall I know even as also I am known.'[12] The second is described thus: 'But we all with open face beholding as in a glass the glory of the Lord, are changed into the same image from glory to glory, even as by the spirit of the Lord.'[13] The description of the third stage is given in the words: 'I am crucified with Christ; nevertheless I live; yet not I, but Christ lives in me.'[14]

Here we have a very exact description of the three stages of the transformation of the etheric body into the mirror of supersensible perception. A completely transformed etheric body is a perfectly pure and shining mirror, reflecting the spirit in its fullness. To begin with, however, after only one stage of transformation it is two-thirds dark — that is, it assimilates most of the light of Christ's being, reflecting only a part of His glory. The first impression received by Christ's illumination reveals the darkening death forces woven into man's life-organism. Man knows, therefore, that what he sees as the first supersensible experience is only preliminary and partial. When one works one's way further, then the partial vision can be extended into a greater wholeness: 'But when that which is perfect is come, then that which is in part shall be done away.'[15] In the second stage, self-knowledge changes into self-transformation. Man knows himself to be known by Christ, i.e. an active cognitive interrelationship is established, in which man no longer sees only himself (darkly) by means of Christ's light, but he knows himself as Christ knows him, that is, not through death but through resurrected, eternal life. But this means that man can now see openly in the glass the glory of the Lord, the true soul-image of the Christ, reflected inwardly in the perfected etheric body. And this sight works creatively as a conscious transforming power, changing man into the likeness of that image. Here man truly knows as he is known by Christ, because the Christ gives him his creative, reality-sustaining power of sight. In the terminology used often by St Paul, man puts on the new human image, the new Adam, participating consciously in the wonder of humanity's reshaping in and through Christ.[16] This is where we find St Paul's second, most sacred ground of being: when the 'I' holds fast to true self-knowledge, seeing still only partly and darkly but knowing clearly what is the source of his partiality, namely, seeing without delusion his active, opaqueness-creating Death being. If, in other words, the self-conscious

'I' in the midst of supersensible illumination, consciously holds itself in the full light of Christ, without fainting or plunging back into ordinary consciousness, man must be able to ground himself firmly in his consciousness-preserving and awakening abyss of death and duality. Then he can participate consciously in the second state outlined above, being granted the grace of seeing into the mystery of humanity's re-creation through Christ.

Now we are in a position to follow St Paul to the highest realization of his Christ experience: the complete union and penetration of his being by the Christ. He is actually saying: participating as I do in my reshaping by Christ, and knowing perfectly well, through His light of self-knowledge, who this 'I' is in reality without Him—that is, my Saul soul being—I can rightly celebrate Christ's life and being within me as my true self. Yet this is not I, as Saul, but I in and through the consciousness-awakening Death being of Saul that became Paul at the gates of Damascus, who is a completely new being moulded according to Christ's likeness from the very roots of human existence. Saul-Paul in me is thus perfected as my unshakeable anchorage of freedom and love, consciously bridging the infinite abyss between the Son of God and the Son of Man, the first and the last Adam in me. And because also the third part of his etheric body was transformed, St Paul could faithfully testify: the life which I now live in the flesh is no longer mine because I experienced my absolute Death being in Christ's death in me, and therefore my ordinary Saul self no longer lives by himself alone, but he, the new Christ-permeated soul-and-life form of my newly achieved wholeness, lives in me.

In this way St Paul became the greatest apostle of the living death and resurrection, because as the other apostles did—but unlike them in full supersensible consciousness—he received into himself the seal of the resurrection in spirit, soul and body. What he first saw he also assimilated and made his own as the first germ of Christ-filled being, which, historically, from the twentieth century on, all human beings can—and must—more and more develop, in order to complete in the right way their earthly evolution.

When we delve in such a way into St Paul's experience at the gates of Damascus, bearing in mind that only a very brief example could be given here, we discover the seed and archetype of the modern Christ experience: the beginning of that which will be completed only in the distant future but that must begin now, i.e. the self-conscious transformation of man through a free collaboration with the helping, guiding and initiating being of the Christ, building around His sacrificial life-model an ever-growing community of human beings who consciously work together under His direct guidance.

Now according to St Paul, two things await the Second Coming

(Parousia) of Christ, his etheric reappearance from the twentieth century onward. The first is of a cosmological nature: the redemption of the planet Earth and its natural kingdoms through the new Christ consciousness of humanity: 'For the earnest expectation of the creature waiteth for the manifestation of the sons of God; for the creature was made subject to vanity not willingly, but by reason of him who hath subjected the same in hope; because the creature itself also shall be delivered from the bondage of corruption into the glorious liberty of the children of God.'[17] Here St Paul speaks unmistakably about the death processes of the old Earth and the birth of the new Sun: the creation of a new planetary sphere of everlasting life, the new Earth and Heaven, through the 'glorious liberty of the children of God' — that is, through the free co-working of self-conscious human beings with the Christ.[18] The second prophecy of St Paul has to do with the mystery of evil: 'For the mystery of inequity doth already work: only he who now letteth will let, until he be taken out of the way; and then shall that Wicked be revealed, whom the Lord shall consume with the spirit of his mouth, and shall destroy with the brightness of his coming.'[19] This means that the problem of evil is to be experienced in our time on a much deeper level than was possible in the days of St Paul. The difference is the following. Whereas in the past evil was mainly a problem of man's bodily sheaths,[20] in our own age evil is becoming, through the consciousness soul, a direct temptation of the ego itself.[21]

Therefore, as we shall see later, it is not the overcoming of death as such that is the most difficult mystery inherent in Christ's appearance today. This was, to a certain extent, already accomplished in the fourth cultural epoch and must only be recapitulated and adapted to the level of the fifth, present epoch. The overcoming of death is, in a sense, an actual given reality in the modern Christ experience today. But the struggle with evil is another matter altogether, because since Golgotha the forces of evil active in human evolution have penetrated much deeper into the very core of man's self. This future, apocalyptic struggle was clearly seen by St Paul: '[He] opposeth and exalteth himself above all that is called God, or that is worshipped; so that he as God sitteth in the temple of God, shewing himself that he is God.'[22] The experience of the being of evil so deep in one's soul that he appears to be sitting as God in the temple, in the holy of holies of the human soul — this is the new reality not yet accessible to self-knowledge gained in the Pauline illumination through Christ. Therefore, the redemption of man's inmost soul, together with the redemption of the heart of planet Earth, are the two spirit legacies of St Paul and early Christianity as a whole for our time. We shall now begin their closer exploration.

Chapter 3

The Conditions of the Modern Christ Experience — The Evolution of Freedom

In the past, the direct inner co-workings of the Christ, in and with the human soul, was neither necessary nor possible, because he worked upon humanity when it was still part of a living and ensouled Earth. The Earth still carried within it the rudiments of the living and sentient evolutions of her cosmic past. Being still young and growing, the Earth was recapitulating early stages of evolution in which its embryonic warmth, light and life sheaths were till being shaped. It was only after the separation of the Earth from the Sun and, later, from the Moon, that the hardening, densifying and death-bringing forces slowly but surely gained the upper hand. The warmth-, light- and life-giving beings, the higher leaders of young humanity, then began to withdraw their direct external guidance, leaving man to realize his freedom as an earthly being. The gods enabled man to experience death and extinction by inviting these forces to participate in human evolution. But they themselves could not experience their earthly influence; death itself remained an absolute riddle to them.[1]

In this way man was taught self-consciousness and egohood: through learning to experience death as the final ending of life and as the ultimate darkening of his soul and spirit vision after death, which, in its turn, could lead to a real death of the human soul.[2] A veil of forgetfulness was spread over his spiritual origin, and the gates of birth were closed; a veil of fear closed the gates of death, and man's spiritual destination was darkened and suppressed. Deprived of the knowledge of his spiritual origin and destination, cut off from the living memory of his cosmic past and from the living stream of its future, humanity began to learn to value the present earthly life, and concentrated its attention increasingly on the physical plane, discovering and mastering the forces and beings of the Earth.[3]

The more this process intensified itself, the more conscious man became of himself as an earthly, separate personality. And the more he individualized himself, the more he felt himself independent of his divine origin and destination. He wanted from now on to know himself and the world purely by means of his own cognitive forces, resting solely on his outer sense perception and intellectual analysis. He felt that any regression to older, atavistic forms of consciousness would mean a losing of his free and modern humanity. He began to feel his earthly freedom as his most precious moral possession, defending it against any external spiritual intervention, be it religious or otherwise.

However, as historical time advanced from the nineteenth to the twentieth century, from Kali-Yuga to the new age of light, many human beings could no longer suppress the feeling that humanity must find a way to combine harmoniously its freedom with its deeper spiritual nature. Otherwise, they felt, man would be deadening ever more his creative human nature.[4] It is in this sense that we have to understand the approach of Christ to modern man. Ever since the Mystery of Golgotha, He was establishing Himself in the *unconscious* depths of the human soul, waiting until the ripening of man's earthly freedom.[5] A free striving for spiritual knowledge and human love was to arise first from the depths of human nature itself, leading man out of his free initiative to seek a modern way to the spirit. Therefore, any modern experience of the Christ, be it as mighty and transformative as it often is, must be seen as a friendly approach, fully respecting man's freedom and self-conscious responsibility for the totality of his life, offering him an experience of himself that might serve as an *example or model* of a possible future evolution. The Christ plants a potent seed in the human soul, but He does so in such a way that this seed can only become fruitful in humanity's future life, when man himself, out of his own free, cognitive and moral initiative, takes hold of it and independently carries it further.

Seen cosmologically, Christ brings to humanity the enlivening Sun forces of its bygone ages, but He does so only in order to awaken man to his own inner, independent Sun nature. As we shall see later, if the Earth is to become a new Sun, this depends not only on the initial, redeeming act of Christ, nor alone on his present modern revelation, but also on its being ever strengthened and continued by humanity. It is a co-working, a mutual labour and sacrifice, uniting Him and humanity ever more closely, that will be increasingly called for and consciously recognized as the right spiritual advancement for the Earth's future. But for this co-working, man's absolutely free position in the universe must first have been firmly grounded and assured. As was mentioned above, it is the unique destiny of Lucifer and Ahriman[6] that enabled man to find his independent self in that empty void of creation,[7] where the will of the Fathers from Heaven ceased to rule.[8]

In the past, in the old Mysteries, a real death experience of the human soul was purposefully prepared and consciously carried forward, reaching its dramatic culmination in the final act of initiation: in the three days of deathlike temple sleep, by means of which the soul and spirit of the neophyte — and also a part of his etheric body — were separated from the physical body and transported by the hierophant to the supersensible worlds. But in this process the aspirant had to be completely dependent on his teacher or guru. According to Rudolf Steiner's investigations, he would be unable to make even the smallest advance in his spiritual training without entirely surrendering his personality, suppressing his ego and eventually, at the final initiatory act, also his awakened daily consciousness and very life. His consciousness was lowered and a trance-like state of consciousness prevailed, darker and more unconscious than in ordinary deep sleep. This means that his spiritual eyes and ears were opened without his self-conscious participation.[9] It also means, as a necessary correlate, that the pupil remained dependent on his teacher in all his subsequent supersensible experiences.[10]

But when the Christ approaches modern man, He does so exactly in those moments in which man's self-consciousness, through pain, loneliness and despair, is enhanced — in the moments in which he experiences the necessary consequences of his having been freed from the living forces of the universe.[11] Rudolf Steiner also describes how in the old initiation the hierophants had to take care that during the initiation the pupil did not encounter alone the forces of death and evil that are released from his soul and bodily sheaths. They had to hide them from his opened spirit eyes by lowering his self-consciousness and sacrificially protecting him from his lower self.[12] Here again, the reverse of our own time is obvious. Among the most important events of the modern initiation as described by anthroposophical spiritual science[13] are to be found exactly those fully conscious and direct confrontations with one's own death and evil-creating forces. And so it stands also with the natural but anthroposophically penetrated modern initiation through Christ. The same flash of light that kindles the light of living spirit consciousness also illuminates the deadening, hardening forces in man's being. And the word of life, when streaming into man's awakened heart, shows him, in the most exact manner, the existence of evil as a mighty reality in the depth of his soul.

Only through this intimate self-knowledge can man rightly understand and utilize the blessing that Christ confers on his being. He understands that Christ shows him in pictures, words and deeds what he can *become* if he will work on himself by his own free decision and continuous effort. The so-called 'redemption' through Christ is, therefore, something quite different from what is commonly believed and preached. Many people, unfortunately, see in it an end to their spiritual striving. In reality, however, Christ shows man the depths and heights of his soul in order to place him in a balanced, humble and realistic position in regard to the burdens of the past and the hopes of the future. The modern Christ experience can thus be rightly termed the revelation of man's real and living, balanced present.[14] But to be balanced in such a way in regard to one's evolution in time means also to realize one's true humanity. Therefore, the modern Christ experience can most aptly be described thus: 'It is the Christ who gives me my humanity.'[15]

So we can say: the conditions of the experience of the etheric Christ from the middle of the twentieth century onward are derived directly from the inner, organic laws of the evolution of humanity towards freedom. So far, only Rudolf Steiner's investigations concerning the body, soul and spiritual evolution of humanity offer, in the most varied and manifold ways, a coherent and scientific explanation of its essential features, which are — and this is historically and esoterically demonstrable — the ever-growing, self-enhancing and self-accelerating emancipation and individuation of the human race, both as a whole and in the development of each single individual. This individuation process is, however, from an esoteric point of view, *evolution and involution together*.[16] The advance in self-consciousness is achieved at the cost of the natural, intimate and sacred participation of humanity in the living reality of the cosmic and earthly worlds.[17] Let us now briefly look more closely at the main features of this individuation process.

Especially significant for the post-Atlantean evolution of humanity is the beginning of its inner soul development, starting with the sentient soul epoch and extending five to six thousand years later up to our fifth cultural epoch (a quarter of which is already behind us). It is interesting to realize that it was the old Ancient-Indian wisdom that designated the development of man's self in soul inwardness as Kali-Yuga, or the Small Dark Age, which lasted from 3001 BC to AD 1899.[18] Darkness, for the true eastern mind, is everything that has been developed in the West since then, in the Egyptian-Chaldean, Hebraic-Grecian, Latin-medieval and Anglo-German cultures, up to our own day. The reason for this eastern conviction lies in the fact that it could more clearly perceive the external, negative results of this evolution but not so clearly its inner, hidden justification, which can only be grasped through understanding the Christ impulse, past, present and future.

The true essence of the Christ impulse means: the spiritualization of the ego-evolution of humanity.[19] And it means, therefore, that the ego must first be there, directly available to such a spiritualization. This ego must work its way through the bodily sheaths of man, creating its soul-inwardness and personal subjectivity by transforming them through its own forces. Such a work also brings with it as an unavoidable corollary a certain devitalization, a suppression as well as corruption of the sheaths' original constitution. But only through this overcoming of its bodies does the ego gain its full independence and self-consciousness.

In the sentient soul evolution (2907–747 BC) this was relatively unperceived, because the healing forces of the Mysteries were still strongly active. The ego imprints in the astral body are, from a certain

43

point of view, the shallowest, and at this stage its influence on the etheric and physical organizations is almost nil. But with the onset of the intellectual or mind soul cultural epoch (748 BC–AD 1314), the ego influence began to be more strongly felt: positively as the beginning of the development of free thinking, fantasy and the personal dignity of the individual in Graeco-Latin times,[20] and negatively as the clouding of the last remnants of the old atavistic supersensible perception, resulting also in the growing inability of humanity to understand the cosmic Sun nature of the Christ.[21] This point of time was also the turning point in the evolution of the etheric body. Up to the Mystery of Golgotha it was still actively forming man's physical body according to the cosmic wisdom of the Kyriotetes, the Spirits of Wisdom — that is, working still from the power of the original impulse of the Old Sun.[22] But it exhausted itself through the growing materialization of the physical body,[23] and then, after Golgotha, as an increasingly empty and dead form,[24] it began to release itself from the physical body. For the time being, however, up to the beginning of the fifteenth century and, in a sense, still up to the middle of the nineteenth century, it was still powerfully supported by both the very last forces of the old eastern Mysteries and by the strong feeling and devotion aroused in the soul by the Jewish, Christian and Islamic religious scriptures, ritual and belief.[25]

The most decisive step in man's individuation began when the ego became so powerful that it could begin to penetrate and transform — also devitalize and corrupt — the physical body. This has become possible since the fifteenth century,[26] and reached a certain climax in the nineteenth and twentieth centuries of our modern culture. Now this stage brought with it a number of important transformations of the *whole* being of man. Physically, with the help of the Gabriel Moon forces (1529–1879), the brain was transformed as a necessary foundation to enable purely physical thinking to provide the basis for the free and active spirit thinking in the coming Michael Sun epoch.[27] This led to the magnificent developments of the mechanistic, materialistic natural sciences, and their implementation in the no less fantastic achievements of modern technology. As a consequence of this special forming and deforming of the physical body, a further loosening and emptying of the etheric body took place, now not only from the head (this process was, of course, also accelerated) but also from the heart and lung region, that is, from the central rhythmical system of the human organization.[28]

This loosening of the etheric *from the head down to the heart* has a most decisive influence on the astral and ego organizations of the whole human constitution. It causes a real division of lower and upper man. We can discover an excarnating-dispersing effect on the upper part of the ego together with a parallel, too strong incarnation in the lower pole. This growing polarization brings about a far-reaching transformation of the fourfold human organization and with it an enhanced separation of the soul forces.[29]

It is a remarkable, extraordinarily interesting process. Taken as a totality, it amounts to this. It causes 1) a hardening of the physical body, 2) a loosening (and emptying, devitalizing) of the etheric, 3) an animalization through dismembering of the astral, and 4) a dispersing–condensing split by an uncontrolled excarnating–incarnating swing of the ego. Now the combined effect of this fourfold process on the soul of man is first reducible to a threefold and then to a basic twofold soul symptom. In ordinary consciousness it remains mostly hidden, showing itself only in psycho-physical pathological conditions.[30] Through self-achieved initiation or through the naturally given, but then anthroposophically spiritualized modern Christ experience, it is brought clearly into full self-consciousness and knowledge.

The first element of the threefold soul symptom is experienced as a growing feeling of death and dying. This is the result of that which is taking place in between the hardening physical and the loosening etheric body. The second symptom appears as an augmentation of the first and is not always easily distinguished as a separate element, which it nevertheless undoubtedly is, namely, the experience of a mighty inner fissuring and opening of a bottomless abyss in between man's physical-etheric bodies on the one hand and his astral body and ego on the other. But the third element is still more inwardly experienced. It results from that which happens between man's astral and ego beings: man experiences the whole drama of the dismemberment of his soul (and life) forces as a growing fading of his self-conscious ego unity and ego control, or, which is the same, as an evaporation, disappearance of the ego centre altogether. Now this threefold process can be understood only if we pay careful attention to Rudolf Steiner's indication that since the middle of the nineteenth century—and increasingly as time moves on—humanity's individuation as a whole, and the individuation of each individual as a part of this overall evolution, compels it to begin the crossing, unconsciously, of the threshold of the etheric, astral and spirit worlds.[31]

The visibility of the Christ as a purely supersensible (etheric) figure in the soul (astral) world[32] is thus a perfectly natural result of these necessary evolutionary stages, which are the building stones of humanity's path of individuation and freedom. It can therefore be understood why the Christ appears always before 'the sick and sorrowful', that is, before those who experience most intensely these evolutionary changes.[33] From 1933, these changes became externally visible through humanity's unconscious—and therefore destructive—crossing of the threshold in middle Europe. From 1966, these changes reached the point of universality and are becoming—and will ever more become—a global, daily, common human experience of humanity as a whole.[34]

We can now reduce the above described threefold soul experience into a twofold, major modern soul experience. There are two main groupings, or soul-poles, moods or existential life experiences that every man experiences to some degree in the twentieth century, though here they are described in their archetypal form. The one pole is concentrated especially around the growing awareness of what takes place between the physical and etheric bodies, as well as to a certain extent also between these bodies and the higher members. Above we referred to these as death-like experiences of the human soul. Its subjective manifestations are to be seen in a growing sense of devitalization, emptiness, up to complete despair, coupled with excarnation experiences that can lead to an acute sense of inner duality and disharmony between one's earthly being and one's spiritual being. Rudolf Steiner referred to this experience as the greatest inner disharmony ever to be experienced in human evolution.[35] Man, in a sense, experiences himself as continuously dying in 'ordinary' life itself. He dies in living and lives in dying as his natural state of being in the—no longer purely physical—world.[36]

Around the other soul-pole there are grouped all those still deeper experiences that emerge from man's unconscious crossing of the threshold. This means, above all, the symptoms caused by the separation of the soul forces and the losing of ego-centring and control,[37] which eventually might lead to a real, unavoidable and, unfortunately, so often deeply tragic experience of the problem of evil in the soul itself. Since the middle of the century and now, at its end, this ever deeper—because more inward—process might reach the intensity of an inner, unconscious identification of *oneself* as an evil being.[38]

Only when these two fundamental states of soul (the further investigation of which lies beyond our limits here) are firmly established in man through his natural evolution does the modern, Etheric Christ come to meet him. And then, as we shall presently see, 'if man had only really sharpened his eyes through Anthroposophy',[39] they are transformed, *in the moment of the meeting itself*, into the two pillars of the bridge of consciousness-continuation: securing man's remembrance, awareness and conscious supersensible seeing and comprehending of the living Christ. The Christ is then *seen* through the metamorphosed forces of death, and is *experienced* through the mystery of man's evil.

When the anthroposophical spiritual scientist wishes to study the modern Christ experience as a fully conscious 'I' experience, he knows quite well that these two basic soul experiences—the result of the threefold process between his members that comes about through their fourfold involutionary transformation—must serve him as the foundation stone on which he strives to build his conscious bridge of spirit remembrance and self-conscious imaginative sight.[40] For him, the situation of modern man at this differentiated abyss of the threshold is a

46

personal spiritual-scientific observatory, the only guarantee of his being able to remain awake when he stands before the inner etheric cross of the second, modern Golgotha, which is composed of his own forces of death and evil.

He knows that through the meeting with the living Christ his being of death becomes the guarantee of steadfast supersensible cognition; his soul is awakened from death into the light of true and free anthroposophical-imaginative knowledge. And the being of evil becomes his only guarantee of consciousness creating and sustaining spirit morality: the dismembered soul is remoulded according to His healing presence in him. In this way the moral sacredness of anthroposophical knowledge and cognition begins to illuminate the modern Christ experience. We shall, therefore, begin now its deeper study.

Chapter 4

The Modern Christ Experience —
The Meeting with the New Initiator

There are three basic elements or stages in this meeting which, while forming a unity, will be described here separately for the sake of clarity.[1] The first might be described as the awakening from the death of the soul through the Imagination of Christ's etheric *appearance*; the second is the soul's remoulding through the Inspiration of His living *words*; the third might be characterized as the kindling of the eternal fire of the self by the Intuition of His active *presence*.[2] The first — imaginative — element is brought to consciousness by means of the forces of death. As we saw above, the growing separation of man's subtle members from his hardening physical body is the cause of the modern deathlike experience of the human soul. It thereby gradually loses the unconscious, half-conscious, living and sentient immediate connection with the living and sentient outer universe. The human soul is thereby prepared for the first inner and free experience of the spirit. The second — inspirative — element is the outcome of man's intensive discovery of the existence of evil in himself and in the world. This is one of the greatest mysteries of the present time, which will be increasingly experienced in the future.[3] Here there is not only a separating of man's members from one another and man's separation from the outer living world but a real inner splitting and degradation of man's innermost soul. This split, however, for the first time enables a real inner, free spiritual experience of the mystery of the soul's remembrance of itself as an 'I' form in the stream of supersensible world-becoming. The third — intuitive — element can only be understood if we accept the fact that man can actually step out of himself and completely externalize his own being, so that he might — as a result of the foregoing trials and probations — be directly penetrated, as a pure spiritual being, by another, purely spiritual presence. Being penetrated in this way by the actual movements, acts and inner touch of the Christ means the final and conclusive rebirth and reshaping of man's total constitution, in spirit, soul and body, sowing in him the seed of his — and the Earth's — possible complete self-transformation in the future.[4]

The first stage of the experience is dominated by a thoroughly etherized physical vision.[5] It is a real (objective) sight, a delicate and yet strikingly powerful visual perception, in which man can become aware of his share in creating Christ's visual aura or form of appearance. He can actually see how the form that emerges out of the surrounding darkness clothes itself in the substances taken from his own being. His partly released etheric and sentient bodies, being in a state of the highest, most intensive, inner movement, pour themselves out and lose themselves in the engulfing and sucking emptiness. And out of their whirling dynamics the Christ weaves His luminous body of manifestation; He ignites and lights up man's wasted sheaths and becomes visible in them. By so incorporating Himself in man's released and devitalized members, the Christ weakens and subdues His mighty living presence in order to be consciously grasped and seen by man.[6] It is this incorporation that is experienced as an awakening from the death of soul; consciousness is kindled of which man is from now on assured that it is a consciousness of living light in the soul itself. The soul begins to be light-giver, radiating its own light into its surroundings.[7]

The second stage is a 'hearing' experience. Christ's words assume such an inner potency that a consciously experienced dismemberment of man's soul, and then its re-membering into a new self-identity and consciousness, takes place. This remoulding is a result of Christ's sacrificial flow of being. Man knows: the power that flows in me through His words unites my separated soul forces. That which must have been seen as the evil being in one's own soul—the distorted, twisted form of the separated soul forces—is transformed and shaped by the magical power of the word gestures into a soul-being of pure, quickening and re-membered spiritual life. Life begins to pour through man's heart, transforming the forces of healing into knowledge and vice versa, demonstrating in the spiritual core of the soul the reversal and metamorphosis of moral and cognitive forces into one another.[8]

The third stage is a direct transference of creative identity and responsibility from Christ to man, caused by a definite act, the mysteries of which are the hardest to describe because our language is not at all adapted to describe purely spiritual relationships. We must imagine not only a visible, dynamic soul-awakening appearance, not only the flowing power of soul remoulding words (all of which represent still a form of dualism, of linking separated beings) but an actual mutual penetration, 'a passing through' of a spiritual being that penetrates man's deepest being, and kindles in him—while 'passing'—the fiery spirit of eternal selfhood, or unified spirit, soul and bodily identity.[9] It is this third stage, as was mentioned above, that made it possible for St Paul to declare: 'Not I, but the Christ in me.' In the threefold structure of the meeting are to be found united the three aspects of Christ's relationship to man in our time: Christ the friend and helper *appears* as man's brother who joins him 'on the way' of his life and destiny; Christ the teacher, who *speaks*, teaching the secrets of His kingdom of eternal life; and Christ the initiator, who *acts*, demonstrating in man the sublime goals of his future evolution.[10] We can now begin to investigate more closely the three stages of the meeting and the three roles of Christ.

In the preceding chapter was a description of the inner soul conditions necessary for preparing modern man for the meeting with the 'new' initiator.[11] In order to characterize once again this existential situation, let us use here a term which, beside its common meaning, received a special content in modern physics. As was pointed out above, at the moment of the meeting with the living Christ in the soul world, man is no longer identified with his physical organism; he has actually lost his home in the physical world and become 'homeless'.[12] Unconsciously he has already passed the first threshold, standing, unknowing, in the midst of the still darkened, but strongly felt, soul world. He is, therefore, in his human state of *singularity*, where all familiar laws of physical space and objectivity have collapsed, and new, unexpected laws begin their reign.[13] But this implies that man has died without dying. He consciously experiences what everyone experiences after ordinary physical death: he dies in, and into, life, from space into living time.[14]

So we can now say: at the moment of the meeting, man is in *a situation of singularity*, in his absolutely unique, individualized space of freed, excarnated, life-time. He is no longer fixed and objectified as a physical point in three-dimensional space. He is already — though still unconsciously before the meeting — livingly flowing back and forth in between the two banks of the river of his life.[15] In ordinary life this is felt only as deprivation and loss, the source of self-annihilation and despair. Through Christ, this state is revealed as man's new space, or home, his new, uniquely personal identity, externalized in, through and around him as the substance of his past and future living physical life, in the time he was — and is yet to be — in space. And as mighty cliffs on either side of his flowing, dynamically circulating life-time river, he touches and feels — before being granted, through the meeting, the awakening soul light of seeing — the mighty, unfolded and infolded cosmic spaces of his pre-earthly and post-earthly existence. The one, on his left, is felt as extensively luminous, unfolded, everywhere present, formatively shaping one's lifetime into realized and therefore transparent timespace. The other, on his right, is felt as intensively dark and infolded, on the one side still pregnant with potential, and therefore opaque, future physical realization and manifestation, and on the other towering majestically into the future time-worlds of the stars.[16]

What has been described is man's experience of his loosening etheric body. But all this is, at this stage, before the great illumination, still only felt, touched, sensed in the surrounding darkness. It is as if, wandering in an underground maze of rocky mountain caves, one hears and feels, knowing oneself to be immersed and surrounded by flowing waters, sensing, touching[17] the dark walls of the stream but having yet no spark to ignite the oil that nourishes the light of one's soul lamp. The appearance of the living Christ in the soul world is the saving fiery spark, kindling and awakening the dormant light of the excarnated soul. And in this illumination consists the first part of the first stage of the meeting.[18]

Let us draw this picture in all its concreteness before our soul eyes. In a single flash of lightning, the whole scene is lighted up in a dazzling, blazing illumination that seems to break into the clearing of one's soul landscape all at once, from all directions of the engulfing dark soul atmosphere.[19] The flowing river of one's life-time, the rocky cliffs of cosmic time-spaces on right and left, give birth, as it were, in their midst, to a pure Sunlike, sublime auric presence that presents itself through one's now joyfully expanding, soaring life-stream.[20] At this moment man feels the mightiest, irresistible upward attraction and is penetrated to the deepest core of his soul by lightness. Knowing himself in pure light, he ascends to the Sun-sphere and blends completely with its radiating abundance.[21]

In the heart of the Sun, man finds his true home,[22] where he experiences eternal peace. And when he looks down through the living light-eyes of his gentle host, he sees how the totality of his life takes its leave from the earthly globe; iridescently streaming and shimmering with magnificent colours, rhythmically expanding into the enveloping cosmic sphere, it merges with the starry firmament that assimilates man's transformed life-time.

According to Rudolf Steiner, this is the most important experience man can have after his death: to see the living Christ essence, in and through his released life-stream, inscribed into the radiating starry firmament.[23] It is, however, also the first element in the modern, anthroposophic meeting with the living Christ in the soul world: the awakening of man from his soul-death by submerging, or 'baptizing', him in his freed, Christ-permeated life-body. This is also the essence of the first stage of the modern 'Damascus' experience.[24] Here is to be found that living 'oasis' of the resurrection of the human soul, where the withered soul life of our time, intellectualized and materialized to death since the nineteenth century, comes to life again,[25] clearly, consciously illuminated by means of that living light which has bathed and penetrated the earthly soul atmosphere from all directions since the beginning of the age of Michael and the new cosmic age of light.

The awakening from the soul-death described here[26] can serve him from now on as his awakened spirit consciousness. In the near future, more and more people will learn, through Christ's comforting, brotherly help, the secret of their soul's redemption during their earthly lifetime. This health-bestowing, life-giving impulse is being increasingly poured into our disintegrating culture, society and the planet Earth, and incarnated human beings will become life-, light- and warmth-givers, drawing the oil for their lamps of soul from the inexhaustible earthly-Sun source of Christ's spirit nourishment. At the end of the twentieth century and the beginning of the next, this source must be openly, exoterically seen, understood and consciously utilized in all fields of life if we are to heal the planet and humanity. And Anthroposophy will become the mothering, nourishing and fostering being of the most important spirit revelation of our time .[27]

Until now I have described only the first, more external side of the meeting with the new initiator. So long as man stays at this stage, however, the process by means of which the Christ becomes etherically, imaginatively, visible remains a mystery surrounded by impenetrable darkness. Only when looked at from the other, inner side — from its back, as it were — does it disclose its secrets.[28] Here we reach that stage where the Christ experience can no longer be termed 'natural' or 'given', because from now on it will be increasingly evident that it is the anthroposophical spiritual schooling that supplies the necessary reserve of consciousness-sustaining and strengthening forces, by means of which the Christ can be consciously known and studied.

That such descriptions as we must put forward here will be considered by many people today to be fantastic, illusory, or worse is perfectly understandable. And yet one would do a great injustice to the modern spiritual reality if one wished, out of fear of such reactions, to remain in the realm of abstract generalities, or conventional, long outmoded religious images. Consciously penetrated and meaningful imaginative sight is, and will be more and more, an absolutely necessary spiritual language of our times. As we shall see in the next chapter, it is exactly the development of this imaginative faculty of the human soul that Rudolf Steiner considered to be the specific contribution of western, scientific spiritual life to the present stage of the historical evolution of human consciousness.[29] Through consciously formed pictures, therefore, we shall try to reawaken in our soul that mighty, shattering impression which reveals itself at the height of the soul's illumination in the Sun-sphere of the living Christ.

Being at the peak of his spiritual excarnation, awakened and released from the long-lasting soul desolation, man is normally, in the usual Christ experiences, immediately pulled down back to the Earth, bringing the health-giving forces of the experience with him into his daily life. As a matter of fact, most of these Christ experiences do end here, and rightly so, for otherwise they wouldn't bring with them healing and blessing. But with the anthroposophically motivated spiritual guest it is different. The end of the usual Christ experience is only the very first beginning. It is this motivating power that, as a hidden reserve of forces, *bursts forth from the depths of the awakened soul, enabling man not to assimilate the whole of the awakening light into his astral, etheric and physical bodies but to reflect most of it back and transform its healing forces into cognitive forces capable of creating and sustaining conscious supersensible knowledge.*[30] This means that the healing power of the living Christ streams back, reflected from the soul onto its bodily sheaths, and then, reversed in its direction, is sent by them backward, *illuminating its source*. In this way man is able to know the Christ with Christ's own light of knowledge.[31]

Only now is real conscious imaginative sight possible, which, because of its surplus of motivated forces, begins to condense and make manifest objective spiritual reality. And what is there revealed is of such a nature that it transforms man's bliss into a profound inner pain.[32]

What transforms the surface vision of the Christ into meaningful imaginative sight is the awareness of what might be termed the Mystery phenomenon of Christ's body-cross of visibility.[33] This appearance, which must be distinguished from all other objects of ordinary imaginative perception, is an active, consciousness-creating and enhancing visibility, in the creation of which man plays a major role.[34]

In the first aspect of the meeting described above, the Christ appears in His full radiance, incorporating Himself in man's freed *living* etheric body. But the other side of this appearance reveals itself immediately thereafter; here Christ *conceals* Himself and, in doing so, strengthens human consciousness and deepens it by incorporating Himself in man's *dead* life forces.[35] It is, then, the first secret that completely escapes the non-anthroposophical Christ experience. First, man sees the glorious Sun-figure of the Christ incorporated in his youthful life forces. But he does not see *how* this appearance is being made possible, that is, what the actual process is that enables him to perceive the etheric, visible form of the Christ at all. Now, however, this becomes visible, namely, *that this body of visibility is woven and condensed from man's own sheaths* which have degenerated through the increasing intellectualization of modern man. What he sees and experiences as his devitalized and deadened etheric substance[36] is externalized before his eyes, devouring the radiating light being of the Christ and darkening—as in a Sun eclipse—His Sun aura.[37]

The essence of the death forces of the soul is drawn out as an impenetrable dark cloud that assumes a powerful, parasitic might. It sucks in the newly kindled, radiating soul light of man and conceals the light's living form. In the ensuing total darkening of the world,[38] in the disappearance of one's newly gained soul foundations, one sees how a Being, stripped of all beauty and might, merges Himself, unites and clothes Himself—annihilates Himself—by surrendering His life-giving heart to darkness's vacuum. He blends with death, and sinks down, suffocated, in its bottomless, whirling soul morass. And man observes that his sight actually grows clearer and more conscious the more this situation develops. The more the Being sinks, the clearer one sees and understands what one sees: one *awakens* ever more through Christ's demonstration of living death.[39] But this awakening is not comparable to the first. It is not a blissful release of one's higher being in a Sun-filled world but a sombre, painful soul contraction, accompanied by a think-ing-like clarity of sight. In the repeated recapitulations of this moment, man realizes that the essence of conscious spirit sight itself is here demonstrated and can therefore be made into the object of further anthroposophical study.[40]

The experience that Christ's light and life die in the living world because of one's own self-created death being, that one is, simply as a man of the consciousness-soul age, a death bringer to the world's living, redeeming light, and the instant realization that one must radiate one's darkness out into the world in order to be consciously awakened in spirit reality, causes, through the deepest pain, an inversion and frac-turing of far deeper layers of one's being than was hitherto experienced by man. In this experience is to be found a further, deeper key to the understanding of the nature of the spiritualization of the consciousness soul into a seeing, or imaginative soul.[41]

This means that man perceives clearly, exactly at the place where formerly the living and light-radiating river of his freed life-body flowed, the abyss of the suffocating and annihilating forces of his spirit forgetfulness. As a real valley of death-forces, it cuts its way directly through man's lifeblood and soul substance.[42] And when the living Christ — as was described above — pours His being into this abyss, *it is this abyss itself which becomes man's eye of self-conscious imaginative sight.* In other words, through Christ's sacrifice the consciousness-awakening power inherent in the consciousness soul, which in physical life makes possible the perception of the outer sense world, is penetrated and assimilated by the power that, through its capacity to preserve life in death and death in life, lifts the conscious human soul to that same sphere. When the consciousness soul is being penetrated in this way with the etheric body of the Christ, its forces are so transformed that it begins to transfer to man's etheric body what usually takes place in the physical body alone.[43]

As we shall see in Chapter 5, the above process is that to which Rudolf Steiner referred under the name of the Second Mystery of Golgotha, out of which the 'Christ consciousness', or the new clairvoyant etheric sight of humanity in the twentieth century, will spring forth.[44] It is this event that makes the Christ visible and penetrable by conscious human sight. The major discovery at this (first) stage of the modern Christ experience is, therefore, that this body of etheric visibility is woven out of the threads that Death spins around Christ's eternal life-tree, and that its workshop is to be found above all in the human brain, which always

54

'murders to dissect' in order to know.[45] In the anthroposophically penetrated Christ experience, the Christ thus lives man's death-producing being before man's externalized mind's (consciousness soul's) eye, and gives, through His sacrificial spirit suffocation, an awakening impulse to man's materializing, withering cognitive forces. At this point there begins the modern, anthroposophical knowledge drama, because the Christ unveils thinking's other, unseen side. While remaining always self-concealed,[46] this escapes ordinary conscious knowledge but is the powerful foundation of this knowledge. For our daily thinking spreads its proudly radiating and conquering light over an outward, external world; the intellect's world, as Goethe said, is the world of finished dead objects and concepts. At the same time, it necessarily blinds our seeing into the world's living, ethereal light. Christ's suffocated luminosity, His humbly darkened living light, opens the eyes of the soul to active participation in its own self-induced awakening to freedom in its experience of death.

The karma of freedom and knowledge is thus experienced and understood. What is inwardly experienced as Christ's etheric bodily cross, created out of man's death forces, awakens in the consciousness soul the strongest desire for true self-knowledge, and the deepest moral obligation and responsibility towards freedom and knowledge in the modern sense. *Every act of knowledge, sensible or supersensible, must become, from our time on, a conscious participation in the modern Mystery of Golgotha.* It must become a conscious consecration of thinking and sense-perception, a sacrificial lifting and carrying of the cross of conscious knowledge and free moral action, which is Christ's gift to humanity in the twentieth century.[47]

This first aspect of the modern Christ experience, His soul-redeeming appearance and knowledge-bestowing crucifixion, makes Him the most intimately comforting friend and helper of modern man in his cognitive struggles and crises. That is, He is our brotherly comforter and adviser in our anthroposophical strivings towards knowledge of the spiritual worlds. He is waiting to be consulted, speaking from the spirit abyss concerning man's spiritual daily initiatives.[48] But the pupil of spiritual science is confronted daily, both while awake and asleep, with the continuous crisis of spiritual knowledge, namely, with the everlasting fight against his spirit forgetfulness. He is dramatically involved in all the difficulties and impossibilities in his efforts to kindle enough light in his soul lamp. The oil-giver, the light's source and nourishment, is the living crucified Christ. In the pictures described above of Christ's second, etheric crucifixion, the earnestly striving anthroposophical student can find an openness to the source of his serious cognitive strivings. This openness can lead him to confront consciously the greatest obstacle to any conscious spirit sight: *the problem of the ever-*

broken, ever-to-be-newly-constructed bridge of living memory over the abyss of spirit forgetfulness.[49]

We can now summarize the foregoing. The first stage of the meeting with the etheric Christ has two aspects, one exoteric, or given, and the other esoteric, which can only be experienced consciously through anthroposophical spiritual schooling. The Christ appears in His majestic light aura and His living light awakens and heals the human soul from its soul and spirit death. For the uninitiated, this appearance is an objective event; he knows himself in the experience to be a participator in a given situation. In this experience he is healed, redeemed or born again; his attention is turned entirely to his own transformation and not at all to the nature of the Being who appears before him. He receives, therefore—and this is, from our time on, completely justified—the blessing of the Christ in a most intimate and sacred way. And he does not wish for more than this grace.

The truly Pauline approach is, however, different. As we saw in Chapter 2, in this case—as in the case of the modern anthroposophical aspirant—the given Christ experience coalesces with a consciously striven-for supersensible experience. The result of this is the development of the 'Pauline method' of investigating the modern Christ event. This method was, for our time, brought to its highest perfection by Rudolf Steiner's anthroposophical spiritual science.[50] And when we use it in order to penetrate beyond the visible appearance of the etheric Christ, we begin to unravel its deeper, hidden nature. This penetration, as was shown above, brings to light not only the subjective transformation of man but also the objective evolutionary struggle and sacrifice of the Christ Himself when He wishes, in our time, to intervene rightly in the course of human evolution.

The first stage of this investigation brought to light that event which, as a necessary background, remains concealed behind Christ's radiating Sun aura. What makes Christ etherically visible is not perceived so long as we see only His external, surface light picture. A special strengthening and deepening of the naturally given etheric perception is necessary (and today only spiritual science offers the means to achieve this aim) in order to penetrate *through* the powerfully shining illumination and to see its actual source. But this source—and this is the unique anthroposophical discovery—is the event of Christ's living death in man's own dying life. It is this aspect which raises the most difficult and anthroposophically crucial questions in regard to the nature of the consciousness soul in general and its transformation into the imaginative soul in particular. That is, here one begins to create one's knowledge drama out of the source of Christ's etheric visibility in the soul world that borders immediately on our physical world. With the help of the imaginative consciousness soul forces developed in this way, further, still deeper aspects of Christ's being are made available to detailed anthroposophical investigation.[51] We shall now consider their main features.

We might prepare our study of the second stage of the supersensible meeting with the etheric Christ in the soul world by contrasting it with both the ordinary sensible and the given supersensible consciousness of man in our time. If we consider, in the light of the objective, daily consciousness of modern man, the first form in which man experiences his supersensible perceptions, we stand before the following riddle. This experience is a *conscious* experience, that is, it is fully meaningful, directly containing its essence within itself. On the other hand, the degree of *self*-consciousness in this experience is, to begin with, extremely low. Man is always on the verge of total self-forgetfulness. Therefore, the supersensible experience eludes any effort of conscious recollection. It is at once more and less than the ordinary conscious experiences of daily reality. The supersensible experience is not, in contradistinction to the daily experience, a riddle *in itself*. On the contrary, its main characteristic lies exactly in its being wholly a self-sufficient, self-sustaining reality.[52] Here is to be found its 'more'. But its 'less' is to be found in its unrepeatability. An ordinary soul experience is characterized by its voluntary and reflective character. We can always a) repeat or reawaken in ourselves a specific connection of thoughts, feelings or will impulses, and this is so because we can remember them voluntarily; and b) our 'I' image — or self-consciousness — must be able to accompany, as Kant rightly said,[53] all our mental images (*Vorstellungen*). But the supersensible experience darts away from us at the moment of its happening. It lights up abruptly in the soul in order to flicker and die immediately. It strikes through it as a lightning bolt does in a stormy night sky, lowering, sometimes completely suppressing, man's self-awareness, leaving behind it a reverberating, rumbling inner echo. Such an echo, while passing, can deeply shatter and transform man's inner soul constitution, but, on returning to normal consciousness, one has only a vague and evaporating shadow of the reality experienced.[54]

The appearance of the Christ stands as a unique phenomenon of its kind when compared with the sharp dichotomy between the ordinary supersensible and sensible experiences. With the supersensible experience it has in common the fullness of meaningful content as well as the 'lightning' character described above. But it also has a remarkable affinity (not sameness by any means) with our normal daily consciousness. Not that it is in any ordinary way voluntarily repeatable as such, but it has a very peculiar and mysterious relation to man's capacity for preserving his conscious 'I'-awareness through memory — an affinity that brings it, *in this respect,* closer to our daily consciousness than to the normal supersensible consciousness. In this experience, self-consciousness not only does not diminish, as in ordinary supersensible experience, but is rather dramatically *enhanced,* so that we can actually say that man is for the first time consciously 'taught' the original secrets of the constitution of self-consciousness as such in the organization of man and of the world.[55]

This is the true and deeper meaning of Christ's 'teaching' that takes place at the second stage of the meeting. His imaginative appearance, which we studied above, is the source of His soul-awakening, comforting and 'saving' influence. He resurrects the soul from its utter death in life. But this aspect is, on this level, only of a personal and subjective significance. Its objectivity lies deeper and is revealed only when the Christ becomes not only a comforter but demonstrates Himself as He is for Himself. He emerges as if resurrected from a long-lasting suffocation and dumbness, and He begins to speak with a wholeness of being that goes far beyond the light-filled Imagination of his auric appearance. His whole being becomes expressive, silent speech. He pours his life-words directly into the heart of man, and thereby He shatters and builds anew, moulding and fastening the secret of the preservation and consolidation of self-consciousness in supersensible experience. And this creation culminates in an act of offering the seed of this consciousness to man as a seed of the faculty of spiritual self-consciousness. This gift then becomes a model for independent supersensible research, enabling a free and voluntary construction of identity and remembrance in self-motivated, not given, supersensible experiences.[56]

In the second stage we have to do, therefore, not only with the kindling of the light of spiritual (imaginative) consciousness in the etheric world. This kindling occurs rather passively through a given event of 'seeing'. The mere appearance of the Christ causes the awakening. But one can only refer to a 'teaching' from the moment an inner spiritual activity begins on the side of man. Christ's supersensible teaching is an actual 'talk', a flow of creative, destructive and constructive, man-and-world-shaping meanings that stream from teacher to pupil. The real teaching begins when man no longer needs Christ's light in order to awaken his own self but can reflect a surplus of this living light back, as already indicated above, *illuminating the illuminator.*[57] In this mutual illumination the field of polarized tension is created in which not only a visible, two-dimensional but also a 'speaking' Being, a Being experienced in spiritual depth, can be made manifest in His independent identity as a self-transforming, dynamically self-creating, erasing and re-creating Being.[58]

The real experience at this stage must be imagined as a dramatic event. Man is actually transformed into two different beings. The one crosses the field of the polarized soul-tension and merges with the triumphant[59] Christ at the infinite horizon of man's soul. The other stays behind as a personalized stage of experience. Through the performing-speaking figure on the other shore of man's surfacing inner abyss something is spoken, or enacted, which, not yet clearly 'heard', effects nevertheless an inner change in the subjective side of the event. And the more pronounced and precise the mysterious gestures of silent speech, the more profound becomes this inner experience of an external and visible event. This event can be described as an increasing 'twisting in dismemberment' of the soul members of man. And this dismembering process advances up to the periphery of a thorough scattering of 'many' out of a dismembered 'one'.[60]

In the 'former' stage, so man realizes 'now', one saw one's being of Death still abstractly, in the form of a dark, light-sucking and annihilating cloud. Now one not only 'sees'. One acts and lives in a multiplicity of separate, hostile beings that attack and multiply themselves in oneself, thus externalizing man's moral abyss. This abyss not only annihilates light but also transforms all the best desires, wishes and hopes of man for the good and the humanly true into their complete opposites.[61] This splitting and disjoining of the soul forces and beings creates a reversed and autonomous — and therefore evil — metamorphosis of each of man's soul members and beings. And it is enacted, spoken and guided from the horizon of man's now infinitely growing longing to be.[62]

Man is becoming aware, at this stage, of the fact that he is always possessed by these inner soul beings, and that they are usually only concealed, suppressed and tamed by that other being of himself that left and joined the risen, awe-inspiring etheric Christ on the other shore of the inner division of man.

Only now can man begin to 'hear' the meaning of the words enacted and performed on the other side of his inner abyss, from where the living gestures begin to pour forth as healing beings. They stream into his 'den of thieves' and mould there a new form of inwardly composed being. The composition of this being can be heard as follows: 'I am your true "I"-builder and preserver, through absorbing and carrying your evil in my heart of love; I am becoming your new "I", recreated in the destructive core of your evil, shaped in the image of my eternal Life Spirit. Remember yourself in me.'[63] And man then beholds and experiences, through his most intimate soul rhythms, how he consciously partakes in the articulation and re-membering, re-covering and renaming of his innermost being. He feels himself created anew as a real being out of gathered, healed and transformed fragmentation. He knows that he is transformed inwardly into his future image, shaped in the likeness of that living and pouring spirit Identity that reaches into his heart through his primordial soul-and-self division and gives him back — but for the first time as self-conscious 'I' — himself.[64]

In this experience we have before us, albeit in a pictorial and dramatic form — but nonetheless accurately[65] — a preliminary description of the deeper foundation of the knowledge drama of the Second Coming and of conscious spirit knowledge in general. It is the permanent spirit activity that is responsible for the hidden ongoing creation of preservable self-consciousness which, while taken for granted as a given natural fact on the Earth, must always be spiritually maintained through a higher sacrifice. We discover that it is the Christ Being Himself in man that constantly reaches across the stream of Lethe and connects the spirit being of man with his earthly and daily consciousness. What always takes place normally behind our daily consciousness is seen here in its true light. Behind the memory mirror of objective, reflective and voluntary self-consciousness, the process described above is continuously renewed.[66] "In the anthroposophical, modern Christ experience, it is taught as a supersensible conscious art of self-conscious self remembering. This happens through the lifting of the human self to the place where he undergoes the experience of self-conscious self-deconstruction, followed by an exemplary self-conscious self-reconstruction of identity. Only a self that can consciously erase itself and consciously rebuild itself from its very foundations can be the builder of the bridge of consciousness over the abyss of forgetfulness that separates man from his true home and being.[67]

The first stage of the meeting, as was shown above, reveals the moral ground of the modern Christ-cognition of man: the sacrificial act of Christ, assimilating into Himself man's consciousness-kindling death forces. In the second stage, in the light of the imaginative sight that was secured before, the pure moral reality is revealed that forms the ground of the 'I'-being itself in the soul world — that is, not only for the kindling of the light of spirit sight but for the recreating and remoulding of the moral ground forces of the soul so that a preservation of self-conscious identity will be possible in actual spirit life and existence. If the experience of the moral ground of the Christ cognition is the result of the first stage, so, in the second stage, this hidden moral background of spiritual cognition becomes the cognitive power itself. Not only the light of the soul but its very fabric of being is consciously awakened. Not only its death forces, but the far deeper forces of its primordial division and fragmentation are consciously confronted and transformed. The soul light of seeing that was born through Christ's appearance is, through His teaching, condensed into an 'I'-centre that consciously partakes in its own creation and supersensible preservation.[68]

After describing in some detail the first two stages of the modern Christ experience we shall try to indicate also the third stage, in so far as this is possible in book form. The third stage is the final initiatory act, and it takes place when supersensible self-consciousness is firmly consolidated as described above. The higher being of man, which separated itself from him while joining the figure of the risen Christ on the other shore of man's original world abyss, returns and unites itself again with the now consolidated and newly moulded subjective being of man on this side of the abyss. And when this happens, and through this reunion, the Christ Himself virtually 'steps over' and crosses the bridge of remembrance that stretches in man's inner being from Heaven to Earth. And for 'one' ever-present moment, He splits the spirit of man's body in two, passing 'physically' through man. In passing, however, He leaves behind a fiery bodily seed of Himself as a permanent token of remembrance.[69]

Above I characterized this stage as a 'bodily' (heart, blood or limb) experience, comparable to the third element of the disciples' experience at Emmaus: the opening of the eyes in the breaking of Christ's bread of life, by means of which Christ becomes the 'initiator', completing the whole initiatory process of modern man. We can now advance to a more concrete examination of this. As the imaginative appearance of Christ is the awakening of man to conscious spirit reality, and his inspirative outpouring of soul-transforming words is the crystallization of super-sensible self-identity, so his bodily penetration is the awakening back to physical reality, but awakening in the body as in a conscious spirit reality. This means the cancelling of all differences between spirit and matter by making of 'spirit' an 'Earth' and from 'matter' a new 'Heaven'. A crystal-clear transparency is demonstrated when man is passed through and spiritually penetrated at the most opaque and lowest point of his being. A special state of consciousness is realized in this process, which can only be expressed in the following words: 'ultimate creative freedom experienced in heavenly transparency, in the heart of absolute, coarse density'. As in the first stage darkness was transformed into light, and in the second a new being was shaped out of evil, so here beingness as such, the ground of all cosmic heaviness, streams lightly through its infinite zero point of transubstantiation in man himself. 'Beingness, the Father ground of the worlds, finds its return and reversal of home-coming in and through man.'[70] One can also express that which resounds in the omnipotent silence of this stage as follows: 'In your bread of life that I broke in twain while passing and in the fiery spirit of your life I have seeded the fiery seed of My life. This you can assimilate into your being, and in it the world is resurrected from the dead. I thereby transfer to your creative hands and feet the responsibility to nurture and mother the Earth and all its kingdoms of life. I give to you that which until now was protected under My care alone: the future world-seed, containing infinite evolutionary riches and possibilities.' So reverberates the ever-remaining echo behind the disappearing One on awakening back to physical reality after the final stage of the meeting with the etheric Christ.[71]

The healed and remembered, self-conscious bridge over the abyss of spirit forgetfulness, constructed from the transformed life and soul forces of man, is thereby crossed for the first time consciously. The higher, Christlike being of man, followed by the highest etheric aspect of the Christ Himself, descends from man's Heaven down to his Earth. This process might be termed the etheric 'descent'. It awakens man back to earthly consciousness and reveals the future inner bodily spirit resurrection of man and the Earth. This spirit-fire resurrection occurs now from within the innermost core of the spiritual soul. Through this final initiatory act man learns the future significance of bodily incarnation in the physical world. In each new awakening in the body every morning, and in each new soul that awakens in the body in the physical reality of earthly birth, he learns to see this seed of new physical life, the fiery, embryonic, future evolutionary centre in every last particle of matter and in every incarnate being and substance. And he learns then, by means of that final demonstration, how to make use of this new life in practical, moral and cognitive work, in order to bring it into outward expression in all fields of our modern civilization.[72]

The awakening through the purely spiritual descent of Christ, undergoing the fiery spirit resurrection as an inner spiritual body experience, reveals a world-man spirit for which 'Heaven' is in the Earth, that is, real and substantial, and an 'Earth' which is becoming Heaven, spiritual and transparent. Man knows: Christ transfers to humanity his creative, cosmic role. From now on it will depend upon man what kind of Heaven and Earth there shall be. The new Earth and Heaven shall be moulded consciously according to the Christ-permeated model of the transformed being of man.[73]

Chapter 5

The Knowledge Drama of the Second Coming

Our study of the knowledge drama of the Second Coming will be divided into three major parts:

1 the transformation of thinking, or the opening of the gates of thinking;
2 the transformation of sense-perception, or the opening of the gates of perception;
3 the construction of the bridge of memory and continuation of consciousness over the abyss of spirit-forgetfulness.[1]

When we try to recreate, or recapitulate, the modern Christ experience voluntarily, we are confronted with two major problems, the nature of which is determined by the nature of our daily consciousness, namely, the problem of thinking on the one hand and the problem of sense perception on the other. These two are experienced as the main obstacles, but, at the same time, as the only legitimate gates of entrance into the sought-for land of the Etheric Christ.[2] When a self-conscious bridge is to be built between the normal, wide-awake and rational modern state of consciousness and the inspired and intuited imaginative appearance, speech and acts of the Christ in His Second Coming, so must the consciousness soul itself — which, according to Rudolf Steiner, is the soul of free sense-perception and free Imagination[3] — be our only solid ground of construction. There are, therefore, two closed gates to be opened: the gate of thinking and the gate of sense-perception.[4] We shall have to explore, to begin with, the reason for the specific problem of modern thinking and sense perception. To do this, we shall turn to Rudolf Steiner's philosophical-anthroposophical investigations concerning the nature of modern, thinking self-consciousness.[5]

The most fundamental result of his anthroposophical investigation in this regard can be described as follows: the fully incarnated organization of modern man, in body, soul and spirit, functions in such a way that when confronting reality it does so in a partial and subjective manner. Without being aware of it, man achieves his awakening in the physical world by reducing a former, pre-physical state of consciousness to an earthly one. This is done so as to create the proper conditions for the coming into existence of his wide-awake, sense- and brain-founded thinking. Thus the given daily consciousness is truly 'given' only as

63

regards its limits. From a higher, imaginative consciousness, man can see and follow the process of its consolidation out of a state of pre-physical, etheric consciousness. This means that in every activation of this organization in the physical world a psycho-physical process occurs by means of which a change of consciousness is brought about. This is a real 'fall'[6] in every opening of the eyes and in every act of conscious seeing and of forming mental pictures of the seen.

In Rudolf Steiner's fundamental book *The Philosophy of Freedom*, this process is described as follows:

> Nowhere are we satisfied with what nature spreads out before our senses. Everywhere we seek what we call the explanation of the facts. The something more which we seek in things, over and above what is immediately given to us in them, *splits our whole being into two parts*. We become conscious of our antithesis to the world. We confront the world as independent beings. The universe appears to us in two opposite parts: I and world.[7]

And further:

> It is not due to the objects that they are given to us at first without their corresponding concepts but to our mental organization. Our whole being functions in such a way that from every real thing the relevant elements come to us from two sides, from perceiving and from thinking. The way I am organized for apprehending the things has nothing to do with the nature of the things themselves. *The gap between perceiving and thinking exists only from the moment that I as spectator confront the things.*[8]

> Our mental organization *tears the reality apart* into these factors ... If our existence were so linked up with the things that every occurrence in the world were at the same time also an occurrence in us, the distinction between ourselves and the things would not exist. But there would be no separate things at all for us. All occurrences would pass continuously one into another. The cosmos would be a unity and a whole, complete in itself. The stream of events would nowhere be interrupted. It is owing to our limitations that a thing appears to us as single and separate when in truth it is not a separate thing at all ... for us, however, it is necessary to isolate certain sections of the world and to consider them by themselves ... this separating off is a subjective act, which is due to the fact that we are not identical with the world process, but are a single being among other beings.[9]

The splitting of man's whole being into two parts is modern man's basic act of individuation. In the resulting process of objective knowledge, we overcome this gap by reuniting our thinking with our sense-perceptions.

We then have an objective picture of the world, solid and secure enough to enable us to understand and master the physical world.

This picture is, however, necessarily lifeless. The living, ensouled and spiritual worlds, in which also the deeper being of man is rooted, are concealed by this picture — concealed behind the act of condensing, through splitting, an objectified world, which is made to appear as consisting of distinct, separated physical objects and fixed, well-cut mental concepts.[10] It is Rudolf Steiner's most essential anthroposophical contribution towards a new foundation of the science of epistemology to discover this underlying supersensible act, which creates the ground for the dualistic split of modern consciousness and which alone produces both an individual self-consciousness as well as the objective scientific foundations of natural science.[11] In the last chapter of his book *The Riddles of Philosophy* (1914), Rudolf Steiner describes this process directly out of his anthroposophical research. Let us follow him, therefore, further.

> ... At a certain stage of his development [man] must give a provisional form to his ego in order to suppress from his consciousness the forces that unite him with the world. If these forces exerted their influences in his consciousness without interruption, he would never have developed a strong, independent self-consciousness. He would be incapable of experiencing himself as a self-conscious ego. The development of self-consciousness, therefore, actually depends on the fact that the mind is given the opportunity to perceive the world without that part of reality which is extinguished by the self-conscious ego prior to an act of cognition.
>
> The world forces belonging to this part of reality withdraw into obscurity in order to allow the self-conscious ego to shine forth in full power. *The ego must realize that it owes its self-knowledge to a fact that spreads a veil over the knowledge of the world.* It follows that everything that stimulates the soul to a rigorous, energetic experience of the ego conceals at the same time the deeper foundations in which this ego has its roots.

This unconscious, supersensible, concealment of the real and living man-world being, so as to create an objective world picture that can be experienced in full self-consciousness and self-possession, is a process that prepares, and therefore precedes, the conscious act of knowledge:

> ... The human soul does not deviate from reality in its creative effort for knowledge, but ... prior to any cognitive activity the soul conjures up a world that is not real. Man is so placed in the world that by the nature of his being he changes things from what they really are ... the unreal character of the external sense world is caused by the fact that

when man is directly confronted by things of the world he suppresses something that really belongs to them ... it is due to the nature of the soul that, at its first contact with things, it extinguishes something that belongs to them. For this reason, things appear to the senses not as they are in reality but as they are modified by the soul. Their delusive character (or their mere appearance) is caused by the fact that the soul has deprived them of something that really belongs to them.[12]

Three years later, in his book *The Riddles of the Soul*, Rudolf Steiner brought this idea to a higher, more explicit anthroposophical formulation:

[The soul] must suppress its own life, in order to have the conscious soul experience of the ordinary consciousness. This suppression takes place through every sense-impression. When the soul receives a sense-impression, there comes into being a suppression of the life of the mental pictures [*eine Herablahmung des Vorstellunslebens*]; and it is the suppressed mental picture which the soul experiences consciously as the carrier of knowledge of external reality. All the mental pictures that the soul relates to an external world are inner spirit-experiences whose life was suppressed. With everything that man thinks about an external sense-world, he has to do so with deadened mental pictures.

The real world gives man something living. He kills from this that part that enters into his ordinary consciousness. He does so because he would not have awakened to self-consciousness in the external world if the relation to this world was experienced in its full vitality. Without the suppression of this full vitality, man would have to be a member in a wholeness far greater than himself; he would be a member of this greater organism.[13]

Seven years later, in the *Letters to the Members*, Rudolf Steiner described this process of man's individuation in a way that brings us directly to the cliffs of the world-man abyss that is opened in our time *inside* the building processes of self-consciousness:

Thus in his momentary ideation or forming of ideas man lives not in an element of real being, but only in a mirroring of being — in picture-being. In this fact the possibility of the development of freedom lies inherent. All that is being in consciousness has power to compel. But a picture cannot compel. If anything is to be brought about through the impression that the picture makes, it must happen quite independently of the pictures. Man becomes free through the fact that with his consciousness soul he rises out of the ocean of being and emerges in the picture-existence which has no being ... *We are here pointing to the abyss of nothingness in human evolution* which man must cross when he becomes a free being. It is the working of Michael and the Christ-impulse which makes it possible for him to leap across the abyss.[14]

Up to now we have described the foundation of objective self-consciousness in general, in regard to thinking as well as sense-perception. We can now begin the study of thinking as such, in order to observe the process of its transformation. After this, we shall turn our attention to the transformation of sense-perception and then to the construction of the bridge of supersensible remembrance over 'the abyss of nothingness in human evolution' by the combined forces of metamorphosed thinking and sense-perception.

Turning our attention to ordinary, brain-bound thinking, we can ask: what is this ordinary thinking, and what is it not? Taking our start from what was said above about the empty picture nature of this thinking, we can say that it is produced by means of a continuous devitalization of the living flow of creative, biologically active time. The abstract concept and mental picture are life-organs of the vital organism of man that have been abstracted and separated from the totality of his unconscious life-process and thereby made conscious. As Rudolf Steiner described it in the above-quoted passage from *The Riddles of the Soul*: whenever we open our eyes and minds in order 'to picture'[15] the world and to reflect it conceptually, we let our primordial, pre-conscious, enlivened and ensouled 'original participation'[16] in the real living world be transformed into a conscious and disconnected, non-participatory knowledge of an external and dead world. Consciousness is thus awakened, ignited, and reflected back upon itself as pure thought: it becomes self-consciousness, viewing its self-active thinking as subject, over against the external object.[17] Externalizing and objectifying himself as self-conscious self, man achieves individuation, experiencing himself as a separated, divided self over against a non-living, non-animate and non-human world, which is there, as it were in space, outside of himself. Self-conscious thinking and sense-perception, when mutually combined in this way, provide the secure and solid foundation of everyday reality and rationality, including its elaboration and extension in science and philosophy, as *The Philosophy of Freedom* shows.

In mathematics and logic, thinking reaches its highest level of abstraction, freeing itself from the last remnants of bodily and sentient life.[18] In the clear and logical membering of concepts or numbers, man consciously members what he first unconsciously dismembered: the living, creative life-organizing and life-sustaining mathematics, geometry and logic of his body.[19] The ancient cosmic, starry evolutionary wisdom of our embryology, which moulds, forms and deforms our organism from conception until death, is continuously emancipated, dislocated and dismembered, providing both the conceptual material and the formative force of fantasy, memory and thinking.[20]

In each mathematical formula and logical relation, there appears a fragmented and devitalized remnant, picture or corpse of an embryonic, pre-personal life. And the more we dismember, member and remember our lifetime, the more we die into conscious freedom; the more we become conscious of our separated self, the more we lose our hold on instinctive life and the stronger we bind ourselves to our self-conscious, free and reflective self—we individuate ourselves in dying, and our daily, rational identity is this flower of continuous unconscious death, receiving its pure light of knowledge from the suffocated creative life of man's total world being.[21]

For the daily consciousness of modern man, the origin of the dismembering of his life-organism—the destructive splitting and dismembering of his life organism in every new act of intellection—conceals itself in the very act of its coming into being. The force that creates it, as well as the life-stream suppressed in the act, are both to be found, therefore, at a deeper level than that of ordinary thinking and sense-perception. We must, in other words, try to find the life element, the active power concealed by, but still inherent in, the source of thinking. But we must confess, to begin with—if our striving is experientially sincere—that this task is rather an impossible one. Our effort again and again shatters itself on the tough fixity and condensed solidity of our finished and formed memorized thinking.

We must, so we feel, livingly seek to immerse ourselves in that power that creates thinking, shapes its concepts and links them logically to one another, without being itself ever revealed. We must step out of the dead end of thinking! This soul striving must be felt so intensely that it is able to give birth to an inner anguish, as if man was inwardly burning with soul thirst and wandering helplessly in the light-filled, clear and arid desert of modern intellectualism. Man will need this soul force—cooled down, of course, powerfully concentrated and peacefully directed to thinking's source—but nevertheless as energizing, existentially motivating power.[22]

Into this inner burning soul thirst, Rudolf Steiner's indications concerning the transformation of thinking pour themselves as refreshing, enlivening water of life. Already in his *Philosophy of Freedom* he directs our attention to the sought-for opening of active will life in thinking. There we can begin to experience the riddle of the transformation of death into life and life into death in our awakened self-consciousness.

It can be asked: why is the new Christ experience, described above, 'modern' at all? We might now propose the following answer: precisely because it takes its place of time—it appears—within our living and deadened life at the boundary of consciousness. As we saw in Chapter 4, the Christ incorporates Himself in the non-permeable soul membrane of consciousness where we continuously rebound back and forth, hitting both the inner as well as the outer borders of our daily consciousness. It appears, in other words, at the modern abyss of reflectivity, or at our intellect's blind spot of rationality, and therefore remains 'occult', unseen, by most of our contemporaries.[23] This means, however, that the Christ takes on Himself today the fate and destiny of self-conscious thinking. That is, He is continuously crucified at the place where we continuously kill our living time in order to know that which we have killed, consciously and freely. Thereby our most solid foundation of objectivity and, at the same time, the most secure concealment of our living, active self is achieved. Whenever we link two concepts with one another – or an objective sense-impression with its related concept – we structure a firm, objective, rational ground on which to stand mentally. Behind that firmness is concealed humanity's ever-active, pulsating logos of life: the etheric Christ. We shall begin, therefore, the experiential exploration of the knowledge drama of the Second Coming at this point.

The self-concealing openness in thinking[24] is clearly indicated in the third chapter of *The Philosophy of Freedom*. There we read:

> I am never able to observe my present thinking; only the experiences that I had in the process of thinking can I later make into an object of thinking. If I would like to observe my present thinking, I would have to split myself into two personalities: into one that thinks and into another that observes itself in its thinking. This I cannot do;[25] I can do this only in two different acts. The thinking that is to be observed is never that which is thereby in activity, but another ... Two things do not suffer one another: active creativity and standing over against it in observation.[26]

What would happen, then, if we cancelled our act of concealment, our reflection? We would in this case cancel the concealment of the actively creative,[27] and open the gates of the abyss beneath and in between our future time-stream and our past time-stream.[28] In this way we break the continuity of normal consciousness and focus our attention on the present creative activity alone. We ceased living in the coherently combined, logical production of thinking and immerse ourselves in the experience of thinking-in-the-making. In doing so, we have made our first step towards the transformation of thinking: we begin to open one of the gates to the reality of the living spirit.[29] And among the most important first results of this experience is the discovery of the nature and workings of the will as the unseen regulator of the forces of life and death at the hidden source of thinking. The essential riddle that stands before us now is this: how is reflection made possible at all, and what exactly is its inner nature?

It seems to be immediately evident that, before such an inner veiling and concealment of the creative present, no self-consciousness would be possible, otherwise the self would only experience the world in thinking and not himself as self over against the world and over against himself. But how is this self/world occultation generated? What suppresses the experience of the future 'I'-being, darkens the presently active and living 'I' and illuminates its dead past alone? From the experience of the will in thinking this can be answered as follows. *There 'is'* (the real, living 'is' is precisely what is annihilated) *a freezing and preservation of the difference of time that has elapsed, a stretching and spacing of time – a killing of time and a temporal immortalization and preservation of the killed time – in every act of ideation and perception.* We see a continuous transformation of the concentrated, non-spatial being of the active living present into a dead time-being that endures as past.[30] That is, there lights up into conscious, clear perception that which was and 'is' no longer (living now), and darkens down into an unconscious sleep that which creatively *is*. Every moment of our life-time that is raised into self-consciousness is in this way always split in two,[31] into a living and creative unknown element that is immediately concealed and suppressed, pushed back and preserved as future potentiality, and into something that is fixed, made non-living and, hence, remains as an available element for later recollection.

Before reflection was historically born in ancient Greece, biographically, in early childhood, there could be no consciousness of this negativity of elapsed time; there could only be the experience of an untimely and universal ever-present, non-broken duration, a flowing stream of positive reality, in which thinking could never have become our inner personal possession. Thinking would have remained similar to digestion or biological growth – an unconsciously regulated activity as an expression of an integrated organism-environment wholeness.

A self-conscious self is *thinkable*, therefore, only when the universal self can, as the condition for fully conscious cognition, actively suppress its living participation in the streaming reality of the living world.[32] Here we have *the first* experiential result on our way to a modern anthroposophical, fully-conscious transformation of thinking: the seeing of that process by means of which our life-time organism is continuously divided into two half-brothers or twins, a mortal and immortal, in every conscious moment of life. A fully incarnated (past) life brother, and a fully excarnated (post) life brother are standing one over against the other on the two banks of the river of time's annihilation and await their conscious meeting and rebirth in and through each other.[33]

In this splitting of our life we awaken to objective reflection. We construct on its objectified and devitalized time the foundation of daily separate identity and rational behaviour. But now, after having experienced consciously this unconscious splitting, we can also begin to follow with our earthly time-self the second immortal being of our life-time that entirely escapes—futurewards—our daily consciousness. We find this being united with our deeper, active will. He then becomes our guide, showing as the way, consciously illuminating the further spiritualization of thinking.[34]

However, before we continue our research deeper into Life, we must feel ourselves wholly at home in Death. We must strengthen our ability to stand consciously poised in between the divided halves of our life, that is, in the present momentary core of our life's destruction and resurrection. There we have to build a provisional[35]—but essential—bridge, or rock, at the moment of splitting and division. We must steel our newly awakened consciousness in the midst of that annihilation of our life-time, because here we begin to practise and experience our own, always present, event of etheric crucifixion, death and resurrection as the mystery of *modern* cognition. The act of knowledge becomes Christ's Mystery Place of the second, etheric coming. Let us, therefore, hold fast to this Mystery Place of time and explore in greater detail some of its basic features.[36]

The stream of time that has elapsed remains connected with our earthly being: used, devitalized, and therefore always readily available to be voluntarily recollected. As that portion of our life that was fixed or 'nailed' to the cross of our dying tree of knowledge in the nerve-sense system, it is held as such, as 'elapsedness'—as past life—in the closest possible proximity to the actively living present. Here the source of dying life (cognition) and the fountain of living death (the active will) are superimposed and coalesced. That mortal 'I' which is born out of this division might be designated as a decomposed, half-time 'I', the child of our continuous living death. This 'I' can sustain itself only on the decayed past. It must always be possible for it to re-member this halved life of man's total being into itself, in order to be—and remain—awake and self-conscious in the physical world.

We see, therefore, that the universal flowing life of the world-creating, world-sustaining ancient Logos must first become a separated, fixed object for us and in us.[37] It must be represented objectively in front of our mind's eye in order to be known. But in being objectively known it is being put to death in order to awaken us. In awakening us, Death has spread its opaque veil of concealment over the living source of all reality. When we consciously incorporate our living being into this veil, we make it transparent again. We begin to transform the being of Death into our cross of supersensible perception, which is the gate of vision that thinking has opened within our soul.[38]

A remarkable perspective opens itself imaginatively in our soul when we have completed this first stage in the transformation of thinking. We see ourselves hovering over the abyss that opens under our 'mind's feet' in-between the dark and sinking, life-carrying will seed, and the birth of the abstract, clear daylight of thinking; in-between the creative present moment and the next creative moment, dividing *ourselves* consciously into two selves, viewing both from the two directions of future-in-the-making and past-in-the-making. We die consciously in living vision when we observe how our objectified lifetime continuously dies 'in the grey spirit abyss' in order to be available, consciously-earthly, as remembered halved-time, a time that *was* a member of life's primal world-man constitution, that *is* consciously dismembered in us and through us in order, when we return to objectified time-in-space, to be *re-membered as past preserving being* — the being that conceals and thus also protects the Michaelic knowledge drama of the living present.[39]

Our true and whole 'I' is then seen, from the point of view we have achieved so far, as a dark, ever-active, world-creative self, artfully masking its potent darkness within the luminous garments of abstracted dead life. In this way it incarnates in the flesh of objectified time and space, identified with external reality in complete self-surrender and forgetfulness of its true nature. It is thereby born out of the spirit wholeness and finds itself as a separate and independent earthly self.[40]

This capacity of the World Self to imprint on the living flow of the Logos the seal of dismemberment means also that it begets, and begetting devours, and in devouring preserves, its dead time-children. The living, non-broken flow of world creativity is broken down by the 'I' in each cognitive activity, thus begetting logic out of Logos, continuously creating dying, light-irradiated and thought-transparent 'dead spirit children' [41] which, as such, remain bound to the self.[42] They supply it with the solid foundation of identity, being always ready to obey its voluntary control of thinking, feeling and willing in the physical world.

The unique process in this crucial 'abyss of time annihilation',[43] where living physical and etheric substance is perpetually killed and dispersed in man in order to enable the engraving of his daily, objective sense-perception and brain-conditioned thinking, was described by Rudolf Steiner as follows:

> ... When the human being works over external impressions, makes them into a memory pictures, and in doing so thrusts them into his ether-body, how does it happen that he actually brings down into the ether-body what the astral body [and ego] has first worked over and what now presses against the ether-body? How does he transfer it? ... We see currents developing everywhere in the ether-body, taking a very definite course, as if they would join the blood flowing upward from the heart to the head. And in the head these currents come together, in about the same way ... as do currents of electricity when they rush towards a point which is opposed by another point, so as to

neutralize the positive and the negative. When we observe with a soul trained in occult methods, we see at this point ether-forces compressed as if under a very powerful tension — those ether-forces which are called forth through the impressions that now desire to become definite concepts, memory-pictures, and to stamp themselves upon the ether-body.

I shall, therefore, draw here the last out-streaming of these ether-currents, as they flow up towards the brain, and show their crowding together somewhat as this would actually appear. We see here a very powerful tension which concentrates at one point, and announces: 'I will now enter into the ether-body!' ... thus we have in the brain, whenever a memory-picture wishes to form itself, two ether-currents, one coming from below and one from above, which oppose each other under the greatest possible tension ... If a balance is brought about between these two currents, then a concept has become memory-picture and has incorporated itself in the ether-body.[44]

The time-place we described above as the place in which the human life-time organism is continuously broken and divided in each moment of dying time is precisely this workshop of the making of memory. For ordinary consciousness this time abyss is tightly closed and concealed. Its unity is given and natural, because it does not consciously experience the process of its becoming through the forces of living Death. It knows only its last and finished result in the form of the faculty and contents of remembrance. This blessed unknowing is the necessary condition for the daily experience of *a solid and continuous, always unbroken and remembered*, self-consciousness. But the very first enhancement and transformation of thinking through the will unveils the hidden, self-protecting veil of forgetfulness that is spread over the process of the making of remembrance, and lifts it into consciousness.

When we succeed in cancelling the instinctive engraving process of memory, we are able to stand etherically fast between the poles of the normally tightly closed circuit of our flowing etheric currents. Then we can consciously space its hidden *time difference* out, as we showed above, precisely at the most intensive point of its inwardly sealed tension. We then break down and overcome the intense mutual attraction holding sway between the two main poles of our astral-etheric activity in the head centre — physically seen between the epiphysis (pineal gland) and hypophysis (pituitary gland).[45] This means that we actually separate the higher (astral and ego) organization of man from his lower organization (physical and etheric bodies). That is, in the moment we cancel *at will* the ordinary activity of sense-perception, reflecting and memorizing, we free our astral body from its commitment to the destructive engraving process of sense-perceptions and thinking in the etheric body. A lightening of excarnation[46] is then experienced, and our physically hardened cognition dissolves in the nothingness of its own, now powerfully surfacing, empty abyss. We consciously enter, in other words, the empty grave into which the etheric corpse of our normal objective consciousness — our deadened life-time — has disappeared, and out of which the resurrected, consciously moulded new body of resurrected Christ consciousness emerges.[47]

In the inner calender of man's supersensible soul life, the arriving at this 'abyss of time' in soul-seeing of past death in life and future life in death is the seasonal, spiritualized inner recurrence of the Easter experience celebrated *through* the autumn festival of Michael. It is at the *same time* — the mutually penetrated autumn-Easter time — the beginning of the inner, always recurring celebration of the Christ-Mysteries of the future. This inner experience was described by Rudolf Steiner as follows:

> The man of the future has before him two possibilities. The one possibility is this, that he will look back in memory to the time when he had experiences in the physical body and will say to himself: only that was real ... man will then look at the forsaken physical body as on a grave, and what he will see in the grave is a corpse — but for him the corpse will represent reality. This is one possibility. The other possibility is that man will look again at what he experienced in the physical world as on a corpse, but so that he feels it deeply and will be able to say to those who believe that the physical alone is truly real the following words of truth: 'The one ye seek is not there.' *The empty grave and the resurrected Christ: this is the mystery of prophecy*; and so we have in the mystery of Easter the mystery of prophecy.[48]

So far we have indicated the zone of the first (etheric) abyss or threshold into which man enters as a result of raising the modern Christ experience into full anthroposophical consciousness. This abyss is intimately close to man's daily life: it exists 'right behind' his ordinary thinking and memorizing. As we showed, when he begins to turn his attention to thinking's creative, hidden source, he may enter this abyss consciously and open — for the first time voluntarily — the gate of thinking to the living spirit. But at this threshold's abyss the still largely hidden Guardian of the Threshold may, nevertheless, assume his first conscious form. We cannot, therefore, advance further without, however briefly, referring to this struggle at 'the cliffs of thinking's abyss'.[49]

Modern man's most secure foundation of thinking self-consciousness, his 'I think therefore I am' as anchorage of rationality, might, at this point, be irredeemably shattered. The losing of this 'single vision and Newton's sleep' (W. Blake) may lead man either to 1) rebound back in fear upon his convenient and secure daily consciousness or scientific and philosophical convictions, determined never again to approach thinking's end, or 2) he may be tempted into the other extreme, namely, to deny thinking, self-consciousness and objectivity altogether, in which case he might end as a total sceptic, or mystic, or both.[50] But the selfsame crisis may also lead to another, more promising possibility, as indicated above: man can learn to live, move and have his being *at* the limit of thinking, *over* the abyss of consciousness, and *in* the actual birth, death, and rebirth process of self-consciousness. It means: willing, feeling and thinking making a home in that land between the poles of the dividing, annihilating and self-individuating higher being of man. To establish oneself firmly at this point of extreme instability means to anchor self-consciousness in its singularity, from which alone real spiritualization of thinking is possible.[51] At this zero point of rationality, [52] which is neither its logical negation nor affirmation but rather its conscious *for*-mation, man enters the knowledge drama of the Second Coming. This entry requires a courageous delving into the abyss of the structure, dis-structure and re-structure of self-consciousness.[53]

What was until now in the hands of the old gods (the lunar teachers of young humanity) is transferred from our time on into the conscious spirit hands of man himself. He must become increasingly ready to take full cognitive and existential responsibility for the creation, consolidation and preservation of his self-conscious self and clear spirit sight in the living stream of the world-man becoming of the universe.[54]

The further transformation of thinking, shortly to be described, can only be based on what we recognized above: that what we call 'thinking' in our modern intellectual science, philosophy and general culture is but its devitalized, weakened shadow, on which we awaken to full, clear-cut self-consciousness.[55] In this devitalized inner soul atmosphere alone can modern man consolidate a world picture and an identity that separates and thereby protects him from the reality of the real world, in which, at the present stage of human evolution, he would be overwhelmed and submerged in continuous unconscious sleep. And only because our mental pictures and concepts are mere picture-shadows, devoid of living content, can we be truly free and active in them alone; we wake up out of our world sleep in the thin air of the abstracted and lifeless image of the real, and exercise our independent volition with their help.[56]

But the act of the creation of thinking, the will element that brings it into existence and shapes its course, remains unthought. Thinking can grasp, reflecting, only formed thinking. When we combine one concept or mental image with another, we are focused positively in our mental creations, oblivious of the source of their active formation. We do not consciously experience the original formative power that shapes concepts and links them creatively to one another.[57] If we could photograph the etheric counterpart of thinking—and such a photo-graph does actually always exist in the light-ether component of our etheric body—

we would see our dead concepts appearing as isles of light surrounded and bathed by a dark fluid medium — as white icebergs surrounded by the dark ocean of living waters.[58] Our daily consciousness is aware only of the light spots, or ice isles of finished concepts, and would perceive the will only as its negative, as thinking's nothingness.[59] A transformation of thinking must begin, therefore, through the resolute effort to give up our stubborn fascination with the finished conceptual results of our thinking and focus our awareness only on its creative dynamics. It is, at the same time, the transition from the intellectual soul, still committed to reflection, to the consciousness soul, which begins to reveal its true being as a will- and -warmth soul, as active, dynamic and future-orientated being.[60]

In reality, therefore, behind every light-filled, crystallized conceptual condensation there lives and flows the deep water of active, dynamic and thought-formative will power, which brought it into being but remains hidden, concealed behind its own creations. Thinking's conceptual crystals free our consciousness; here it can have its existence only for itself, unconcerned or unaffected by any real force and influence. *But the dark will is reality through and through*: self-active, potent and, for the daily consciousness, extremely repellent and thereby self-concealing. Like a living tree or shrub, it pushes our thought away, continuously abstracting and condensing concepts and mental images as a non-living, lignified bark that thickens more and more around its living, creative heart. The transformation of thinking into pure will must, therefore, break through this sedimented, dead soul-and-life layer into life's living core.[61]

From the point that we reached above we can, standing at life's dividing threshold, consciously control the metamorphosis in both directions: into the death of the organism in the full growth of thinking, and back into deep life in the spiritually active will seed. Imaginatively, this polar transformation can be pictured as follows. If pure thinking is, in its highest (Hegelian) manifestation, fully structured light, differentiated conceptual finished work, so pure willing is — to begin with — the opposite of thinking; chaotic, wholly structureless potential, a source of unlimited, yet completely unspecified, possibilities of future becoming and creativity.[62] When we now leave behind us the place of our lifetime's annihilation, but carrying it henceforth with us as the engraved, consciousness-awakening and preserving 'wound'[63] of imaginative remembrance capacity, and we delve ever deeper, searching in the direction of the sinking will-seed,[64] there dawns in us a new understanding of thinking's fate and mission in the evolution of human consciousness on the Earth.

Usually, in ordinary daily consciousness, we have thinking always 'in front' of our eyes, guided by the unseen will at our back. This thinking leads us outward into the external world. But now we have turned around at life's threshold; we look inward into the dark of spirit night, as we formerly looked out into the external light of day. At noon time, we had thinking's impetus, the will, behind us: now we have thinking's memory behind us, guiding us, as Ariadne's thread, into the inner labyrinth of living will.[65]

We may now say to ourselves the following. The ancient role of thinking was to divert man's attention from the living spirit and fix it on the external world. In doing so, thinking was man's guide to modern self-consciousness, the scientific and technological mastery of the world of the senses, and personal freedom and estrangement. But this was only the first part of thinking's true sacrificial mission. In uniting itself with man's emancipated personality, thinking helped bring about, out of a fully justified evolutionary necessity, the dividing of man's self in two, sharply demarcating his ever consciously growing day (half of) self, from his increasingly unconscious becoming night (half of) self.[66] Since the end of Kali-Yuga at the end of the nineteenth century, however, man's daily self, the child of thinking's sacrifice, has been mature and strong enough to be turned around and outside-in, and directly face, without losing himself, the sublime and terrible truth of his other, night will-self, while always remaining true to thinking's guidance. But reversing and *internalizing* the self of thinking — pouring its external light inwardly — means, at the same time, reversing and *externalizing* the hidden night-self of the will: until one can cross them inwardly together and hold them fast at their crossing point, regulating from there their future internalization and externalization, according to man's free thinking in willing and free willing in thinking.

A magnificent Imagination lights up in us when we succeed in this. We see our transformed, spiritualized and reversed thinking as a triumphant being, striving mightily with its Michaelic sword to secure its future ruling in the castle of the consciousness soul. And in every new victory won, with every new temptation suffered, the deeper it penetrates towards its spirit goal the more profound and clear resounds its call and grows its power of attraction for its other, which is man's other (half of) self, or dark brother. It summons and invokes ever mightily its dark brother from its unconscious night depths into the crossing point of battle in the whirling vortex of the reversal of the soul forces, in order to be remembered *of* him, *by* him and *into* him again, but consciously for the first time.

With the greatest awe and wonder man stands before such inner, spontaneous imaginative revelations of the human soul, when it shapes and condenses into mighty pictures, and thus summarizes and preserves, the decisive moments of its evolutionary breakthroughs. The transformed thinking, reversed, matured by experience and spiritually enlivened, becoming darker and heavier, makes its way from the death world of the brain-bound intellect into the inner fountain of eternal life; the dark, hidden will-brother—lightening and lighting—surfaces, externalizing himself. And the two beings meet face to face at the crossing-reversing (*Umstülpung*) point, fighting fearfully with one another: '. . . each bore the heart of the other, and in their strangeness to one another they were still intimate enough', until they consciously recognized the true nature of their 'other brother'. 'One may say that "they" were fighting this way if one wants to speak of them as two, *but they were indeed only one*, for "my brother and I" that is one flesh.' And yet, before this union can be consciously realized, the two brothers must learn to bow down in surrender before one another, committing themselves to their *future* destiny. The day-thinking self must be inwardly humbled and fall to his knees; and then break his proud thinking's sword on the tough, potent will-core of his night-will brother, thereby bringing him, in his turn, 'to a posture of prayer on his knees'.[67]

Then the brothers intermingle, interchange, cross and recross each other's heart way, and replace each other in each other, united from that moment forever as man's remembered total day and night, will and thinking self.[68]

In this 'battle' we shall have henceforth another, more advanced, but still provisional, sign or rock of memory, an inscribed mark of remembrance in the landscape of the process of thinking's transformation. As we shall see later, man will have to come again and again to this place of soul battle, and deepen its engraving in the etheric counterpart of the soul's point of inner reversal. On the same halved-time spot that we learned to know above as the place of time's annihilation—but now far deeper in the fabric of the life of the soul itself—man has to superimpose the new landmark.[69] As he formerly consolidated his soul stronghold of awakened imaginative self-consciousness in life's division zone—in the time-place of its annihilation in thinking and resurrection as will—so he has now to engrave and consolidate systematically the point of the reversal of his soul forces, in order to ever again in-spire and re-member his separated life and soul (etheric and astral) members into an ever-conscious unity of ever-increasing Spirit Self diversity.

When this crossing and reversing of thinking into will and will into thinking is accomplished, a new, more inwardly inspired soul balance is achieved, on the foundation of which a more advanced imaginative soul observatory is established. The soul vision now revealed is experienced as the metamorphosis of the three soul forces, when they are freely woven and replaced through and in each other.[70]

It must be clear by now that any future development of thinking can only proceed through thinking's returning and recoiling back on to its potent will core. Imaginatively speaking, this means that a darkening of its infinite luminous periphery and a condensing, energizing of its finite personal centre takes place, dynamically reversing centre and periphery, light and darkness, into one another in an inner soul battle of opposing soul forces. *So thinking exercises an active study of beginnings.* It must learn to find — in a thoroughly modern way — its own sensitive chaos of *tohu wabohu*, of early, primordial, creation.[71] It learns in this way to weave and live in its preconceptual, embryonic warmth ether, creatively immersing its aged intellectuality in its childlike and youthful origins. We begin to practise soul remembrance in the world-man process of man's becoming.

That is, we learn how to annihilate the tomb of thinking in the fertile and fresh depth of the will's womb.[72] We complete a full circle, now consciously re-membering our primal beginnings into our present life-and-soul time. Out of God we are consciously born.[73]

This means, to receive into the dark and fertile earthly tomb-womb of the soul of man the purest ashes of the burnt-down and abstracted, but thoroughly spiritualized, corpse of thinking. That is, to have the death and resurrection of the Etheric Christ as inner, conscious soul experience.[74] This means, at the same time, to experience the illumination of the dark inner soul night with the most intimate and sacred universal light of spirit resurrection: to experience inwardly the awakening of the light of the new spirit-will of thinking, which is the future guiding force of man into the land of the spiritualized consciousness soul and Spirit Self.[75]

The foregoing can also be portrayed in the following picture. Man gathers one by one the purest rays of the ancient light of thinking that are crystallized through analytic intellect and sense-perception, oxidized and devitalized in the dead matter of the external brain, and then lets it dissolve in the deep waters of life. When the brain-bound pure salt crystals dissolve in the intensive fire of will and feeling, and are chemically reduced to chaos, they are transformed into the fertile soil of a new inner, human cosmic beginning.[76] A new Sun is being born out of thinking's old stellar dust and cosmic ashes.[77]

Only now, after having established ourselves in this threefold weaving and reversing of our soul forces, metamorphosing the soul members one into the other as described above, do we achieve a soul state which, for the first time, might be designated as 'peace of soul'.[78] This is a most essential inner acquisition. Without being grounded in this new state of peace-giving soul harmony no further deepening of the transformation of thinking can be healthily carried out, because the next step will be a direct penetration into the most potent spirit core of the will in thinking. Such a penetration, as we shall presently see, throws man completely out of his soul balance. His firm anchorage in life's birth-death-rebirth *hypomochlion* (the zero-point of a balance) and the harmonious regulation of the metamorphosis of the soul forces into one another will from now on be his only safeguard when sailing into the turbulent and stormy open ocean of the soul world.

The experiences described above were brought about by means of an intensive unfoldment of the will activity in thinking. Now a new start shall be attempted, retaining the new soul capacities that were gained, while disregarding both the pictorial content and the dynamic soul metamorphosis described so far. We shall begin, therefore, with the pure soul force as such, with the will element of thinking itself. We start our meditation with a seed-thought, with a single concept. But instead of unfolding its pictorial or ideal elements as in the first stage, or actively recreating its dynamic inner movements as in the second, we use it here solely as an external means for the initial focusing of our will. We have placed it in the centre of our most awake and intensive consciousness. Now, bypassing any further activity, we let it disappear altogether, but we keep intact — without any will effort — *its negative thought space.*[79] In complete passivity, without falling asleep, we hold this state. Now we suddenly begin to feel that our self-created thought emptiness takes on immense sucking power that inhales us into itself, turning us actually inside out. We realize now that we no longer have empty thought space in us, but rather that nothingness is emptying us, while itself growing to be — now no longer a centre, because we have become its (emptied) centre — but our increasingly filled and incredibly potent circumference.[80] And if we preserve our presence of mind in this remarkable *Umstülpung* (turning over) process, we begin to feel: now He (the will) wills; He strives to penetrate my emptiness and take me over for itself, boring its way into me with the unlimited power of its infinite periphery.[81] No battle at this stage can help us — not in the least — but only a sacrificial surrender to the instreaming will, listening most attentively to its commanding weaving and speaking in our centre.

Until now the will has always been a dark potency, repellent and opaque; the more we penetrated inwardly, the more we felt in the will our densest bodily heaviness and impenetrability. Now an unexpected invitation resounds into us from our externalized will. It increasingly invites our attention, calling us back as if from afar, reaching us in the infinite periphery of our externalization. And when we dare to look into the place where in daily and imaginative life our heaviest element was, and where just a moment before our total evacuation was experienced, and if we succeed in keeping our complete stillness, the more friendly and welcoming it becomes. Now we feel ourselves secure enough to return home, joyfully delving and swimming in and through our long-forsaken centre, freely expanding into its inmost point, as if following an unseen guiding spirit hand. And before too long we find ourselves dancing in inwardly expanding, radiating light circles, streams and pools, being buoyantly carried and blissfully suffused by gentle, ethereal beings of thoughtlike quality. We suddenly know: *now we live in the other side of our ordinary will of thinking*, which is the pre-earthly, prenatal life of the formative power of our thought.[82]

Grotesque as it might sound, the factual truth must still be expressed. We find ourselves submerged and surrounded on all sides by many unborn thought-like babies, each beseeching us — some lovingly and gently, some flatteringly, some treacherously — to conceive them, to breathe them in and transform them into mature thought organisms and crystals. But in the light world of their joyous ethereal life, they do not yet know what awaits them out there — such a half-mocking, half-warning thought being might then cross our inner soul horizon, and its appearance shock us out of our joyful mood and quench our inner soul light. As if at the speed of light we are hurled backward to the border of our earthly shore of consciousness, experiencing on this backward journey the destiny and fate of thinking. We see how thinking sacrifices itself continuously in us, guiding us from our ancient cosmic dwelling down to the external light of the senses.[83]

The shock of this backward journey and reversed *Umstülpung* (see p. 78) is immense. When we find ourselves at our cross of etheric remembrance and imaginative self-consciousness, we feel that on this way back, following inwardly the fate of thinking through the reversed will, the whole inner structure of our soul has been shattered. A moment of powerful soul dismemberment overwhelms us, which, we now realize, would have completely crushed and dispersed us had we not prepared in advance the solid and condensed etheric rock of our remembrance and anchored it firmly on the shore of our physical existence.

Prior to this stage we have established in the centre of our consciousness two spiritual layers, or sediments, superimposed on one another. The first was our solid etheric identity in the stream of time's annihilation. The second was the crossing and metamorphosing of thinking into will and will into thinking. The soul experience, differentiated and divergent as it came to be, was still unbroken, running in its steady course by means of having its reflection, or inscription, kept intact in the condensed stream of time's annihilation. We had a united perception, though radically transformed at both poles, of our presently living self. This perception now comes to an end. After the liberation of the will from thinking, and of thinking from the will, the unbroken, dynamic soul unity is broken and rent in two; and this rending occurs at the same place as the increasingly surfacing world-man abyss. But now our own soul is this place and is becoming this abyss itself.[84]

The inspired imaginative unity of the soul is rent asunder. Out of it emerge two independent soul-like beings, one-sidedly emancipating themselves from 'us' but, in reality, scattering our sense of self into an endless periphery. Man feels how the poles of his soul being, until now

81

held through his willed activity, speed away from his vanishing and emptied will centre, opening a gap of unlimited and bottomless division between his former unity of self and his present scattering of many selves. Man feels: what evaporates 'me' upwards is what was my 'thinking'; and that which condenses 'me', pulling irresistibly into the abyss below, is now 'my will'. But 'I' – where is my 'I'? And no answer to this inner cry is heard until, from this helpless division, from the midst of man's intensive self-loss, a third being from the abyss is born. And it is out of this third being that the liberated and opposing 'will' and 'thinking' selves of man will gradually have to shape the astral equivalent of what we usually designate as 'feeling'. Here feeling appears as the last soul-self-being to be released, and as the most mysterious of all.[85]

Man knows that when the thinking and willing halves of one's two selves succeed in the future in creating between themselves a commonly agreed upon 'centre', they will *feel*: this third being carries within its divided, abyssed soul the secret of our primordial world-man abyss. And it is this recognition of the mysterious nature of 'feeling' that now becomes the most unstable and vulnerable, but the *only* uniting soul sense of coherent identity, which can be articulated in the following way in inner perception: 'I only exist as an "I" when my two divided poles recognize in the third my surfacing abyss. *I am* only when I consciously feel the division in my broken soul centre; when I am not, I am. In constant decay, I am whole.'[86]

Now when this inner experience is repeatedly established in the soul, there appears before the new selfhood a spirit-imbued, real picture, through which man hears the inner soul aspect of his participation in the etheric Mystery of Golgotha. Man knows himself to be united in his inner soul drama of knowledge with that same Being whom one meets at the *second* stage of the modern Christ experience. Man sees it articulated thus: 'Out of the opening abyss of your thinking's grave I arise. I was crucified in your thoughts; now I am resurrected in your self-consciously incurred soul death and dissolution. You are dismembered now out of Me; it is your future task to re-member yourself – by means of your own forces – into Me again. Otherwise you would lose your human soul form entirely, and slide increasingly into the world-abyss of your soul.'[87]

The transformation of thinking in the anthroposophical knowledge drama of the Second Coming has reached here a certain culmination. Between the poles of man's freed will and thinking, feeling has emerged, giving birth from within its dual-fissured heart to an inspired Imagination of the etheric resurrected Christ. When this Imagination is deeply inscribed in the free threefoldness of oneself, it becomes the means of navigation in the soul-world ocean, independently regulating the separated soul beings. With its help alone man can pull his evaporating thinking back to the Earth, and elevate his sinking, heavy will up to the stars, rescuing himself from complete inner disruption and collapse. From now on it must be possible gradually to work freely with any one of the soul forces, supported according to need by the others. As we shall presently see, beside the work done by the metamorphosed sense-perception — to which the freed being of thinking readily allies itself — the will being must be able to sacrifice itself in order to make possible the final act of construction in the supersensible building process of the bridge over the abyss of spirit forgetfulness.

And feeling? When the metamorphosed thinking and sense percep-tion, supported by the liberated, sacrificial will being, constructs the first etheric layer of the bridge, it will be feeling's task to prepare, working again at first in a hidden way, the ultimate moral crisis of the spiritual strivings of modern man, in order to ensure the deepest and strongest conscious anchorage of the bridge. But before we can advance so far, we must first open the second gate to the spirit reality of the knowledge drama of the Second Coming, which is also the second pillar of the bridge, namely, the gate of sense-perception.[88]

The Gate of Sense-perception

In order to construct consciously the supersensible bridge of self-conscious remembrance over the abyss of spirit forgetfulness (Lethe), we need a metamorphosed sense-perception[89] as well as thinking. These two are the main pillars and foundations, the Joachim and Boaz, on which the bridge that unites consciously the spirit land of Christ (Shamballa) and our physical Earth can be securely built. *Man as a cog-nitive being of thinking and sense-perception, taken as a whole and consciously transformed, is the twofold bridge* — a being that can, on the one side of the abyss, be firmly anchored in the physical-etheric worlds and, having individualized the abyss consciously and made it his own inner world, can carry the fruits of Earth to the heavens and plant the seeds of Heaven in the new Earth in a fully conscious and balanced way. Only when transformed thinking (as living, free will being) and transformed sense-perception (formative world thinking) blend and enhance each other do we have the building materials and the formative power needed for the 'great work' of construction.[90]

As the great problem in thinking is the finished, sedimented, light-filled concept and mental picture, hiding behind it the dark spot of willed, unperceived activity, so in sense-perception the object fulfils the same role.[91] And as we overcame the death of thinking by delving into the living creative activity of the embryonic will, effacing the effacement of life brought about by the light of thinking, so must we proceed in the case of the organization of the human eye. We have to overcome the continuous inner devitalization process of the external sunlight, which dies in the eye and its connection with the brain. In its death it creates the devitalized light of sense-perception which enables our objective consciousness to perceive an opaque object, presented in space. Our ordinary sense-perception—as part of our total psycho-physical organization, as was shown above—interacts with the light (or sound, warmth, life) of the world in such a way that what we self-consciously perceive is the dead corpse, or remnant, of the world's creative, elemental quality of being. The light that we (physically) see and (mentally) comprehend is not the living but the dead, not the vital-sentient but the devitalized, soul-emptied real light of the world. Plants and animals would never have thrived with the light we see; they would have died immediately, suffocated, lifeless and lightless. In every sense-perception, therefore, we murder in order to dissect (understand, remember). This subject was investigated in the most manifold ways by Rudolf Steiner. We can bring here, however, only an example:

> Death takes place, for the air we breathe, in every inhalation of the air. But this is only one phenomenon. The ray of light that enters our eye must die in the same way; and we would have in the world no light rays if our eye had not placed itself over against the light, as the lung does with the air. And every light ray that enters our eye dies in our eye, and by means of the death of light in our eye we are enabled to see... In our eye the ray of light is killed. We murder it in order to have the perception by means of the eye. *So we are filled with what must die in us in order that we can develop our earthly consciousness.*[92]

We are reminded again of that essential passage from *The Philosophy of Freedom*: our total organization functions in such a way that it separates, in each cognitive act, the (living, ensouled) sensible element of 'the thing' from its (living, spiritual) ideal element. This 'separation' between perception and thinking gives us our self-consciousness: the freedom between the (dead) sense-data and the (dead) concept. And when we combine the two we have reached, thereby, the truth of the objective—object-like—world but lost the reality of the living, ensouled and spiritual world in which we, as whole human beings, move and live and have our true being. External objects are therefore not real as such; that is, we make them into what they appear to be *for us* in every act of perception.[93] Objects are maya, illusion, when compared with their appearance to the higher, enlivened, ensouled and spiritual perception. They are our (unconsciously, livingly killed) dead creations. An object must, therefore, be readily redeemable and dissolvable. In the moment we cease its unconscious consolidation, it etherizes, becomes transparent and rent in twain, revealing the real living and ensouled world-man behind it.[94]

In the case of thinking we can, at any moment, reverse and shift our attention from its hardened light surface and immerse our consciousness in its dark and potent will core. We open, as it were, the door of miracles between every two concepts by holding them apart and spacing out their time difference, as was shown above. Through this space of livingly deadened time we delve into the dynamic reality of living spirit. We shall now practise the same miraculous act of liberation in the field of sense-perception, in order *to pass through* the external physical object and reach the spirit of the world in the etherically extended and expanded being of man.

Experienced by supersensible consciousness, true, substantial being-ness, as Rudolf Steiner often indicated, is created and deposited only in the will-organism of man.[95] Already in his Goethe editions he pointed out that the objective sense-world is nothing but the metamorphosed sum of our sense-perceptions as appearances, without any abstract (ideal), unqualified, imperceptible and only hypothetically deduced matter 'behind' it.[96] As a (the) matter of fact (as mother, or matrix of every fact), we project continuously — though unconsciously — our bodily will-activity onto the external sense-appearances that are, taken purely as sense-perceptions, light-filled and evanescent. An 'object' is, in the purely sense-world, an etheric-elemental flowing reality, fixated, cemented and sedimented, made dense and heavy through — and only through — our bodily, willed touch,[97] from which we abstract, con-ceptually, all our metaphysical material notions.[98] Rudolf Steiner described how the united sensations of our body, perceived through the bodily senses of life, movement and balance, penetrate into and are held fast by touch, smell and taste and eventually reach also into sight in order to create in our conscious mind[99] two solid convictions. The first is that we are solid, material beings,[100] and the second — projecting this conviction outwards — is that the tree out there is a real, heavy material body similar to what we imagine ourselves to be. As Rudolf Steiner showed — opening again one of the greatest riddles of epistemology and ontology of all times — the conscious concept of real beingness, the riddle to which Heiddeger's entire philosophical life was bound with such bewitchment, is created unconsciously through our body-senses, whose perceptions give to our sight and thinking a feeling- and will-like experience of density and opaqueness that causes us to shape the con-scious judgement that out there something absolutely physical-material exists.[101]

At this point we may begin the living deconstruction process of the opaque, external object. Here we have the point of attack clearly outlined before us: in each conscious act of sense-perception we should be able to hold back our unconsciously working will-power in order to avoid its unconscious metamorphosis into dead thinking when we open our senses to the world. Were it possible for us to separate completely the 'is' as *bodily*-will affirmation — which flows into the half-conscious Being judgement — from the etheric-astral essence of the 'object' grasped purely in the sense-activity, we should be able consciously to control and liberate the living flow of will in sense-perception itself. That is, if we could stop mingling unconsciously and instinctively our external and internal sense-perceptions and, as a result, free our thinking from its metaphysical abstractions, we should find that openness, or gate, of pure sense-perception that Rudolf Steiner indicated.[102] We should, so he said, penetrate through the 'zone of opaqueness', of impenetrability (touch, smell, taste) created at the place where, on the one hand, the external senses (seeing, warmth, hearing) are sucked in too deep into the body and, on the other hand, the bodily, inner senses are projected too far outside, obscuring the clarity of spirit sight. We should be able to find our way through touch, smell and taste, freely and consciously separating the outer senses from the bodily ones, making the senses of touch, smell and taste transparent.[103] A pure sight (warmth, hearing) of a living, non-objectified 'external' world would emerge on the one side, and a deep transparent sight of the inner man would be made possible, revealing the true world dynamics of our body, on the other.[104]

After this initial unfolding of willed thinking in the effort — of which only a very brief and abbreviated extract could be presented here — to clarify on the level of pure thinking the problem of the object in the knowledge process within the sphere of perception, we shall proceed to offer a more practical spiritual example of the real process involved in the spiritualization and opening of the gates of sense-perception.

Our method has as its goal, first, the achieving of *the fullest crossing and interpenetration of the death and life forces and processes* in the total organization of man,[105] and then, second, the focusing of this process (in the service of our purpose here) specifically in the field of sense-perception.[106]

The guiding indication for this work is given by Rudolf Steiner in the following way:

What is experienced in the spring and what is experienced in the autumn was, in the past, completely independent of each other: this outward radiation in the spring [of new planetary, elemental life forces, whose appearance since the end of Kali-Yuga was described earlier in this lecture] and this wistfulness in the autumn. What the cosmos gives out of its memory enables us to carry something from what we experience in the autumn into spring. When we let work in us the elemental forces of autumn, we can feel in a new way what will be given to us in the future. Everything will be renewed in the future... In that the etheric body develops itself, also through the autumn impressions that man takes in and weaves into himself, the Etheric Christ will be perceived.[107]

Condensely described — the actual experiential details are always manifold and many-sided and must be developed further elsewhere — the spiritual strength needed for the opening of the gates of sense-perception is forged in the soul through the following stages:

1 The impressing into man's organization, in meditative activity, of the two basic time-situations of life in the physical world, as given to the senses in the fully developed plant (maximum materialization and objectification of living time), and a small seed (maximum liberation and expansion of the living-time forces in connection with the physical world). This stage leads man to experience the two 'time-cliffs' described in Chapter 4 as the pre-earthly (past) and post-earthly (future) time-streams, between which flows the living, present lifetime river emanating from the eternal fountains of life within the Christ-permeated part of man's etheric body. When this river is lifted up into self-conscious imaginative consciousness, it is perceived as a continuous, rhythmical pulsation, expanding and contracting, lighting-up and darkening-down according to the subtle excarnation-incarnation rhythms of the human astral body and ego.

2 In the second stage man should bring the two 'time cliffs' into movement in the direction of each other: the fully expanded physical time formation (externally impressed in space through the full-grown plant) is moved through the withering autumn process into the seed-time formation, and vice versa; the concentrated etheric time formation (tied mysteriously to space with only a thin thread through the life-secret of the plant seed) is developed through the spring dynamic into the young, sprouting shoot and up to the fully developed plant. This process is intensified until the two streams not only reach and touch in each other's infinite end point but, pouring themselves *through* the other's infinity, merge into *one* stream that circles and reverses itself through a central point for both time formations at once. So man has a pulsating time formation whose one pole is etherically the weakest (the full-grown plant) and the other pole etherically the strongest (the seed), as the two poles of the year's solstices, winter and summer, respectively; and in the middle is a crossing and *Umstülpung* point when summer flows into winter (autumn) and winter into summer (spring) *at the same time.*[108]

3 When the dynamic-organic survey of the whole life-cycle has been achieved in the way described, the inner attention is lifted from the etheric-time process to the astral-soul process. In this way man learns to experience — holding fast to, and flowing with, the life-stream — the soul mysteries of the etheric lemniscate as duration-being, as etheri-

87

cally spaced-out time process. That is, living and weaving in the time process at the same time in both poles and in the *Umstülpung* point with its two time directions, man learns to experience the soul drama of life, death and rebirth, meditatively formed by Rudolf Steiner in the soul language of the yearly cycle in the *Soul Calendar*.[109] This stage culminates in the awakening of inner sight in the depths of *feeling*, illuminating the consciousness-astral forms of natural death and natural life in their flow in and through one another. This means to go through the whole range of feelings and grades of soul awakenings, from the most refined natural sympathy, warmth and love, expanding inwardly beyond time and space, and contracting in inner clarity of soul experience into the earthly depths in awakening pain, coldness and antipathy. It means learning the soul processes of falling asleep and the waking up of the astral body in its inner daily, yearly but also momentary incarnation-excarnation breathing rhythm in the elemental world of natural life.[110]

When this soul experience is carried through long enough, however, man begins to feel — to begin with this is a subtle, self-effacing experience, but it grows gradually into a mighty mood of soul anxiety — that the harmonious, rhythmical flow of the life forces is losing its momentum ever more. He feels that the autumn and winter experiences increasingly gain the upper hand over the youthful spring and summer forces. More and more he feels that in every new return and rebirth of life there is less power and vitality than in the former cycle. The dark, cold abyss of life's annihilation stream begins to be inwardly experienced, slowing down and gradually freezing the dynamic reversal moment of life-and-soul breathing and pulsating, down to the point of complete inner lameness and helplessness. And man learns gradually to understand that, in the whole natural life cycle, and in the whole elemental range of soul experiences, *there is no power to break this overwhelming spell*. He must feel his whole being coming to a total stop at this point.[111]

4 The life-and-soul natural experience in man is thereby cancelled and neutralized, and is therefore lifted to the ego level. There man must struggle to discover the inner point where no vital change and no change of consciousness can overpower him and carry him along. In this point — pictorially expressed in the 'eye point' of the lemniscate of time — man can freely master the natural streams in his elemental body, and freely direct his soul attention and so *cross the time streams at will*. He learns thus to carry consciously the autumn impressions into the spring, which means to let the Michael spirit of autumn inwardly illuminate the Raphael healing spirit of spring and so realize not only the repeated yearly rebirth of the forces of nature but the resurrection of the ego of the human being through Christ on Golgotha, and

88

through Him the resurrection of the whole Earth and its kingdoms. That is, the anthroposophical experience of the fate of living and ensouled nature has led us to the point of awaiting the new appearance of the etheric Christ in the astral world as an inner ego experience of man.[112]

Having come so far in the crossing of the life and death streams in the organization of man as a whole, we can return, strengthened through this experience, to the problem of sense-perception.

Let us then begin again, but remain now 'with open eyes'. This means that now we shall hold on strictly to sense-perception and focus our efforts entirely on this level.

We carefully place a real physical, externalized time being before us.[113] It may be an unfolded time object — such as a full-grown plant — or an infolded time object — such as a seed — as the case may be. (As we saw above, in the course of our practice we will have to oscillate harmoniously between the two time situations.) After carefully observing the sense qualities — colours, hardness, warmth, and so on — of the object, we concentrate our attention on its external shape and limits.[114] But we then suppress all of these, and begin to think actively, as Rudolf Steiner recommended, the object's unseen essence.[115] That is, we do not begin by suppressing objective thinking and sense-perception. On the contrary, we first enhance them as we did in the case of pure thinking (above). But we should note the following: when we sense, we must learn truly only to sense (and not to think); and when we think, we should only think (without sensing). The clearer we begin to experience the gap between the two, the better. It is perception's abyss: it leads us gradually to the indicated openness of the gate of sense-perception.[116]

If we have already transformed our thinking into pure will, as was described in this chapter, the next step is possible. If not, *this will first have to be achieved*. Now when thinking the essence of the object is completely willed, it must be arbitrarily suppressed: one must step outside of thinking *but remain fully conscious and awake in sense-perception*. When one no longer takes hold of one's organism in order to engrave the sense-impressions in the physical body through the forming of sense-mental pictures that can be later remembered, one loses it altogether; one becomes body-free. But in holding onto perception, one does not evaporate into thin air.[117] One sees with the etheric counterpart of the physical eyes, that is, with eyes that have been disconnected from the automatic connection with the nervous system and the brain (and therefore also from the bodily will that is bound to the blood in the case of the regular physical-bodily sense activity).[118]

In other words this can be formulated as follows. Man opens the tiny time-space that always elapses — at the speed of light — between the reception of a sense-impression in the eye and its registration (reflection) in the brain, where it is immediately devitalized and fixed in the organism as mental mirror picture that can later be memorized. But if we cancel all reflection we open wide this tiny time-gate between perception and brain registration and reflection. We step through it out of space (and deadened, objective, measurable time) into the flowing, living light of time, where light and colours live and move and have their true being outside the human physical body in the external etheric and astral worlds. In these worlds the human etheric and astral bodies always weave in the majestic, purely qualitative sensible-supersensible tapestry of world-man Imaginations and formative thoughts. This opening of the gates of sense-perception through which the human soul in the physical world is usually bound to the dead illusion of matter, and the resulting transformation of physical seeing into living etheric and astral imaginative perception, is nothing other than the modern, Michaelic way to open the gates of *Hades* and release the mourning Persephone-Natura from her natural seasonal captivity in Pluto's kingdom. This task belongs today to the endeavour to spiritualize the fallen and materialized forces of world thoughts, ruled by Michael. When modern man learns to open and close these gates freely, and steps out of himself to the worlds of free-flowing, weaving light, colours, sounds and all the other sense qualities, experiencing himself as world-man in the macrocosmic Man of cosmic reaches, he will redeem the fallen seeing soul within him — the Earth-bound Persephone-Natura, and out of his 'living soul'[119] see the Etheric Christ in His majestic new cosmic revelation.[120]

The opening of the gates of Hades in sense-perception is described by Rudolf Steiner as follows:

> The possibility lights up to use the tiny time-space [between sense perception and brain registration] that otherwise man cannot use at all ... It is already known today by experimental psychology that a certain time elapses between the influence on our eye and the registration of the mental picture of blue ... There elapses a certain time-space. In this time we do not yet experience the colour blue ... but we experience in this time-space the moral impression of the colour ... The soul element of the colour really works earlier, only it remains in the unconscious. The human being does not perceive it ... At the present time it can happen that man is given the grace — and we are always in a certain sense blessed with grace in our existence in the world — *to hold this moment fast* ... But for the ordinary life what happens in this small time-space lies beyond consciousness, beyond the threshold. In the moment in which man can bring to consciousness what really is beyond the threshold of consciousness, in this moment he makes an important spiritual discovery ... In the world of which I

have just spoken, that always exists around us, that we do not perceive because it remains unnoticed when the impression reaches us, *in
this world are to be found the etheric bodies of the Dead*, on which the Dead
are looking. What the Dead see of our world, what they gaze upon, is
contained in the etheric word that surrounds us. And we could always
see this world if we could see [the pure sense-impressions] before we
see in the physical world, if we could only cross over this threshold a
little.[121]

At this moment of crossing the threshold of sense-perception a most
beautiful and immensely rewarding experience takes hold of us. Human
perceiving consciousness becomes light,[122] gently radiating and circulating, weaving — and that is the unusual impression — inside and
around, the centre and circumference of what *was* the object. It merges
with the expanded essence of the object that was formerly only thought,
but now is experienced in living light. But now also the eye becomes an
'object' of perception for an expanded, new eye. The eye is experienced
detached, separated from the body, and it swims on the rays of its own
light[123] into the living, light-pulsating space of the object, *becoming its eye
of etheric appearance, serving its unfolding being.*[124] And this is a matter of
direct vision: the object, dissolving, evaporating, transparently shining
and teaming with infinitely coloured light sparks, pools, streams and
clouds, sails the sea of light in the same manner as the eye but in the
opposite time direction, reversing the eye's movement, exchanging
places with it, crossing it on its own way 'backward', uniting with man's
light of sight.[125]

This 'future' meeting and blending of subject-object in etheric sense-
perception overcomes the gap in space and time between man and the
objectified, dead world.[126] When this experience is repeatedly condensed and brought again and again to the focus of etheric-time (imaginative) perception, that is, when the crossing movement of the eye
outwards into the dissolving object, and of the living object back into the
expanding eye organism, is held fast, man can begin to experientially
understand Rudolf Steiner's insistence on the epistemological claim that
man as thinker and perceiver alike is not to be located in the space-time
of his physical body, but that his true 'I' is always moving, living and
having its being inside the living, ensouled and spiritual fabric of the
real world. And that the physical body, with its devitalized nerve-sense
system, serves only as a mirror in order to devitalize, reflect and
objectify the 'I' and the beings in which he weaves and lives unconsciously, thereby enabling the development and forming of clear self-
consciousness in the age of the consciousness soul.[127]

At the above indicated crossing circumference of physical and etheric
sight, man meets the real world for the first time outside his dense

physical body. He impregnates it and is being impregnated by it.[128] Man is creating the world, and is being created at the same (life) time. Man becomes a world-human being, and the world becomes a human world.[129]

Through this experience man can gain the deeply fulfilling conviction that the process of human knowledge, when grasped livingly, as described above, is a direct, willed participation and creation *inside* the core of the becoming Sun process of the new earthly-human Sun. Then one can feel also how, resurrected through the Life Spirit of Anthroposophy, Goethe's living essence comes to life again in the following words of Rudolf Steiner:

> So the knowledge process becomes a member in the shaping of world reality. Man co-creates in this world reality, when he knows ... In knowing, man does not create something for himself alone, but he creates, together with the world, in the realization of real being ... Goethe stands in creative life and being when he activates himself in the knowledge process.[130]

It is this circumference of crossing in *Umstülpung* of subject-object in sense-perception that becomes the situation of perceiving meditation,[131] when the first stage, described above, is firmly grounded and becomes consciously repeatable. The new object of meditation is this crossing reversal out of space into living time and vice versa.[132] And what is revealed is of the greatest importance for our study here on both its levels. It leads, on the one hand, to the conscious ability to control the devitalization and revitalization of sense-perception. This is, as was the case with thinking, the necessary condition for the conscious construction of the bridge. But it also leads, on the other hand, to the conscious illumination of the role of living sensing in creating the planetary sphere of living light, which is, as will be shown in the next chapter, its Christ-permeated imaginative atmosphere, the new Heaven of the new earthly-human Sun. But first we must continue our exploration in the same direction, asking: at the crossing of dimensions, at the reversal inside out of objectified space into living time, or at perception's threshold of man-world being, what else is dynamically revealed?[133]

Through the radiating, space-filling illumination of living sense-perception, moving dynamically from within outwards, there appears, from the vanishing object-space, the living, formative spaces of creative world time.[134] In other words, into the expanding (vitally awakened, etheric) eye streams the real world of form-creating, object-moulding cosmic formative thought-pictures. And it is possible to determine in this sight, by learning to focus (etherically condense, devitalize), or unfocus (etherically vitalize, expand) — that is, by moving at will the living time organism of the eye — the exact crossing moment (in time) or gap (in objective space) *where the etheric cross, now in perception, is erected*: the spirit cross of the stabilization and anchorage of supersensible sense-perception. It is the gate of sense openness that leads from space to time and back, now firmly controlled by man's awakened spirit will in seeing.[135] And man can here quite objectively, livingly perceive how, at the gate's openness, the cosmic, world-creating and infilling Christ is continuously crucified in every single, objectified and devitalized sense-impression.

Rudolf Steiner describes in the following way how man's Angel, or his true, higher (spirit) self, is penetrating him in every pure etheric (and therefore unconscious) perception:

When the Sun ray penetrates our eye and things become visible, on the Sun ray the place is to be found where our Angel lives. But it is so: in the oscillations of sounds, in the radiance of light and colours, in the other sense-perceptions, lives the being of the Angel. Only, because man must transform his sense-perceptions into mental pictures, the Angel cannot enter into them, and man does not know how he is surrounded by the being of the Angel ... Through this fact we are exposed, in the time between birth and death, to the penetrating attacks of the ahrimanic forces in our intellect.[136]

When we bear in mind that since the Mystery of Golgotha the Christ lives in the form of an Angel in the hierarchy of the Angels, and that in the etheric world he undergoes his renewed etheric death and resurrection in the ahrimanic thinking forces of our time,[137] then it immediately clarifies the experience of the transformation of sense-experience, described above. As Christ is continuously crucified in our daily thinking—and is resurrected through the liberated will being of thinking—so He is objectively, as world-human self, also crucified in every ordinary sense-impression and resurrected in the process of its spiritualization. This is truly the real, in our time absolutely necessary, Michaelic 'Christ-relation' to external nature.[138]

Preserving and bearing the living light of the formative, cosmic love as the source of world thinking, He is experienced as infinitely narrowed and condensed, in utter suffering nailed inside out and upside down, and fixed as a dead picture on the human physical retina. Ordinary sight is revealed as a continuous crucifixion, in order that man might consciously see a dead world—in freedom. This is the shattering experience at this stage of the transformation of sense-perception.

The place of the cross in sense-perception, and the second, etheric Mystery of Golgotha in this sphere can, therefore, in imaginative observation, be exactly grasped. In ordinary consciousness it enables, working from out of man's unconscious soul life, the objective process of sense-perception. This process was described by Rudolf Steiner as follows:

Sense-perception can be understood as a fine interaction between the external and inner ether; as enlivening of the outer ether that is killed in the sense-organs by the inner ether. In this way what the senses kill from the ether of our surroundings, is inwardly made alive again through the etheric body, and we come in this way to the perception of the external world.[139]

When the point of killing the external ether is consciously *seen*, the etheric Golgotha in perception is seen; when it is consciously *grasped*, we go through it livingly, uniting the inner and outer etheric streams through life in death and death in life in conscious imaginative 'I'-activity, and experience the etheric resurrection of Christ in the etheric world as man-world united resurrection in joyful expansion into the macrocosmic worlds of living light, colours and sounds.[140]

Without advancing in sense-perception to this etheric crucifixion and resurrection, man cannot, in our time, achieve conscious, voluntary imaginative sight. He will remain a dreamy, 'auric' visionary clairvoyant,[141] or intellectual materialist. But then he would have missed Christ's etheric resurrection in the imaginative planetary life-and-light sphere, woven out of humanity's Christ-permeated perceptions, livingly crystallized around the fiery core of the new earthly-human Sun. But here, as in the case of the transformation of thinking, the etheric crucifixion experience is what enables us to create the living/dead/resurrected bridge of remembrance over the river of our released—and livingly annihilated—life-time, that as the abyss of the 'greatest disharmony ever to exist in the being of man' continuously threatens to destroy any conscious knowledge of the interrelationships between the spiritual and the physical worlds.

The Construction of the Bridge

Now that we have at our disposal the forces of metamorphosed thinking and sense-perception, that is, the forces of the body sustaining spirit-will and world-shaping imaginative thinking, we can begin the work of construction, because we overcame the life- and time-annihilating river of spirit-forgetfulness, which is, according to Rudolf Steiner, 'the power of mental-picturing and of memory that separates the sensible from the supersensible'.[142]

The great difficulty before which we stand now was described by Rudolf Steiner in the epilogue to the new printing (1918) of the book *The Threshold of the Spiritual World*. What follows is the relevant text that will serve as the background for our present study (the italics are mine):

The power of memory, which plays in the soul-life of ordinary consciousness a special role, does not constitute an active human force in supersensible perception ... The human soul has this power of memory in the life in the physical world because it can activate it by means of the organization of the physical body. When the soul stands in the supersensible world in connection with the beings and processes of this world it cannot use the power of memory. The soul would, to begin with, only stare at what stands before it in this world without retaining a memory of it when diving back into its body. But this does not remain so. The soul takes with it, out of its experiences in the physical world, *an echo of its memory-capacity*, by means of which it can know in the supersensible experience: I am the same being here in spirit as I am there in the sense-world. This power of memory is necessary for the soul, because, without it, it will lose the connection with its self-consciousness. But, what is more, the self-consciousness that is raised to the supersensible world develops also the capacity *to transform the impressions received in this world* in such a way that it would be able to make in the body inscriptions of the same kind that the physical impressions make in the physical world. In this way it is possible that the soul retains for itself a sort of memory of its supersensible experiences. Otherwise the world it experiences would be continuously lost. But while the sense-impressions gained in the physical world influence man in such a way that, after the experience, they can be remembered by means of the physical process that brought them about, *in the supersensible realm man himself has to control the process with the impressions*, so that it will be possible later to know them also in the ordinary consciousness. In the supersensible experiences, therefore, everything must take place in the full light of consciousness.[143]

This passage makes it clear that our bridge, as any bridge, must have two sides, or pillars. The one must be firmly anchored in the earthly consciousness, but lead the 'echo' of daily memory into the spirit. The other must be firmly grounded in the supersensible world, but be orientated earthward; it has to condense the spiritual experiences to such an extent as to give them the consistency resembling the physical sense-impressions, in order to enable their remembrance in earthly consciousness.

In other words, this means the following. Our earthbound memory, capable of inscribing and sedimenting thinking and sense-perception, must be first vitalized and then spiritualized; our cosmically released, flitting spirit experiences must be consciously despiritualized and devitalized.[144] And the work, proceeding from both sides of the abyss of consciousness, must meet, be superimposed on and cross at, above and in the stream of spirit forgetfulness. At this point there takes place the conscious crossing, reversal and—as was pointed out above, both inwardly for pure thinking and outwardly for sense perception— crucifying of the living into the dead and the dead into the living. But this means to stand wide awake on the threshold. There lights *up* the earthly darkened will, and darkens *down* the heavenly shining thinking interchangeably, continuously revealing man's primordial fissured being. And there he experiences, deeper still, his moral dismemberment. And only in this superimposition of what awakens in death, and in awakening dies, namely, the *cognitive* (etheric) capacities, with the most intimate fragmentation and recollection of the *moral* (astral) being of man is the bridge hardened and stabilized, so that it can stand the storms sweeping across the zone of the abyss of time's annihilation and spirit-forgetfulness.[145]

This effort must, naturally, break down many times before man begins to receive and preserve the first, flitting and shadow-like spirit intimations and recollections in his waking consciousness. But morally strengthened by the modern Christ experience, and cognitively awakened through the transformation of thinking and sense-perception, man works his way steadily and confidently to the desired goal. Building now on the foundations that were hitherto acquired, let us proceed to explore the bridge-building process in some detail.

The twofold work on this side of the abyss—the spiritualization and vitalization of thinking into the free will being, and sense perception into formative world thinking—has already been accomplished. They must now be woven tightly into *one* spiritual force, in order to a) anchor firmly the whole construction on this side's shore, and b) throw, or project, the capacity of self-conscious imaginative self-remembrance far enough onto the other side. This capacity will be used, then, working from the other side back, to complete the work. Again, we should not shrink from the use of consciously-formed pictures; they are, in any case, our only means to describe truly spirit reality.

We have already referred twice to such 'crossing circumferences'. The one was delimited by us at the inner limit of consciousness—at thinking's end. We saw that when thinking is dynamically reversed and turned outside-in, the hidden will, energizing unrecognized the whole process, turns inside-out, is inwardly, spiritually awakened and consciously grasped. This is the cross of the first of the two 'thieves' crucified on Christ's left and right at Golgotha and, in a certain way, the more easily redeemable by modern man. The second cross delimits the crossing and reversal of perception. Here we have to cross through that resisting power that hides spirit reality outside, in the sense-world. At this point of reversal, where our vitalized seeing gaze moves, lives and has its being in the space-time of the transformed object, and the object— woven formatively of the world's living, streaming time-pictures—

flows into the transformed eye; when the two are no longer objectively separated, devitalized and deadened, *but are not yet completely mutually replaced* (retimed), when they openly show each other at the moment of their crossing, there we know how our second limit—or cross—of consciousness is sealed and made opaque.[146]

Now, after having carefully penetrated and exactly delimited the two border zones of inner and outer consciousness opacity, we might proceed as follows. We shall strive ever more to intensify interchangeably sense-inbreathing and will outbreathing to such an extent that they will be more and more brought to cross each other.[147] When the two crosses cross, coalesce and become one, we are transformed into the central, eternally living cross.[148] This is, finally, the rock on which alone the bridge can be securely anchored in supersensible self-consciousness.

It is the eternal, but now fully self-conscious, soul breathing and spirit pulsating of the 'I' at, over and in the mystery of world-man bridge creation—phoenix-like ever vitalizing, devitalizing and revitalizing itself in order to awaken, create and increase cosmic self-consciousness. Only now are we in the position to substantiate and form the first— cognitive—layer of the bridge of spirit remembrance.[149]

Rudolf Steiner described this process, which, as our experience shows, creates the self-conscious 'I' centre in supersensible reality, as the new Michaelic yoga breathing in the soul-and-spirit elements of sense-perception and will:

> When our sense-processes become ensouled again, we will have established a crossing point, and in this crossing point we shall take hold of the human will that streams up, out of the third [inspirative] stratum of consciousness, as I described to you recently. Then we shall, at the same time, have the subjective-objective element for which Goethe was longing so very much. We shall have the possibility of grasping, in a sensitive way, the peculiar nature of the sense process of man in its relation to the outer world ... In reality, there takes place a soul process from the outside towards the inside, which is taken hold of by the deeply subconscious, inner soul process, so that the two processes overlap. From outside, cosmic thought works into us; from inside, humanity's will works outwards. *Humanity's will and cosmic thought cross in this crossing point, just as the objective and the subjective element once crossed in the breath.* We must learn to feel how our will works through our eyes and how the activity of the senses delicately mingles with the passivity, bringing about the crossing of cosmic thoughts and humanity's will. *We must develop this new yoga will.*[150]

We can now say: when we have firmly grasped this crossing and reversing of world-thoughts and human will, we can establish there the first fully matured station on the path of our bridge construction. This means: standing still at the point of man's singularity, founding self-consciousness in the zero point of space and the breaking through of living, cyclically self-annihilating and self-resurrecting time. Such a self produces its consciousness in being selflessly, and without fear, open to the stream of time's annihilation in the production of space, and in the annihilation of space through lightning time. It is a world-self, self-consciously consciousness producing and suffocating, coming to its self in the midst of the ever-renewed destruction and rebirth of the human, Christ-permeated world.

And when man has gained the capacity, out of his own free will, to place himself voluntarily, repeatedly, in this situation — living at the crossing, moving dynamically over its whirling, opposing forces,[151] and having his being in its abyss — he can, basing himself firmly on his own ground, arch the arc of his freed and consciously reversed lifetime, and consolidate, sacrificially freezing[152] and sedimenting,[153] the marvellously shining crystal bridge of his consciously deadened — and resurrected — etheric body.[154] This etheric body is the solid ground of spirit remembrance, safely connecting the spirit and earthly worlds, untouched by the storming, life and time annihilating forces of the abyss of Lethe.[155]

At this point we might insert — as we did above in regard to the preparatory spiritual work that was necessary for the opening of the gates of sense-perception — a more technical and condensed description of the actual meditative anthroposophical practice that leads to the final consolidation of the bridge. But first we must be reminded of the true nature of the being that fights with Michael for the mastery of the cosmic intellectual forces in the human being.

This enemy was described by Rudolf Steiner as follows:

> The dragon has the most manifold forms; he has all possible forms. Those springing from human emotions are damaging enough, but they are not so damaging as the form that the dragon assumes through the dead, deadening knowledge of the present. There the dragon becomes absolutely, especially abominable ...[156]

And further:

> It will be nothing else but this misguided understanding, this misguided intelligence, which can prevent man from coming to the Christ-principle. And if those who finally succumb to the two-horned beast could look back on what has dealt them the worst blow they would say: the tendency to descend into the abyss only came later, but what darkened the Christ-principle for me was my intellect.[157]

Practically, then, this process can be described as follows. Man takes a specific thought process which expresses a typical ahrimanic connection of concepts in pure scientific or philosophical conceptual formation and formulation. For this purpose the great classical materialists of the nineteenth century are the best, because their thoughts were the last remnant of classical times, but already transformed into the new ahrimanic element.[158]

As an example to learn from, one can take the already prepared material to be found in Hegel's logical dialectic, 'which is torn free from Ahriman for humanity's sake, because humanity needs it in order to advance further'.[159] But this is, as we have said, already achieved *for us*. Everyone must, therefore, if he wants to create *his own* drama of knowledge, also find his personal intellectual enemy, who can be his personal teacher in the great battle of our time over the fallen cosmic intelligence.[160]

Now the first stage of the work consists in the analytic study of the chosen material through pure brain activity. Man must make sure that he activates the *physical* brain, and not the etheric brain alone, and this means, from an anthroposophical point of view, a real battle of the will: to follow down deep into the grey, and deeper still into the white, matter of the brain the thought process, until one has the inner certainty that the intellectual operation is firmly materialized.[161]

When this preparatory stage is accomplished, we take the following measures. First we separate carefully the intellectual *content* from the intellectual *form* of our chosen thought material, and concentrate entirely on the last, the pure *force-dynamic* of the thought process concerned. This separation takes place in the head-centre, behind the eyes,[162] and advances still deeper into the middle of the brain. The result will be a growing feeling of the existence of a hollow 'tunnel'[163] connecting the forehead with the middle brain and eventually pouring its waters into the spinal column. When this is achieved, it is a sign for the release of the etheric brain from the physical brain at the point of its tightest bondage to the latter since the fifth, Semitic, race of Atlantis.[164] Now, after this 'etheric brain operation' is successfully carried out, we turn to the second measure, namely, we begin to impress the above-mentioned thought dynamic rhythmically and repeatedly into our etheric body so that, after due practice, we can consciously follow our spiritualized thinking from the head process down to the heart in the following way.

We 1) begin to experience the thought's *forms* around the larynx region in inner light-shade perception; 2) we begin to feel the thought's warmth and frost formations and emanations as direct inner contact in the heart region;[165] and 3) we can voluntarily enhance this process and condense it to such an extent that, in and through the heart, it radiates its coldness or warmth forces into the whole body, into the hands and then back into the eyes and inner head, until the circle of freed etheric activity, started in the brain, is – through heart and limbs – closed *and made thereby etherically, imaginatively visible as a totality.*

When we are securely grounded in our meditation so far, we can begin the actual 'heart confrontation' with the inner ahrimanic forces dwelling in the force-dynamic of the thought process which we have worked through. This confrontation is brought about through the most intensive condensation of the freezing-cold atmosphere that emanated from the forces released in the meditation described above, extracted from a thoroughly assimilated materialistic thought dynamic. Man gathers and guides all the sub-earthly head forces, which assume in the larynx region a darkening arrow or spear form, and then – being morally and cognitively permeated with the Christ-impulse – condenses its cold spirit like metal further still and thereby also sharpens its cutting astral edge. He thrusts it consciously into his warm, luminous heart centre[166] until it begins to *bleed etherically.*[167] Imaginatively speaking, the drops of blood freeze in bleeding and are transformed into the shining *Quint-Essentia* pearls and diamonds on which the bridge is constructed.[168] When this process begins to ray itself in pictures back to the head centre – circulating backwards and upwards in the consciously transformed and thereby closed etheric circuit – it becomes imaginatively visible.

In the backward radiating inner imaginative pictures we perceive now the etheric bridge of remembrance arched majestically over the abyss of time's annihilation stream, shining with pure spirit light in the ahrimanic night of our age. This imaginative faculty is achieved as the result of the transformation process of the world intelligence that fell into the claws of Ahriman, now returned to its source as fully humanized Michaelic intelligence. *This faculty is the Michael sword,* and the process described above is the inner work of its conscious spiritual-scientific steeling.[169] As we saw above, its metallic substantiality was won for the Michaelic forces in the inner fight with the materialistic and intellectual ahrimanic forces that control the modern human brain. It was then etherically transfigured and steeled in the fire of the human Christ-permeated heart. This sword is the power that serves both to perceive and to overcome Ahriman's presence in the physical-etheric subterranean world, where he unfolds his mightiest power as the guardian and lord of all elemental intellectuality that is immersed and externalized in objectivity, far from its original source in the macro-cosmic heart centre.

The process described above is precisely that to which Rudolf Steiner referred in the moment when he fierily exclaimed: 'We must find the possibility to turn to our supersensible heart!'[170]

Man thus repeats microcosmically, freely and out of his fully conscious knowledge drama of the Second Coming, Christ's macrocosmic sacrificial deed for modern humanity. Man has, consciously, killed a part of his life-time, assimilating his death livingly into himself, mastering his death and preserving the capacity of living death *preservation* self-consciously intact in the stream of spirit-forgetfulness. This is 'that kind of memory' created out of the capacity 'so to transform the impressions received in this [supersensible] world', and retain them as if they were physically, bodily perceived sense-impressions. 'In the supersensible realm one must transform the experiences so that it will be possible later to know them also in ordinary consciousness'.[171]

Rudolf Steiner described this process, the first aspect of the Second Mystery of Golgotha, as follows:

That which will be gradually revealed to human beings is a memory or recapitulation of what St Paul experienced at Damascus. He saw the etheric form of Christ. But that it shall be visible for us now is based on the fact that in the etheric world a new Mystery of Golgotha took place. The crucifixion that took place in the physical world as a result of the hatred of the people who could not understand Christ, this repeated itself on the etheric plane through the hatred of the people who, as materialists, entered the etheric world after death. Man experiences how, at the Mystery of Golgotha, a cross made of dead wood was raised, on which the body of Christ was hanged. And when we see this wooden cross, that through the flames of hatred turned to coal, and on which the seven flowering roses still appear representing the sevenfold nature of the Christ,[172] then we have the picture of the Second Mystery of Golgotha taking place now in the etheric world. And through this dying, this second death of Christ, it was made possible that we shall see His etheric body. *This condensation, this dead part of the etheric body of Christ Jesus human beings shall see.*[173]

We said earlier that the bridge over the abyss of consciousness has etheric and astral levels. So far we have described the first stage of the work, namely, the achievement of supersensible self-consciousness, and with it the capacity of memory in supersensible experience. In the modern Christ experience it was that part of the etheric body of Christ that, by assimilating man's death forces, dies and becomes visible, that made possible the awakening of man from the death of soul (see Chapter 4). And so it was His *resurrected* etheric body, making visible His reappearance in the soul world on the other shore of man's surfacing world dividedness, that consolidated, as was described above, man's fragmentation into coherent spirit identity. At this second stage, the given modern Christ experience and the consciously achieved anthroposophical supersensible experience must be carefully compared and distinguished. Both begin through the moral shattering when facing the burnt down and suffocated living etheric cross. When one returns to this place consciously, after being there first through grace, the profundity of the impression does not diminish. On the contrary, because it is now brought about voluntarily in man's own heart, its moral impact is deepened. But now, in the self-achieved experience, it is man himself who must carry forward that process which was demonstrated and conferred on him by the Christ in the second stage. In other words, after the transformation of the etheric body, he must learn how to control consciously his total moral breakdown, to which we have already referred when we described the results of the transformation of thinking and the separation of the soul forces. This experience is the second act in the consolidation process of the bridge of conscious spirit memory, now not in the life-stream, but in the soul (astral) world itself. It is actually the soul steel that holds the whole construction together in self-consciousness. We turn now, therefore, to this second stage.[174]

In order to advance to this stage, we must first give up our place of the cross—the head centre, or Calvary—though not entirely; we learn henceforth to carry it with us into the sojourn in the soul world, as our 'earthly' (relatively speaking) anchorage of imaginative spirit sight.[175] We must now find the soul-force that will enable us to bring the process of soul metamorphosis to its fulfilment. This force can only be the liberated will being. Our task now is to pour our inner liberated soul life actively over and beyond the edge of our whole existence, and so send a willed ray of our self[176] over the surfacing inner soul abyss, described above. But this means, conversely, that one fully takes in the abyss, so that one lives with the decentered will being completely externalized, with the world's space and with the world's space-forming Imaginations as one's inwardness. The self-directed will being projects a ray of the soul-self through and over the nothingness of the astral void; as a result, the world pictures condense themselves within the emptied centre of the fragmented self until they become themselves this self. We can also say that this process fully individualizes man's primordial abyss, and thereby deepens it still further, splitting now the very core of the soul-self itself. It thereby conjures before man a picture of all the lower aspects of his astral nature.[177]

Only now, however, can the bridge over the abyss be firmly grounded. The realization gradually grows that both the degree of consciousness's light (the degree of spirit seeing), and the capacity to darken it in consolidation of memory (by returning to the cross-place of time) depends absolutely on the measure of the control that man can exercise over his new, firmly divided soul-self condition. This control is, to begin with, virtually non-existent. It means to learn anew, now on the soul level and reversed, to regulate the movements of the soul from the very beginning: to move the soul body left and right, back and forth, up and down—that is, to learn how to move freely at, over and between the two shores of one's divided soul-self existence. The agility required here

102

is morally dependent. One learns, for example, that to go backwards (which is actually forwards by earthly standards) is to strive towards the moral soul state that can stand upright under the living-dying, burning-freezing etheric cross; one has an upward, morally self-sustaining force in the soul world only then. Without it, one drifts helplessly, losing oneself, being hidden from oneself by one's lower self in shame in face of one's infinite soul ugliness. One has to achieve, therefore, in this case, the upright moral 'I'-faculty in order to recreate, in retracing one's steps, the cognitive bridgeway back to one's memory of oneself, which only the sight of the physical and etheric crosses can grant.[178]

But if he wants to move forwards (which in earthly life means backwards, towards the spirit), he discovers that he lacks the necessary moral trust and confidence in the world's goodness, being under the cruel impression of his fragmented, evil multiplicity of self-created soul beings, who seem to destroy all his future hopes of the true, the beautiful and the good. He knows that, although he established himself firmly behind, at the bridge's shore of the truth of life's death and its living preservation, that is, having on his soul back — or body — firmly inscribed and engraved the etheric body's cross that he can carry independently everywhere in the storming soul-world atmosphere, *he still lacks the ability to (morally) see the being that can overcome his evil in the soul world.* And it is this realization of moral inability that, when repeatedly experienced and grounded, offers, paradoxically, the required moral firmness for the future completion of the bridge.

Here we reach the crucial moment of crisis. It is the most difficult test of man's forces, and the greatest question in regard to the possibility of completing the work of construction. Let us picture this situation in concrete detail. We now have man's being so divided that his lower Christ-permeated being (physical and etheric bodies) appears in the form of the cross of consciously living death. This being anchors him securely in his self-conscious imaginative memory. But his higher being (ego and astral body) takes on the form of a world-man riddle and doubt.[179] Being inwardly situated and stabilized in his moral abyss, this being appears as a self-less mystery yet to be understood, but, at the moment, completely transcending the farthest shore of his spirit existence; and this experience becomes man's identity, or 'I' *feeling*, that gives him the only possible stable form of being in the soul world.[180]

This feeling is the only real possession that man has at the most crucial state of the anthroposophical knowledge drama of the Second Coming. By means of the surrender of any further striving, man gathers the inner moral force needed to complete the work of construction.[181] Only when we are grounded in this absolute dualism[182] and fragmentation of our moral being may we be granted the Christ experience at this stage. This weakness and helplessness is, therefore, the strongest preserving force of self-consciousness over and in the abyss of soul-devouring spirit forgetfulness. It alone enables the presence and preservation of mind necessary in order to stand firmly on the bridge of the consciousness soul in the morally fragmented reality of the soul world; and, in face of one's externalized, burning moral abyss — or astral 'wound' — *to articulate oneself as question: as a pure world-man question that one can offer to one's higher Christlike self*.[183] This self-articulated and shaped soul being in the soul world is, paradoxically, the only expression possible of the wholeness of man at this stage. And when this question has been self-lessly spoken by man *himself*, becoming his self, it reaches, carried on the wings of his self-less will being, the farthest shore of man's primordial world dividedness. Then there resounds, as a spoken, cosmically articulated answer, a spirit-filled affirmation from the other, higher spirit side of oneself.[184]

Anthroposophically expressed, we can say: the will being of man that was arched over the soul-world abyss anchored itself in the spirit world (Devachan), becoming one with man's highest archtype. But this achievement remains unconscious so long as the inner abyss, opened between man's (now cosmic) will being and his (now human, inner) cosmic thinking, has not given birth from its midst to the third soul being, namely, man-world *feeling*. When this happens, that is, when the feeling soul-being is articulated as man-world question, shaping the soul in the face of its evil wound into a moral mystery,[185] then this soul feeling-being, penetrated and consumed in its very core by the astral fire of burning self-knowledge, resurrects, or brings to full inspired imaginative consciousness, the voice of the higher, Christlike archetype of man. And this being then begins to speak. His spirit speech, however, awakens in man, for the first time in fully conscious spirit experience, the meaning of the second and the third stages of the modern Christ experience.[186]

It is this soul being, consciously articulated and composed of man's highest, self-created, strongest realization of moral weakness, that sails the ocean of soul infinity in order to make visible again, appearing at the shore of a much higher world, the figure of the etherically resurrected, life-giving and soul-transforming 'teaching' Christ-self. On this last constructed soul chain of the bridge, of purely moral spiritual character, man's will being, now healed, remembered and resurrected, comes back, united with the higher aspect of the Self and — for the first time — crosses the bridge of conscious memory backwards, descending and filling the earthly being of man with the creative power of the new Heaven and the new Earth. It bridges man's primordial world abyss in self-conscious memory, and thereby confers on his united cosmic-earthly self the capacity to mould the basic being and consciousness structure of the new earthly-human Sun.

What we called here the completion of the bridge through the moral act of soul metamorphosis, and the resulting meeting, sacrificial teaching and then the earthly penetration of man with his higher, Christlike Self, a process that is comparable first to the second and then to the third stages of the modern Christ experience described in Chapter 4, was expressed by Rudolf Steiner in the following words:

A spiritual decision ripens. The spiritual decision that ripens is that man should carry his loneliness to this second Being and that he should let his frost be warmed in the warmth of the other Being, so that he unites himself with this other Being. For one moment man has the impression as if now consciousness would be annihilated, as if he would bring about a sort of killing of his own being, a burning of his own being. Then ... there breaks into the self-consciousness, which felt itself already annihilated, something that man learns to know for the first time: Inspiration. Man feels himself inspired. It is like a conversation, like a special conversation, that now develops with a Being that man learns to know only because he allows man to share His Inspiration. Is man really capable of understanding what this Being brings forth through His inspired voice? Man can translate what this Being says into the words: because you found the way to the other Being, and united yourself with His offer, so you are permitted to go back with Him, in Him, to the Earth, and I will appoint you on the Earth to be his guardian. And man has the feeling that thereby he receives into his soul something of untold significance, that he has been found worthy to hear these words through Inspiration ... There is in the spiritual worlds a Being that has greater value than man himself, that can rain down His astral element in blessing. That man is permitted to unite himself with Him, and that man is permitted to be His guardian when he comes back down to the Earth: it is through this impression that man first really learns to understand how he, as a physical man that wanders on the Earth, is related with his physical and etheric sheaths to what impregnates him with higher forces in his self and astral body. Man is, with what he has as physical and etheric bodies, the guardian of that which, in the higher spheres, shall develop itself further and further.[187]

This 'descent' (physically seen, the so-called ascension) of man's remembered higher nature, and its resulting outpouring of the Holy Spirit fire of resurrected earthly spirit consciousness, is that which, now returning towards the new earthly-human Sun, makes man into world creator. His Christ-permeated Self has offered and conferred his cosmic creative role on earthly man. Out of the *knowledge* drama, the *creative*, world-shaping and transforming drama begins.

Chapter 6

The Creation of the New Earth and Heaven of the Earthly-human Sun

In this chapter we shall look closer at the forces and dynamics that create and shape — out of man's knowledge drama of the Second Coming — the new Heaven and Earth of the new earthly-human Sun. That the Earth has been, since the Mystery of Golgotha, at the beginning of its Sun-becoming process belongs to the essential results of Rudolf Steiner's researches in Christology and cosmology — but no less so, though this is as yet little explored, to his theory of knowledge and study of man. In the light of the modern Christ experience, however, the role of man's cognitive and moral activity in the Christological-cosmological process of the creation of the new earthly-human Sun becomes ever more conscious. During the last 2,000 years humanity has unconsciously participated in this process by means of its accumulated religious and spiritual strivings.[1] But this was, after all, precisely the problem of medieval Christianity, that it was not able to unite the moral-religious and the philosophical-scientific streams. Its moral-religious life and thought and its philosophical-scientific thought and life did not fully converge.[2] This convergence has been possible, as we know from the various indications of Rudolf Steiner, only since the beginning of a) the new Michael epoch (1879–c. 2330), b) the end of Kali-Yuga and the beginning of the new age of light (1899–4499), c) the beginning of Christ's etheric reappearance (1933–4933) — events that fall together after d) the end of the first quarter of the consciousness-soul epoch (1413–3573).[3] The consciousness-soul age provides the overall evolutionary period and the basic soul structure in which these impulses converge. The much shorter age of Michael provides the decisive impulse to spiritual awakening, the kindling of spiritual consciousness in the consciousness soul as a foundation for the whole period. The much longer new age of light provides the cosmic light atmosphere that enables the reintegration of humanity's evolution into the evolution of the cosmos as a whole. And the reappearance of the Christ is the expression of His eternal relationship to humanity and the Earth in their current evolutionary cycle.

The convergence and synthesis of these four influences — the investigation of which does not belong to our study here — creates the beginning of a totally new situation for humanity in its own evolution and in the evolution of the cosmos. Through the mutual penetration and fertilization of its waking, conscious thinking and sense-perception with its sleeping moral will, humanity becomes for the first time a creative factor, a co-creative element in the cosmos, joining — for the first time consciously and freely — the ongoing creation-process of the gods.[4]

In the last chapter I tried to show this from the point of view of the modern knowledge drama of the Second Coming. We saw how man's abstract and dead, past cosmic thinking can become a consciously directed and controlled, morally active supersensible will being, and how his ordinary will element, present always in every sense-perception, can lead him to a conscious creative participation in the formative living thought element of the cosmos. It was indicated further that, beside the role of thinking (will) and sense-perception (thinking) in the self-conscious construction of the bridge of remembrance over the abyss of spirit forgetfulness, they have another creative function. The supersensible will-being, after completing its doubled *Umstülpung* — out into the higher worlds and back into earthly man, reversed — becomes a powerful creative force, the fountainhead of a new Earth. And the new supersensible cosmic thinking element, after completing its own doubled reversal — from the far cosmic time spaces into man and then, individualized, streaming outward again — becomes the radiating sphere of a new planetary Heaven. Both together constitute the creative fiery core and the reflecting light atmosphere of the new Sun.

The emerging structure of the new earthly-human Sun is threefold. It has its new Heaven above, which is created out of man's transformed sense-perception, working in the new Sun's periphery with the power of world-Imaginations. It has its new Earth below, which is created out of man's Christ-permeated will-being, working in the new Sun's centre, united with the creative will power of the Christ. And it has a budding middle sphere, which is created out of the forces of transformed social life, weaving from human heart to human heart as the new Sun's breathing and outpouring of its life, light and warmth forces through world-man being.

Our study here, though in many respects preliminary and incomplete, can nevertheless be of value to anthroposophical spiritual science, which was characterized once by Rudolf Steiner as a '... modern initiation-science that can move itself in rhythm between Heaven and Earth, that asks the heavens when it seeks knowledge of the Earth, and asks the Earth when it seeks to know the heavens ... The modern initiates have to look for the knowledge of the rhythmic connection between Heaven and Earth.'[5]

It will now be our task, before we show in greater detail how this creative process unfolds itself out of the united and metamorphosed cognitive-moral stream of man's Christ-permeated consciousness, to prepare our study through Rudolf Steiner's description of the evolution of the Old Sun, and its continuation in the evolving earthly-human Sun.

This is the central Imagination of the creation of the Old Sun: in its depths the fiery Old Saturn sacrifice of the Thrones to the Cherubim, forming in the process the time beings of the Archai as the smoke clouds of their sacred offering; and then the Kyriotetes that, through their devotion to this sight, offer their wisdom-filled, life- and beauty-bestowing grace, which the Archangels individualize and reflect back as light from their time-place at the Sun's periphery.

> So we have, over against the Spirits of Wisdom, which in the Old Sun times are the giving, offering beings, to imagine the Archangels as the receiving beings ... think about a picture of an inwardly closed sphere, from the middle point of which something radiates outwards, that is offered; that radiates up to the periphery, and is reflected back from there to the centre. On the inner surface of the sphere are the Archangels, which reflect it back ... What is it that radiates back into the inner space, as the backward reflected offering of the Spirits of Wisdom? ... this is light. And so the Archangels are the creators of light as well.[6]

In the same way the Christ Mystery of the Earth constitutes the centre and periphery of the evolving earthly-human Sun process. But now other beings stand at the Earth's time periphery and reflect back as life and light Christ's sacrificial, outpouring source of new Sun life. And these beings are human beings.

> Let us think that what was described of the Old Sun could be wholly concentrated, could be gathered together and carried forth, in order to appear later. And it would have appeared again on the Earth and worked so that it would have brought with it out of the ancient sacrifice and smoke offering, and out of the light-creating time and the grace-bestowing virtue, an extract of grace forces, and would have radiated it again to all the world as warmth bliss and light beauty. Let us think of all this concentrated in one soul that gives it to Earth existence, around which are gathered all those that are now called, as Earth beings, to reflect it back, to retain it until the end of Earth existence: in the middle the one who bestows out of sacrifice and offering, and around him those that should receive it ... and on the other hand the possibility to destroy this offering, so that everything that is given to human beings as grace can be rejected as well as received ... We can have such a feeling towards the *Last Supper* of Leonardo da Vinci: the whole Sun grasped with the soul, with the sacrificing beings, with the beings of the offering virtue, with the

beings of the warmth bliss and light beauty — radiated back by those who are chosen to retain it from early times to later times.[7]

This is, then, the centre and periphery, Earth and Heaven, of the new earthly-human Sun process. Man stands in regard to the centre (Earth) building process and the periphery (Heaven) building process in the following ways. At the periphery he creates the reflecting etheric-astral atmosphere of Christ's (Holy) *Spirit* of the new Sun, out of his transformed sense perceptions; in the centre he works on the building of Christ's new planetary *bodies* with his liberated will-being; and in the middle man develops his sevenfold microcosmic-macrocosmic *soul* activity united with the sevenfold soul nature of the Christ.[8] Breathing and pulsating in continuous *Umstülpung* process between centre and periphery, he thus makes of the new Earth and Heaven the living Sun organism of the earthly-human Sun.

First, we shall bring before us Rudolf Steiner's indication in which he describes the beginning of the new *Earth* experience as follows:

> The youth of today strives for ancient knowledge of humanity, which already on Old Saturn was connected to man and, in the time of the Sun and Moon evolutions, entered into a kind of world slumber, into a sleep consciousness, in order to shape out of its own spirit substance the foundations for the Earth. And so this earthly nature, for the soul that can feel it but not see through it to the spirit, for the young feeling heart, is also like a snow-cover in summer which, though it shimmers as bright spirit crystals, carries Death within itself, that is, unconsciousness, which urges the soul to perceive deep under the soul snow-cover that which has its origin in still older times: *the fiery blazing, living workings of the Word that radiates outward from the middle of the Earth.*[9]

Now we shall try to describe the way that leads to the new Earth experience through the active and formative participation of the liberated will being of man in the human-creation process of the new Earth element of the earthly-human Sun.

As we saw in Chapter 5, man's liberated, macrocosmic will being comes back (re-membered) over the bridge of moral self-knowledge and cognitive, self-conscious remembrance as spiritualized, creative love. In its still microcosmic form as transformed thinking it appears, imaginatively speaking, in the picture of a life-giving fountain streaming out of a rocky cave or well into the darkness and density of which man descends through the meditative practice of active, dynamic and living thinking. The unseen dark spot of will that creates, unknowingly, man's ordinary thinking is then illuminated by the reversed, darkened light of thinking's reversal in and upon itself. External physical Sun light as well as the light of abstract thinking is reflected back from objects; it illuminates their concealment. It creates their occult nature. The dark light of will penetrates objects right into their real, substantial spirit core. The human will-self, self-active, is the first world being to be thus penetrated and experienced. It is revealed as the pulsating, living core of the real world.[10]

In so doing, we have followed the guiding thread of thinking's transformation. It leads us again to grasp the powerful will being holding sway esoterically between every two concepts, as the fountain of life in death, now opening the way to the mysteries of the formation of the new Earth of the earthly-human Sun. The descent into the depths of the new Earth begins *when the two will beings unite* consciously for co-ordinated earthly-Sun work — the world-man will being returning from above, and the man-world will being of earthly man. A new will being is thus created, and this being is the creator of the new Earth. This new will-love-being works cosmically-creatively with a human-cosmic will in the spirit depths of the new Earth. We shall now follow the traces of its world creativity downwards, grasping its active workings through intuited Imagination.[11]

We begin again at the point of pure will meditation that was described in the last chapter. But we now have at our disposal the seed-potentiality of the united world-man, man-world will being from the very start. When our concentration penetrates deep enough into our absolute void, it becomes the pure will-dynamics of complete self-reversal described in Chapter 5. But now it becomes spiritually audible in a specific manner. Instead of leading us into the pre-natal life of our *thinking*, as was the case with the microcosmic transformation of thinking into will, it reveals the true earthly-cosmic nature of the will substance itself. The Saturnian warmth element is now not only formatively *imagined* but is cosmically-humanly acted upon. This virgin and young, wholly future-orientated warmth element[12] is inwardly, spiritually *awakened and ignited*; it breaks the shells of old cosmic crystallizations and reveals an embryonic inner fiery core of concentrated circumference, an intensive, intuitive inner cosmic infinity, gleaming in the bluish depth of matter as if in the power of a mightily evolving Sun. As a bodily-earthly, all-penetrating thunder it resounds and reverberates in the dimly radiating depths, articulating the first Word of the newly impregnated and seed-like Earth of the new earthly-human Sun.

But how is the *awakening and igniting* of the Saturnian warmth-will element carried through in actual inner soul-and-spirit activity? The secret of this process lies in the peculiar nature of the doubly reversed will of thinking, described above. Because this doubly reversed and cosmically liberated will-being was originally the will-force of human thinking, if united with the human, unconscious will element, it has an awakening influence *in* it. When it returns and unites itself with the ordinary, unconscious, will of earthly man, it begins to think inwardly inside this will, and it bores its way into the opaque will-substance of man and Earth in the same way as an electric current moves inside an electric wire. The subjective soul experience that accompanies this process can only be compared with the physical experience of electrification, at least in so far as the will-and-feeling reaction is considered. But as far as the cognitive side is considered, man's consciousness becomes aware of an awakening *light* impulse that penetrates the dark inner opacity of the bodily substantiality as if it were a hollow, inner emptiness.

Especially the inner head structure and the spinal cord are experienced as hollow, in such a way that their hollowed inwardness spreads itself to the body as a whole and into the limbs; and then, through them, it overflows the bodily limits and strives to merge to a greater or lesser extent with the physical world as a whole and in particular with certain lines of force or veins inside the Earth. And though a *concrete and differentiated* esoteric investigation of the supersensible qualities of matter as such requires a much higher cognitive force, namely, real spiritual Intuition, the intuited imaginative faculty we follow here can at least offer us some indications concerning the inner soul aspect of the beginning of this process. Abstract as it still is, it *is* a beginning and it must be undertaken as part of the modern Christ experience and the knowledge drama of the Second Coming.

The awakening of the warmth element inside the bony system of the skull and skeleton occurs, to begin with, in the dark. But then inside this experience man strives to awaken the memory of the higher stages of the knowledge drama of the Second Coming, and especially of the last stage of the spiritual descent into the depths of the body and the Earth. The moment such a memory becomes concrete enough, and provided that the other soul-and-spirit conditions are appropriate, man can experience how the inner, awakened hollow darkness is also *ignited*. Man has a subtle inner experience of a burning, fiery process that spreads itself through the whole body. This is a living, inner sprouting, a weaving and transforming of darkness into light and warmth into active fire.

This interplay is transformed into *rhythmical* movement the more it becomes conscious. Man experiences how the inner centre of his being begins to pour its heart-and-lung activity into the rhythmically warming and lighting hollow darkness of the inner skull and limbs. And at that moment man discovers that the 'bony man' within him, to which in ordinary imagination thinking is mainly related and attracted, has an inner heart activity and sensitivity of its own and that it begins to have certain inner, dark supersensible perceptions of a wholly unique kind.

111

And it is this unique power of perception that then brings about a measure of conscious awareness of — and formative influence on — the inner creative processes inside the Earth.

If the 'young heart' spoken to by Rudolf Steiner at Koberwitz is able, in the way indicated here, not only to *feel* but also to *see* into the now Christ-permeated and resurrected primordial depths of the Earth, it can say to itself: now thinking has fulfilled its ancient cosmic mission, which is to lead man into the youthful spirit core of himself that can be consciously active in the will-centre of the Earth. As a loyal and pure representative of the Old Sun evolution within the Earth, resurrected thinking opens the gates to the creation of the *new* Sun in man. As a result of *the conscious awakening and igniting process of the will through thinking in the heart centre*, a real subterranean Imagination crystallizes and lights up through man's cosmically imbued limbs and feet, extending his will-being vision into an increasingly transparent and articulated Earth. But he knows that it is his own planetary will-being that speaks. This cosmic speech of the humanized planet Earth shapes a being in the depths: an articulated embryonic will-seed organ of a new world, as an extension of the creative heart of world-man himself.[13]

The imaginative appearance of this world-man embryo as the life-giving seed of the new Earth can be better understood if we bring it together with the description given by Rudolf Steiner of the imaginative appearance of the Earth before and after the Mystery of Golgotha:

> The spiritual scientist sees the Earth, before Christ came down, in the form of a cross, and really as a human form ... We are reminded there of the wonderful words of Plato that were formed out of the Mysteries, that the world soul is crucified on the world body ... [then] the Christ died on the cross; and thereby the Earth advanced *from a mere form into life*. Before Christ, the Earth appeared to spiritual sight as a form only; after Christ the Earth appears as newly enlivened through the Christ principle.[14]

This newly enlivened, once-dead form of the Earth — the world-man soul crucified on the world-body — appears again, now shaped out of the new Mysteries of Anthroposophy at the threshold from the twentieth to the twenty-first centuries. In appears in the Imagination of the living, future-orientated embryonic being of world-man that is born, rejuvenated, out of the now resurrected and virgin world-man soul. That is, man's newly awakened imaginative soul faculties (his awakened Persephone-Isis nature), fertilized and redeemed through the modern Christ experience, grasp actively in intuited Imagination the creative work of the Christ-permeated will-being of humanity (Dionysus) in the depths of the new Earth (the Pluto-Ahriman kingdom) of the earthly-human Sun. It belongs to the essential aspects of the modern Christ experience, transformed through the knowledge drama of the Second Coming, that man should become ever more conscious of his planetary role in creating anew — out of the sacrificial will-being of his Christ-permeated self — the earthly-Sun core of the new Earth, and know himself in the process as a world-Sun man, as a free collaborator in the shaping process of Christ's new planetary bodies of resurrection.

What was described above is an aspect of the objective world formation that originates in the anthroposophical spiritualization process of the *naturally given* Christ initiation in our age. It was shown how the forces that result from the knowledge drama of the Second Coming can be used in the formative transformation of the old Earth into the new earthly-human Sun. This transformation has its pure spiritual archetype on the highest level of modern initiation, of which the modern Christ experience described here is the imaginative reflection. This pure Christ initiation, experienced through Intuition, is described by Rudolf Steiner in an esoteric lecture entitled 'The Mission of Man on the Earth'.[15] Because of its central relevance to the theme of the building of the new Earth, we shall quote a lengthy passage from it.

First, Rudolf Steiner describes the pure spiritual relationships that prevail between the fully liberated, Christ-permeated man and the Earth:

When man steps out of his three sheaths and experiences himself in the cosmos as newly born, the first thing he feels is the being of the great Mother, the Earth Mother, out of whom he grew; and he experiences earlier evolutionary states in which he was more dependent and more intimately connected with the Earth.

The first man to experience this Mystery through the Christ was Jesus of Nazareth, and after Him the beloved pupil, Lazarus-John, the reborn Hiram Abiff:

And in his Gospel it is said how Christ-Jesus with the last words that resounded from the cross gave His mother to this youth, of whom she was not the bodily mother. As the Son He gives to the human 'I' the Earth Mother, after He enlivened Her with His forces, that he shall protect and take care of Her. As a mother he gives to this 'I' the Earth, to which the Son gave His forces. The human 'I' should redeem the Earth, lift her up with his forces to spiritual regions with the full consciousness that without this Earth he could not have developed himself to what he is and to what he must become.

And now comes the intimate description of the nature of Christ-permeated man and his sacred future mission in the building of the new Heaven and Earth of the earthly-human Sun:

113

With the event of Golgotha, when the blood flowed from the wounds of the great Redeemer, when the cosmic heart-blood penetrated the Earth and its forces poured down to its middle point, the Earth became a shining being, radiating light on its surroundings. The possibility was given for *every human individuality* to experience this light in itself. When the Earth became the body of the great Sun Spirit, in that it permeated itself with It's spiritual forces, then were all the beings of the Earth endowed with these forces. The seed was planted for the reunion of the Earth with the Sun. The physical body of Jesus of Nazareth was the vehicle through which the forces of the cosmos united themselves with the aura of the Earth. And when the blood of this body streamed forth on Golgotha, the Earth was received again into the power of the Sun. Since then the Christ power has radiated out of the Earth's middle point into the surroundings, and out of the Sun the Christ power streams into the Earth. Man can experience this power, this light in himself as earthly human being if he recognizes himself as part of the Earth, which, as the physical body of Christ, is permeated by His being. Then there shines in him the white light from his inwardness, as it radiates also from the middle point of the Earth.

Man can experience the Christ power and the Christ light as though it shines over him from outside and penetrates him with higher forces. Then it enfolds and penetrates him as it enlivens the Earth when it radiates out of the Sun. Then man feels himself united spiritually with this Sun power; he feels himself, from his heart outward, growing together with the great cosmic heart. As a higher being, living in this spiritual Sun, he recognizes his true Self, united with it as the earthly man is united with the Earth itself. And as the Sun forces shine through and enliven the Earth, so this higher being radiates into and enlivens the earthly man with its forces … Because man lives as a twofold being, he can pour the spiritual Sun forces into the Earth and become a connecting link between the Sun and the Earth. As from the life-centre, the heart, the enlivening blood flows and pours itself through the whole physical organism down to the bone-system, which man can conceive as the opposite of the living, ever active heart, so must every human individuality be a channel for the blood that flows out of the cosmic life-centre that penetrates the solid Earth with life. The Earth can be thought of as a cosmic bony system. It would have been completely dried up and ossified if the cosmic heart had not let its life-blood stream out through a human body and rejuvenate it anew.

What once the great Sun Spirit experienced in a human body, every man should live again in himself. The possibility to do so is given through Him. To fill oneself with the Christ Spirit, to experience oneself as a middle point, living in this Spirit through which spiritual light, power and warmth can stream forth into the Earth: this is the mission of the single man and of humanity, because in this way it will redeem the Earth and lift her up to spiritual realms.[16]

Linking these profound anthroposophical truths to the knowledge drama of the Second Coming, we can say: when the dead, frozen (ahrimanic) snow-cover of the earthly intellect is broken through in the being of man, and he penetrates to the place where 'the fiery, blazing, living workings of the Word [Logos] that radiates outward from the middle of the Earth' resounds in his liberated will being, man fertilizes with the new Christ Impulse, the 'lost Word'[17] inside the Earth and awakens it to new earthly-Sun life. And what is here revealed can be described as follows. Every free moral deed of man contains a seed essence that penetrates and fertilizes this living embryonic earthly growing point. A new soil is thus created that mothers and nourishes many human individual love-seeds. Its pulsating planetary embryonic will-seed is thereby gradually transformed into a germinating planetary heart centre: a Sunlike Christ-permeated, golden essence is seen to be maturing out of human acts of love. In the new Sun's veins, flowing warmly, branching dynamically from seed to seed, circulates man's moral impulses: as a growing, life-giving network of thoughts, feelings and acts of goodness and practical healing of the Earth through man.[18] Creative freedom assumes here an elemental power; it builds and shapes the nourishing metabolic system[19] of the new Earth, whose life's blood forms the Sun-heart of a new cosmos.[20] Every free human creation of truth is a direct formative power, working in the depths as the purest food for the sprouting new Sun.[21]

Rudolf Steiner described this creative world-Sun process in philosophical terms as the conclusion drawn from his spiritual investigations documented in his doctorial dissertation *Truth and Science* (1892) as follows:

The result of this study is that truth is not, as man usually assumes, the ideal reflection of something real, but a free creation of the human spirit that would never have existed if we had not brought it forth ourselves. The task of knowledge is not to recapitulate in conceptual form something that already exists somewhere, but *to create a wholly new realm that, together with the given sense world, forms the full reality for the first time.* The highest activity of man, his spiritual productivity, is membered organically into the general world happening. Without this activity the world happening could not be thought of as a complete wholeness in itself. The human being is not a mere spectator that stands over against the world and recreates in pictures in his mind that which takes place in the cosmos without his participation; he is

115

the active co-creator of the world process, and knowledge is the most perfect organ in the organism of the universe.[22]

When this willed 'I' activity, embodied in *Truth and Science*, is worked through into the inner earthly substance of the germinating will-seed of the new Earth of the earthly-human Sun, the transformed spirit of *The Philosophy of Freedom* appears again, as it were approaching from the 'other side' of the Earth, gathering in its wings the unfolded old time-spaces of the dying macrocosmic intelligence, while at the same time embracing and receiving the infolded, seedlike future earthly macro-cosmos. This is Anthropos-Sophia, the man-created Mother of the new Earth, the bearer of the new Heaven of the earthly-human Sun. Every active thought that is metamorphosed into spiritual good will and love repeats this Christ-permeated spirit gesture, sending its condensed darkened will-rays into the budding infinite life germ within, to be resurrected in the interior of the Earth as an evolving embryonic Sun. And the more man realizes himself in the conscious dynamics of pure moral Intuition, Imagination and practice, the more the embryonic Sun of the new Earth warms and lights up under his feet.[23] To experience that every lightening up of pure thought 'up above' (in the planetary Heaven or 'head') creates at the same time a fiery, concentrated, Sun-earthly will-seed below, this is the conscious human participation in the creation of the new Earth of the earthly-human Sun. When this Sun is complete — through the weaving of the new Heaven and Earth together in the wholeness of the new planetary Sun — it will form the heart of the Michael-Christ reality of the next century: the heart-Sun organ of the present Michael age.[24]

The scientific, cultural and social significance of this experience that is now available to every human being through the anthroposophical experience of the etheric appearance of the Christ is immense. And the more conscious we become of the esoteric nature of the real activity of our deeds of love through free thinking the more will our culture draw its sustenance from the only true future source of our cosmic evolution — from the new heart of the Sun inside the new Earth, from the planetary earthly-human Sun.

So far we have described only the contribution of the liberated will-being of man to the creation of the new Earth as the Christ-permeated Geo-logia of the new Sun.[25] But the new Sun has also its germinating 'Heaven', that is, the living (etheric) and light (astral) corona or envelope that reflects and augments the fiery-golden radiation of the embryonic will-centre of the earthly depths. It is the task of the transformed sense-perception, expanded into the creative time-spaces of cosmic thought, to build this new Heaven. We shall, therefore, refer now to this aspect of the creation of the earthly-human Sun in some detail.

As we saw above, what we perceive through our physical senses is only the veil of illusion that our own Death-being spreads over the true mysteries of the Earth and the starry cosmos.[26] But the self-consciously awakened etheric and astral sight reveals the germinating, ever-self-regenerating elemental qualities of the real external world in which we participate continuously by means of our active, interested and loving perception. We shall try now to show that man, as an incarnated etheric and sentient organism of sense-activity and perception, creates the living and light-filled Sun circumference for world creative being. It will be our task to explore the creative act of perception as man's actual construction of the new earthly Heaven — the life-giving and light-reflecting sphere of the new earthly-human Sun.[27]

The pupil on the spiritual path learns, as he advances to a certain stage, how to extend his consciousness into his etheric body.[28] What we described above (Chapter 5) refers to the same process, beginning in the sphere of thinking and sense-perception. The more the pupil succeeds in consciously moulding and preserving his earthly etheric life-stream, the more he is enabled to construct the bridge of self-conscious self-remembrance at, over and inside his released and annihilated life-stream of spirit forgetfulness. Now it is by means of such an inwardly organized life-time body that the world's new planetary life and light sphere is both created and preserved. The new 'Heaven' is, therefore, basically an extension of man's etheric-sentient sensory organism.[29]

As was demonstrated in Chapter 5 (p.91), the meeting, crossing and reversing of the time-places between 'subject' and 'object' in etherized sense-perception takes place in the *future* time-stream of world-man, man-world being. The living, resurrected eye — so we pointed out there — moves, redeemed from its physical past bondage to objectified time and space, towards its own future dimension in the external light world of flowing and living universal time; and the object moves, released from its man-made frozen appearance in physical sensing, into its own etherized time element. And the two redeemed, Christ-permeated time movements meet and cross each other's time path in a specific middle point, through which they are immediately thereafter *re-timed and re-placed*: man *sees* himself from the object's future time-place, and man *is* the object, being incorporated into its etheric corporeality, experiencing its world-essence from a human world, eternal spirit perspective. The dead, crucified form of the world enlivens itself in and through this activity of human sense-perception, and man experiences himself as Earth and world creator through his etheric gaze. In looking and seeing he learns to awaken, enliven and heal the dying Mother Earth. Now when man extends and applies this experience — in the manner that is indicated by Rudolf Steiner in his book *Knowledge of the Higher Worlds* — to the three natural kingdoms and also to the anthroposophical knowledge of man himself, he learns to discover and impregnate the specific creative future seeds of the different earthly kingdoms.[30] In this way we find the formative heavenly forces of the earthly-human Sun as the result of the co-creation of the Christ power within spiritualized nature and the Christ power within the spiritualized cognition of man:

> The life of this earthly realm becomes clear and transparent when we feel at its foundation the germ of a new universe. Every plant form, every stone appears before the human soul in a new light when he becomes aware how they contribute through their life, through their form, to the existence of the Earth as a whole as an embryo — the seed of a macrocosm newly rising into life.[31]

When man has advanced in his etherized sense-perception so far that this experience becomes his essential life and soul experience, he can proceed further in the building process of the new Heaven. Above (Chapter 5, pp.90–91) it was pointed out that, becoming etherically conscious in the tiny time-space between living perception and the deadening brain registration and reflection, man enters into the etheric world where the Dead live, beholding their departing etheric bodies, seeing all that is perishable, but also the eternally preservable, Christ-permeated parts of their etheric bodies. *Now this place — at the gates of Hades of ancient lore — is exactly where the planetary 'etheric ring', constructed out of the Christ-permeated remains of human etheric bodies since the Mystery of Golgotha, is to be found as the planetary bridge of remembered, preserved lifetime.* It is part of the Christ power, active especially in the plant kingdom — and forming itself through the mineral and animal kingdoms — through which we enter directly into the living etheric-time core of each natural object. Spiritualized sense-perception leads us, therefore, actively into that Christ-permeated etheric realm itself. But this means that every redeemed, etheric-imaginative act of perception becomes part and parcel of the construction process of this heavenly ring, which up to the end of Kali–Yuga was constructed by the higher Hierarchies only after man's death. Now man participates in it with full self-consciousness while still incarnated and living in the physical-etheric world. It is the Christ force, streaming from the centre of the Earth outwards, raised by man to conscious imaginative sight through the transformation of sense-perception, that lets him work consciously in the building process of the new earthly-Sun Heaven, weaving into the etheric ring his own Christ-infilled sense-perceptions and living and sentient world-Imaginations.

However, here another aspect is involved, which takes place between the purely spiritual Earth work referred to above, and the purely imaginative building process of the new Heaven. As we saw in Chapter 5, the actual construction of the bridge of the green snake—its 'freezing' and 'consolidation' (p.98 and p.100), which in itself is of a purely etheric nature, must be carefully anchored in the unique time-space gap between the physical and etheric bodies. That same process, only externalized and membered into the Earth's enveloping time-spaces, applies also to the construction of the foundation of the new planetary Heaven. In the limits of our study here, we can only point to the direction indicated by Rudolf Steiner in connection with the work already practised in the past, though in another state of consciousness, by the pupils of true Rosicrucianism. In their case, too, as in the knowledge drama of the Second Coming today, man could begin the direct transformative work in the macrocosmic realm only after thinking and willing were duly transformed. This process was described by Rudolf Steiner as follows:

> Man could begin with a wholly new observation of the world, thanks to the radiations of the wonderful etheric body of Christian Rosenkreutz. What was then carried out up to our time by the Rosicrucians is both an external and an inner work. The external work had as its goal the task to find what lies behind the maya of matter ... At the foundation of the whole macrocosm there is an etheric macrocosm, an etheric body, as man had his etheric body. There is a certain crossing of the border from a dense to a finer substance. Nothing in the world is similar to that which is found between the physical and etheric substances. It is neither gold, nor silver, nor lead, nor copper. There we have something that is not comparable to any other physical substance but is the essence of all physical substances ... So these substances can be thought of as modifications of this one substance. To see this substance supersensibly was the striving of the Rosicrucians. They looked for the development of such a sight in a strengthened activity of the moral forces of the soul, which could make this substance visible. In the moral forces of the soul they found the power needed to see it. This substance was really seen and discovered by the Rosicrucians. They found that this substance lives in a certain form in the world, the macrocosm, as well as in man. Outwardly, in the external world, they revered it as the mighty garment of the macrocosm. They saw it arising in man when there is a harmonious interplay between thinking and willing. The Rosicrucians sought the strength to achieve such a harmony between thinking and willing in their own soul in the force radiating from this etheric body of ... Christian Rosenkreutz.[32]

So far we have distinguished *two* elements in connection with the new planetary Heaven. First, there is the Quintessential element developed in man through the etherization of the blood and its special sacrificial condensation described in Chapter 5. And second, there is the etheric element itself, thoroughly penetrated and transformed through the living Christ, projected and separated from man and, as an independent element, woven into the planetary etheric Heaven of the earthly-human Sun. But to these two a third, sentient-astral element must be added, without which no complete new 'Heaven' could arise. The inner-human production of this astral element of the bridge was described in some detail in Chapter 5 (pp.103–4). We might now briefly mention one relevant perspective concerning the external macrocosmic aspect of this work.

For this purpose let us open again the tiny time-space between sense-perception and brain registration and enter once more the time-place of construction of the etheric bridge of remembrance over the storming waters of Lethe, where the Dead are gazing at their expanding and dissolving etheric bodies. As Rudolf Steiner pointed out, the deepest soul pain is experienced by the Dead in connection with the destructive appearance of the unspiritual parts of the etheric body, and the highest soul bliss is experienced here when man sees how the individualized life-giving, radiant Christ essence in his etheric body becomes a living part of the living etheric body of the macrocosm as a whole.[33] When this process is accomplished, man continues his journey into his Kamaloka period. But the greater the part of his etheric body, which is membered into the Christ-permeated planetary etheric ring, the stronger and clearer will be his ability to perceive and act by its means on the astral-etheric and elemental-physical happenings in the spiritual, ensouled and living-elemental Earth while sojourning in the spiritual worlds in the time between death and rebirth. Now what we mean here as the soul component of the new Heaven is that same experience, but it is now also available — through the anthroposophical modern Christ experience — to incarnated human beings between birth and death. This fully conscious etheric meeting and living with the Christ and His human and angelic brothers and co-workers in the soul world, normally experienced only after death, becomes here a sensible-supersensible Earth experience, *but on an Earth that is in its Sun-becoming process.*

As was shown in Chapter 4 (p.51), the man who experiences the death of the old world-soul in his physical soul life as his own personal death of soul is awakened out of it through the living death in Christ's body-cross of etheric visibility. And when he recapitulates this experience independently and pours his etheric-sentient being into the macrocosm through the gates of his transformed sense-perception and experiences himself consciously in the planetary sphere of living, weaving and radiating world thoughts, and is then able to develop voluntarily the external imaginative sight of the Earth as seen through the eyes of the cosmic, Sunlike Christ, then the following occurs. Man learns to see and experience the Earth while living, as do those human souls who have already passed through the gates of death and who, from the spiritual world, protect and sustain the mystery of the new Heaven of the earthly-human Sun. He is consciously accepted in their company and takes a self-conscious part in their sacred creative work. He begins to participate in that aspect of the life of the resurrected Earth in which the Dead are living:

> When a soul of the Dead in our present time-cycle observes certain points [on the surface of the spiritual Earth], then he sees how out of the place that here on the Earth is designated as Palestine, Jerusalem, out of the midst of the bluish-purple, something like a golden formation emerges, *a golden crystal formation that then enlivens itself.* This is Jerusalem, seen from the spirit! . . . Spiritually seen from the world-all, the event of Golgotha was the lighting of a golden star in the bluish Earth aura of the eastern half of the Earth . . . When you try to think with one departing [with someone passing through the gate of death] of the crystal formation of heavenly Jerusalem building itself in the gold radiance of the blue-purple Earth aura, then it brings you closer [to Him], because this is something that belongs to the Imaginations into which the Dead dies: *Ex Deo nascimur – In Christo morimur!*[34]

The weaving together of the three elements created above in the spiritualized process of sense-perception—the fifth or Quintessential element, the etheric element and the sentient-soul element—is the beginning of the conscious macrocosmic construction process of the planetary Heaven of the earthly-human Sun, in a form that will become part of the universal spiritual and social life of awakened humanity in the coming millennium.

In other words, the most fundamental discovery concerning this aspect of the modern Christ experience, achieved through the knowledge drama of the Second Coming, is this: that man can begin today consciously to create the new vital and sentient sheaths of the Earth through his actively awakened sensible-supersensible cognition. This means that since the end of the twentieth century the esoteric knowledge ideal of Goethe[35] and Rudolf Steiner[36] can be realized, through Christ's direct cognitive and moral help, in the life-time of ordinary, self-initiated people.[37] This sphere of the spirit of knowledge and truth, aglow with the human-Christ created flames of spiritualized love in the depths, illuminated outwardly by the astral light pictures of world-thoughts, is opened in and through human eyes. Where objectified old cosmic space dies in our physical sense in-breathing as devitalized living time, and where sprouting sense-life produces in etheric sight majestic world-pictures through the formative forces of conscious human Imagination, man acquires the conscious capacity to imprint them—member them—

into the planet's garments of resurrection.[38] Indeed, man knows himself fully justified when he articulates and moulds himself, in expanding and pouring his living being, consciously crossing and reversing space into living time, into the form of those world-creating words that were kept until our time under the protection and care of the Earth Spirit alone.[39]

So schaff ich am sausenden Webstuhl der Zeit
Und wirke der Gottheit lebendiges Kleid.[40]

The ringing loom of Time is my care,
And I weave God's living garment there.

Let us place again before our eyes the picture of the Christ incarnating His Sun being in the centre of the Earth, making of the Earth His body. Around Him are gathered all His pupils, 'the human Archangels' of our earthly evolution, who reflect through their knowledge drama of His Second Coming, and all future comings as well, in their active, imaginative sensing in world-thought-pictures the life, light and love flowing from His heart. Their freed will being works, united with Christ's own will, in the depths of His earthly body, transforming it through the power of free moral intuition and love into a planetary resurrection body. At the periphery, in the new earthly-human Sun Heaven, in the substance of their etheric and astral offering of imaginative perception and knowledge, they imprint, consolidate and preserve their Imaginations in the etheric ring of their own life-giving perceptions and in the astral light of their living world thinking.[41]

In this more 'Goetheanistic' way of entering the spirit reality of our time through the gates of sense-perception, we might receive a non-traditional, more individualized and fresh experience of what Rudolf Steiner described (for the first time in exoteric human history) as the creation of the planetary Sun-sphere of the Holy Spirit — the new Christ-permeated Heaven of the new earthly-human Sun:

Since that time [the Mystery of Golgotha] there has been in the etheric body of man something that does not go through death, that does not fall prey to the death forces of the Earth. And this something, that does not suffer death, that human beings gradually gain through the influence of the Christ-impulse, this streams back, streams outwards into world space and builds, according to its strength in man, a power that builds around the Earth a sphere that is in the process of becoming a sun. Just as the Christ light radiates out from the Earth, so we have a kind of a reflecting back of Christ's light in the periphery of the Earth. What is here reflected back as Christ-light, and what began as a result of the Christ event, is that which the Christ calls the Holy Spirit. Just as it is true that through the Mystery of Golgotha the Earth began its process of becoming a Sun, so it is also true that from then on

122

the Earth begins to be creative and builds around itself a spiritual ring that will later be a kind of a planet around the Earth.[42]

This creative activity of the Earth, taken into the spiritually trans-formed activity of the consciousness soul, is that which was described in this chapter as the conscious creation of the new Earth and Heaven of the earthly-human Sun. At the threshold of the twentieth and twenty-first centuries it becomes the spiritual-esoteric and social-public task of a reborn anthroposophy. This process must become the living scientific, artistic and social practice of the next century.

To see this living — and therefore holy — spirit light up in every sense-perception,[43] this is a most essential Goetheanistic-anthroposophical task of the present and the near future. Stars, mountains and seas, plants and animals, seeds and crystals and, above all, the human form itself — they all harbour, in their frozen physical separation and estrangement, the seeds of living resurrection, waiting to sprout into new life in man[44] through his living sense-perception.[45] As we saw in the Introduction and in Chapter 2, the Pauline Damascus experience — the archetype of the modern Christ experience — is the seed for both *The Philosophy of Freedom* and Goethe's theories of colour and metamorphosis of plants and animals. In the peripheral spirit of universal resurrection there appears at the end of the twentieth century the results of man's immortalized stream of life (his Life Spirit) carrying the transformed consciousness soul's forces of pure sensible-supersensible perception and free Imagination. In his active sense-perception, imagining and formative thinking in the world's shaping forces, man fertilizes and awakens new world activity that, as a new 'Heaven' begins — when it becomes dense and saturated enough — to reflect and augment the Earth's new willing-moral, fiery-golden core. As this humanly-created sacred time essence lives actively on, humanity will perceive and create, and in creating perceive and receive back, reflected from the atmosphere all around, its own Christ fire from the earthly-human Sun. A cosmic-earthly 'holy' atmospheric and anthroposophic living light creation and reflection will descend onto man's heads and senses, moulding plane-tary nature through the imaginatively awakened spirit of man himself. He will consciously form the 'Heaven' of his future Earth — the luminous envelope of the new Sun — when he weaves into it more and more conscious threads of living time out of his vitally Christ-permeated sense-organism.

As the single pupil learns to weave his own indestructible etheric garment, so will humanity increasingly weave the Christ-permeated holy garments of the new Earth. What poured itself forth 2,000 years ago into the Earth's astral aura will receive in this way its creative-reflective, etheric counterpart from human activity below, from the streams of conscious sensory will that are consciously transformed into world-shaping sight. Until now, this etheric ring, embodying the new planetary Holy Spirit, was constructed in piecemeal fashion from the Christ-filled remnants and fragments of the etheric bodies of human beings who had passed through the gate of death. The modern Christ experience, when anthroposophically developed through the Life Spirit of Goethe and Rudolf Steiner, will enable man to create it while physically incarnated, fully conscious, out of his sacrificial deeds of cognition.[46] The scientist as well as the everyday person will more and more be able to transform every look into participatory, creative world consecration. As thinking was transformed into the pure will being of love, that creates in the Earth's depths the germ of the new Sun, so will sight, hearing, touch and all bodily sensations be increasingly spiritualized, irradiated and purposefully woven into the evolving future life-time organism of the Earth. A headlike planetary sensing and imagining sphere organ will thus be created above, enabling the reflection and enhancement of the human-earthly Christed fiery core below. In the place-time of their dynamic mutual union, penetration and fertilization, the illuminated heights and the fiery depths touch one another in every attentive, love-filled gaze, and in every morally free act of will on whatever level of human existence they occur. In the zone of the continuous crossing and reversing of world-man will inside out and human-world perception outside in, there will arise 'the temple' of the active, humanly and socially open Mysteries of Michael in the heights of his present first post-Golgothean age. This temple is where cognition is direct human-social action, and social practice a conscious formation of the new earthly-human Sun. And this place-time of reversal and exchange between the new Sun centre (Earth) and periphery (Heaven) will be most clearly revealed when, through metamorphosed thinking and sense-perception, 'every two or three human beings' shall meet one another in the name of the new earthly-human Sun Spirit: in the new heart and lung zone of the new Sun, which is its new social life.

Chapter 7

Christ's Appearance Between 'I' and Thou

At the heart of the mutually crossing and turning inside-out and out-side-in of the new Earth and Heaven—the centre and periphery of the new earthly-human Sun—there is still another, probably the deepest and most difficult, threshold or abyss that must be consciously bridged before a full realization of the Second Coming and a firm grounding of the Michael age will be possible. This abyss cuts its way of spirit-forgetfulness between every two human beings that—the rational con-tent of their daily consciousness notwithstanding—confront each other in modern social life. As the history of the Anthroposophical Society shows in many cases, this abyss surfaces clearly when a community strives to ground its spiritual life in the true existential situation of the consciousness soul. And this could not have been otherwise, for it is where the social-planetary wound behind the last two World Wars (and the current Third World War of the planet's survival) burns strongly. It becomes, imaginatively speaking, a virtual dark sunspot that emerges from the circulating rhythmical social heart and lung zone of the earthly-human Sun, at the most sensitive and vulnerable crossing and reversing place-time of the new Heaven and Earth.[1]

This is the reason, therefore, for the absolute necessity of a radically new social life in our time.[2] The etheric crucifixion, resurrection, teaching and initiatory acts of the etheric Christ are nowhere more readily perceived—and, because of that, also ignored—than here. The more crucial it becomes for our evolution the more we turn away from its cruel as well as exhilarating reality. But as long as we do so, we can acquire no conscious Imagination or intuitive power of realization in order to make the new earthly-human Sun a truly productive and life-giving cosmic being.[3]

To transform social life into Christ-permeated daily reality: this is the most serious responsibility that human beings who have experienced the true nature of the Second Coming can take on themselves today.[4] The modern Christ experience, as described in Chapter 4, is also the archetype and hidden ground of the new human meeting. The three stages of the meeting with the new Initiator are—on a different level—the same stages that are found in every spiritually awakened human meeting. In the field of the powerful spiritual tension of morally active cognition, and cognition radiating morality, i.e. surrounded and penetrated by the new Earth and Heaven of the earthly-human Sun, the awakened human meeting can acquire a potency and depth hitherto unknown in human history.[5]

In such a meeting every person that I meet is for me my initiator, bearing and suffering my cross, awakening me from my death of soul, profoundly teaching me my mysteries of evil, and gracefully blessing me with the mutual penetration and creative reversal of karmic responsibility.[6] But I can do the same for the other person. I can be his cross-bearer as well as his crucifier; I am his initiator as well as his pupil, for good or ill.

As Rudolf Steiner pointed out, this was and is the fundamental, basic rule of occultists; it must become the life habit of all those human beings who experience concretely and consciously the weaving and pulsating of the living Christ between members of the social community: 'It is a fundamental maxim of occultists to see the other person as the revelation of one's own Higher Self, because he knows then he must find the other in himself.'[7]

The anthroposophical foundations for our study here are to be found in Rudolf Steiner's researches concerning the deeper esoteric nature of the social question, communicated especially after the First World War, in the years 1918–19.[8] The most important discovery of Rudolf Steiner, as far as human encounters are concerned, is especially crucial for our considerations here. In every meeting, Rudolf Steiner says, unconsciously-supersensibly, the participators always mutually cross the threshold as a result of the powerful spirit impact of the other. That is, they metamorphose their state of consciousness continuously with only very short, purely physical awakenings in between, changing their roles from being put to sleep by the other to being the 'sleep inducer' of the other. The remarkable thing is, however, that a person is out of his balanced physical place (bodily space and time) in *both* cases. As sleeper, his soul and spirit members are briefly separated from the physical and etheric bodies, as in normal sleep. But as sleep inducer he incarnates *too* strongly, so as to suppress, or frighten, the other out of his skin into sleep. If excarnation in sleep means that we lose our stronghold in space and in physically measurable time — that is, we become space-and-timeless — so the reverse is true in our excessive incarnations. We are not satisfied with only *one* space-time centre; we wish, and do, overtake another. We actually strive to achieve unlimited space-infilling omnipotence by extending our physical soul might in order to conquer, by spiritually-spatially densifying ourselves, the body of another, sending him to sleep — and vice versa. In the one case, sleeping, we become too social; we efface our presence altogether, giving way completely to the other by annulling our daily consciousness. In the other case, we become fearfully awakened and antisocial, suppressing the other's independent self-consciousness.[9]

Rudolf Steiner described this process as follows:

> You perceive a man for a short time; he makes an impression on you. This impression disturbs you inwardly; you feel that the man ... makes an impression on you like an attack. The result is that you 'defend' yourself in your inner being, that you oppose yourself to this attack, that you become inwardly aggressive towards him. This feeling abates and your aggression ceases; hence he can now make a fresh impression upon you and so on. That is the relationship that exists when one man meets another and perceives his ego: giving yourself up to the other human being, inwardly warding him off, giving yourself up again, warding him off; sympathy-antipathy, sympathy-antipathy ... The soul vibrates. Sympathy-antipathy; sympathy-antipathy — they vibrate too.
>
> In that sympathy is active, you sleep into the other human being; in that antipathy is active, you wake up again, and so on. There is this quick alternation in vibrations between waking and sleeping when we meet another person. We owe this alternation to the organ of the ego sense. Thus this organ for the perception of the ego is organized in such a way that it apprehends the ego of another in a sleeping, not in a waking will, and then quickly carries over this apprehension accomplished in sleep to the region of knowledge, i.e. to the nervous system ... For we are constantly weaving moments of sleep into the act of perception of another ego. What lies between them is indeed knowledge, which is immediately carried over into the domain of the nervous system; so that I can really call the perception of another a process of knowledge, but I must know that this process of knowledge is only a metamorphosis of a sleeping process of the will. Thus this sense process is really a process of the will, only we do not recognize it as such. We do not experience in conscious life all the knowledge that we experience in sleep.[10]

As indicated here, this whole process takes place unconsciously, supersensibly-sensibly — only the transition between the stages is taking place, in a twinkling of an eye, in daily consciousness. Imaginatively, that is, taking living time consciously, a real knowledge and life drama reveals itself here, which is always happening beneath the threshold, motivating, moulding and destroying our social life. And into this drama the appearance, words and acts of the Etheric Christ are most intimately woven. Let us, then, look closer at the secrets of the new human encounter.

What is the first impression that we receive when we observe rather objectively, spiritual-scientifically, every 'normal' human meeting today? It is the feeling of an ominous, profound spiritual sleep and forgetfulness. Man is completely outside his karmic reality, is most oblivious of his being so intimately interwoven with his fellow human beings.[11] The more we observe this phenomenon, nowadays taken as a matter of fact, the more we begin to realize the depth of the abyss of forgetfulness and the measure of disconnectedness prevailing here. What is suppressed, we feel, is the common origin of human beings as such. We might feel that the more karmically connected they are and the more intricate is their pre-earthly interweavings with one another in a previous life and in the life between the present birth and the last death, the more they are tempted, unconsciously, to break their bond of mutual spirit loyalty and brotherhood. This is one of the most shattering spiritual impressions of our times — man's self-willed and self-imposed social blindness. And the clear knowledge that this state of affairs is a necessary by-product of his increasing and accelerated individuation in the last centuries cannot in the least temper this experience.[12]

Out of this death of the social soul, however, there emerges, for the first time in human history, the burning human need for conscious ego-confrontation and penetrating mutual recognition,[13] without which both sides of the social abyss become absolute riddles — the subjective no less then the objective, I no less than thou, and vice versa.[14] The key to unlock this mystery is to be found only in the anthroposophically experienced Christ event of our time.

Let us be reminded that, as was pointed out in Chapter 3, all human beings, since the middle of the *last* century, have begun unconsciously to cross the threshold of the spiritual world. Since the middle of *this* century, this process has been deepened and externalized. What took place as a result of the natural advance of this process is nowhere more evident then in the case of that mutual 'excarnation-incarnation dance' of the human encounter.

When we go to sleep normally as well as socially, we are directly confronted by the Lesser Guardian of the Threshold. Man then experiences the seed of his karmic future, and on awakening he becomes aware of his past karma.[15] Now these two revelations are the limits, or polarities, in the field of tension between which any human meeting continuously oscillates. A further investigation of this reveals the following scene. When I am strongly impressed (or, actually, outpressed) by another person, I am immediately put to sleep. My abyss then surfaces in the twinkling of an eye. At that very moment, if I am quick enough and can remain conscious in the experience of excarnation, when, as if in a flash of lightning, my ego breaks through with the obliteration of its ordinary self-consciousness, I can see and hear my shadow, or double, articulating itself right behind me. And out of him emerges a twofold picture. The first one is the physiognomical seed of my true moral form in the cosmos, which always surfaces out of the empty abyss of the Guardian's centre of being.[16] And within this picture I see, secondly, the picture potential emerging out of that judgement. This is the self-shaped form of my future.[17]

But now — and here is the difference between this experience and the normal night sleep — in the encounter I see my future picture forming itself in a specified way in relation to this concrete and unique aspect of this meeting. It is a *future* picture of my moral form in relation to the other person related to *this* aspect of our shared destiny. This creates a burning desire to know why and how this future is what it is, and this desire pushes me towards the other, who, I strongly feel, must have the answer. And in that moment I am shaken out of my sleep.[18] I find myself awakened in the other and at the flash of lightning of awakening I perceive my lower karmic *past*. It appears as the answer to the question that arose earlier in my soul. I am awakened back to the physical world with a balanced karmic impulse, which can be later transformed through patient meditative practice, and brought to full self-consciousness. It will gradually ripen into an increasingly concrete picture of the reasons, conditions and context and the ensuing moral duties of our interwoven destiny, now perceived as being deeply rooted in the reality of the world. A conscious pictorial conscience can then take hold of me, motivating me from now on in a specific moral direction, which I know that I want freely to follow and realize.[19]

Through the modern Christ experience and the knowledge drama of the Second Coming man can develop those soul forces which enable him to delve still deeper into this process, entering the moral-karmic abyss that opens between 'every two or three' people who come together in our time. A still closer look at the above described meeting reveals a decisive and crucial moment. A powerful temptation overwhelms us at the moment when, out of our moral abyss, our real future debt to the other suddenly surfaces and takes shape. It is extremely important in our time to raise this moment into full self-consciousness. When man sees and experiences the true impact of his moral self-knowledge and the resulting future moral obligations, he usually succumbs to the irresistible urge to deny and betray this moral debt. This denial is, again, a most essential event in the whole drama of the social problem today. It takes on a specific, independent, moral form, comparable to the one created as the second (moral) layer of the bridge over the abyss of consciousness described in Chapter 5. This self-same astral being, appearing out of our own world-abyss of evil, is articulated as a soul question, dreadfully tempting, speaking thus: Am I my brother's keeper?[20] And as this question resounds — one cannot put it otherwise — it is immediately transformed into another question, asked as it were in the voice of spirit conscience: Do you love *me*?[21]

When this event becomes the centre of our conscious social training and we return to its emergent point in our moral abyss again and again, and if we learn to live, move and have our being at home there, having established the bridge of supersensible consciousness continuation firmly under our soul-feet, we gradually begin to behold – in hearing – the destiny of Christ, fulfilling, unrecognized and therefore fearfully maltreated by man, his new social-karmic role in the chaos of man's immense modern capacity for social evil.

As blind captives of our liberated demonic shadows we now see ourselves and our fellow human beings in each encounter. The more one is captivated, however, the more one inclines to answer the question above in the negative, in the original, biblical manner of Cain, 'I am not my brother's keeper!' (implying instinctively and wildly, *no, I do not recognize nor love the Christ Being*! and then one rushes down aggressively to overwhelm, control and devastate the other, continuing and enhancing the modern social war of all against all.[22]

This is what is literally heartbreaking in this scene: that Christ, who continuously approaches our maladjusted karmic chaos in order to transform and heal our unresolved karmic situations, is not at all recognized, nay, is even feared and is pushed away from one's being,[23] and – this must be simply stated as a fact of our century – is crucified again and again, not only in the hatred of man's materialistic thinking of the last century but in man's totally irresponsible moral excarnation and continuous sleeping, far beyond the threshold.[24] There, where as blind captives of their Guardians men unleash the most evil impulses in face of the other, Christ is condemned to a continuous torture in the spiritual world.[25] Only through consciously undergoing such experiences again and again can man create the social aspect of the bridge, which is at the same time the true healing force of the modern social dilemma.

The question shaped out of this moral perplexity and the resulting experience of the denial of Christ is the only one that burns in the astral world so powerfully that it can never be forgotten. And the burning condenses, consolidates and engraves itself deeply into the etheric body in order to be transformed into the fountain of moral-social continuation of consciousness, bridging the abyss between the meeting's true (Christ-permeated) spirit reality and everyday social maya and spirit-forgetfulness. The experience of denial described is thereby transformed – through the vision of the self-incurred suffering of Christ – into the rock (Peter) on which the new community can be, for the first time in the modern age, firmly and securely built.[26]

Now up to this point we referred only to the experience of the single participator in the meeting. And indeed this is the first stage of the future social evolution that can always take place, in any meeting, also when only one of the partners is consciously aware. But when this process becomes a conscious social-communal practice, a whole new dimension is added. Instead of the usual ahrimanic-luciferic, uncontrolled chaos of mutually induced soul death of sleep and forgetfulness, people can consciously create a social dance of mutually induced spiritual-soul awakening and healing. Rudolf Steiner pointed towards this possibility, urgently trying to resurrect and awaken the Anthroposophical Society from the physical ashes of the burnt down First Goethanum and the parallel dissolution of its inner social structure and meaning.[27] However, before first consciously undergoing the experience of mutual spirit betrayal and forgetfulness — as striving, independent, human beings at the first dawn of the consciousness-soul age — and before experiencing the reappearance of the Christ out of the evil of the Second World War, the new cognitive, spiritual-scientific and moral-social forces were not yet available. The situation today is, therefore, completely different, and a significant deepening and clarification of the challenges ahead is necessary.

When two human beings meet each other in order consciously to awaken and humanly to transform and heal their relationships, and if they experience the first awakening experiences in soul and spirit, they might press further, exploring with one another the mysteries of the Second Coming of Christ a) as the awakener of the social soul from its death of forgetfulness, b) as the supersensible teacher of the morally created self-conscious bridge of karmic duty and continuation — or remembrance — over the abyss of our karmic temptation and transgression, and c) as the archetype of self-offering in the *Umstülpung* and mutual reversal of creative karmic responsibility.[28] We have already described the first — individual — stage of the meeting: the self-induced awakening in the meeting with the other. We might now describe the further stages that are possible, though only when the two-or-more partners are already self-awakened and can begin consciously to transform, heal and weave anew their common web of destiny.[29]

When two people awaken at the same time, and stand together before their own Guardian, viewing interchangably their common future and past destinies, together suffering and sharing their own and their brother's mutual temptation, betrayal and overcoming; when, in other words, they reach together that experience described above, a remarkable metamorphosis sets in, the understanding of which can only be achieved through our former studies of both the given and acquired modern Christ experience.

The second stage of the *given* Christ experience can be said to be grounded in the fact that Christ, appearing, as we saw, on the other shore of man's (moral or astral) abyss, attracts to Himself man's hidden, unseen second, higher, self.[30] And when this self leaves us, merging with the Christ at our infinite horizon, we feel our lower self mightily excarnated and externalized, surrounding and attacking us from all sides.[31] This is experienced as an unforgettable 'teaching', the purpose of which is to let us see clearly the true moral form of our being; we realize that our daily, earthly form is kept intact unconsciously, as an act of sacrifice and grace, by that other, Christlike being of our self. Seeing and feeling now our true moral form, we are enabled to compare it objectively with its higher other — or brother — that stands on the spirit-world shore of oneself. And only then, after undergoing this 'comparison'[32] and experiencing its implications deeply enough, do we come (as a gift of grace in the case of the given, natural Christ experience, and consciously in the case of the anthroposophically developed experience) to our new re-creation, as world-man question of man-world destiny. In the astral world we are transformed into an astral riddle by the being of the Christ in the given, natural initiation, or by our own independent efforts. This happens at the moral turning-and-reversal point, where the inner and external sides of the soul are mutually reversed and replaced. This *Umstülpung* process shows us that our moral form, after being judged objectively according to its true moral value in the soul world, is lovingly returned to us, re-membered into us as a being whose essence can from now be spiritually remembered. In this way a soul form is given to us, or produced by us, that will constitute an archetype for all our future self-transformations and serve as the foundation for our awakening spiritual conscience.[33]

So that we can say: in the given Christ experience this archetype is 'given' in the second stage of the experience itself; in the anthroposophically developed experience we work on it gradually through our own self-acquired self-knowledge. That is, in the first experience it is a given archetype but in the second it is a self-created and assimilated archetype of our own moral form.[34]

In the awakened encounter, however, it becomes our common, mutual creation: *the forming and moulding of the common destiny being of our karmic relationships*. The details of this work can be described as follows.

When another person puts me to sleep, I awake, intuitively, with my will being in his higher being; I see in *his* Ego *our* future. And at the same time, he (the sleep inducer), pressing downwards, awakens imaginatively in *my* etheric body, seeing *our* past from my 'point of view'. And vice versa, when I put another person to sleep, it is he who awakens in my future karmic picture of our shared destiny, and it is I who see the imaginative past pictures of our karma in his etheric body. Through changing perspective, we gradually acquire the possibility to work consciously on the moral destiny form of our united karma. We learn to view our web of relationships from future to past, gaining a growing measure of objectivity through the fact that we learn more and more to see—and thereby mould—our united destiny through the *whole* being of one another.[35]

This creation is the *inspirative* element of the new social life: forming the common astral-moral being rhythmically, in the mutual soul breathing between the intuitive Ego future karmic perspective and the etheric body's imaginative past karmic perspective. A new form of a living, ensouled and spiritual *present* will in this way become socially true.[36]

When we confront our other—our at first unrecognized and betrayed but later rediscovered, resurrected and therefore Christ-permeated brother—we have to do not only with our individual moral form but especially with our common and shared moral form. Such a common moral form—the destiny question, temptation and judgement of our primordial connectedness and its betrayal—does exist. It remains unconscious, pressed together with all our karmic pasts and futures, united in the general moral being of our Guardian, and is differentiated and specifically released into action—comes to specific articulation—in every single life situation and meeting.[37]

To begin with we see this being only from our own side, and our partner sees his side alone. But as we continue to awaken in the soul world, and as the awakenings undergo an ongoing development, both in physical social life and in our awakened, imaginative-intuitive spiritually bridged meetings, this being becomes morally transparent and inwardly luminous, readily agreeing now to be turned around, actually to be reversed inside-out for me and outside-in for the other, and vice versa, in both directions at the same time. It reveals to me my partner's moral form of our connection and reveals to him *my* moral form of our connection. Thus we actively create and shape our own united being of destiny. We begin to raise to full consciousness, our karmic question, temptations, transgressions and mutual betrayals. And we can begin the mutual work of healing, creating, spiritually-morally the soul-being archetype of our united, communal rock of karmic remembrance as a foundation for our social life together on the Earth.[38]

From such a meeting one emerges with the firm resolution: I shall awaken into physical reality as my brother's keeper and shall consciously take his karmic cross upon my shoulders, not possessing his daily consciousness aggressively but consciously exchanging our earthly destiny abode, awakening inversed, incorporated in the karmic web of each other. This is, then, the foundation of what Rudolf Steiner meant when he described the future, conscious karma experience and regulation in the new human community:

The community can bear the destiny of the individual. Karma can be brought together in such a way that the community will bear this destiny. From the moral point of view, in other words, the following may occur. A member of the community commits a wrong. This will, of course, be inscribed in his personal karma and be worked out in the great setting of world existence. However, it is possible that someone will come forward and say: 'I will help you to work out this karma!' The attitude of the community may be: you as individual have done wrong, but we will enter the lists for you; we take upon ourselves whatever will bring about the adjustment of your karma ... This is the establishing of human community on the 'I' nature of the human being.[38]

To penetrate each other's place of karmic space-time in physical awakening means to place oneself in the centre of the other's cross of destiny. This means, therefore, *the actual seeding in each other of a soul-woven life germ of united and reversed moral creation*. This actually means to implant in me your true karmic will for my healing, and to implant in you my true will of your transformation. Thus human beings can increasingly learn to dance in a lemniscatory way in and out and through each other: to enter into conscious world-man morally creative social sleep, and awaken into the conscious earthly human-world creation of the new social heart of the planetary Sun. They can learn to oscillate dynamically, breathing in this painful and joyful life-dance, bestowing social maturity and health through the rhythmical exchange of the pupil/teacher, initiator/initiated roles with each other. I can learn to find my true 'I' in and through you and vice versa, and see in your eyes my true, karmically and socially responsible self, hearing in your words my conscience's commandments, feeling in your physical nearness the deepest body-spirit foundation of my destiny: this is the deeper aspect of the future social communion, the new sacred social ritual of humanity.[40]

Rudolf Steiner describes this social 'sacramental act' as follows:

Today much is spoken of social reforms, social progress. Who will be the great reformer of social life if the acts among people take place in social life in the service of the Christ, so that the world can be Christed through? It could be the Christ Himself, if people live socially in such a way that in certain moments their social life becomes for them a consecration, where they look up to the Christ and do not say 'I', but say 'when only two or three, and when many are united in Christ's name, so is the Christ in the midst of them'. So when social activity becomes a sacrificial act of consecration it continues what was the ancient act of worship. The Christ must, in that he is active today in a lively way in the being of man, also Himself become a great social reformer.[41]

As the single pupil learns to weave his consciously preserved, living etheric body, as the bridge of consciousness-continuation, and as humanity as a whole learns to weave Christ's planetary, Sunlike, new heavenly and earthly sheaths, so too, working on the same project, 'every two or three' that come together in 'His name' will learn to create the new social etheric body of the Earth and Heaven of the earthly-human Sun. Being articulated and articulating, spoken and speaking themselves and thereby shaping together their being of karma, weaving around, in and through His 'name' as the eternal 'I' archetype, so shall real earthly human beings weave the sacred threads of the Holy Spirit of community from person to person.

In their social relationships human beings will be ever more Sun-creating, Sun-nourishing and fostering. Ever more will they grow to recognize that their life connections can be developed into branching, warming, radiating blood vessels, activated through the pulse of Christ's universal Life Spirit. They will then be able to say to themselves: when we build firmly on the rocklike, mutually created, social-ther-apeutic, karmic 'I' archetype of Christ's etheric reappearance, we shall weave the living garments for the descending (heavenly) spirit of future brotherhood.[42]

So shall every two or three human beings be able to create, between and over their abyss of karmic disorder and forgetfulness, their soul-and-life being as a social resurrection body, in the likeness of that self-consciously remembered, Christ-infilled remaking of man, which is at the same time the 'I' bridge, or the morally-cognitive created 'I' arche-type, given, developed and socially moulded through the modern Christ experience and the knowledge drama of the Second Coming.[43]

To carry one another's destiny in this way — to balance and heal our own and our co-workers' anthroposophical and human one-sidedness — means to unite consciously the divergent, different, but spiritually and humanly complementary and refreshing experiences of the being of anthroposophical spiritual science.[44] This is the present social anthro-posophical task, written with fiery spirit letters in the heavenly spirit of our anthroposophical karma. It speaks now unceasingly from the depths of our spiritual conscience, striving to awaken us to the courageous fulfilment of our self-chosen and self-directed mission for the humanity of the next century. Then shall we be able, at the place-time of the modern, estranged, forgotten and deadened human encounter, to con-sciously and scientifically create the embryonic heart and lung rhyth-mical system of the new earthly-human Sun. This social, karmic creation will become *the heart-and-'I' centre of social resurrection for the Michael age.* It will propagate itself from heart to heart, weaving — in the most vul-nerable and wounded middle heart zone of the new but still darkly spotted earthly-human Sun — a planetary etheric heart, where the new Heaven (descending) and the new Earth (ascending), will meet, be consciously sensed and perceived, integrated and made fruitful for human culture: in and through every conscious, planetary creative, human meeting.[45]

Notes and References

Introduction, Part I

1 GA 118, 18 April 1910. An indication concerning the spiritual background of those souls who today develop the new faculties of supersensible perception, and experience thereby the modern Damascus event, is given by Rudolf Steiner in the following passage: 'All the souls who in the Middle Ages cultivated in themselves the Christ-impulse, who experienced the deep Christian Mysteries of the Middle Ages, will then experience the Christ-impulse in the sense of Paul: "It is not I who lives, it is not I who works, it is Christ." They will see their own inner life illuminated by the light of Christ ... Those who received the Christ-impulse into their souls then, who permeated their will, feeling and thinking with this impulse in the Pauline sense, will come again. And the fruits of their rebirth will show themselves in such a way that what they lived through then will be enlivened anew as a force in their souls.' GA 106, lecture of 16 June 1920.

2 Verlag am Goetheanum, 1991–93.

3 'Often, my dear friends, I am asked by our members: how do I bring myself into a connection with the Christ? This is a naive question, because everything towards which we can strive, every line that we read in our anthroposophical science, is a bringing of oneself into a relation with the Christ. We are actually doing nothing else but this. And the one who wishes to have a special connection [to the Christ Being] only shows, in a naive way, that he really would have liked to avoid the somewhat uncomfortable way of study and reading.' (GA 169, lecture of 13 June 1916.)

4 See GA 26, 'A Christmas Contemplation: the Mystery of the Logos' (1924).

5 GA 109/111, lecture of 31 May 1909.

6 The loftiest region of their eternal union is to be found beyond the higher Devachan, in the Budhi sphere, or world of macrocosmic archetypes (*Ur-Bilder Welt*) — that is, in the realm where the 12 Bodhisattvas surround the being of the Cosmic Christ. The task of the 12 is to reflect, as light of wisdom and knowledge, the living stream of Christ's pure presence. This spirit light of wisdom is the Holy Spirit in its macrocosmic form (GA 113, lecture of 31 August 1910, GA 116, lecture of 25 October 1909, GA 123, lecture of 6 December 1910, and GA 130, lecture of 9 January 1912). This is also the realm from which springs the original spirit force that shapes the imaginative, supersensible faculties of perception (GA 119, lecture of 28 March 1910).

7 'So we feel ourselves standing, in full understanding, in the coming together

of two streams of world conception. The one should bring us a deepened conception of the Christ problem, the Mystery of Golgotha, and the other should bring us new concepts and ideas about reality. The two stand under the necessity to flow together in our time. This will not be possible without the worst hindrances ...' (GA 124, lecture of 13 March 1911.)

8 About the creative connection that exists between the being and workings of Anthroposophy, the Holy Spirit and the Christ, Rudolf Steiner says the following: 'The Holy Spirit is the great teacher of those whom we call the Masters of Wisdom and the Harmony of Feelings ... what is brought forth as wisdom through the spiritual scientific movement, in order to understand the world and its spirits, flows through the Holy Spirit into the Lodge of the Twelve, and this is that which will, eventually, bring humanity to a self-conscious, free understanding of Christ and the event of Golgotha.' (GA 107, lecture of 22 March 1909.) This means, in other words, that the truly anthroposophical knowledge of the Christ is a new, free spiritual creation of the age of the conscious soul, which streams, for the first time, as Holy Spirit substance *from the Earth upwards* to the highest Budhi plane. Or, which is the same, it is the first realization of the Holy Spirit in the new, Christed earthly-human Sun-sphere, in which Christ has established His Heaven and Kingdom, and around which the new circle of the future Bodhisattvas is being formed, led by the three great Masters of the West (GA 264).

    Anthropos-sophia is, therefore, the spirit of man as such, in his archetypal form and perfection, as he develops from Saturn up to Vulcan, reflecting through the free act of knowledge, and embodying, through the free act of love, the being of Christ. When man confronts today the etheric Christ in the astral world it is really the following words that resound to him from out of his own, deepest human nature: 'It is not the Christ that we miss, but the knowledge of Christ, the Isis of Christ; the Sophia of Christ we miss ... What has caused the misfortune of civilized humanity in the new age is not the loss of the Christ, who stands before us in a higher glory then Osiris stood before the Egyptians ... no, what we have lost is the knowledge, the sight of Jesus Christ. We must find it again by means of the power of Jesus Christ which is in us. The Christ will appear in the twentieth century in his spiritual form, not because something external will enter [into human evolution] but because human beings will find that power represented by the Holy Sophia.' (GA 202, lecture of 24 December 1920. And see also GA 221, lecture of 10 February 1923.)

9 The spiritualization of thinking through the renewing of Anthroposophy is the main anthroposophical task of the end of the century: 'And so we have, I would say, in the Anthroposophical Society a further working of Aristotelianism, only now spiritualized and awaiting its further spiritualization ... That which today can shine as if only through tiny windows must, in the future, become a unity through the coming together of the leaders of the School of Chartres and the leading spirits of Scholasticism, when at the end of the twentieth century that spiritual renewing will come to pass whereby intellectualism is lifted to the spirit.' (GA 240, lecture of 18 June 1924.)

    The despiritualization of the Christ experience can only be carried forth through such a spiritualization of thinking. But such a spiritualized despiritualization is possible only when the two major streams of Anthroposophy *consciously* fertilize and enhance each other.

10 This veiled secret is the secret of the new Isis legend, the mystery of the new, resurrected being of Anthropos-sophia, described by Rudolf Steiner in GA 180, lecture of 6 January 1918. Philosophically expressed, this secret is formulated by Rudolf Steiner thus: 'Such a way of knowledge can be termed anthroposophical, and the knowledge of reality gained by it Anthroposophy, because it must take its departure from the fact that *the truly real man* (anthropos) lies hidden behind what is revealed by the knowledge of nature and what is found in the inner life of ordinary consciousness. In obscure feeling, in the unconscious soul life, this truly real man expresses himself; through anthroposophical research it will be lifted into consciousness.' (GA 35, *Philosophie und Anthroposophie*.) This 'truly, real man' is the one referred to also in *The Philosophy of Freedom* as the whole, man-world being, that embraces and cancels the subject-object dualism of ordinary consciousness: 'In that we sense and feel (and also perceive), we are single beings; in that we think, we are *the all-one being that penetrates everything*' (GA 4, Chapter 5). Or in the book *Mysticism at the Dawn of the Modern Age*: 'I live, therefore, a double life, the life of a thing among things, which lives in its body and perceives by means of its organs what takes place outside this body; and above this life a higher one, which is not limited by such inner and outer, which reaches across and extends beyond the external world and itself. Therefore, I would have to say: first I am an individual, limited "I"; then, secondly, I am a general, universal "I".' (GA 7.)

11 The term 'Pauline method' was used by Rudolf Steiner in the following way: 'The first who could perceive the cosmic significance of the Christ was Paul, who could perceive how the power of Christ's being streamed into the aura of the Earth. That which was grasped by Paul as a specific point of the knowledge of Christ can, if we deepen the occultism of our time, be grasped by man in wider fields of Christ knowledge. If the vision of Paul ... be extended from what for Paul was almost only the perception of Jesus Christ, to the life of Jesus Christ as a whole, then the Pauline method will be extended from a single centre over the total event of Jesus Christ's life. If today we can reach the position, by means of devoted occult research, making the Pauline method a general method of Christ knowledge, a real advance in the knowledge of the Christ will have occurred.' (GA 152, lecture of 27 May 1914.) If this should happen, then in the future, through anthroposophical spiritual science, the Christ will 'appear again in His whole grandiose world splendour as the cosmic Christ' (GA 238, lecture of 16 September 1924).

12 GA 211, lecture of 2 April 1922, my italics. In the nineteenth century the death process of thinking had reached a further, mighty acceleration: 'The Fall into sin ... influenced at last the intellect as well. The intellect felt itself [in the nineteenth century] at the limits of knowledge. And if the theologians speak about sin, or Du Bois-Reymond speaks about the limits of knowledge of nature, it is the same, only in somewhat different form.' (GA 220, lecture of 21 January 1923.) The second Mystery of Golgotha (which is

studied in Chapters 4 and 5) has its roots in this intellectual second Fall of man.

13 GA 211, lecture of 15 April 1922, my italics.

14 GA 116, lecture of 8 May 1910.

15 GA 176, lecture of 4 September 1917, and further GA 60, lecture of 25 January 1912. And see also Frederick Hiebel, *The Epistles of Paul and Rudolf Steiner's Philosophy of Freedom* (Spring Valley, New York: St George Publications, 1980).

16 GA 194, lecture of 30 November 1919.

17 GA 322, lecture of 3 October 1920. The same method was described again — from a somewhat different aspect — in *Anthroposophical Leading Thoughts* as the anthroposophical method that can make of the Anthroposophical Society a preliminary school of true modern initiation, in the spirit of the Christmas Foundation Meeting. (GA 26: 'Understanding of the Spirit; Conscious Experience of Destiny', 13 July 1924.)

18 About the unique nature of pure thinking, in relation to the traditional spiritual paths, Rudolf Steiner writes the following: 'There is, however, still another path [than the paths of *Knowledge of the Higher Worlds* and *Occult Science*] that is safer and above all more exact, but it is also more difficult for many human beings. This path is presented in my books *A Theory of Knowledge Based on Goethe's World Conception* and *Philosophy of Freedom* ... These writings stand at an important point intermediate between cognition of the sense-world and that of the spiritual world ... whoever permits these writings to act upon his entire soul nature stands already within the spiritual world ... through it he is able to gain a feeling towards the higher world that will bear for him the most beautiful fruits throughout all future time.' (GA 13.) On *The Philosophy of Freedom* as the way to the purification and transformation of the astral body into the Spirit Self, or Holy 'Virgin Sophia' (the Holy Spirit) and therefore as a direct way of spiritualization of the consciousness soul into Spirit Self, see GA 94, lecture of 5 November 1906, and GA 103, lecture of 31 May 1908.

19 GA 152, lecture of 5 March 1914.

20 It was the same Krishna-Nathanic-Jesus being who taught both Arjuna and Paul — the one before and the other after the Mystery of Golgotha — the secrets of Ego self-consciousness and its spiritualization: 'Krishna, that is to say, the spirit that works through Krishna, appears again in the Jesus-child of St Luke, out of the Nathan line of the house of King David. This personality bore, in essence, everything that exists as impulses for the emancipation of man, for the release from external reality.' (GA 146, lecture of 5 June 1913.) In the first lecture of this cycle Rudolf Steiner speaks of Krishna as the spirit whose mission is to teach man the secret of 'universal egoism' (28 May 1913). This was the most mature pre-Golgothean form of the appearance of the all-human 'I', or the archetypal paradisiacal man, namely, the primal Adam-Nathanic pure Being of heavenly humanity that became the vehicle for the Christ: 'As Paul journeyed to Damascus it was the Christ who appeared before him. The light-appearance in which the Christ clothed Himself was Krishna. And because the Christ used Krishna as His own soulsheath, through which He then continued to work, *His radiance contains*

everything that once was the sublime content of the Bhagavadgita ... the teaching
of Krishna became thereby a thing that belongs to the whole of humanity ...'
(GA 146, lecture of 1 January 1913.)

When the etheric Christ appears again today in His radiant light-soul
aura, it is an important anthroposophical research project to understand in
detail how He actually appears, speaks and acts as the teacher of the new
Michaelic soul-and-spirit yoga breathing, in the rhythmical etheric life and
light elements of the new earthly-human Sun.

21 'Under him [Dionysius] the school had its time of blossom, because
Dionysius taught these mysteries in a wholly special way, while St Paul
spread the teaching exoterically.' (GA 264, lecture of 7 March 1907. See also
Note 8 to Chapter 2.) Compare Wolfgang Müller, *Dionysius Areopagites*,
(Verlag die Pforte, Basel 1976).

22 Nikolaus von Kues found in John Scotus Erigena's Latin translations of
Dionysius the spiritual support he needed in order to consolidate and
ground the experience of illumination which he had on the sea coming back
from Constantinople to Venice (1437). His *De Docta Ignoranta* (1440) was
already based on the writings of 'the pupil of St Paul', as he used to name
him. (E. Meffert, *Nikolaus von Kues*, Verlag Freies Geistesleben, 1982).

23 GA 74, lecture of 23 May 1920, my italics, and see also the lecture of 27
August (GA 129).

24 GA 176, lecture of 4 September 1917, my italics.

25 GA 131, lecture of 14 October 1911. See also GA 212, lecture of 7 May 1922.

Introduction, Part II

1 *Briefe*, Vol. 2 (Dornach 1953), GA 39, my italics.

2 'For although, *on the one hand*, intuitively experienced thinking is an active
process taking place in the human spirit, *on the other hand* it is also a spiritual
percept grasped without a physical sense organ. It is a percept in which the
perceiver is himself active, and a self-activity which is at the same time
perceived. In intuitively experienced thinking man is carried into a spiritual
world also as perceiver.... the experience of thinking, when rightly
understood, *is* in fact an experience of spirit.' (Rudolf Steiner, GA 4,
Author's Additions, 1918, 'The Consequences of Monism'.)

3 'Will and feeling still fill the soul with warmth even when we live through
the original event again in retrospect. Thinking all too readily leaves us cold
in recollection; it is as if the life of the soul had dried out. Yet this is really
nothing but the strongly marked shadow of its real nature—warm, luminous, and penetrating deeply into the phenomena of the world.' (Rudolf
Steiner, GA 4, Author's Additions, 1918, Chapter 8.)

4 This is the modern Pauline, Christ-permeated 'I' experience, thoroughly
strengthened and penetrated by the living spirit power of Fichte: 'The
source of all reality is the 'I', for this is the straight and simple law. The
concept of reality is only given through and with the 'I'. However the 'I' *is*
because it *puts itself*, and *puts itself* because it *is*. Accordingly, *putting itself*
and *being* are one and the same thing ... So all reality is *active*, and all *activity*

is reality.' J.G. Fichte, *Grundlage der Gesamten Wissenschaftslehre* ('Basis of the Complete Doctrine of Knowledge'), 1794, second part, Felix Meiner Verlag, 1988, p.55.

5 About the natural evolutionary separation of the etheric body from the physical and the resulting transformation of the whole human constitution, see Chapter 3.

6 GA 3. [Numeration added by present author.]

7 '... what that really is which we hitherto considered as our ego. It presents itself as a web of recollections, produced by the physical, the elemental and the astral bodies in the same way as an image is produced by a mirror ... The web of recollection which we now regard as our former ego may be called the "ego-body" or "thought-body".' (GA 16.)

8 'In reality, the most fatal thing of all for a true occultist is to long to penetrate into spiritual science without desiring at the same time to do so differently than in the case of knowledge concerning the physical world.' (GA 162, lecture of 29 May 1915, 'Characteristics of Man's Occult Development'.)

9 'It is not possible, however, to acquire a knowledge of the spiritual world in this way. On the contrary, the books dealing with the spiritual world should stimulate our inner activity anew each time we read them; they should each time bring new life and movement into our inner forces ... We permeate ourselves with the activity leading towards knowledge ... Freedom, as something exterior, as an exterior condition, would at some time or other in the near future become a heavy chain for humanity. Freedom is something that can be held fast only through constantly arising anew. Freedom is something that a human being must acquire anew at each moment, and as a matter of fact he can really acquire it only when there arises in his soul at each moment a trace of his coming into contact with the spiritual world. Look it up in my book *The Philosophy of Freedom.*'

10 The decisive year through which the two periods must be mutually crossed is 1908 (1892–1908–1924), in which the article 'Philosophy and Anthroposophy' was written: 'Fichte may at this point supplement Aristotle.' (GA 35).

11 'We can say therefore that in the person who is developing spiritually the consciousness soul is transformed into the *Imagination Soul* [...] and the consciousness soul makes use of the brain of the physical body ... the Imagination Soul actually enters into the physical body and permeates it ...' (GA 145, lecture of 29 March 1913.) And also: 'But occult training will, by the transformation of the physical body, show the Mystery of the Living Christ in a new way ...' (GA 121, lecture of 17 June 1910.)

12 Rudolf Steiner, *Von Seelenrätseln* ('Riddles of the Soul'), GA 21, my italics.

13 Ibid.

14 See GA 157a, lecture of 14 December 1915.

15 See GA 153, lecture of 11 April 1914.

16 'What man stores up in his memory is a curtain woven across the spiritual reality ... A far greater striving must arise for a ceaseless activity and an active participation in things, and the tendency to say "We have understood this, now we can carry it about with us through life" must disappear.' (GA 162, lecture of 29 May 1915.)

17 See Chapter 5, concerning the transformation process of sense-perception.

18 The primary separation of 'I' and world is the theme of Chapter 2 of *The Philosophy of Freedom*.

19 '... But, unless *self*-consciousness had been purchased in the first place from *ordinary-level* consciousness it could not be achieved in supersensible consciousness.' (GA 21.)

20 See in this connection Chapter 9 of *The Philosophy of Freedom*: 'The essence which is active in thinking has a twofold function: first it represses the activity of the human organization, and secondly it steps into its place.'

21 'What makes initiation such a shattering experience is that we perceive this destruction, that we know that if we bring ourselves into relation, let us say, with an Angel or an Archangel being of the spiritual world and want to gain some ideas concerning that being, that is, if we want to perceive the being truly, we must first destroy something in ourselves ... If the spiritual is to appear in the beings, processes of destruction must take place.' (GA 162, lecture of 23 May 1915, 'Whitsuntide').

22 GA 198, lecture of 2 April 1920.

23 GA 161, lecture of 3 April 1915; and see also GA 243, lecture of 22 August 1924.

24 This process is the *reversing* of the process by means of which self-consciousness is brought about in the consciousness-soul age. This is described by Rudolf Steiner in the following words: 'The past [thoughts] throwing its shadows, the future [with its will-forces] fraught with the germs of a new reality meet in the human being. And their meeting constitutes the human life of present time [the full, free human self-consciousness in the epoch of the consciousness soul].' (GA 26.)

25 *Von Seelenrätseln* ('Riddles of the Soul').

26 See the details in Chapter 4.

27 'Within a perceptible realm, every integral expansion of a unified force capable of change ... is inspirationally and intuitively certain ... Imagination.' (Herbert Witzenmann, *Verstandesblindheit und Ideenschau*, ['Blindness of Understanding and Vista of Ideas'], Gideon Spicker Verlag, 1985 p.120.)

Chapter 1

1 GA 112, lectures of 4–5 July 1909.

2 'In very ancient times the Sun shone down as a uniform disc of light. There were no Sun-spots. After thousands of years, the Sun will have many more spots than it has today; it is growing ever more spotted ... In the increasing number of Sun-spots in the course of cosmic evolution, the gradual decay and the old age of the Sun is revealed.' (GA 237, lecture of 8 August 1924. On the gradual weakening of the Sun through the Moon forces, see GA 150, lecture of 23 March 1913: 'In every new spring, the Sun has weaker forces than it had in the previous spring.')

3 GA 13; and also GA 110, lecture of 14 April 1909.

4 This process can also be termed the re-timing of the evolution of humanity and the Earth, in regard to their true, living, cosmic time: 'In the inner Sun is

Time. And out of this weaving time of the inner Sun the Christ descended to the space of Earth ... the Christ brought to man the time element ... because humanity, at the time of the Mystery of Golgotha, had become so strongly a space-being that it lost the time! The Christ brought time back to humanity.' (GA 236, lecture of 4 June 1924). But re-timing means, at the same time, enlivening, because the time forces are the etheric life forces in the cosmos and man. Those life forces that were separated from man in order to protect him from complete corruption as a result of the Fall were securely guarded in the great Sun-Christ oracle until, through the being of Christ-Jesus, they could be brought back to man and the Earth (GA 13; and GA 114, lecture of 21 September 1909).

Living in full self-consciousness in (living) time means, therefore, having the faculty of time regulation, preservation and harmonization – that is, enabling the past to be vividly presented and remembered, and being able, in the present, to harmonize it with the living weavings and streamings of future life-potentials. In this sense we can see in the Etheric Christ the living presence of the present. Rudolf Steiner described Him from this aspect in the following way: 'What happened in Jesus of Nazareth was a continuous manifestation of the horoscope, because in each moment [of his life] occurred what in other cases takes place [only] at the birth of man [the imprinting of the cosmic constellations of the living moment into the brain of the new-born baby]. This could be so only because the whole body of the Nathanic Jesus remained capable of being continuously influenced by the forces of the cosmic spiritual hierarchies, who guide our Earth as a whole ... And when the Mystery of Golgotha took place, that which radiated from out of the cosmos passed into the spiritual substance of the Earth and has been united since then with the spirit of the Earth.' (GA 15.)

5 'The receiving of Death into life: this is the secret of Golgotha.' (See GA 211, lecture of 2 April 1922; and see also GA 112, lecture of 6 July 1909.)

6 This double relationship of the Christ with his disciples shows itself in the night walkings on the sea of Galilee (Matthew 14:22–33; Mark 6:47–54; John 6:16–20), and in Peter's identification of the Christ on the physical plane (Matthew 16:13–28; Mark 8:27–37; Luke 9:18–27). In the night the Christ appears before the disciples in His supersensible form, but is not recognized or identified as the one with whom they go around physically. They see only a 'ghost' before them. In the day they see His physical form but do not know His true spirit and nature. As Rudolf Steiner described it, Peter's flash of recognition was an intuition that far surpassed his actual conscious-soul capacities, as indeed the betrayal scene was clearly to show only a short while later (GA 123, lecture of 11 August 1910).

7 'I came forth from the Father, and am come into the world; again, I leave the world, and go to the Father. His disciples said unto him, Lo, now speakest thou plainly, and speakest no proverb. Now are we sure that thou knowest all things, and needest not that any man should ask thee: by this we believe that thou camest forth from God. Jesus answered them, Do ye now believe? Behold, the hour cometh, yea, is now come, that ye shall be scattered, every man to his own, and shall leave me alone ...' (John 16:28–32).

8 Thus, through the ahrimanic being that possessed Judas, it is Ahriman

144

himself who participated in Christ's bread of life: '... and when he [the Christ] had dipped the sop, he gave it to Judas Iscariot ... And after the sop Satan [Ahriman] entered into him. Then said Jesus unto him, that thou doest, do quickly.' (John 13:26–27). This participating in the Bread of Eternal Life by Ahriman is, however, the first germ of his own transubstantiation and redemption in the far future (see GA 148, lectures of 6 October, 18 November and 10 December 1913).

9 GA 112, lecture of 6 July 1909.

10 'With this lecture we have placed ourselves on one bank of the stream which separates the evolution of humanity into two parts. We have come from the direction of this evolution as far as the bank; we stand upon it, and what this standing there signifies has been brought home to us through the frame of mind of the later Egyptian initiate, the 'Son of the Widow', who was initiated in order to experience mourning and resignation. It will now be our task, in the boat of spiritual science, to cross the stream that separates the two shores of human evolution. In the last lecture we shall see what is on the other shore when we push off our boat from the place where we have experienced the mourning for the God who is dying in the heavens, when we leave that place in order to traverse the stream and arrive at the other bank. When the boat of spiritual science has carried us across, with the remembrance that we have previously experienced the dying of a God in the heavens we shall see what is offered to our view on the other side'. (See GA 144, lecture of 5 February 1913; and see also Chapter 4 and Note 13 on p.157).

11 The bridge was historically preserved. But this was achieved through retaining some elements of the old form of initiation, as in the case of Lazarus-John (GA 8), and also, later, in the Rosicrucian initiation (GA 233a, lecture of 13 January 1924). Today, in the age of the consciousness soul, no such half-conscious bridging is possible or permissible. In this age the bridge can only be the creation of self-conscious and free human beings. This new form of 'earthly-human' initiation was first lived through and made available to humanity as a whole through the life of Rudolf Steiner (see his autobiographical sketch, given in a lecture of 4 February 1913, published as *Self-education: Autobiographical Reflection*, Mercury Press 1985).

12 As with any bridge, the anthroposophical one must have an anchoring on either side of the stream. In this way we may also understand the double nature of the anthroposophical Foundation Stone: the physical one, laid in the earthly elemental foundation of the physical Goetheanum (1913), with its intimate connection to the fifth gospel of anthroposophical knowledge; and the spiritual one, laid at the Christmas Foundation Meeting (1923/4) of the General Anthroposophical Society, as a free spiritual creation of spiritualized human consciousness of the future. The first was shaped out of Christ's divine-human life, death and resurrection, and the second was a free human-divine deed of knowledge and love. From another point of view, the bridge is the living remembrance, awareness and seeing that must be developed in order to link consciously the anthroposophical work at the beginning of this century with the work at the beginning of the next, over the abyss of this century's spirit forgetfulness (see the description of this

bridge over the abyss of the twentieth century in my book: *The Spiritual Event of the Twentieth Century*, Temple Lodge Publishing, 1993).

13　These lectures are collected in the volume GA 148. The three pre-Golgotha sacrifices of the Christ, and the present, modern fifth sacrifice, belong essentially to this gospel, namely, they describe the past and future pre-conditions and outworking of the Mystery of Golgotha. And because the Nathanic being of Jesus is the bearer of these sacrifices, the reader is referred here also to the lectures given in GA 114 (18, 19 and 21 August 1909), GA 130 (12 October 1911), GA 143 (24 December 1912), GA 146 (3 June 1913), GA 150 (21 December 1913), GA 153 (2 May 1913, and 5, 7 and 30 March, 27 May and 1 June 1914).

14　From another point of view, what has been described is actually the process of the etherization of the blood, with its resulting unification of the moral (macrocosmic) stream with the intellectual (microcosmic) stream, that causes the illumination and activation of the modern conscious anthro-posophical Christ perception (GA 130, lecture of 1 October 1911). The point where the two streams cross and fertilize each other (around the pineal gland) is the psycho-physical place of the Second Coming (described in detail in Chapter 5). Where death becomes eternal life, and life becomes quickening death, the first anchorage of Goethe's bridge is firmly con-solidated.

15　Already, at this early stage of our study, we can turn our attention to the fact that it was, according to Rudolf Steiner, the imaginative pentecostal sight of the 'body on the cross' by means of which Christ-Jesus was first identified, recognized or remembered by his disciples in the moment of their spiritual awakening. Here lies a great mystery of Christ's being and appearance in his etheric appearance today. As we shall see in detail later, 'the body on the cross' remains his vehicle of visibility and identification in his etheric crucifixion and resurrection in the astral world (see Chapters 4 and 5).

16　GA 148, lecture of 2 October 1913.

17　About the moment of purely spiritual illumination through the imprinting and reflection of the purified higher members in the prepared etheric body, see, for example, GA 104, lecture of 18 June 1908. About the special nature of the modern, Christian and anthroposophical initiation as a self-conscious process taking place in the physical world, beginning in and returning voluntarily to full earthly bodily incarnation, see, for example, GA 103, lecture of 31 May 1908, and GA 112, lecture of 30 June 1909.

18　John 16:7–16.

19　GA 148, lecture of 3 October 1913.

20　Here a subtle transformation of all other members takes place as well, including the physical body (GA 13; GA 10).

21　GA 104, lectures of 18 and 19 July 1909.

22　GA 148, lecture of 2 October 1913.

23　GA 226, lecture of 17 May 1923.

24　A further, deeply related aspect of the ascension event is described by Rudolf Steiner in the lecture of 7 June 1923 (GA 224) as the redemption of the human etheric body. This redemption means, however, exactly this: that the Christed etheric body does not disperse itself completely in the cosmos after death but receives the power to remain intact, at least in part, and connected to the spiritual Earth (see also GA 176, lecture of 4 August 1917). Thus the Christ offered, through His own redeemed life-body, a degree of 'weight' to man's etheric body. He consolidated it and enabled man henceforth to weave its forces more and more into the planetary etheric sphere of the Christed Earth.

25 GA 165, lecture of 16 January 1916.

26 See further the detailed study of the subject in Chapter 4, and in S.O. Prokofieff, *The Cycle of the Year as a Path of Initiation* (Temple Lodge Publishing, 1991), Chapter 7, Part 2.

27 GA 96, lecture of 1 April 1907, GA 97, lecture of 2 December 1906, GA 103, lecture of 26 May 1908, GA 112, lecture of 6 July 1909, GA 223, lecture of 1 April 1923.

28 GA 181, lecture of 1 April 1918.

29 GA 130, lecture of 1 October 1911.

30 GA 113, lecture of 25 August 1909.

31 GA 204, lecture of 16 April 1921.

32 'This is something that the Christ-impulse conferred on the human etheric body. Ever since that time, the human etheric body has held something that is not subject to death. Since that time there has been given to the human etheric body the possibility that, as a result of Christ's light, something new appears, something living and breathing and immortal, something that can never suffer death ... And this something which does not die with the rest ... streams back—out into cosmic space, where it builds, according to its strength in man, a sphere around the Earth that is in the process of becoming a Sun. A sort of spiritual sphere builds itself around the Earth composed of the enlivened etheric bodies.' (GA 112, lecture of 6 July 1909.)

33 'And in the same way that the light of Christ streams out from the Earth, we have a kind of reflecting back of Christ's light in the surroundings of the Earth. What is here reflected back as Christ's light, and what entered as a result of the Christ event, is what the Christ calls the Holy Spirit.' (GA 112.) We shall study the building process of this etheric sphere or 'ring' of the Holy Spirit (the new Heaven of the new earthly-human Sun in our terminology) in Chapter 6.

Chapter 2

1 GA 103, lecture of 20 May 1908; GA 185, lecture of 7 December 1918.

2 Colossians 1:16 — 'For by him were all things created, that are in heaven, and that are in earth, visible and invisible, whether they be thrones, or dominions, or principalities, or powers: all things were created by him and for him.'

3 Philippians 2:6–7 — 'Who, being in the form of God, thought it not robbery to be equal with God; but made himself of no reputation, and took upon him the form of a servant, and was made in the likeness of men.'

4 Rudolf Steiner described the ongoing creation of humanity as the cosmic religious ideal of the gods in the following way: 'There hovered before the

147

gods the picture of humanity as the goal, as the highest ideal, as the religion of the gods. And as if at the farthest shore of their existence, there hovered before the gods the temple that shows the highest creative achievement of the gods as a picture of divine being in a human form.' (See GA 153, lecture of 10 April 1914, and also GA 134, lecture of 27 December 1911.) That means that Christ Jesus has been, since He became fully man on Golgotha, the complete temple and realized goal and religious ideal of the gods, as well as of humanity. He thereby brought together for the first time both the human and divine religious strivings into harmony, mutual penetration and fulfilment. St Paul was the first man to experience this secret.

5 Before Golgotha, what separated the gods from humanity, and humanity from the gods, was the mystery of death that, as an opaque, impenetrable veil, shut off their sight in both directions. After Golgotha, Christ Jesus brought the gods and humanity the secret of death, being Himself the first god to have experienced death through eternal life, and the first man to have experienced eternal life through death: '... The Mystery of Golgotha meant for the gods the enriching of their wisdom through the wisdom of death ... they themselves learned to know death through the being of Christ' (GA 211, lecture of 2 April 1922). And also: 'It had to come to pass that the being of Christ, who lived three years in the body of Jesus of Nazareth, said something to this body that can only be said in the moment of death, because only in the moment of death can all that constitutes the mystery of human consciousness be condensed together ... In the death on Golgotha, Christ Jesus revealed to Jesus the mystery of the coming human consciousness' (GA 176, lecture of 28 August 1917).

6 'What has made Saul into a Paul? Not the teachings, not the events in Palestine, but the event of Damascus, a supersensible event. Before, he could not have believed that the one who had departed so miserably on the cross was the Christ. But he knew, as an initiate of the Cabbala, that the Christ, when he shall come to the Earth, will be visible in the Earth's aura. And this was the experience of Paul. Thus was Paul created out of Saul.' (GA 109/111, lecture of 31 May 1909.)

7 GA 103, lecture of 23 May 1908. The knowledge that Christ is the bringer of man's true 'I am' to maturity was contained in the deeper understanding of esoteric Christianity through the ages. And again it is one of the 'open secrets' of Christ's etheric appearance and the being of Anthroposophy in the fifth post-Atlantean epoch. This is the Grail mystery of the 'I am' (see GA 109/111, lecture of 11 April 1909, and Chapters 4 and 5 below).

8 In the historical-evolutionary perspective of the changing relationships of the Mysteries to humanity, Rudolf Steiner distinguishes three main stages. Firstly, there are the *Ur* or Spirit Mysteries, where the superhuman ancient teachers of humanity taught the pre-individual man. Secondly, there are the Son-Mysteries, where the Christ Himself is the teacher in person (as, for example, in the esoteric school of Paul and Dionysius in Athens). And thirdly, from our own times, we have the 'future Mysteries', where free, ego-endowed human beings are taught by purely human teachers, as in the Rosicrucian-anthroposophical spiritual-scientific stream, in which the secrets of both the first and second Mysteries are given in a new way (GA 97,

lecture of 7 March 1907). That is to say, if man today has the modern Pauline Damascus experience (which is possible only through the exoteric influence of the etheric body of Christian Rosenkreutz, according to GA 130, lecture of 27 September 1911), and doesn't rest content with the *given* form of this experience but endeavours to spiritualize it through the lifework of Rudolf Steiner (as is described in Chapter 5), then he works actively on the transition from and unification of the second and third stages of the Mystery evolution of humanity.

9   Acts 8:4.

10 GA 134, lecture of 29 December 1911.

11 Romans 7:15–26. In 2 Corinthians 12:7–9 we can realize how humanly deep and esoterically exact St Paul's self-knowledge was. He actually identifies the ahrimanic death as being the 'thorn' in his own life and physical bodies, and sees in this permanent dualism a Christed necessity: 'And lest I should be exalted above measure through the abundance of the revelations, there was given to me a thorn in the flesh, the messenger of Satan, to buffet me, lest I should be exalted above measure. For this thing I besought the Lord thrice, that it might depart from me. And he said unto me, my grace is sufficient for thee: for my strength is made perfect in weakness.' (See also 2 Corinthians 4:10–11.) That is, in order to live permanently in the event of Golgotha, *in Christo morimur*, man needs the conscious experience and seeing of his ahrimanic thorn in the flesh. This remains so also today (see Chapter 4). (About the essential nature of the ahrimanic double, see GA 158, lecture of 20 November 1914, GA 178, lectures of 16, 18 and 19 November 1917, and GA 144, lecture of 6 February 1913.)

12 1 Corinthians 13:14. This important verse is inserted at the end of Paul's great hymn about love. And right thereafter the three virtues (faith, hope and love) are mentioned, and love is declared to be the greatest. We see here how intimately the moral and cognitive elements are interwoven and mutually penetrate in the Etheric Christ experience. Morality is a cognitive awakening and sustaining power, and cognition is morally productive.

13 2 Corinthians 3:18.

14 1 Galatians 2:20.

15 1 Corinthians 13:10.

16 Romans 8:29; 1 Corinthians 15:49; Ephesians 4:22–25.

17 Romans 8:19–22.

18 The anthroposophical task of saving the Earth at the end of the twentieth century is mentioned by Rudolf Steiner for example in GA 238, lecture of 16 September 1924.

19 2 Thessalonians 2:7–8.

20 That is, Lucifer attacks the astral, Ahriman the etheric body of man, as described in GA 13.

21 GA 107, lecture of 22 March 1909.

22 2 Thessalonians 2:4. The reference is to the book of Daniel 11:36–37. Concerning the nature of this being that will appear as God in the place of God, that is, as a Satanic ego possession in place of man's Christed ego, which the prophet Daniel — because of his special Hebrew and Persian initiation — was the first to recognize, see further GA 184, lecture of 11 October 1918. About

the special, evil connection of this being to the etheric Second Coming of Christ in the fifth post-Atlantean epoch, see GA 178, lecture of 18 November 1917.

Chapter 3

1 See Note 5 of Chapter 2. About the invitation that the Hierarchies offered Ahriman in order to involve him in human evolution, Rudolf Steiner says the following: 'We, the higher Hierarchies, are capable of shaping out of the Moon an Earth in which human beings shall not know of death, but in which they shall also not be able to develop the intellect ... Here we have to turn to a wholly different being, the ahrimanic, that comes here through other paths than we ... Ahriman knows death ... he is a knower, a knower of death. He is thereby also the Lord of the Intellect ... It has to do with accepting Ahriman into evolution ...' (GA 211, lecture of 2 April 1922.) On the role of Jehovah in this process, see GA 203, lecture of 13 March 1921, to which an important deepening is given in GA 212, lectures of 5 and 28 May 1922.

2 GA 211, lectures of 13 and 15 April 1922.

3 GA 184, lecture of 21 August 1918.

4 See GA 26, letter of 9 November 1924, on the difference between the ahrimanic and the Michael-Christ experience of freedom.

5 It is the task of the new Michael epoch, as the founding cornerstone of the whole epoch of the consciousness soul, to bring the unconscious being and workings of Christ in humanity to full self-consciousness (GA 152, lecture of 20 May 1913).

6 See, for example, their destiny in the light of Rudolf Steiner's lecture about love and its mission in the world (GA 143, 17 December 1912).

7 GA 26, letter of 12 October 1924.

8 GA 245, lecture of 20 August 1913, and GA 148, lecture of 5 October 1913. And then also GA 110, lecture of 18 April 1909: 'So to speak, in the middle of the Angel hierarchy the possibility of freedom begins; in man it is developed for the first time in the right way.'

9 GA 112, lecture of 4 July 1909.

10 GA 12.

11 GA 130, lecture of 1 October and 20 November 1911.

12 GA 119, lecture of 26 March 1910.

13 GA 10, GA 12, GA 13, GA 16 and GA 17.

14 See Note 3 above.

15 GA 26, letter of 9 November 1924.

16 GA 107, lecture of 17 June 1909, and see also GA 204, lecture of 24 April 1921.

17 'Man must, therefore, in order to be able to realize the impulse of freedom, ward off certain influences that work on him from the cosmos ... man pushes away from himself those cosmic forces that would have liked to build him further, that would have liked to give his "I"-being the physical support that they gave him before the Michael epoch' (GA 26, letter of 9 November 1924). Those forces that create in man the physical, bodily

foundations for the 'I' are the Jehovah-Gabriel Moon forces. From the sixteenth to the nineteenth century, they brought the consciousness-soul development of the human ego to its highest *physical* expression.

18 GA 118, lecture of 25 January 1910. Rudolf Steiner speaks in the lecture from 29 June 1908 (GA 104) about the much greater period of darkness—from the middle of the Atlantean (fourth) epoch up to the middle of the sixth ('seals') epoch.

19 GA 13, GA 103, GA 104, GA 113, GA 116 and GA 129.

20 GA 126, lecture of 29 December 1910.

21 'For all that humanity gathered as knowledge [through Plato and Aristotle] in pre-Christian times has its symbol in the Moon ... because for all higher stages of human cognition this knowledge has acted, not as a light-bringer or solver of riddles but rather as a bringer of darkness, just as the Moon darkens the Sun during a solar eclipse ... one feels the darkening of the Sun of humanity in the earthly evolution, engraved into the cosmos in a stupendous sign of the occult script, in that darkening of the Sun in the moment of the Mystery of Golgotha.' (GA 148, lecture of 2 October 1913.)

22 GA 13.

23 GA 129, lecture of 25 August 1911.

24 GA 112, lecture of 5 July 1909.

25 In the Mysteries, however, this process was deeply experienced, and no more so than in the Mysteries of the Grail. There, the initiate of the fourth cultural epoch could experience this dead etheric-physical element in man's nature as the 'thorn in the flesh' over which St Paul had no conscious spiritual control (see Chapter 2, Note 10). Anthroposophically, this element was described by Rudolf Steiner in the following way: 'In the physical and etheric bodies there exists something that penetrates them as streams running in different directions ... That is dead—so dead that man really has something in his body like a piece of dead substance ... There is something in man that escapes the control of the soul ... Therefore, the Middle Ages saw in the Grail Mysteries something related to a recapitulation of the Graeco-Latin period in the experience of the intellectual or mind soul, for there is rooted mostly those parts of the soul which are now forgotten and dead ... Everything brought about by the duality of human nature lays hold, in the place, first of the intellectual or mind soul, which divides itself truly into "two souls"...' (GA 144, lecture of 6 February 1913.) About the knowledge that Aristotle and, through him, his pupil Alexander, still had of this corruption of the bodily sheaths in the intellectual soul epoch as a necessary correlate of man's increasing individuation process, see GA 26, letter of 25 December 1924.

26 At this time, when the consciousness-soul age was founded, a much greater cycle of human evolution began, which gives to this epoch a special, far-reaching importance. The forces of cosmic intelligence, which in Atlantis were grasped and experienced in the not yet totally materialized human *heart*, were implanted now, through the cosmic-earthly power of the First Hierarchy, in the hardening physical human *head* (GA 237, lecture of 28 July 1924), from which the etheric body had already released itself at the beginning of the *fourth* post-Atlantean epoch (see below, Note 28).

27 GA 152, lecture of 18 May 1913.

28 'Since the third century BC, the old intimate connection between the etheric head and the physical head of man has been lost. But an intimate connection was still maintained between the physical heart and the etheric heart. However, since the year 1721, the connection between the human physical and etheric heart dissolves in a remarkable way ... and until the third millennium, when the year 2100 has arrived, [the etheric heart] will be completely released ... this released etheric body will acquire a right connection to the spiritual world only when man strives for spiritual knowledge ...' (GA 190, lecture of 5 April 1919, and also GA 102, lecture of 13 October 1908 and GA 171, lecture of 14 October 1916). On the one hand, this condensing and hardening of the physical body and the separation of the etheric is the condition for the new etheric vision of the Etheric Christ (GA 130, lecture of 17 August 1911). On the other hand, when the released etheric body is not consciously strengthened and transformed, it might lead to a growing separation of man's members and soul forces. As Rudolf Steiner often showed, the heart and lung region (rhythmical system) is the harmonizing, balancing, health-giving foundation of the whole incarnated organization of man (GA 21; GA 293). When it is in itself disharmonious, it loses the natural capacity to harmonize the inner connections between body, soul and spirit, and such a disruption must cause diverse and severe symptoms. For example, the etheric head is continuously preventing man's animalization, in that it takes into itself from the etheric streams of the etheric body only the pure moral impulses, and pushes down to the unconscious limb-metabolic system man's lower nature. That is, it protects man's daily consciousness and purifies it (GA 221, lecture of 17 February 1923). But this can be done only when the middle, heart and lung rhythmical system is functioning properly. When this is not the case, then unconscious contents erupt out of the lower body through the damaged middle zone and penetrate into the conscious nerve-and-sense system, bringing about characteristic pathological results. (About the function of the rhythmical system in regulating the sleeping-waking, incarnation-excarnation balance of consciousness, through the blood circulation and breathing, see GA 137, lecture of 9 July, 1912. The disturbance of this function through the unconscious separation of the etheric from the physical heart must also lead to the most severe psycho-physical symptoms.)

29 This splitting of the astral-ego organization into a lower-higher polarity is a natural nightly event, that is, it takes place unconsciously in healthy, life-giving sleep. In this process the lower pole comes strongly into the ahrimanic, the higher into the luciferic, sphere of influence (GA 141, lecture of 10 December 1912). When this normal, balanced nightly process enters unconsciously into daily consciousness, it causes the splitting and fragmentation of the soul as described below. When it is consciously transformed and perceived, however, it enables the imaginative perception of the Etheric Christ.

30 See the detailed account given by Rudolf Steiner in GA 174, lecture of 14 January 1917, where especially the results of pathological excarnation in relation to the four members of the human constitution are described.

31 GA 190, lecture of 11 April 1919, GA 192, lecture of 1 May 1919, GA 203, lecture of 6 February 1921, and GA 204, lectures of 2 and 3 June 1921.

32 This exact — and most important — indication as to the true nature of what is usually taken to be only 'the etheric' appearance of the Christ is to be found, for example, in GA 130, lecture of 4 November 1911, and in GA 143, lecture of 14 January 1912.

33 'When the union with Christ is achieved, we will know that all previous sufferings were necessary conditions. For the Christ union to take place, suffering must be there; this is an absolute factor in evolution. In that man overcomes suffering, he overcomes the feelings of depression and lameness. In this phenomenon man can see something good: how power grows out of helplessness.' (GA 110, answer to a question on 21 April 1909.)

34 'The years 1933, 1935 and 1937 will be especially important. Then there will be seen in man, as natural endowment, completely new faculties. In this time great changes will take place, and biblical scriptures will be fulfilled ... everything is changing. But the most important event of our time is a *deeply decisive change in the soul faculties of man.*' (GA 118, lecture of 25 January 1910.) That our time is the time of 'great decision, of the great crisis', of which 'all the sacred scriptures of all times spoke', see GA 237, lecture of 3 August 1924. And see further in my book *The Spiritual Event of the Twentieth Century* (op.cit.) for the *results* of this crossing of the threshold for humanity as a whole.

35 'So shall be the resolution of the most significant disharmony in human feelings that ever existed in human evolution: the disharmony in the feeling of man between his experience of himself as an earthly being and his knowledge that he is a super-earthly, cosmic being. The undergoing of this experience will prepare him to know how, out of the grey spirit depths, the Christ Being will be revealed to him ... But [human beings] will be prepared for this only ... if they feel the described split, in that this being split in two will weigh them down terribly ...' (GA 200, lecture of 31 October 1920.)

36 Psychologically, the central symptomic complex here is the so-called 'derealization-depersonalization experience', the losing of the sense of reality of the objective world and of the self, separately or together, to whose growing prevalence in human soul life a considerable body of scientific literature beginning with the 1890s testifies. That is, when the first symptoms of man's unconscious crossing of the threshold began to be noticed but are still not understood in their true nature even today. This situation, however, is slowly changing, as the following quotation might show: 'Depersonalization and derealization phenomena are of great theoretical interest, since they are concerned with the core of personal experience. They are linked up with the sense of unlimited reality of the external world and the self and, therefore, they are of great importance for epistemology, ontology and other problems of philosophy of mind. Because of the metaphorical language in which they are described and because they belong to a field in which the physical world and the world of symbols overlap, and where mythical thinking interpenetrates reality thinking, depersonalization phenomena offer great difficulty to an experimental attack. For this reason

they have been largely ignored by experimentally oriented psychologists.'
(T. Weckowicz, 'Depersonalization', in: *Symptoms of Psychopathology*, a
handbook, NY, 1970, p.163.) The following publications will give the
interested student an overall survey of the main researches in the field:

Paul Shilder, *Introduction to a Psychoanalytic Psychiatry* (Nervous and Mental
Disease Publication, NY, 1928).

Konstantin Oesterreich, 'Die Entfremdung der Wahrnehemungswelt und
die Depersonalization in der Psychasthenic', in: *Journal für Psychologie und
Neurologie*, 7–8, 1907, and also 'Die Phenomenologie des Ich', in the chapter
'Das Selbstbewusstsein und die Depersonalization'.

Karl Jaspers, *Allgemeine Psychopathologie* (Spring Verlag, Berlin, 1913).

A literary expression for this symptom is to be found in *La Nausée* (Nausea)
by Jean-Paul Sartre.

For anthroposophical perspectives, see, for example, B. Lievegoed, *Man on
the Threshold* (Hawthorn Press, 1985) and the basic psychiatric researches of
Rudolf Triechler.

37 As described, for example, in GA 10, in the chapter on the separation of the
soul forces by means of esoteric training.

38 This might lead to severe pathological disturbances of the soul, the deepest
source of which is to be found in the fact that — as a result of the unconscious
crossing of the threshold — man feels, unknowingly, the surfacing of the
Lesser Guardian of the Threshold. Eventually, in radical cases, he might be
led to believe that he must call this being 'I'. A real possession by the Lesser
Guardian is then developed which might be compared from a certain point
of view with the 'captivity by the Lesser Guardian' described by Rudolf
Steiner in GA 13, and by Bulwer Lytton in his book *Zanoni*.

39 GA 130, lecture of 1 October 1911.

40 In the above described fourfold, threefold and twofold disjointed being of
man, lacking, as it is, the one, uniting 'I' centre, the student of anthroposophical spiritual science will recognize the basic characteristics of the
Lower Guardian of the Threshold, whose exact study is one of the principal
tasks of the future. This lies, however, beyond the scope of our present
work.

Chapter 4

1 This unity of the threefold structure of the modern Christ experience, to be
described here, should be understood in the sense of Rudolf Steiner's
indication given to W.J. Stein in reply to his question concerning the nature
of Rudolf Steiner's original experience of the being of Anthroposophy.
Rudolf Steiner answered: 'In any experience of freedom, three things are
woven. They appear as a unity in the moment in which the experience takes
place, but the later course of life lets them become separately conscious ...
These three experiences, woven as one, later separate themselves, become
isolated and conscious, so that the Imagination, Inspiration and Intuition
become conscious as acts of knowledge.' (See W.J. Stein/Rudolf Steiner,
'Das Haager Gesprach', in: *Dokumentation eines wegweisenden Zusammen-*

wirkens, Verlag am Goetheanum, 1985.) I have endeavoured to show in the preceding chapters that the Christ experience—though a 'given' experience—is worthy of being described as one of freedom when I pointed out that it occurs at the summit of man's individuation, in the most crucial moments of his evolution towards freedom.

2 The three interwoven levels have to do, therefore, with the following elements:

   i) radiating light appearance;
   ii) a speaking life activity;
   iii) an active fire presence.

These three elements belong more to the external side of the revelation of one spiritual, Sunlike Being, and the clear differentiation between them is possible only through the assimilation of anthroposophical spiritual science (for example, through the description of the threefold nature of the Sun, GA 208, lecture of 29 October 1920, and through everything that belongs to the being and strivings of the individuality of Julian the Apostate and his continuous struggle to combine the old Mysteries with the cosmic Sun Being of the Christ, according to GA 238, lectures of 14 and 16 September 1924).

3 The main indications of Rudolf Steiner concerning the problem of evil are to be found in GA 93, lecture of 11 November 1904, GA 93a, lecture of 17 October 1905, GA 94, lecture of 13 June 1906, GA 95, lecture of 29 August 1906, GA 104, lecture of 13 June 1908, GA 113, lecture of 31 August 1909, GA 273, lecture of 3 November 1917, GA 185, lecture of 25 October 1918, GA 207, lectures of 23 and 24 September 1921, and GA 264.

4 Here the more inward, moral threefolding of the experience is indicated:

   i) the experience of death;
   ii) the experience of evil;
   iii) the experience of the possible complete transformation of man.

5 We refer here intentionally to a 'physical' aspect of the perception of Christ's etheric appearance, because of the wholly unique nature of this body, which in some cases *can* cause it actually to appear as a real physical body. As Rudolf Steiner indicated, in such cases 'only if man has sharpened his eyes through Anthroposophy' will it be possible to know that what is seen is not a physical but a unique etheric body (GA 130, lecture of 1 October 1911). It will become clear, however, that in the case studied here, as in the case of St Paul's original Christ experience at Damascus (Acts 9:3–9), a pure supersensible appearance is meant, which, because of its powerful etheric illumination, is perceived to begin with also *through* the (etheric part of) the physical eyes but does not take on a bodily physical appearance.

6 This is the reason why, in all the stages of a given Christ experience—even when spiritualized and consciously penetrated by an awakened supersensible sight—man should be careful to note that he perceives the Christ only *in his etheric form in the astral world* through a sight brought about through the transformation of the consciousness soul, intellectual soul and sentient soul into the imaginative, inspirative and intuitive *soul* faculties described by Rudolf Steiner in GA 145, lecture of 29 March 1913. In other

words, in this case, the Christ is still conditioned in his appearance, words and acts by man's own soul beings and sheaths. The true being of the purely spiritual Christ is to be found only on the Budhi plane, 'where man can find the Christ, stripped of all that He became on the Earth or in its surroundings', 'where we, in the dazzling spirit heights, can find [Him] as an object of initiation ...' (GA 113, lecture of 31 October 1909.) And see also in GA 13, on the purely objective perception of the Christ through the highest form of Intuition, as 'the great Ideal of man on Earth'. (About the etheric picture-character of Christ's imaginative appearance in the astral world and its preparation through the special activity of Michael, see GA 158, lecture of 9 November 1914). On the other hand, another essential difference between the natural, given meeting with the Christ and the see-ing of His Being through initiation should be pointed out. Rudolf Steiner refers to this difference in the lecture of 17 September 1911 (GA 130) as follows: 'There is a great difference between what the trained clairvoyant experiences and what ... is experienced in a natural way. Since time immemorial the trained clairvoyant experienced the Christ by means of certain exercises. On the physical plane, when I meet a man he is there in front of me; through clairvoyant sight I can perceive him in quite different places and we do not actually meet. Clairvoyant perception of the Christ was always possible. But to meet Him, now that He stands in a different relationship to humanity, in that He helps us from the etheric world, this is something which ... is independent of our clairvoyant development. From the twentieth century onwards, in the next three thousand years, certain people will be able to meet Him, they will meet Him objectively as an etheric form. That is very different from experiencing a vision of Him by means of inner development.'

7 This stage is the *equivalent* of the illumination stage, the kindling of the inner imaginative light through the development of the soul-body organs, as described in GA 10. In the lecture of 1 May 1913 (GA 152), Rudolf Steiner refers to this stage as the activation of the centre between the eyes, which comes about through the transformation and liberation of thinking from the physical brain. It gives man the faculty by means of which he can experience his free spirit self expanded into the far ethereal spaces. (Compare also GA 232, lecture of 23 November 1923 on the supersensible result of the trans-formation of pure thinking through the 'Philosophy of Freedom').

8 This second stage of the Christ experience is *comparable* to the 'hearing of the inner word' of GA 10. In the lecture referred to in Note 7 above, Rudolf Steiner describes it as the activation of the larynx centre, by means of which man begins to comprehend the origin of speech, time and the significance of the Mystery of Golgotha for the evolution of the Earth.

9 This stage can be *compared* only with the descriptions given by Rudolf Steiner in GA 10 concerning the results of the transference of the active etheric centre from the eyes (first stage) to the larynx (second stage), and eventually to the heart, its permanent location in the vicinity of the twelve-petalled lotus flower. It is a heart-limb experience (limb in the sense of the blood pulsation and circulation, and the force dynamics of the muscles) which, according to Rudolf Steiner (see lecture of 1 May 1913 in GA 153),

leads man to the fiery Saturnian origins of the Earth and of his own body. (This past evolutionary perspective gives, at the same time, the foundation for a future prophetic vision of the cosmic metamorphosis of the Earth and humanity through the Christ.)

10 In the story of the Christ experience of the two disciples on the way to Emmaus on Easter Sunday, the three elements are most clearly represented. First, Christ, unrecognized, *appears* and joins them on their way, and is questioned and rebuked by them ('Do you live alone in Jerusalem these days and know nothing of what's going on?') He hears *their* story concerning the events of Golgotha and, rebuking them in His turn, He *teaches* them the secrets of His being and destiny through the Old Testament scriptures. Now their hearts begin to burn inwardly, when He 'opens before them' the inner Christ secrets of the Bible. But they still do not recognize Him. Only after they exercise their active initiative and invite him to eat bread with them (the process of awakening begins to penetrate their will in the metabolic-limb system) do they recognize Him through His *active presence* when He blesses and breaks the bread (Luke 24:13–35). These three elements: a) His appearance, b) His words, and c) His acts — or a) joining them in a brotherly fashion on their way, b) teaching, and c) initiating them — have remained ever since, though in very many variations, the basic elements of His meeting with man.

11 The term 'new' is used here to refer specifically to Christ's appearance in the Second Coming. Originally the term '*Ur*-initiator' designates the esoteric nature of the meeting with the Christ in the Johannine and Pauline sense. Rudolf Steiner uses it in his book *Christianity as Mystical Fact* (GA 8).

12 He has lost his physical home; he has to strive consciously to build a new home for himself in the spiritual world. See GA 10.

13 See the important conception of quantum gravity collapse and singularity, and the role of the observer in quantum physics, developed by John A. Wheeler in J.A. Wheeler, K.S. Thorne and C. Misner, *Gravitation* (San Francisco: Freeman, 1973), and also the popularization of the singularity concept in Stephen W. Hawking, *A Brief History of Time* (Bantam Books, 1988). Anthroposophically speaking, this state of 'singularity' is described by Rudolf Steiner imaginatively as the standing on the precipice of a high mountain on the brink of a bottomless abyss, created through Lucifer and Ahriman on man's left and right (GA 210, lecture of 1 January 1922). In our account below, the same scene is actually described, but from another imaginative perspective.

14 On the moment of death — the release of the etheric body from the physical body — as the moment in which the *Christo morimur* experience can overtake man, see GA 176, lecture of 28 October 1917. The riddle of thinking self-consciousness, as a continuous life in death and death in life, is then understood through the personal experience of the Mystery of Golgotha. The awakening from the death of soul, referred to in our study of the first stage of the modern Christ experience, is actually that same experience, only condensed into a single moment (the epistemological consequences of which are explored in detail in Chapter 5).

15 The Imagination of the released etheric body as the river that runs its course

between the physical bank of the physical world and the astral-spiritual bank of the spiritual world is both ancient and modern. It appears in Greek mythology as the river of Lethe, whose waters, when drunk after death, bring about the total forgetfulness of all earthly memory, and when drunk before conception bring about the total oblivion of all spirit knowledge. (Plato incorporated the myth in the important story of Aer the son of Armineus, who could cross and re-cross the river of forgetfulness, and consciously remember his supersensible experiences on coming back to the Earth [see *Politae*]). the self-same river appears again in Goethe's legend of the Green Snake and the Beautiful Lily as 'the stream — the force of mental picturing and of memory — that separates the sensible from the super-sensible' (GA 22); and Rudolf Steiner referred to it, for example, when describing both the 'drink of forgetfulness' (erasing the memories of the physical world) and the 'drink of remembrance' (retaining the experiences of the spiritual world) taken after the fire, water and air ordeals had suc-cessfully been gone through in the process of initiation (GA 10). As we shall see later, this problem of remembrance stands at the centre of the knowledge drama of the Second Coming, because, as Maria tells Thomasius in the ninth scene of *The Guardian of the Threshold*:

> Knowledge, in truth, will only come to life
> and manifest itself within the soul
> if it can bring to men, in earthly bodies,
> the memory of life in spirit realms.

(See also Chapter 1 and its Note 10.)

From another point of view, it is one of the principal tasks of Anthro-posophy to enable man to develop this faculty of supersensible remem-brance so that he will be able in the future to consciously look back on his previous earthly lives: 'Then [in the next earthly life] he is reborn with this developed ego and remembers himself as this ego. And the deeper task of the anthroposophical movement today is to send over to their next incar-nation a number of human beings each possessed of an ego that enables them to remember their own, individual identity. And these will be the human beings who will form the kernel of the next cultural epoch.' (GA 117, lecture of 4 December 1909.)

16 Unfolded time is transparent and light-filled, because it has been exhaus-ted in past physical life. Infolded time is dark, opaque and seedlike, because it is still unmanifested physically. (GA 202, lectures of 4 and 5 December 1920.) The two cliffs are also our Scylla and Charybdis. The time cliff on the left (bright, expanded) is the luciferic, conserving the past as temptation. The time cliff on the right side is the darkened, suppressed future, made heavy and impenetrable by Ahriman. Only the Christ-impulse in the etheric time-body of man can make both cliffs consciously graspable. (For the left and right dimensions of Ahriman and Lucifer in the being of man, see GA 158, lecture of 21 November 1914. For the past and future from the luciferic and ahrimanic perspectives of human evolution, see GA 184, lecture of 21 September 1918, and GA 193, lecture of 27 Octo-ber and 4 November 1919.)

17 In GA 21, Rudolf Steiner describes the first perceptual experience beyond the limit of sensible reality as a kind of soul-spiritual touch experience.

18 This twofold division of the first stage is most important, because it exactly delimits the place where the Christ experience, without initiation science, is given and natural. This is what, in non-anthroposophical contexts, is usually designated as *the whole* Christ experience. We must carefully distinguish this first part of the first stage of the modern Christ experience from the second part of the same first stage, and, of course, from the second and third stages themselves, all three of which can only be consciously experienced through anthroposophical spiritual schooling.

19 This experience of illumination is archetypally portrayed in the Book of Isaiah 9:1–2, and also in 59: 10–11 and 60: 1–3.

20 In other words, this experience can also be described as 'the birth of the eternal light-form in the resurrected ether'. (See Adalbert Graf von Key-serlingk, ed., *Koberwitz 1924 – Geburtsstunde einer neuen Landwirtschaft*, Nifern-Oeschelbronn, 2nd ed. 1985. About the 'resurrected ether' in which Christ's eternal etheric form appears, see the description of the new Heaven of the new earthly-human Sun in Chapter 6.)

21 That man directly experiences the Sun spirit in experiencing Christ's being has been described by Rudolf Steiner from many different points of view. A characteristic example is to be found in his letters to the members of the Anthroposophical Society about the Michael-Christ experience of Anthroposophy in the consciousness-soul age: 'Man knows himself in reality when he stands over against the physical Sun and receives from it warmth and light. So he must live with the spiritual Sun, the Christ, who united His existence with Earth existence, and receive from Him that living element which, in the spiritual world, is the equivalent of warmth and light.' (GA 26, lecture of 9 November 1924.) Or, somewhat later in the same book: 'In this cosmic year the cosmic Christmas is at the point when the Sun not only works towards the Earth out of the spirit of nature, but where the Soul of the Sun, the Christ Spirit, descends onto the Earth.' (GA 26, lecture about New Year, 1925.)

22 About the Sun-sphere as the true home of man's soul-life, see GA 141, lecture of 1 April 1913. As man experiences the Christ today as a Sun-being, so we can say that it is only possible to find the true being of the Sun in the cosmic Sun-sphere (after death or in initiation) if man has first found Him on the Earth, in the budding earthly-human Sun. Otherwise, man finds in the Sun only Christ's empty Akasha picture, devoid of His real presence. (GA 141, lecture of 20 November 1912.)

23 GA 148, lecture of 10 February 1914.

24 This experience is also described by Rudolf Steiner as follows: 'If we have awakened the Paul experience in ourselves, then we have developed a soul element that is already an outer one in ourselves. If we are outside the body, then we feel the Christ experience as an inward one. This can be called: the first meeting with the Christ-impulse in the macrocosmos.' (GA 150, lecture of 5 May 1913.) The 'soul element' mentioned here, by means of which the Christ is experienced as *inner* soul experience when outside the body in the

macrocosmic world, is the imaginative soul whose formation is described further below.

25 GA 198, lecture of 2 April 1920.

26 About this 'soul-death' and its overcoming, see GA 211, lecture of 25 April 1922 and, further, GA 175, lecture of 3 April 1917, GA 182, lecture of 16 October 1918, GA 226, lecture of 21 May 1923, and GA 224, lecture of 7 May 1923.

27 Here one aspect of the specific contribution of the Platonic-orientated anthroposophical stream might be of value, because, as we learn from the Chartres' Masters, their dedication to the more feminine aspects (if one may be allowed this expression) of the Michael-Christ spirit, was profound. It may not be without significance, therefore, that the riddle concerning the Isis legend was described by Rudolf Steiner in the same lecture cycle—only a week later (GA 180, lecture of 6 January 1918)—in which he spoke for the first time of the great teachers of Chartres, linking them directly to the Mysteries of Persephone (GA 180, lecture of 30 December 1917). This theme is again linked with the Mystery of Persephone-Natura in the lecture of 14 August 1924 (GA 243) and the Karma Lectures.

28 The supersensible looking 'from the back' on a specific supersensible content means that a higher, more inner sphere of observation has been gained; a deeper, inspirative one, in contradistinction to the more external, panoramic imaginative view. Rudolf Steiner uses this terminology in GA 237, lecture of 4 July 1924, in order to differentiate between the ordinary 'frontal' view of the etheric body after death and its view from the 'other side' by the initiate.

29 GA 322, lecture of 3 October 1920.

30 On the transformation of the forces of healing (rhythmical system) into the forces of conscious spiritual development (through the nerve-senses system), see GA 230, lecture of 9 November 1923.

31 This process is that to which St Paul referred to when he said, 'then shall I know even as also I am known' (see Chapter 2, and its Note 11). As was described in Chapters 1 and 2, it is the transformed etheric body, being consciously condensed and preserved, which begins to reflect purely spiritual events and beings. In the case of the modern Christ experience, it is the true being of the etheric Christ in the astral world that is thereby reflected.

32 Pain is the messenger of—and the gateway to—any true spirit knowledge. According to Rudolf Steiner, pain is behind our physical sense-perceptions, though unconsciously. When man consciously shapes his imaginative and inspirative sense-organs, he becomes conscious. It is the condensing and thereby the *wounding* of the bodily sheaths which bores into them the senses; and pain is the soul expression of the ever closer and intimate relationship established with the real, objective world. (GA 83, lecture of 1 June 1922, GA 231, lecture of 15 November 1923, and GA 317, lecture of 28 June 1924.) Specifically relevant to our study at this point is the lecture of Rudolf Steiner of 17 May, 1923 (GA 226), where he describes the inner soul experience of the disciples who lost sight of the Christ in the ten days after his ascension: 'All real knowledge is born out of pain and sorrow. When man tries to enter the

spiritual world with the means of knowledge given by anthroposophical spiritual science he can also reach his goal only when he goes through such pain. Unless man suffers, and, in suffering, thereby becomes free from the oppression of pain, he cannot know the spiritual world.'

33 See Note 44, and also Chapter 5, pp.100–01.

34 In all imaginative perceptions, man's organization still plays a major role, subjectively colouring everything perceived (GA 13). But in a normally given (natural) Imagination, this activity of the subject is largely unconscious; one has to spiritualize the given Imaginations in order to see one's contribution to its creation. In the case of Christ's etheric appearance, this perception of man's share in His etheric visibility is of the greatest importance to man's self-knowledge.

35 This twofold nature of the etheric body has already been alluded to in Chapter 1. In one part are to be found all those destructive forces that also lead eventually to the dissolution of the physical Earth in the heat death at the end of its evolution. In the other part are to be found the living etheric forces into which, since the Mystery of Golgotha, the Christ forces have been streaming, and by means of which the Earth will give birth to a new cosmic Sun-star centre. (GA 148, lecture of 10 February 1914.) (Regarding how the destructive forces are to be found more in the warmth and light ether, the upbuilding forces more in the sound and life ether, see GA 114, lecture of 21 September 1909, and GA 155, lecture of 16 July 1914.)

36 See the description of this substance as 'more dead than dead' in GA 144, lecture of 6 February 1913. This is the stronghold of the Klingsor forces in man that fight against the Grail Mysteries and caused Amfortas' wound. The dead forces they use are the delicate organs that served in the past ancient, atavistic supersensible star wisdom of man; this is the dead cross in man on which the Christ is etherically crucified.

37 In northern mythology, this Imagination was presented through the Fenris Wolf that devours the Sun Being in every Sun eclipse. According to Rudolf Steiner, the same Fenris forces are trying in our time to obscure the new etheric appearance of the Christ. (GA 121, lecture of 17 June 1910.)

38 This darkening of the etheric world can only be compared to the darkening that took place at the time of the first, physical Mystery of Golgotha, in the special 'Sun-eclipse' state described by Rudolf Steiner in the lectures on the Fifth Gospel (GA 148, lecture of 2 October 1913).

39 In other words this means that the surface, auric imaginative impression is 'hollowed out' and 'bored' through pain, and thus becomes transparent to Inspiration. But only an Imagination that is irradiated by an inspirative element can be called a true Imagination, that is, where *through* the picture an essential element of the being concerned is consciously perceived.

40 In this experience is to be found, therefore, the starting point of the knowledge drama of the Second Coming, to be described in the next chapter. It is, as was seen above, the basic Pauline experience of the existence of Death in—and as—man's cognitive foundation. When penetrating unconsciously man's organization, it brings about his normal, wide-awake objective consciousness, but, when brought to full conscious imaginative sight through the confrontation with Christ's etheric body of visibility, it

shows how Death is the ever-wakeful guardian of all steadfast and clear thinking and conscious supersensible perception. (That is, St Paul was actually the first seer who was able – to some extent – to see and think Ahriman in the light of Christ. This theme is dramatized in Strader's tragic life and Benedictus' victory over Ahriman, as portrayed in the fifteenth scene of the Fourth Mystery Drama, *The Soul's Awakening*:

Ahriman	It is high time for me to turn away
	in haste from his horizon, for when his sight
	can think me as in truth I really am,
	there will arise and grow within his thinking
	part of the power that slowly will destroy me.
Benedictus	I recognize it now, it is Ahriman
	who flees from here, creating in myself
	the knowledge of his being in thought form.
	[...]
	As yet he does not know that he will find
	redemption in the future, if he only
	can find his Self reflected in this [human] thinking.

(Translated by Ruth and Hans Pusch, Steiner Book Centre, Toronto, 1973. To understand why it is the necessary task of the death forces to help man develop his consciousness soul, see, for example, GA 185, lecture of 26 October 1918.)

41 On the transformation of the consciousness soul into the 'imaginative soul', through consciously penetrating into the imaginative forces active in the physical body of man, see GA 145, lecture of 29 March, 1913. (This means, therefore, that any *true* spiritualization of the consciousness soul *must* go through and illuminate in detail the cosmic and human fight with the ahrimanic forces active in the etheric-physical foundations of this unique soul being.) And see also GA 121, lecture of 17 June 1910: 'But that which shall be given as the [new, anthroposophical] Mystery schooling will show the Mystery of the living Christ in a new way, *through the transformation of the physical body ...*'

42 This is the first opening of man's fourfold, threefold, and twofold abyss that was described in Chapter 3. It is created through the unceasing efforts of man's ahrimanic being to transform living time in man into dead space, to objectify and materialize – and therefore annihilate – the etheric forces of the world in man. (About the cosmic Imagination of Ahriman's being concerning this great mystery, see GA 26, lecture of 16 November 1924.)

43 In order to draw closer to an understanding of the mystery of the conscious imaginative perception of Christ's body of visibility, it might be of value first to recall the way in which man's ordinary self-consciousness is produced in the physical world. This is described by Rudolf Steiner in the following way: 'The self-consciousness that is centred in the "I" arises out of [the general, astral] consciousness. The latter arises when the spiritual [astral] in man enters in such a way that it destroys the forces of the etheric and physical bodies. Through the destruction of these bodies, the ground is prepared on which consciousness can unfold itself. But after the destruction

162

must come a renewal, if the organism is not to be [completely] destroyed. And so, after a destruction has taken place in order to make possible conscious soul experience, it is precisely the destroyed part that must be again regenerated. *In the perception of this regeneration process lies the experience of self-consciousness ... self-consciousness enters when the emptiness is filled again from within. The real being that is able to achieve this refilling is experienced as the "I".'* (GA 26, lecture of 16 March 1924.) The same process is actually transferred into the etheric world through the etheric death of the Christ as described above. It thus becomes the foundation of supersensible self-consciousness in the etheric and astral worlds. The Christ fills in man's etheric emptiness, through His incorporation in the death forces of man's etheric body. Only this fact can explain why, the more he is seen to be doing so, the more self-conscious and awake becomes man's conscious seeing and understanding in the supersensible worlds. We refer here to this process when we say that the still largely unconscious process of the 'I' experience in the physical world described by Rudolf Steiner — which comes about through the consciousness soul — is transferred, through the interaction with the etheric body of the Christ, to the etheric body of man, so that the consciousness soul is transformed into the imaginative soul. The faculty of a self-conscious imaginative perception is thus engraved into the withered and freed etheric body of modern man.

44 GA 152, lectures of 2 and 20 May 1913.

45 These are the famous words of Wordsworth in the poem 'The Tables Turned' (1798). About the necessity of the deathlike processes in man's physical and etheric organization for the coming into being of conscious perception both in physical *as well as* in supersensible cognition, see the detailed account given by Rudolf Steiner in GA 162, lecture of 23 May 1915.

46 This self-concealment of the origins of the most manifest powers of the modern mind, that is, of the origin of its intellectual capacities, is referred to by Benedictus in the last (fifteenth) scene of the Mystery Drama *The Soul's Awakening*, from which we quoted above, when he says of Ahriman '... so he shows himself *revealing and concealing* ...' As I shall endeavour to show in the next chapter, this is the hidden abyss into which collapses again and again the best efforts of the modern, self-conscious mind, whenever it tries to uncover and consciously grasp the living origins of thinking.

47 See GA 170, lecture of 7 August 1916.

48 See GA 175, lecture of 6 February 1917.

49 This 'ever broken, ever to be newly constructed bridge of living memory of the abyss of spirit forgetfulness' is man's etheric body, in which the death forces (working mainly in the warmth and light ethers) again and again erase the engraved supersensible impressions, so painstakingly imprinted there by the disciple. He feels as if he was writing his picture-script in vain on an ever-restless, turbulent and chaotic watery element, which he is yet unable to condense into an even and peaceful mirroring surface capable of consolidating and preserving his spirit remembrance. In other words, he has not yet been able to drink fully the 'draught of memory' (GA 10), or 'to walk on the waters' after stilling their stormy night surface. When we take into consideration the fact that the main stronghold of the consciousness soul is

the brain (in the metabolism of the sense-and-nerve system—see, for example, GA 181, lecture of 30 March 1918), we may imaginatively-physiologically point to the centre of the brain as the time-place where the etheric cross is erected and the struggle with the death forces, the crucifixion, death and resurrection of the Etheric Christ in the cognitive forces of man, is taking place. When this process is consciously carried through, the microcosmic (intellectual) and the macrocosmic (moral) spirit streams merge, and the etherization of the blood is brought to a certain completion, as far as the head organization is concerned. This is also, at the same time, the completion of the first stage in the moulding of the etheric body, which finds its expression in the shaping of the (impermanent) etheric centre between the eyes (GA 10). (On the etherization of the blood as the place of the etheric crucifixion and resurrection of the Etheric Christ, see Chapter 5.)

50 An essential aspect of Rudolf Steiner's epoch-making spiritual achievement was the fulfilment of the Rosicrucian initiation for the age of the consciousness soul. The novelty of this initiation is, as Rudolf Steiner pointed out (GA 15), the bringing to complete harmony of the principle of initiation with the principle of imaginative sight, so that the traditional separation between the initiate (and adept) and the seer would be cancelled. Initiation—the *knowledge* of the higher worlds—and supersensible *seeing* in imaginative pictures of these worlds must henceforth become *one* in training as well in practical supersensible research. The higher knowledge must lose its oriental formlessness and be steeped in the concrete manifoldness of spiritual colour, sound and shape, etc., of the beings and events of the higher worlds. And imaginative seeing must lose its unconscious or half-conscious character and see its objects with the clarity and self-control of initiation, or, in other words, it must be steeped in the inspirative and intuitive elements to be found in the modern basic initiatory training of pure thinking. (GA 117, lecture of 13 November 1909.)

51 A firmly prepared imaginative consciousness-soul is shaped through the transformation of the first stage of the modern Christ experience. It is therefore a necessary cognitive tool for the study of the second stage of this experience. So long as it is still not firm enough, any effort in this direction will again and again be shattered. In the original experience itself it is—as was remarked above (and this applies as a whole to all the three stages—given, that is, sustained by grace through forces that flow into man from the Christ Himself.

52 'While man here in the physical world has first the separate sums, numerals and denominators, and then gets the result, it is [in the spiritual world] the reverse. In spiritual experience the result is there; it is experienced, and in the spiritual world are to be found the single elements that lead to the result.' (GA 73, answer to questions relating to the lecture dated 5 November 1917.) Here, but only here—that is, in spiritual reality itself—is the concept of the 'evident' in its rightful place, a concept that Franz Brentano applied directly to *any* given inner soul experience. According to Rudolf Steiner, the essential assertions of Brentano's neo-Aristotelian philosophy and psychology can be affirmed only if we take them one step

further into the spiritual world. That is, his division of the soul forces, for example, is in accordance not with the physical state of soul affairs but with the soul's purely astral-imaginative activity, and so on (GA 21). And this applies also to his concept of 'evidence'. (Through Brentano's pupil Husserl and his phenomenology, this concept played an important role in the development of German and French existential philosophy and theology in the second third of this century.) Concerning the fact that any self-conscious elemental-imaginative perception contains its thought element directly within it, inseparably given with its pictorial form — or, in other words, that in imaginative perception the percept and concept are presented in the same, united, act of cognition — see GA 17 in the chapter entitled: 'The Guardian of the Threshold and Some Characteristics of Supersensible Consciousness'.

53 I. Kant, *The Critique of Pure Reason*, preface to the second edition, 1787.

54 See GA 72, lecture of 23 November 1917. This is the source of the justified scepticism of the modern mind in regard to supersensible experience. To the insistence on clear self-consciousness in the process of gaining scientific knowledge we have to thank the foundation of anthroposophical spiritual science through Rudolf Steiner as a spiritually empirical, testable and repeatable method. This method is, however, much more complicated than is often assumed, for example Rudolf Steiner describes how the annihilation of *daily* self-consciousness in supersensible experience takes place, and how, during the experience, a being of the higher Hierarchies sustains and protects man's consciousness within its own. A memory of the experience emerges in man's daily self-consciousness only afterwards, i.e. on returning to consciousness in the physical body: 'So that really those spiritual experiences that are given to us are experienced in one period of time, and become conscious at another time ...' (GA 156, lecture of 5 October 1914). The same difficulty, from another point of view, is dramatized in the fourth Mystery Play, *The Soul's Awakening*, when Capesius almost loses his entire self-consciousness in his first real supersensible experience. (This difficulty of spiritual memory and supersensible self-consciousness stands at the centre of the studies of the knowledge drama of the Second Coming — see Chapter 5.)

55 This is the only given supersensible experience in which the phenomenon of the annihilation of self-consciousness does not happen to such an extent. Because here man meets the only spiritual Being who carries within Him, in spiritual reality itself, the memory of an earthly life and earthly death. And this means that He can sustain human self-consciousness in the supersensible world. The meeting with Him 'face to face' creates in man, inspires into him, such a powerful realization of this self-conscious identity, that man actually experiences this identity as his very own. A further important indication concerning a related aspect of this mystery is given by Rudolf Steiner in the following way: 'The only thing that man can with certainty hold on to [in supersensible experience] is the "I" thought, the thought: you were an "I" down there ... to carry the "I" thought out of the physical world to the consciousness into which man enters is terribly difficult ... this "I" thought when man enters into the other state of consciousness is as a

forgotten dream ... In order to achieve this, help is necessary ... under the present conditions of evolution when the occult aspirant enters the supersensible world, the "I" thought would remain in most cases only as some forgotten dream, if he did not receive help. I will name the help that the present occult aspirant needs today in order not to forget the "I" thought when he enters the supersensible world. For this there is only one expression, and this is the living together on the Earth with the Christ-impulse. This is the help ... You see, the present Christian world has many significant and beautiful things to say about the Christ-impulse. But the one who feels himself entering the higher worlds in a Christian sense knows still more about this Christ-impulse. He knows something of extraordinary importance. He knows that this Christ-impulse is the only help that does not let us forget the "I" thought in Earth evolution.' (GA 137, lecture of 10 July 1912.) (On the Mystery of Golgotha as the redemption and preservation of the human "I", see GA 131, lecture of 11 October 1911. On the Christ as the power that preserves human self-consciousness in supersensible reality after death, until the cosmic midnight hour, see GA 153, lecture of 14 April 1914. On Christ as the teacher of the foundation of thinking self-consciousness through overcoming of death, and Paul's knowledge of this mystery, see again GA 211, lectures of 1 and 15 April 1922, and also GA 132, lecture of 5 December 1911.)

56 We could say that in this active, transformative teaching of self-consciousness preservation in supersensible reality is to be found the spiritual core of the anthroposophically penetrated, new Pauline Christ experience. When this given experience is self-consciously recapitulated through the knowledge drama of the Second Coming (see the next chapter), man has gained the first firm basis for the construction of the bridge of consciousness-continuation between the physical and supersensible worlds, through which, as Goethe's legend tells us, all human beings will freely travel in the future in both directions when they wish to enter the resurrected earthly-human Sun temple.

57 Rudolf Steiner speaks about the light of the soul that illuminates and makes visible the etheric form of the Christ in the astral world in the third lecture of the cycle *From Jesus to Christ* (GA 131): '... So that [through the new power of spiritualized conscience] the soul will be saturated with a light that more and more flows from man himself, illuminating the Christ figure in the etheric world ...' This is also the archetypal picture of the generation of the light of the new Holy Spirit of anthroposophical knowledge, to which I referred in the Introduction and in Chapter 1. This spirit of life that streams through Christ's light aura and is reflected back by man is the source of all supersensible knowledge of the Christ on the one hand, and, on the other, through the work of Christed humanity as a whole, it shapes the light corona, or Heaven, of the new earthly-human Sun, whose centre is the Christ Being and whose periphery is the circle of self-conscious human beings who transform Christ's life into planetary light (see fuller details in Chapter 6).

58 This 'field' is apprehended when the activity of the throat centre, or 16-petalled lotus flower in the astral body, is consciously imprinted on and

reflected by the etheric body in the same region. As shall be shown in the next chapter, this is the point where the crossing and reversal of inner-outer is perceived and therefore where, behind the veil of ordinary thinking and memory, the inner music and word is heard by means of which man's being is originally shaped, in body, soul and spirit, by the Logos, the Christ. But behind this veil of ordinary thinking and memory is to be found also man's centre of evil, the seat of the forces that dismember and continuously destroy him. The opening of man's primordial world abyss is, therefore (see Chapter 3), also the surfacing of his true lower, as well as higher, being.

59 'Triumphant' means here the etherically resurrected Christ, in whose being now, after overcoming His death in the etheric world of materialistic human thinking, a new strength is revealed: to His sacrificial angelic light being, the enduring life-power and creative might of an Archangel is added (GA 154, lecture of 25 May 1914). If we remember that it is the task of the Life Spirit (the Archangel's basic spirit element) to transform and preserve the human soul after death, from one earthly life to another (GA 9), we shall understand the following description of the second stage of the meeting with the Christ in the soul world in the right way, namely, *as a conscious transformation of the astral body through the Life Spirit of the Christ*. (This is, at the same time, the essence of the winter Christ mystery, described by Rudolf Steiner in GA 175, lecture of 20 February 1917 as the meeting of man's astral body with the Christ Archangel; and see Note 63, below.) Linking on to Dionysius and John Scotus Erigena (see Introduction Part I, p.11), Rudolf Steiner expressed this mystery as follows: 'Men behold — namely, imaginatively, the spiritual world — as Archangels. And from now on we have to say, when speaking about man since the last third of the nineteenth century: we perceive as Angels and develop the consciousness soul through soul forces of vision — to begin with unconsciously but yet as the consciousness soul — as Archangels' (GA 204, lecture of 2 June 1921). From another point of view, Rudolf Steiner described this process as follows: 'But our task today is to grasp the occult element in Manas [Spirit Self] in the purest element of thinking. The grasping of the spiritual in this finest distillation of the brain is the real task of our time. To make this thinking so powerful that it takes on some occult power, this is our appointed task, in order to fulfil our role for the future ... But at the same time there must be formed a small group of people who will develop out of the power of thinking the power of Budhi, of Life Spirit, in order to take it over to the new culture ... In our time every single individual must find in himself a kind of a leading spirit in his innermost soul: Budhi, the power of the Life Spirit' (GA 97, lecture of 7 March 1907).

60 As the first stage of the meeting could be better understood when compared to the first stage of the normal life after death, namely, the experience of the Sun of Christ in the three days following the release of the etheric body, so can the second stage be compared to the second stage of the life after death. That is, the Kamaloka experience of the astral body in the astral world, guided and protected by the Sun Being who gradually releases man from his old karmic burden and lets him enter the Sun gate of the pure soul and

spirit spheres. (GA 141, lecture of 1 April 1913; also GA 215, lectures of 14 and 15 September 1922, GA 236, lecture of 16 May 1924; GA 240, lectures of 25 and 28 January and 6 February 1924.) That it is the real higher self of man, which when completely externalized through his uniting with the Christ shows man his true lower self, in other words, that the higher self – through the above-described splitting of man – clothes himself in man's evil qualities and, therefore, can be called the 'teacher' of true self-knowledge or the 'Guardian of the Threshold', was described by Rudolf Steiner in GA 147, lecture of 31 August 1913.

61 The destructive forces – eventually the illness-and-death-bringing forces – of the astral body are necessary in order to create consciousness out of the mere vegetative life of the etheric and physical bodies. In repairing the damage caused in this way, the ego is active, and self-consciousness is experienced. Here we have the unconscious activity of the ego as the foundation of our wide-awake earthly self-consciousness. That is, in man's unconscious destructive evil core is to be found the secret of the awakening of the 'I' to self-consciousness. Rudolf Steiner described it in the following words: 'This "I", how is it created? Because the human being can delve into the chaos of destruction, this "I" can be shaped and built itself. This "I" must be steeled and condensed in that world that exists in man as a world of destructive forces.' (GA 207, lecture of 23 September 1920, and see also GA 173, lecture of 31 December 1916.) This secret is the actual 'teaching' of the Christ in the second stage of the meeting.

62 In order to understand the peculiar influence of Christ's word-gesture on the lower part of man's astral body, described above – an influence that, though it comes 'before' the healing, upbuilding process, emanates from the very same life and love forces of the Christ – we must bring before us the following detail from Rudolf Steiner's description of Christ's physiognomy as he intended to mould it in Christ's figure in the 'group sculpture'. What interests us most in this respect is the formative forces radiating out of Christ's mouth. In the threefoldness of his face, the brow expresses the highest forces of *wonder*, the eyes the highest forces of *compassion*, and the mouth, with the chin, lower jaw and teeth expresses the highest forces of *conscience*. About the power of this mouth Rudolf Steiner says the following: 'With this lower form of the face such a power will be connected that radiates, *dismembers and scatters* the rest of the human body, so that it will become another form, through which certain other [lower] forces will be overcome ...' (GA 133, lecture of 14 May 1912, and see also GA 143, lecture of 8 May 1912. Further, see also the description of the figure of the Christ in Revelation 1:16–17: '... and out of his mouth went a sharp two-edged sword; and his countenance was as the sun shineth in his strength. And when I saw him, I fell at his feet as dead ...')

63 Into the deepest core of evil and destruction in man (in his lower Moon forces) stream the inspirative words of the Sun Being: out of the annihilation of the old, a new moral Sun-world seed is thus created in man (GA 207, lecture of 24 September 1921).

64 Consciously experienced, this is the above-described hearing of Christ's flow of shaping Life Spirit, that creates and condenses in man's evil core his

eternal 'I'-model, that can re-member himself in supersensible reality. (A very similar experience overtakes the astral body unconsciously in every normal sleep; it feels itself entirely fragmented in the soul world, and would completely lose itself if the Christ did not give it the uniting, inner centring 'I' power. See GA 218, lecture of 5 November 1922, and GA 226, lecture of 18 May 1923.)

65 Rudolf Steiner often stated that the experience of the astral world is much more intense, saturated with reality and potent than the physical world (see for example, in GA 243, lecture of 13 August 1924). This powerful character of the astral world was, as recent as the late Middle Ages, still consciously experienced. In the lecture of 30 December 1917 (GA 180), Rudolf Steiner says, for example, that in Bernardus Silvestris' book *De Mundi Universitate* experiences are described that man has when he awakens in him the cosmic night (astral) supersensible (imaginative) consciousness.

66 See the lecture dated 23 January 1914 (GA 151) where details are given of this unconscious preparation of the brain as the basis for individualized earthly consciousness.

67 The bridge is completed when at least a certain continuous part of the etheric body is transformed all the way from the head, through the larynx, to the heart. Through the heart centre, the higher, Christlike Self of man can communicate fully with the lower physical man, and vice versa (GA 10). This means that the normal organic process that serves as the foundation for self-consciousness in the physical world (i.e. the renewal of the annihilated forces) has been consciously transferred into the etheric body; the etheric body can henceforth be killed and made alive again according to man's free and conscious supersensible volition. In this volition is to be found the above-described foundation of remembered self-identity in the spiritual worlds, namely, the inspired and intuited imaginative state of conscious-ness. This identity of man is now the being by means of which the Christ can henceforth be also 'intuited' through imaginative sight, in the third stage of the meeting. His real being can come down and, walking on the condensed and silenced etheric waters of man's etheric body, which is the firm bridge of man's remembrance, find his way to the spiritual foundations of man's incarnated heart life. (The Christ Spirit's 'I' image is the only Imagination that has an independent existence in the sense that it can be inspired and intuited as real being, and taken into the ego, astral, etheric and physical bodies of man as a seed for all future evolution. This is the *esoteric* meaning of Christ's words, St Matthew 28:20, '*I am* with you always, even unto the end of the world'.)

68 The bridge of consciousness continuation is made of these two layers: the moral foundation of imaginative cognition on the one hand, the cognitively inspired moral substance of the soul on the other. This firm etheric web, moulded and steeled in man's evil core through Christ's healing word beings, can now crystallize, yet remain living—serving as a strong and elastic body on which the higher aspect of the Christ can safely achieve conscious incorporation without destroying, through its overwhelming fiery might, man's physical existence.

69 This movement is a movement in both directions at the same time: into a

higher world above, and into a germinating higher world below – in the Earth itself. The 'higher' spirit world and the 'earthly' spirit world are, of course, one and the same spirit world, seen from two different *time* perspectives, where the Earth is the future seed of the spiritual world as a whole, as Rudolf Steiner describes it in GA 10 and GA 26. That the Christ made of the Earth His Heaven has already been mentioned in Chapter 3, according to GA 148, lecture of 3 October 1913. That Christ's ascension is also a descent, and vice versa, St Paul knew clearly: 'Now that he ascended, what is it but that he also descended first into the lower parts of the earth? He that descended is the same also that ascended up far above all heavens, that he might fill all things' (Ephesians 4:9–10). (That the Christ, the Logos Himself, went through an advancement in His own evolution through the Mystery of Golgotha, see Rudolf Steiner's lecture in GA 224, 2 May 1923. That after ascension the Christ could enter a still higher spiritual world than the world from which he came, see GA 112, lecture of 7 July 1909.)

70 Through Christ, Erigena's vision of the completion of God's creation is realized: 'He creates all things and becomes all things, and returns into himself, recalling all things into Himself ...' (*De Divisione Naturae* 2, 25).

71 This devachanic-earthly fire penetration is the final stage of the modern Christ experience. Rudolf Steiner described this aspect of the new Pauline Christ experience in the following words: 'Those that will be *inspired and penetrated by the Christ 'I'*, the Christians of the future ... will understand what, until now, only the initiates understood. They will not only understand the Christ that went through death, but they will understand the triumphant Christ, resurrected in spirit-fire, of the Apocalypse ... those human beings, inspired by Christ, will be transformed from Saul-human beings to Paul-human beings, and ever more will they see the spiritual fire. Verily, as to Moses and his people the Christ appeared prophetically in the physical fire of the burning bush and the lightning on Sinai, so will the Christ appear before us in the spiritualized fire of the future ... human beings will see him in spiritual fire. First they saw him in another form; then they will see the true form of Christ in spiritual fire' (GA 109/111, lecture of 11 April 1909).

72 Rudolf Steiner's lecture of 3 July 1920 (GA 204) is related not only to the modern Christ experience as a whole but specifically to its third stage. In connection with the already mentioned, deeply Christian and spiritualized neo-Platonic stream of Dionysius the Areopagite and Erigena, Rudolf Steiner describes the esoteric spiritual foundations of the Holy Communion as the partaking in Christ's planetary body of the Earth (the new Earth) and Christ's life (the new Heaven), of what we shall call here, in Chapter 6, the earthly-human Sun. And the Holy Communion is understood only if we experience concretely the meaning of Golgotha in the following way: 'What the Earth is, that which man sees as Earth, does not spring from the Father God or from the nature spirits, but from the Son, from the Logos, that the Father let spring out of Himself so that the Logos shall create the Earth ... the Father God let the Son come forth out of Himself and the Son is the creator of the Earth ... [that is] said already in the Gospel of St John; the Logos is the creator, not the Father God.' Indeed, the conclusion arrived at

170

when we study the third stage of the modern Christ experience cannot be put in clearer words than these '... and as a matter of fact, since the beginning of the fifteenth century, we have been living more with the "Godhead at rest" than did Scotus Erigena. The Godhead at rest is waiting until we are active enough to attain to Imagination and Inspiration wherewith we may see the world around us as spiritual, knowing that we are verily within that spiritual world from which the earthly world has been cast off, that we are living *after* the world ending has come to pass and that the new Jerusalem is with us.'

73 The third, intuitive, experience of the Christ as spiritual fire, directly penetrating the densest parts of the physical body of man, brings a still higher aspect of the Christ into visibility, namely, His Spirit Man, or Archai nature. In GA 175, lecture of 20 February 1917, Rudolf Steiner describes man's threefold meeting with the Trinity in the following way: first, the meeting of man's 'I' with the Holy Spirit, or his Spirit Self, the Angel, every night; second, the meeting with the Christ as the meeting of the astral body with the Life Spirit of Christ as an Archangel between Christmas and New Year; and third, the meeting with the Father, or Spirit Man, through the whole of life (but especially in the years between 28 and 42). From our point of view, it is highly interesting to note that all three meetings find their threefold expression in the modern Christ experience. Through the meeting with the Etheric Christ in the astral world, man's 'I' experiences the meeting with the Spirit Self, or Angel (first stage). The astral body is transformed through the Archangel's Life Spirit (second stage). And the physical body is penetrated by the Father's fiery Spirit Man (third stage). This impression is confirmed when we consider the following words of Rudolf Steiner: 'The one who sees the cross on Golgotha must at the same time see the Trinity, because the Christ shows in reality, in the wholeness of His being, that the Trinity is woven into earthly human evolution' (GA 214, lecture of 30 July 1922). In the above mentioned lecture (GA 175), a further indication is given, by means of which the transition from the second to the third stage of the modern Christ experience can be better understood. Rudolf Steiner describes how, in the yearly rhythm, after the meeting of the astral body with Christ's Life Spirit takes place at Christmas, it can best be brought to consciousness at Easter: 'And the great mystery, the mystery of Good Friday, that brings home to man at Easter the Mystery of Golgotha, has ... also this meaning, that the Christ, who walked as it were on our side in the time that I described [from Christmas to Easter], comes now to us in the closest way and, roughly speaking, *disappears into us, penetrates us,* so that He can stay with us for the time after the Mystery of Golgotha, in the time that now comes in summer ...' (Here again the archetypal story of Emmaus lights up: when they recognize Him in the breaking of the bread, He disappears into them, and they lose Him. Had they been able to remain conscious at this stage, they would have followed Him as we described above, wandering further through their being and through the spiritual being of the Earth.) A further support for our description of threefold nature of the modern Christ experience is to be found in the work of Sergei O. Prokofieff. He clearly differentiates a threefold structure, identifying the three bearers of the

171

Christ, and investigates the specific ways of their appearance and workings on the sheaths of man. A detailed comparison between his description and ours lies, however, beyond the limits of the present work, and may be left to the interested student. I shall only mention that Prokofieff identifies the first stage ('the awakening from the death of soul' in our terminology) as Christ's working through the Spirit Self of the Nathanic-Jesus being; the second stage ('the remoulding of the "I"-form of the soul') is identified as the Christ working through the special Life Spirit of the Archangel Vidar; and it is the Spirit Man of Michael, ascending to the rank of the Archai as a new Time Spirit, that gains the power to enable the Christ to work directly in man's physical body ('seeding in him the fiery spirit-germ of the new earthly-human Sun' in our terminology). Compare: Sergei O. Prokofieff: *The Cycle of the Year as a Path of Initiation Leading to an Experience of the Christ Being*, Chapter 12, 'The Modern Mysteries of the Etheric Christ' (Temple Lodge Publishing, 1991).

Chapter 5

1 Our task in this chapter is, as was indicated in the Introduction, to realize in practical experience the Pauline method as the Michaelic spiritual yoga breathing between sense perception and thinking. The bridge of remembrance can only be built with the soul forces gained through the transformation of thinking and sense-perception. In this work, Goethe's method of transforming sense-perception and Rudolf Steiner's experience of pure thinking are brought to the most intimate and intensive interpenetration and mutual fertilization. In this way alone can the given Christ experience be thoroughly spiritualized and individualized and become an anthroposophical 'I' experience in accord with the development of the consciousness soul in our time. The demand for such a fully modern Christ experience was described by Rudolf Steiner as follows: '... in middle Europe, in a powerful way, consciously—that is, in a wakeful state—through what the souls strive for out of their "I" nature, power of the human "I" and the forces of human knowledge should be connected with the Christ-impulse. Only if the German Folk Spirit finds such souls that can in this way plant the Christ-impulse in the astral body and in the "I", only then can that come about for a future culture that must come about.' (GA 157, lecture of 17 January 1915.)

2 Rudolf Steiner repeatedly emphasized the necessity of the limitation of human consciousness both in relation to the outer as well as the inner spiritual worlds. Without this limitation no human individuality, that is no human freedom and therefore no human love, would have been possible. (For example, see GA 199, lecture of 14 August 1920, GA 322, lecture of 27 September 1920, and GA 333, lecture of 22 July 1919.) This is the reason why, if we wish to approach the Christ in the right way today, this can only be done through consciously opening the closed gates of consciousness; because we can then control voluntarily the way in and out of the super-sensible world, and clearly know the difference between physical, objective

consciousness and the higher levels of supersensible experience. As was shown above, the Christ himself is the gate, appearing at the borderline between the worlds, revealing the workings of the two Guardians of the Threshold as two aspects of His own being. This means, therefore, that the practical study of the limits of consciousness, and its overcoming through the yoga breathing of sense-perception and thinking, is the necessary beginning of the true knowledge drama of the Second Coming.

3 GA 171, lecture of 14 October 1916. And see also the fundamental article by Ernst Lehrs, 'The Rosicrucian Foundations of the Age of Natural Science', in: *The Anthroposophical Movement*, Vol. 11, No. 23, 1934.

4 The opening of these two gates is, at the same time, the modern way of going outwards into the macrocosm (through sense-perception) and inwards into the microcosm (through thinking) which, according to Rudolf Steiner (GA 13, GA 113 and GA 119), were the two main ways of the ancient Mysteries in the northern stream (macrocosm) and southern stream (microcosm). But when the two ways are *crossed*—first each within its own being and then, after this small self-crossing, with the crossed being of the other—it is the Mystery of the modern Christ experience that is revealed in the reversed microcosm in the macrocosm and in the reversed macrocosm in the microcosm, that is, in the pulsating world heart experienced through the yoga-will of Michael. The modern archetype of this anthroposophical-Michaelic way—now self-consciously and practically realizable by every striving human being—is the great meeting and uniting of the spiritual streams of the southern Grail Christianity and northern Arthurian Christianity, which esoterically became one in the ninth century through the being of Parsival. The work of building the new Earth and Heaven of the new earthly-human Sun (see Chapter 6), then *esoterically* begun, can be *exoterically* continued today through the transformation of thinking and sense-perception in the knowledge drama of the Second Coming.

5 The greatest question here is: how is the limitation of consciousness generated in the first place? Why doesn't man see and hear and participate consciously in the totality of life around him and within him? These questions, as we shall presently see, can only be answered out of an anthroposophical supersensible research that has understood the limits of cognition as a fully human experience. This is 'the new approach to natural science' of which Rudolf Steiner spoke as arising from the world outlook of Goethe to be found in modern, anthroposophical Aristotelianism and Thomism (GA 74, lecture of 24 May 1920). This is also the fullest individuation of the luciferic fall from paradise—and its subsequent ahrimanic deepening—and its redemption on Golgotha, experienced epistemologically as the knowledge drama of the Second Coming. The modern Christ experience is only spiritualized through Anthroposophy when it leads man's evolutionary drama in each act of conscious perception, thinking and their metamorphosis into clear imaginative sight.

6 GA 153, lecture of 11 April 1914.

7 GA 4, Chapter 5, my italics.

8 Ibid, my italics.

9 Ibid. The becoming aware of the splitting process between sense-perception

and thinking, which 'divides our whole being into two parts . . .', leads to the most significant results in the anthroposophical study of the problem of knowledge as a whole (see GA 78, lecture of 30 August 1921). It is to this 'moment' ('the gap between perceiving and thinking exists only from *the moment* that I, as spectator, confront the things'), where the standing over-against things is generated, that we must direct our gaze: if we could hold it fast (for example, in the first moment of opening the eyes in awakening from sleep), we should be able to see how this split is created out of our 'whole being', and how it is exactly this whole being that is responsible for the dualistic division of modern human consciousness — that is, we should see how out of our primordial world-man wholeness, an 'I'-world abyss of dualism is generated in every moment of wakeful sense-perception and thinking.

10 This process was still livingly-imaginatively experienced by the neophytes in the Eleusian Mysteries, before the first dawn of thinking (Plato) and thinking-infilled sense-perception (Aristotle) externalized the drama and made it into man's — to begin with naturally limited and fallen — individual drama of knowledge. Today, when we stand at the ascending arc of the dawn of spiritualized Aristotelian-Platonic anthroposophical streams, the knowledge drama is returning to its rightful (imaginative, pure, virgin) level, but now as the anthroposophical knowledge drama in the new open Mysteries of the age of Michael. What Orpheus had to sacrifice in his descent to the 'Underworld' (the Euridice-Persephone, the living, ensouled part of the pure etheric and sentient bodies of imaginative sight), is given back to man through Persephone's redeemer, the new, true Dionysius, the Christ, into whose resurrected etheric body (which awakens in man the new conscious imaginative sight) the fiery Sun-lit forces of Michael's cosmic intelligence are most intimately woven in *the knowing heart of man*.

11 This preparatory, pre-conscious and supersensible-sensible act of trans-forming living, world thinking into individual, deadened, brain thinking is described by Rudolf Steiner in the lecture of 23 January 1914 (GA 151).

12 GA 18, my italics. The active suppression of the living reality of the world in each act of conscious perception is described by Rudolf Steiner in his book *Mysticism at the Dawn of the Modern Age* in the following way: 'Sense perception closes off [*schalted-aus*] in the things everything that is not sensible. The things are thereby stripped of everything that is not sensible. When I proceed then to the spiritual, ideal, content, I only bring back what sense-perception previously obliterated [in the things]' (GA 7, on Meister Eckhart).

13 GA 21, Chapter 1, and Appendix 3. The epistemologically most concise and systematic anthroposophical study of the process of sense-perception and of thinking is given in the dissertation of W.J. Stein (1919), written under the personal guidance of Rudolf Steiner. A new reprinting, documented and interpreted by Thomas Meyer, is now available under the title: *W.J. Stein/ Rudolf Steiner: Dokumentation eines wegweisenden zusammenwirken* (Verlag am Goetheanum, 1985). For our study here, this work proved to be of great importance. It is connected in the most intimate way to Rudolf Steiner's book *Von Seelenrätseln* ('The Riddles of the Soul') dedicated to the great

174

Aristotelian philosopher and psychologist Franz Brentano, of whom Rudolf Steiner says that his work indicates in the clearest manner the necessity of metamorphosing the natural-scientific way of thinking into the anthroposophical way: 'If Brentano had recognized the mirror-nature of ordinary consciousness he couldn't but continue his work and lead it towards Anthroposophy, instead of remaining at the gates to Anthroposophy'; (GA 21), and that 'Brentano is a personality destined to work further in the spiritual evolution of humanity ...' (GA 21.) Compare the above with the saying 'Had he [Schröer] attained intellectuality and united it with the spirituality of Plato, Anthroposophy would have come about' (GA 238, 23 September 1924). We can also say: *through* W.J. Stein's dissertation we have an essential continuation and deepening of the philosophical-anthroposophical works of Rudolf Steiner. When combined with the foundations of the knowledge of man introduced for the first time systematically in GA 21, this gives the basis for the spiritualization of thinking and sense perception for the whole Aristotelian stream of Anthroposophy. With such a spiritualized modern Aristotelianism the Platonic spirit of Anthroposophy can readily and energetically unite itself, finding here the deep roots of cosmological knowledge of man with which the new Christ-impulse can harmoniously unite itself.

14 GA 26, January 1925, my italics. And see also GA 203, lecture of 30 January 1921, and GA 214, lecture of 22 August 1922.

15 About the subtle physiology of this picturing process, see, for example, the workers' lecture from 9 August 1922 (GA 347).

16 This is Owen Barfield's term in his book *Saving the Appearances* (Faber and Faber, London 1957).

17 This igniting of self-consciousness through friction on the rock of the physically experienced world is archetypally portrayed in the myth of Prometheus (GA 93, lecture of 7 October 1904).

18 See GA 201, lecture of 16 May 1920.

19 GA 326, lecture of 26 December 1922. It is not without historical significance that it was exactly in the year beginning the new Michael epoch (1879), when the Ahrimanic spirits were overcome and cast down to the Earth (GA 177, lecture of 14 October 1917), that Gutlib Frege published (for the first time in a lecture before the society for medicine and natural science in Jena) his *Begriffsschrift, eine der arithmetischen nachgebildete formelsprache des reinen Denken.* This was to have a great influence on thinkers as diverse as Husserl (who was led thereby to his 'antipsychologist' direction), Wittgenstein, Russell, and on the whole modern analytic tradition, beginning with the Vienna circle, in which a systematic effort was undertaken to reduce both mathematics and language to purely logical-formal algebraic language. This effort—which was foreign to Frege himself, who could still experience and understand pure thinking as reality—was the result of the final death of even the last remnants of the ancient life and logos in thinking. It is really the grave and *tomb* of ancient thinking but, at the same time, it harbours the *womb*, the birthplace and resurrection of the new Christ-life of thinking through Michael, i.e. through the anthroposophical knowledge drama of the Second Coming.

20 This is one of the fundamental results of the anthroposophical study of man and the evolution of consciousness, from the historical-biographical as well as from the epistemological points of view: man thinks with the same forces with which he formerly shaped his biological organism. See, for example, GA 25, Chapter 9 ('The Destiny of Self-consciousness in Connection with the Christ Problem'), and GA 27, Chapter 1. A detailed imaginative picture of this process is given by Rudolf Steiner in the lectures of 14 and 20 August 1921 (GA 206).

21 '... the growth forces of life are transformed into forces of knowledge only by taking into themselves the forces of death.' (GA 35, 'The Chymical Wedding of Christian Rosenkreutz'). Among psychologists, it was Karl Fortlage who, in his eight psychological lectures in Jena, 1869, for the first time expressed this relation between life forces and sleep, death and waking consciousness (GA 21, Appendix 7). Among philosophers, it was only Hegel, *the master of the most living death of thinking*, who could fathom this mystery of thinking: 'The activity of dissolution is the power and work of the understanding, the most astonishing and mightiest of powers, or rather the absolute power ... But that an accident as such, detached from what circumscribes it ... should attain an existence of its own and a separate freedom—this is the tremendous power of the negative; it is the energy of thought, of the pure "I". Death, if that is what we want to call this non-actuality, is of all things the most dreadful, and to hold fast what is dead requires the greatest strength ... But the life of spirit is not the life that shrinks from death and keeps itself untouched by devastation, but rather the life that endures it and maintains itself in it. It wins its truth only when, in utter dismemberment, it finds itself ... spirit is this power only by looking the negative in the face, and tarrying with it. This tarrying with the negative is the magical power that converts it into being' (G.W.F. Hegel, *The Pheno-menology of Spirit*, Oxford University Press, 1977). When the Hegelian experience of the death forces inherent in abstract thinking is fertilized through and through with the youth forces of sense-perception, in the way they are developed by Goethe in his metamorphosis of plants and animals (overcoming the one-sidedness of both, as described by Rudolf Steiner in GA 6), and even more so when Hegelianism is penetrated through the exercises given in the book *Knowledge of the Higher Worlds* (GA 125, lecture of 26 August 1910), then pure thinking becomes the place of Christ's etheric resurrection.

22 In the lecture of 4 February 1923 (GA 221), Rudolf Steiner describes this struggle at the limits of ordinary knowledge in the following words: 'Anyone who would like to enter, in the modern sense, into the spiritual world must begin to struggle with the inner soul tasks exactly where the other [the natural scientist] posits the limits of knowledge. And in that he begins to struggle with those ideas there gradually opens before him the way into the spiritual world. Man must then take what is offered in Anthroposophy in the way that is really intended. Take the first chapter in [my book] *Von Seelenrätseln* ['The Riddles of the Soul']. It is written with the intention that man shall say to himself: If I remain within the limits of the present day civilization then this is rather like choosing to have myself

placed in a wooden box ... the first chapter of this book demonstrates how one can, with the aid of a sledgehammer, learn to break out of this box. If one can have this feeling that it is possible to take a sledgehammer to this box in which man has been encased for many centuries and if one can come to see the words as the sledgehammer that breaks through these boundaries then one can approach the soul and spiritual realms.' (For a detailed description of the cause of the limits of knowledge, as it is seen through imaginative sight in the astral aura of man, see GA 183, lecture of 18 August 1918.)

23 This blind spot became rather a truism of modern philosophy: as the eye cannot see itself, so can the mind never perceive its original source (Wittgenstein, *Tractatus Logicus Philosophicus*, 1922, 5. 633). This problem was already delimited by Fichte: 'Our eye itself stands in our eye's way' (*Anweisungen zum Seligen Leben*, 5), and he called it the 'irrational abyss' (*hiatus irrationalis*). Without entering with our whole soul force into this abyss, and feeling it personally as our own absolute crisis of knowledge there can be no true knowledge drama born out of Anthroposophy, and no true experience of the crucified and resurrected Christ at the limits of knowledge.

24 With this picture we again put in the right place, namely, in the self-conscious 'I' of man that strives for ever strengthened and widened spiritual activity, what Heidegger described from exactly the opposite and wrong side, that is, from the dead concept of Being. If we bear this in mind, we can fully appreciate the — misplaced — truth and beauty of the following: 'Thinking must first learn what remains preserved and in store for thinking to get involved in. *It prepares its own transformation in this learning* ... Philosophy speaks about the light of reason, but does not heed the opening of Being ... no outward appearance without light — Plato already knew this. But there is no light and no brightness without opening ... Still, the opening as such as it prevails through Being, through presence, remains unthought in philosophy ... We must think *aletheia* [truth], unconcealment, as the opening which first grants Being and thinking and their presencing to and for each other ... but the opening of presence concealing itself, the opening of a self-concealing sheltering.' (M. Heidegger, *Zur sache des Denkens*, Max Niemeyer Verlag, Tübingen, 1968, p.61. English translation in: M. Heidegger, *Basic Writing, the End of Philosophy and the Task of Thinking*, Routledge & Kegan Paul, 1978.) The only real element of Being that does not suffer the fate of *total* death and extinction, in the experience of pure, thinking self-consciousness is the self-conscious 'I' activity brought about through the experience of the life, death and resurrection of Christ in the physical *as well as* in the etheric world in the twentieth century. If Heidegger had had *this* experience of the redemption of thinking through the living, fully human Being of the 'I', 'Anthroposophy would have come about'. That is, he would have found in the ego of man, instead of abstract being, the spiritually-substantial Imagination of the 'I' of Christ, which can be found today only in pure, willed thinking, which is 'love in its spiritual form' (*The Philosophy of Freedom*). Then, through the experience of the *real* picture of this 'I' in man's own 'I' he would have cancelled *in a fully Christian way* the self-cancelling of truth (*aletheia*), and could have drunk the 'remembrance draught' from

177

Christ's foundation of new life from the other side of the life-and-consciousness-annihilating stream of *Lethe*, of whose existence he was powerfully aware but could neither rightly locate nor clearly observe it. Through *this* opening—and through it alone—he could have come back to everyday consciousness with Christ-imbued consciousness.

25 'This I cannot do', means here, of course, only within the limits of ordinary, objective consciousness. At this point a crucial moment in the development of the philosophical thinking of our century must be mentioned. It concerns the problem of the relationship between the real 'I' being of man and his ordinary self-consciousness. Through it, we can look deeply into the secret foundations of the spiritual struggle of our times, as it developed itself without any (external) connection with Anthroposophy, and yet is most intimately connected with its fundamental epistemological as well as esoteric problems. We mean here the critical remarks of Heidegger to his teacher Husserl's draft of his intended article about Phenomenology in the *Encyclopaedia Britannica* (written in 1927 and published in 1929). Heidegger asks: 'What is the mode of being of this absolute ego—in what sense is it the same as the factual "I", and in what sense is it not the same?' Husserl answers this in the following way: 'My transcendental "I" is therefore evidently "different" from the natural "I", but by no means as a second "I" which is "separate", in the natural sense of the word, from the natural ego. Nor, conversely, is it in any way an "I" which is "bound" (in the natural sense) to the natural ego or intertwined with it. It is precisely the field (taken in full concreteness) of transcendental self-experience which can, at any time, be changed into the psychological self-experience by a mere shift of attitude. In this shift an identity of the "I" is necessarily produced; in transcendental reflection of the shift, the psychological objectification becomes visible as self-objectification of the transcendental "I", and so it turns out as if it had in every moment of the natural attitude imposed an apperception upon itself.' (Walter Biemel, 'Husserl *Encyclopaedia Britannica* Article', in: F. Elliston and P. MacCormick (ed.), *Husserl, Expositions and Appraisals*, University of Notre Dame Press, 1977.)

We see here clearly that—as was the case with his teacher Brentano (see Note 52 to Chapter 4 and Note 70 to this chapter)—Husserl's philosophy becomes extraordinarily interesting when we lift his descriptions to the imaginative and inspirative levels, but remains untenable, as Heidegger realized, on the level of reflective, ordinary philosophical discourse. When we remember Rudolf Steiner's words concerning the gradual instreaming of the imaginative element into the intellectual life of our time, as an outcome of the influence of Michael (GA 26, January 1925), we can see in the above a certain example of this, which occurs again and again in the European philosophical development of this century, and which, in the light of the modern Christ experience, deserves special attention.

26 GA 4, Chapter 3. It is precisely in this dualistic fact that we have our secure stronghold of self-conscious thinking and cognition in the physical world. We can consciously take hold of our past, dead thinking and, when we harmoniously unite this thinking with sense-perception, we create an

objective picture of an objective world. But in order to reach the spiritual world, we have to cancel the unconscious, original, supersensible-sensible deadening effect on our own physical-etheric organism which occurs before each act of ordinary cognition. The devitalization of time in the brain then stops, and a living experience of time consciously takes its place.

27 To cancel the concealment of the living spirit means to *actively* suppress the suppression of the life of the spirit that takes place in each unconscious act of cognition. And this means, therefore, to *awaken* a real, self-conscious spiritual activity in its place: 'In this suppression activity, the other, the activity of spiritual knowledge, wakes up' (GA 36).

28 That is, we open the abyss of excarnation, because it is the higher being of man, his astral body and ego, that carries the future time-stream, and the physical and etheric bodies that carry the past time-stream. (See GA 124, lecture of 7 November 1910, and GA 115, lecture of 4 November 1910.) The riddle described by Rudolf Steiner in the lecture of 16 May 1923 (GA 226) here becomes actual experience, the higher man remains (from the moment of birth until death) beyond objective time and space, and only the physical man makes his way in them; and the secret of time is contained in the etheric body, that being of man which connects the higher and lower man together through its continuous, sacrificial, death and becoming.

29 This 'intuitive experience of thinking' is described in *The Philosophy of Freedom* as a 'spiritual percept grasped without a physical organ. It is a percept in which the perceiver is himself active, and a self-activity which is at the same time perceived. In intuitively experienced thinking man is carried into a spiritual world also as perceiver', ('The Consequences of Monism'). And see also the important article by H. Witzenmann 'Ein Weg zur Wirklichkeit. Bemerkung zu Wahrheitsproblem' (especially Part 2), in: *Intuition und Beobachtung*, Vol. 2. We see, then, that what was declared to be impossible for *ordinary* human consciousness in Chapter 3 of *The Philosophy of Freedom* is here made possible in the first supersensible experience of the human soul in willed, active thinking — a direct grasp of the presently living and active spirit.

30 See the unique influence of Ahriman on man's thinking described by Rudolf Steiner in the lecture of 25 August 1913 (GA 147): '... to separate thinking from its mortal instrument, the brain, and to make it independent' and so keep it under his control also after man's death, in order to create with its preserved shadow-corpse his ahrimanic kingdom.

31 For Derrida this difference marks the 'abyss of irrationality' that opens in between every two words, or between the living, spoken word and the written word and, eventually, between everything and its own self (or essence). From the point of view of the knowledge drama of the Second Coming (see Note 19 above) it is worth while to bring some of his words before us in their original formulation: 'Differer [*sic*] in this sense is to temporize, to take recourse, consciously or unconsciously, in *the temporal and temporizing mediation of a detour that suspends the accomplishment or fulfilment of "desire" or "will"*, and also equally effects this suspension in a mode that annuls or tempers its own effect. And we will see, later, how this temporalization is also temporalization and spacing, the becoming-time of space

and the becoming-space of time, the "originary [*sic*] constitution" of time and space ... *An interval must separate the present from what it is not in order for the present to be itself, but this interval that constitutes it as present must, by the same token, divide the present in and of itself,* thereby also dividing, along with the present, everything that is thought on the basis of the present, that is, in our metaphysical language, every being, and singularly substance or the subject. In constituting itself, in dividing itself dynamically, this interval is what might be called spacing, the becoming-space of time or the becoming-time of space (temporization ... or differánce [*sic*]).' (Jacques Derrida: *Margins of Philosophy,* University of Chicago Press, 1982, my italics.)

32 This universal self, which kills the living and raises the dead to resurrected spirit life through self-sacrifice in order to know itself consciously as world-self, is portrayed by Goethe in the threefoldness of the one being of the Beautiful Lily, the Youth and the Green Snake of his legend (see GA 22). This threefold death and becoming rhythm exactly portrays the inner relationship between consciousness soul, ego and Spirit Self as it is perceived through the forces of the imaginative consciousness soul in our time that are thoroughly penetrated by the new Mystery of Golgotha.

33 'If this supersensible consciousness concentrates upon the perception it can have at the present time, it becomes evident that, quite by itself, it gradually resolves itself into *two* pictures. One of these presents the shape the Earth had during its Moon evolution ... the other picture ... reveals that it contains a form that is still in its germinal stage and that will only become real in the future ... *Every* picture of the past corresponds also to one of the future.' (*Occult Science,* Chapter 6.) What is here described in connection with spiritual perception of the past and future of earthly evolution as a whole takes place, however, in every truly living supersensible perception. This perception is actually *born* when it takes hold consciously of the living present flow of time and divides it, as described above, into the 'two life brothers' that 'stand one over against the other on the two banks of the river of time's annihilation'. This is always the first step in a *real* process of a spiritualization of thinking.

34 About the life element that is separated off from our awakened self-consciousness in each cognitive act Rudolf Steiner writes the following: 'But the life of the images [that are killed in perception] is, however, not lost: it continues its existence in the unconscious spheres of the soul, separated from the conscious domain. And there it is found again by the organs of spiritual perception. So that as the killed images can now be applied by the soul to the sense world, so can the living images [Imaginations], found by the spirit organs, be applied to the spiritual world.' (GA 21, Chapter 1. And see also GA 153, lecture of 11 April 1914, and GA 208, lecture of 4 November 1921.)

35 That is, provisional in the sense of its *location* alone. The centre itself and its *function* to sustain self-consciousness in the imaginative world must remain, but it will gradually serve as a consciousness-sustaining foundation of still more saturated states of imaginative consciousness, that is, when transformed into the larynx and later into the heart region of the etheric body (GA 10).

36 This is the true foundation of the knowledge drama of the anthroposophical Christ experience, taking place at the limiting, negative, blinding spot of consciousness, at the crossing, reversing of time and space into one another, which, through the ahrimanic Death being of our world, is made into the opaque, impenetrable mystery of cognition. The drama of unveiling this place, and incorporating the consciousness soul into its Death being, was described by Rudolf Steiner as follows: 'Man should not give up the drama of knowledge in favour of the grammar of knowledge; also the fear that he might fall into the abyss of individuation must not hold him back, because man arises out of this abyss united with many spirits, and experiences himself in kinship with them. So is man born out of the spiritual world, but he took in Death, became himself the annihilator of the becoming, experiences it in a spiritual way and is present in its annihilation.' (GA 40) For more about the knowledge drama, see the lecture of 5 November 1917 (GA 73).

37 Historically, to abstract the dead logic out of the living Logos was the destiny of Aristotle, as Rudolf Steiner pointed out in the lecture of 9 April 1921 (GA 204).

38 The modern mind, precisely the most sensitive, must, tragically, have a different experience. A line of Ashbery says:

> Perhaps an angel looks like everything
> we have forgotten.

This truth is beautifully expressed by W. Benjamin: 'The angel, however, resembles all from which I have had to part: persons and above all things. In the things I no longer have, he resides. He makes them transparent.' (In: Harold Bloom, *The Breaking of Form, Deconstruction and Criticism*, New York, 1986). The Christed being of Death, that is, the ahrimanic, unlawful ruler of this world, made transparent to eternal life, thus revealing the true form of the Father source of the world through Christ, is described by Rudolf Steiner in GA 112, lecture of 6 July 1909 ('In truth, Death is the life giver').

39 The release of human consciousness from its living participation in the external world, that is, its individuation in every act of self-conscious cognition, is the work of Michael in the age of the consciousness soul. Rudolf Steiner described it in the following way: 'That which lights up in the human soul in this way [in every sense-impression] must not have a duration. For if man did not eliminate it from his consciousness quickly enough he would lose himself in this content of consciousness. He would no longer be himself. Nor must this content of consciousness crystallize into real being. It must remain a *picture* ... Lucifer strives so to condense the impressions of the outer world in the human being that they may continuously shine as ideation in his consciousness ... Michael's force does not allow that which is painted in the inner light to crystallize into real being, but keeps it in the state of fleeting picture.' (GA 26, 'The freedom of man in the age of Michael', January 1925.)

40 'From a cosmic being man has become an earthly being. He has the potentiality to become a cosmic being once again, when as an earthly being he has become himself ... since the Christ-impulse has been living with the

Earth, man in his self-consciousness is given back again to the cosmos.' (GA 26, January 1925.)

41 GA 155, lecture of 16 July 1914. On the ahrimanic process by means of which these shadow beings are created out of man's thinking, see GA 147, lecture of 25 August 1913.

42 GA 110, lecture of 12 April 1909.

43 The abyss, or the stream of time's annihilation, is the esoteric expression for the ordinary physical and etheric process taking place in the nerve-sense system, which, when the consciousness soul is consciously transformed into the imaginative soul, appears, imaginatively, in the form of an abyss or stream of life-, time- and substance-destroying forces: '... in the human being, his head formation actually annihilates his cosmic past ... so that we can say: in the head extremity the human being annihilates his past. Thereby he becomes, as a being of nerves and senses, the carrier of pictures, has a picture experience; a picture experience that weaves in the [devitalized, abstracted] etheric.' (GA 208, lecture of 30 October 1921.)

44 GA 128, lecture of 23 March 1911. And compare also the lecture of 24 March 1920 (GA 312).

45 'When the hypophysis surrounds the epiphysis with golden streams, it will be the point of time when the transformation of the astral body to Spirit Self, Manas, has been carried so far that the etheric body can be transformed into Budhi' (GA 264, lecture of 7 January 1908). In the far future this process will densify itself to new physical formations: 'The heart organ of the future will be the hypophysis and the future creative eye will be the epiphysis' (GA 93a, lecture of 30 September 1905).

46 'There must the lightning of will strike directly into thinking itself!' (GA 217, lecture of 7 October 1922).

47 Compare with the lecture of 16 May 1920 (GA 201): 'Christianity will not be understood until we can say: precisely in the realm of warmth there takes place in man a transformation through which matter is annihilated and mere picture-being is pressed out of matter. But this picture-being is made into new reality through the uniting of the human soul with the Christ substance.' This is, from another point of view, the inner process of the etherization of the blood, described in GA 129, lecture of 25 August 1911, and GA 130, lecture of 10 November 1911.

48 GA 102, lecture of 13 April 1908. This weaving of the spring-Easter Raphael Mysteries and the autumn Michael Mysteries is described by Rudolf Steiner thus: 'Easter thought: he is laid in the grave, he is resurrected. Michaelmas thought: he is resurrected and can peacefully be put in the grave' (GA 223, lecture of 1 April 1923). And further: 'So that man must find through the resurrection of Christ the strength to die in Christ, that is, to receive the resurrected Christ into his soul during earthly life, so that he can die in Him. That means that man dies not as a dead being, but livingly.' (GA 223, lecture of 2 April 1923.) And also: 'Easter festival: first death, then resurrection. Michael festival: first resurrection of soul, then death.' (GA 223, lecture of 1 October 1923. See also Note 105 below.)

49 That the deeper being of the Guardian manifests itself not only in external fearful Imaginations but in a far more inward, inspirative manner, as a

breakdown and breakthrough of spirit knowledge and supersensible cognition is described by Rudolf Steiner as follows: 'The one who strives towards the supersensible world strives to meet the Guardian of the Threshold. But to meet this Guardian of the Threshold is not such a simple thing as having a dreamy Imagination ... The meeting with the Guardian of the Threshold is a tragedy, a life-struggle in regard to all concepts of knowledge, to all laws of knowledge, and in regard to all the connections of man with the spiritual world, with Ahriman and Lucifer. These life catastrophes must occur when one wishes to meet the Guardian of the Threshold.' (GA 181, lecture of 6 August 1918.)

50 About the mysticism of feeling and will, see GA 4, Chapter 8. On modern physics and its opposite mirror picture in eastern mysticism (also warning in advance against the unlawful synthesis of the two in the style of Fritjof Capra's book *The Tao of Physics*, and its many offsprings), see GA 20, last chapter.

51 See the lectures of 28 and 29 August 1920 (GA 199) on the border zone of the threshold of the spiritual world, where the centrifugal forces (warmth, limb) and the centripetal forces (cold, head) are constantly colliding, and which can only be cosmically harmonized through the rhythmical system of man: 'How man breathes, how his heart pulses, has a meaning not only inside the human being, it has a meaning for the whole cosmos. And when the heart pulse is perceived it is the working together of the different gods or spiritual worlds.' (Lecture of 29 August 1920.)

52 'Where man is zero', see letter 21 in Schiller's *Letters on the Aesthetic Education of Man*. Anthroposophically, we can point to the exact 'space of time' where, in the splitting of every moment that is raised to full self-consciousness, a reversing, i.e. a spacing of time and temporalizing of space, is actually occurring. This happens where (since the fifteenth century) the consciousness soul takes hold of the etheric and physical bodies in each fully conscious act of cognition. In the sense-nerve system, it also separates the life-ether from its organic functions in the upbuilding processes of the physical body, freeing this ether for self-conscious cognition. Rudolf Steiner describes this process in the following way: 'The uniqueness of the present human being is to be found in the fact that a loosening takes place between the life-ether and the earthly elements ... the life-ether of the present human being is not united so strongly to the earthly elements as it was in the Graeco-Latin cultural epoch ... thereby, however, it will come to pass that the released earthly element will enable the pure seeing of the external world. Precisely because the earthly element is loosened, it will enable the perception of the pure *Ur*-phenomena, without hypotheses [in the sense of Goethe]. And because the life-ether separates itself, it will be possible to experience in this separated life-ether that which, rooted in the supersensible world, can penetrate man as Imaginations.' (GA 171, lecture of 14 October 1916.) The first stage in the transformation of thinking (and sense perception) is clearly indicated here. In the bringing to full consciousness of this splitting process that takes place in the life-ether within the physical body through the direct activity of the ego, the consciousness soul is transformed into the imaginative soul, which, as shown in Chapter 4, is the

means of observing and studying the modern Christ experience. It is, in the terminology we use here, the exact time-place spot where the crucifixion of the living into the dead and the dead into the living is taking place. It is, in other words, etheric Golgotha in the place of Calvary, where man experiences the mystery of Good Friday, Easter Saturday and Easter morning as his own personal drama of knowledge in the etheric world.

53 About such a necessary reversal of the activity and meaning of thinking during the crossing of the threshold, compare, for example, with the answering of the question about Marx's materialistic conception of history given by Rudolf Steiner at the end of the lecture at Zurich on 7 November 1917 (GA 73 — one pays attention to place and date!).

54 See the description of this process in Rudolf Steiner's own spiritual development given in GA 243, lecture of 20 August 1924. His struggle in the time of his anthroposophical activity within the Theosophical Society with the Moon teachers who would not accept the new ego-directed and controlled spiritual-scientific research, repeated and in a sense recapitulated on a Christed level the tremendous cosmic fight between Jehovah and Lucifer on the control of the emancipation and individuation process of human consciousness (see GA 94, lecture of 13 June 1906). However, as the later life and spirit struggles of Rudolf Steiner demonstrated, today not only the struggle with Lucifer (in the new way) is decisive but the direct struggle between the Michael-Christ impulse and Ahriman, which takes place not in the Moon-sphere *above* but in the earthly, ahrimanic Moon-sphere *below*, 'under the Earth'.

55 'But if we once succeed in really finding life in thinking, we shall know that swimming in mere feelings, or being intuitively aware of the will element, cannot even be compared with the inner wealth and the self-sustaining yet ever-moving experience of this life of thinking, let alone be ranked above it. It is owing precisely to this wealth, to this inward abundance of experience, that the counter-image of thinking which presents itself to our ordinary attitude of soul appears lifeless and abstract. No other activity of the human soul is so easily misunderstood as thinking. Will and feeling still fill the soul with warmth, even when we live through the original event again in retrospect. Thinking all too readily leaves us cold in recollection; it is as if the life of the soul had dried out. Yet this is really nothing but the strongly marked shadow of its real nature — warm, luminous and penetrating deeply into the phenomena of the world. This penetration is brought about by a power flowing through the activity of thinking itself — the power of love in its spiritual form.' (GA 4, 1918, addition to Chapter 8.)

56 See also GA 76, lecture of 4 April 1921.

57 'It is the will that brings about logic, and logic is not primarily a discipline of thinking but of the way in which the will orders and connects thought-pictures ...' (GA 205, lecture of 8 July 1921.)

58 This is also, from another point of view, the picture of the ahrimanic and luciferic influences in the etheric body, according to Rudolf Steiner's lecture of 22 November 1914 (GA 158). It should be noticed that dark and light are used here in the sense of will and thinking, heaviness and lightness, according to the first natural-scientific lecture cycle (GA 320, lecture of 24

and 29 December 1919), and future and past, respectively, according to GA 202, lecture of 4 May 1920.

59 'The will, which is based on metabolic processes, is not experienced in a much higher state of consciousness than that of the completely dark consciousness of sleep . . . Man experiences the will in a wholly different manner than mental pictures. The latter he experiences as he experiences a coloured surface; the will [he experiences] as if it was a black spot in this coloured field. Man "sees" it in the field precisely because, contrary to the surrounding surface from which colour effects proceed, from this spot no such effects are received: "man pictures the will" because in the experience of the mental image, at specific places, there is added that which is not pictured, that places itself in wakeful conscious experience in a way similar to the experience of sleep in the course of the day.' (GA 21, Appendix 6.)

60 This happens when the two main impulses of the fifth post-Atlantean epoch (the Anglo-German element) truly come together and enhance each other in the human soul: when the instinctive forces of the consciousness soul in the West connected to the nerve-sense system are penetrated and transformed through the forces of the Middle European element, which live and work in the ego-warmth processes of the head (GA 181, lecture of 30 March 1918). Only then can the consciousness soul be spiritualized into the imaginative soul and open itself in the right way towards the instreaming Spirit Self element that comes from the future, from the Slavic East.

61 In the lecture of 22 August 1919 (GA 293), Rudolf Steiner describes the head organization of man as being 'spat in disgust' out of the cosmos, rejected by the living universe in order to be the seat of human freedom. The same repulsion is also taking place within man himself, between his will (carried through the blood) and his mental images (based on the nerve-sense system). Only in the places where the two merge with one another does the higher soul and spirit life develop. And this happens when thinking is truly willed (see GA 293, lecture of 23 August 1919). In the fight against the dead sedimentation process taking place in each act of cognition, the true 'I' of man comes to itself as a free, 'bridged' self (i.e. that consciously links ordinary, objective self-consciousness with its supersensible being and activity). Rudolf Steiner expressed it in the following way: 'We do not gain a sight of the real "I" before we can observe this inner sedimentation process. The "I" lives naturally in man, but man grasps this "I" because he experiences the death process, the process of inner decomposition. And the one who has grasped that the "I" is a tireless fighter against this death process has grasped that the "I" is a being that, as such, has nothing to do with death . . . Man enters a realm where death has no significance . . . So we come to the "I" when we study death . . .' (GA 206, lecture of 20 August 1921.)

62 See the description of this polarity in the third ('astronomical') natural-scientific course, GA 323, lecture of 5 January 1921.

63 The 'wound' is Amfortas's wound in the split mind or intellectual soul, resulting from the decay of the physical, etheric (and also astral) bodies inflicted through the development of individuality, intellectuality and freedom, as we saw in Chapter 3 (Note 24). When it is raised to the consciousness soul, it becomes the kindling power of conscious supersensible

185

perception, and therefore of spiritual healing of the torn and tormented soul. But before this can happen, it must lead to the fully conscious shaping of the human soul as world-man duality, as will be described below.

64 The sinking will-seed, 'the excess of force which presses upwards from within the human being through Lucifer's activity [and is suppressed by Michael], will be transformed in this age of Michael into the force of spiritual Imagination. For gradually into the common intellectual consciousness of mankind there will enter the force of Imagination' (GA 26, January 1925). This letter to the members describes the cosmic background of the knowledge drama of the Second Coming, i.e. the cosmic reality behind the transformation process of the consciousness soul into the imaginative soul in the age of Michael.

65 About the labyrinth as a way of initiation for the activation of the lotus flowers from the head down to the heart, and the role of the priestess Ariadne in the initiatory process, see Diether Launstein, *Die Mysterien von Eleusis*, Urachhaus, 1987, pp.81–86.

66 'Man can also call the [real] "I" "the night of ordinary consciousness". The more man fills himself with thoughts about the external world, the more this "I" experience withdraws ... In these thoughts, however, man lives as if in an "inner day". In the "I" he experiences himself to begin with in an "inner night". But the inner day does not solve the riddle of the night ... And the light must appear in the inner night.' (GA 36, 2 July 1922.)

Rudolf Steiner speaks about a cosmic night self and a daily human self, and their relationships, in GA 107, lecture of 21 December 1908. There, and in the lecture of 12 January 1909 (from the same cycle), the cause of the 'time delay', the 'difference' (or 'the abyss of irrationality', see Notes 23 and 31) between man and world is explained. (And see also Chapter 3, Note 18, about the small and great Kali-Yugas, and also below in this chapter on the overcoming of this time-gap in the transformation of sense-perception.)

67 Wolfram von Eschenbach, *Parsival*, Vintage Books, 1961, Chapter 15. Deep mysteries of past and future human evolution are indicated in this 'fight' and its specific gestures, and the key to their occult understanding is to be found in Rudolf Steiner's lectures of 6 October and 13 and 20 December 1914 (GA 156). The head of man is the product of the Old Sun and especially of the Old Moon evolution; its proud upward gestures—'the tendency to lift the nose unsympathetically upward'—is a luciferic effort to tempt man back to his natural head position on the Old Sun. Now Rudolf Steiner describes how the whole body of today will be the head on Jupiter (the shoulder-blade bones will be the skull, the hands and legs the inner brain parts), but the *knee* contains the future seed of the human being on *new Venus*, when the luciferic-ahrimanic influences will be completely expelled from the *whole* being of man. Now man's future archetype is prefigured in the sacred warlike dance that unites the new Grail King and his eastern brother: 'The praying human being [with bent knees, inclined head and folded hands] is already in the form that the Venus man will be' (lecture of 6 October 1914) ... 'let us think now that man at the same time inclines the head and lifts the hand, but so that the two movements are held fast in one human gesture: man inclines the head, lifts the arm and this lowering of the head is the counter-activity

against the luciferic activity of the head. The lifting of the arm aims to bring the luciferic into the arm. But now it is so: in that man allows Lucifer to enter into the arm, and supports the inclined head with the brow on the arm, he redeems the luciferic power that flows through the arm with the Christ power that works from the head; man redeems Lucifer in the arms through Christ in the head.' (Lecture of 13 December 1914).

68 This dramatic fight of the light and dark brothers, archetypally portrayed in the Grail story of Wolfram von Eschenbach as the fight between Parsival and his eastern, half-Arabic brother Fierefiz, is a real supersensible event that is bound to take place in the middle of the way between head and heart of the consciously transformed etheric body. On the first level, it symbolizes the first, still blind, meeting, but then the re-cognition and re-membrance of the two aspects of the consciousness soul into one another—its light, thinking aspect and its dark, will or warmth aspect, of whose necessary union Rudolf Steiner writes in GA 26, Christmas 1924. It is the will element, resurrected from below and fertilized through thinking, which transforms the light-picture-nature of the consciousness soul into conscious imaginative faculty.

69 Man engraves in the landscape of his etheric body—and later also in the spiritual part of his physical body—the most important events on his initiatory way, in order to be able to re-member them into his being whenever he comes across them again in his seasonal spiritual wanderings. And he must come again and again to the same time- and soul-places in the course of his rhythmical wanderings in the etheric and astral worlds in order to achieve conscious supersensible knowledge. He does so in the same way in which the ancient Atlantean and early post-Atlantean man used to create his memorials in the external, physical world. (About this objective, spatial memorizing, which is now internalized through the consciousness soul and Spirit Self, see GA 233, lecture of 24 December 1923). The engravings of the 'battle of the white and black brothers' takes its place of time around the speech centre, the larynx, through which the reversal of the soul forces in and out is taking place: physically, in ordinary breathing and speech, and supersensibly, through the *Umstülpung* (turning over) of the soul in the further transformation of man's bodies through the deepening separation of the soul forces from one another. (Regarding the relation between the heart and the pineal gland through the larynx see the lecture of 6 September 1919, GA 295.)

70 After the transformation of the consciousness soul into the imaginative soul was accomplished in its first stage in the brain, the way to the further spiritualization of the mind soul into the inspirative soul (in the larynx region) and of the sentient soul into the intuitive soul (in the heart centre) lies open. Rudolf Steiner says that 'It is only when a man has penetrated with his "I" as far as the consciousness soul that he is able to transform his consciousness soul into the imaginative soul; the rest follows as a matter of course because he has already passed through the other stages' (GA 145, lecture of 29 March 1913). (By the 'other stages' is meant here the whole range of preparatory exercises.) As was already pointed out in Chapter 4 (see also Note 5 there), the *whole* soul thus transformed is the basis of the

imaginative perception activated through the modern Christ experience. But we should distinguish this thoroughly inspired and intuited *imaginative* faculty, based on the transformation of the three *soul* members, from the fully developed and independent Inspiration and Intuition, which are the outcome of the spiritualization of the etheric and physical *bodies* respectively (GA 13). On the other hand, it must be clear that a *certain* spiritualization of these bodies is bound to occur through the transformation of the soul members indicated here. This transformation stands, therefore, half-way between the change caused in the bodies by the natural soul development and their full spiritualization in the highest stages of initiation.

71 See GA 122, lecture of 18 August 1910. Rudolf Steiner shows in the second lecture of this cycle (18 August 1910) that in the Hebrew language man has still a direct inspirative-imaginative sounding picture script of this stage of creation. That these stages of world evolution do presently co-exist in the inner being of man, see, for example, GA 234, lecture of 20 January 1924.

72 In the early Christian text *Schazholle*, 'the Cave of Treasures', by Ephraim Syrus, it is described how, in Adam's tomb, the seed of the tree of knowledge was planted from which — on the same spot of earth, at the threshold of the Garden of Eden — the wooden cross was made and raised. There the Christ, the second Adam, was crucified (in the old Adam grave), and resurrected. Old Adam's tomb thus became the new Adam's womb. And so it is also today, in the anthroposophical knowledge drama of the Second Coming.

73 That means: *ex Deo nascimur* — through the transformation of thinking the Father ground of all existence becomes an inner soul-spirit experience.

74 As the physical remnants of Christ's physical body, when received by the earth in the earthquake that took place on Golgotha, enlivened and made manifest the purely etheric forces of Christ's blood that has streamed in the etheric world since then (GA 148, lecture of 10 February 1914), so in the same way, but only microcosmically in human consciousness, the corpse of dead thinking works in the knowledge drama of the Second Coming. This makes visible the forces of Christ-consciousness in the new Sun-heart-feeling process of transformed thinking: *in Christo morimur*.

75 That means: *per Spiritum Sanctum reviviscimus*. When we bear in mind that the goal of modern initiation is to raise to full self-consciousness the pre-earthly supersensible experiences of the soul (GA 227, lecture of 19 August 1923), we can see in the threefold soul experience described here the first imaginative, lower *reflection* of the Trinity experience always undergone in the life between death and rebirth (GA 227, lecture of 27 August 1923).

76 Through the Christ-impulse Anthroposophy is capable of 'giving so much life [to man's emptied etheric body] that it will be able to dissolve the dried-out parts of the brain...' (GA 112, lecture of 5 July 1909). This dissolving and enlivening of the dried and dead parts of the brain is again the function of the (etherized) blood, that carries upward the freed will element of thinking into the head. The above is also the modern experience of the chymical-alchymical process, by means of which an etheric essence is produced, the *Quint-essensia* (GA 130, lecture of 27 September 1911, and GA 227, lecture of

22 August 1923) that is capable of illuminating and enlivening the etheric body of the Christ in the astral world, so that it may *appear* to human imaginative sight. (Compare GA 130, lecture of 28 September 1911 on the Salt, Mercury, Sulphur processes as experienced in the Rosicrucian training of the past, which is transformed today into the threefold separation and spiritualization of the human soul forces, described above. And compare also Note 152 below, on the more advanced aspects of this process.)

77 This is the starting point for the creation of the earthly-human Sun, to be described in the next chapter. From the substance of this humanly Christ-permeated stellar dust of the old Sun forces of thinking, Rudolf Steiner created the Christmas mantram, the first one to be recited by Marie Steiner in an anthroposophical lecture (GA 96, 17 December 1909):

> In darkness dwelling
> Create a Sun,
> In matter weaving
> Know the joy of spirit.

About the process by means of which the building of the new, man-created moral world order is proceeding, when the destruction of old life and matter in every act of cognition is reversed, rejuvenated and a new living, moral (Sun) substance is created instead, see GA 78, lecture of 5 September 1921.

78 This special peace of soul—the result of the most dynamic battle, reversal and metamorphosis of the three soul forces—is the most intimate offering of the Christ to His disciples, promised at the Last Supper and realized after the Mystery of Golgotha. It is the Holy Spirit as the giver of spirit memory (see Chapter 1) and of true peace of soul: 'But the Comforter, which is the Holy Ghost, whom the Father will send in my name, he shall teach you all things, and bring all things to your remembrance, whatsoever I have said unto you. Peace I leave with you, my peace I give unto you: not as the world giveth, give I unto you. Let not your heart be troubled, neither let it be afraid' (John 14:26–27).

79 This negative (empty) thought space, created through the annihilation of external warmth and light in meditation, is a cool, shadowed and refreshing place, the true 'home-base' of the aspirant, from which he goes out on his spiritual explorations (see GA 157, lecture of 9 March 1915).

80 On a much higher level, this *Umstülpung* (turning over) of the whole constitution of man, in the liberation process of the will-being from thinking, is described in GA 207, lecture of 1 October 1921.

81 Some of the important indications concerning the *Umstülpung* process in man and cosmos given by Rudolf Steiner are to be found in the following lectures: GA 84, lecture of 20 April 1923; GA 202, 10 December 1920; GA 302a, 21 September 1920; GA 323, 9 and 10 January 1921; GA 316, 24 April 1924; and GA 318, 18 September 1924. Here lies the secret of the liberated will being, the impetus and director—also the 'educator' of the new-born true 'I' of man, when released to free spirit experience.

82 On the experience of the pre-earthly, Moon-like sphere of living, embryonic elemental thought beings as a necessary experience on the way of thinking's

transformation into pure will, see GA 163, lecture of 4 September 1915, and GA 164, lecture of 17 and 18 September 1915. In this world of 'eternal youth', where also the life- and love-pouring etheric bodies of those who died young are to be found (GA 163, lecture of 5 September 1915), we have the power that can truly unite the south and north spiritual Mystery streams mentioned above (Note 4). That is, this is the inner, microcosmic gate leading the ego to self-conscious reunion with the eternal youth forces of the North, from the Egyptian inner Mysteries through Golgotha to Arthur and Parsival. This means that the inner way of the opening of the gates of thinking leads to the mystery of man's primordial, virgin life, soul and spirit being, individualized ever more when we liberate the youthful will-core of the soul from the older soul forces. It is 'what pours itself into [man's] "I" and which can be ennobled when taken hold of by the Christ-principle. This is what is born virginally in man, which unites itself in the course of human evolution with the Christ ... only that in which today the unconscious in man holds sway, as the last remnant from the evolution of Saturn, Sun and Moon where as yet no luciferic forces were present, streams today as the virgin part into man. But it cannot unite itself with the human being without what man can develop in himself through the Christ-principle ... only what in the present human being is childlike has still the last remnant of that being man had before he fell under the influence of Lucifer ... This the Christ power must newly awaken. The Christ power must unite itself with the best forces of the childlike nature in man, because by the detour through this childlike remnant will the Christ faculty suffuse with warmth the other faculties. We should make the childlike faculties in us wise, in order through it to make the other soul faculties wise.' (GA 114, lecture of 26 September 1909.) In this lecture Rudolf Steiner also describes the Mystery initiation that took place in the awakening of the widow's son from Nain that 'includes the Mystery of the continuation of Christianity', and that the initiated individuality is 'later called more and more to penetrate Christianity with the teaching of reincarnation and karma'. The more we liberate the young will-being in the depths of our soul the more it leads us to an ever-deepening experience of this exalted Being who, according to Rudolf Steiner (GA 264) is Mani-Parsival, the greatest teacher of the free, Christed ego evolution of humanity. (And see further below in the third part of this chapter together with Note 183.)

83 The philosophical-historical survey of the way of thinking's sacrifice, from its first moment of earthly conception and birth in human heads in ancient, pre-Socratic thinking up its eventual death in modern philosophy and its resurrection in Anthroposophy: this is the content of Rudolf Steiner's essential book *The Riddles of Philosophy* (GA 18). The same content is given again, only in an anthroposophic-esoteric form, in the lecture of 10 January 1915 (GA 161), where the supersensible being of philosophy is described as the Old Sun evolution within the evolution of the Earth, and its mysterious connection with the being of Anthroposophy is indicated. (See also the important study of the theme in Rudolf Grosse, *Das Wesen Anthroposophie*, Verlag am Goetheanum, 1986.)

84 A detailed anthroposophical account of this soul splitting on the path of

esoteric training is given by Rudolf Steiner in GA 156. In the first lecture (3 October 1914), the transformation of the etheric body brings about the threefold reflection of the astral body as three separated soul beings that can henceforth freely participate in and hear the cosmic processes and beings. In the next three lectures (4, 5 and 6 October 1914), a detailed account is also given of the further sevenfold and twelvefold splitting of the soul in the much higher initiatory process. Our study here is mainly concerned with the first, threefold, splitting of the three soul forces, with only some preliminary aspects of the sevenfoldness, by means of which the Christ mystery of our time is grasped (that is, His appearance through His etheric body-cross of visibility in the sevenfoldness of the astral world).

85 That this is so we can understand when we consider the fact that feeling's basic inner duality — its sympathy pole and antipathy pole — is brought about and maintained, in ordinary physically grounded soul life, through the balancing, opposing forces of thinking and willing: the will as origin and driving force of sympathy, and thinking as the ground of antipathy (GA 293, lecture of 22 August 1919). When the will and thinking are emancipated as separated, autonomous soul beings and begin to evolve their independent activity and follow their natural attractions in the astral world, feeling is at last released also. With its release, the mystery of the man-world abyss is brought to its first real intensity and crisis. We can also say that, in and through feeling, this abyss shows — at this stage (on the astral plane) — its truest form. This experience (which we have to view as archetypal, i.e. as a recurring experience from the lower stages of initiation up to ever higher stages) was described by Rudolf Steiner in the following way: 'Man stands before the abyss of existence in its true form when he makes the decision, through free inner willing, through an energetic act of will, to suppress himself, to forget himself ... every night [man] must suppress himself unconsciously. But it is really something different altogether to suppress the memory of the self in full consciousness, to submit it to forgetfulness, annihilation, to the abyss: really for a while to stand in the spiritual world at the abyss of existence, over against the nothingness as nothingness. This is the most shocking experience that man can have, and he must approach this experience with great confidence. In order to approach the abyss as noth-ingness, it is necessary that man has confidence that his true self will come to meet him out of the world. And this happens ... this is the inner experience of rising to the higher spiritual world: an experience of a wholly new world at the abyss of existence, and the receiving of the true self out of this higher spiritual world at the abyss of existence.' (GA 147, 30 August 1913.) And see below, when a still deeper, more saturated stage of this experience is realized in the ultimate moral crisis at the decisive moment of the con-struction process of the bridge of memory over the abyss of spirit for-getfulness. On the cosmological-evolutionary origins of this world-man abyss, namely, the 'great rebellion and war in Heaven', see Steiner's description of events that took place between the Old Sun (etheric body) evolution and the Old Moon (astral body) evolution, in GA 13 and, in greater detail, in GA 110, lecture of 14 April 1909. They are bound to surface microcosmically in each human soul in individual form when the drama of

the threshold is consciously experienced. In the old Mysteries—especially in those that 1) brought the macrocosmic and microcosmic ways into a certain harmony, and 2) were still powerful enough at the onset of the fourth cultural epoch to have integrated into their actual practice what in the other Mysteries was celebrated only as spiritual apocalyptic prophecy, namely, the Mystery of Golgotha—this drama was especially strongly experienced. Such Mysteries were Ephesus and Eleusis in Asia Minor and Greece, and Hibernia in Ireland, whose last living echo lasted up to the very end of the twelfth century (in Chartres) and, in isolated cases, still up to the sixteenth century (see GA 232, lecture of 14 December 1923).

86 This is the voice of the Christlike, higher self of man in the astral world, resurrected as if out of the astral tomb of the soul when the soul has consciously begun its dissolution and purification and can clearly grasp its threefoldness on the background of the spiritual, cosmic perspective. That the Christ will appear before man 'out of the grey spirit abyss' when he will *feel* most intensely his cosmic-earthly duality, as an unbearable burden, see GA 200, lecture of 31 October 1920 (the quotation from which is given in Note 5 to Chapter 3).

87 See GA 10, and GA 147, lecture of 31 August 1913. Such a dualism—and its overcoming through the appearance of the Christ out of the midst of man's dividedness—was developed in the most intensive way in the Mysteries of Hibernia. After the pupil experienced the absolute emptiness of ordinary science and art as the losing of all confidence in earthly knowledge and all inner satisfaction in earthly life, his gaze was directed by the initiator to the figure of Christ. And the words of admonition resounded: 'Receive the Word and the power of this Being into your heart.' (GA 232, lecture of December 1923.)

88 It might be objected, perhaps, that no such transformation of sense-perception is actually necessary if man has come so far in his spiritual strivings, and that he can go unhindered in the indicated direction. This is true, but also much more dangerous. In returning to the world of sense, the pupil of anthroposophical spiritual science suppresses, to begin with, everything that he has achieved so far, and begins as if from the very beginning—from the most simple elements of external-physical sense-perception. Were he to continue straight forward with his separated soul forces, *without* the transformation of sense-perception, he would, according to Rudolf Steiner, later have great difficulty in finding the right connection to the physical, etheric and astral worlds, and his faculty of Imagination may be suppressed in favour of the pure inspirative and intuitive states of consciousness. But the development of the firm bridge of Imagination is precisely the unique historical task of western, Goetheanistic and scientific spirituality in the consciousness-soul age, in contradistinction to the ancient pure inspirative consciousness of the East. This eastern, pure and truly sublime spirit consciousness is today wholly incompatible with the real needs of the present and future evolution of human consciousness. Consider, for example, the following verse from Madame Blavatsky's translation of the beautiful ancient eastern meditative treatise 'The Voice of The Silence' (and such an example could, of course, be infinitely multiplied):

192

'The self of matter and the Self of Spirit can never meet. One of the twain must disappear; there is no place for both./ Ere the Soul's mind can understand, the bud of personality must be crushed out, the worm of sense destroyed past resurrection.' (For this aspect of the East-West problem, see GA 262, the Barr documents, GA 322, lecture of 2 October 1920, and also GA 12, in the chapter 'Inspiration and Intuition'.) Through such a modern, anthroposophical training, the rhythmical 'two fronts', fighting and over-coming Lucifer and Ahriman at *both* limits of consciousness, create a fruitful soul and spirit balance, absolutely necessary for the present and future tasks of humanity's true spiritual evolution.

89 This is meant here in a twofold sense. First is the sense of the first School of Spiritual Science cycle (GA 322), as the further anthroposophical develop-ment of Goetheanism, in three stages: 1) the conscious transformation of the pure-sense *Ur*-phenomena; 2) the transformation of thinking in the pure will activity of *The Philosophy of Freedom*; and 3) the crossing of both purely supersensible activities. In this way, sense-perception is transformed into Imagination, pure thinking into Inspiration, and the merging of the two leads to Intuition (see Introduction). Experience has shown that, for the scientific grounding of both the theory of knowledge and the drama of knowledge of the Second Coming, this anthroposophical method is a necessary requirement, *in addition* to the more traditional esoteric training given in *Knowledge of the Higher Worlds* and in *Occult Science*.

The second sense of the transformation of sense-perception is indicated by Rudolf Steiner in the second School of Spiritual Science lecture cycle, in which he pointed out (this can only be mentioned here) how 1) Johannes Müller's misconception of normal sense-activity is, when imaginatively understood, a true one (that is, the creative activity of the senses cannot be physically but only etherically-imaginatively understood); and 2) that Brentano's conception of intentionality, when applied to the same problem, can find its justification, that is, 'to research how far the human sense-organ suppresses itself in its own activity ... cancelling its vitality and thereby creating such a process that makes possible the experience of objectivity ...' (GA 76, lecture of 4 April 1921). The reversal of this devitalization and death process of normal sense-perception is that which will be described below as 'opening the gates of sense-perception'.

90 On the one hand, the consciousness soul opens wide the deepest abyss between the physical and spiritual worlds in man. On the other hand, it offers the clear and focused 'I'-consciousness and activity *between* pure sense-perception and pure spiritual perception, the gap between which man can now begin to bridge actively through the freedom of willed intention and love for the world's phenomena. (See Chapter 36 in Rudolf Steiner's autobiography, GA 28.) When we survey in one gaze the method developed by Rudolf Steiner through his *entire* life, in his introductions to Goethe's natural-scientific writings (GA 1, and GA 1a–1e), in *The Theory of Knowledge Implicit in Goethe's World Conception* (GA 2), *Truth and Science* (GA 3), *The Philosophy of Freedom* (GA 4), *Goethe's Conception of the World* (GA 6), *The Riddles of Philosophy* (GA 18), *Philosophy and Anthroposophy* (GA 35), *Von Seelenrätseln* ('The Riddles of the Soul') (GA 21), and the *Leading Thoughts*

(GA 26), that is, *during 40 years of unceasing spiritual struggle from 1885 up to 1925*, we can say: for the rest of Earth's evolution and thereafter as living remembrance far into all future ages this method will be universally recognized as the first and therefore archetypal *fully Christ-permeated act of free human cognition*, because it contains the everlasting seed of all further individual, Christed acts of cognition that will ever more recreate and recapitulate the *Ur*-Mystery of Golgotha and its living continuation as the free, always uniquely individualized knowledge drama of human cognition.

91 It is characteristic of John Locke, the typical representative of the new world conception of the consciousness soul before its spiritual-scientific transformation, that he finds it impossible to understand either the activity of thinking or the world revealed to our senses. He confesses that he cannot know how concepts, on the one hand, and objects, on the other, are shaped in and through the human mind. But such a confession means that the whole being and becoming of the consciousness soul cannot be carried further, and that the twofold bridge over the abyss cannot be built. (On the impossibility of conscious spiritual activity in the field of thinking, see John Locke, *An Essay Concerning Human Understanding*, A.S. Pringle-Pattison edition, Oxford 1924, Book 2, Chapter 14, section 13; on the unknown object, see Book 3, Chapter 6, sections 5–10 and 47–49.)

92 GA 155, lecture of 16 July 1914, my italics. For further elaboration, see also GA 153, lecture of 11 April 1914, giving descriptions of the sedimentation of a dying, corpse-like mineral substance in the physical body in each sense-perception as a necessary protection against the instreaming spirit of the world, which would have been used by Lucifer to spiritualize man too rapidly. Other important indications on the subject are given in GA 162, lecture of 23 May 1915, GA 198, lecture of 10 July 1920 (see below), GA 312, lecture of 31 March 1920, and GA 243, lectures of 15 and 19 August 1924.) About the objective devitalization of the atmospheric air in the course of the evolution of the Earth, see GA 194, lecture of 30 November 1919. On the necessity of having dead air (in order to be conscious at all) and dead warmth (in order to be clever) around the human head, see GA 327, lectures of 10 and 20 June 1924.

93 See in GA 116, lecture of 8 May 1910. St Paul's knowledge of this fact is quoted in Part I of the Introduction of the present work.

94 Compare also W.J. Stein/Rudolf Steiner: *Dokumentation eines Wegweisenden Zusamenwirkens*, Chapter 2, p.50. That objects are really 'theories' (that is, already the outcome of a half-conscious cognitive process in the sense of Goethe's 'every fact is already a theory') is also known by Karl Popper: 'Every description uses universal names (or symbols, or ideas); every statement has the character of a theory, of a hypothesis. The statement, "Here is a glass of water" cannot be verified by any observational experience. The reason is that the universals which appear in it cannot be correlated with any specific sense-experience ... by the word "glass", for example, we denote physical bodies which exhibit a certain lawlike behaviour, and the same holds for the word "water". Universals cannot be reduced to classes of experience ...' (K. Popper, *The Logic of Scientific Dis-*

covery, Hutchinson, 1986.) On this relationship of thinking to sense-perception, see also Note 27 to the 1924 edition of GA 2.

95 'When we observe the will with the power of supersensible sight it becomes thicker and thicker, and it becomes substance [*stoff*] ... when man penetrates the nature of will, then is revealed the true nature of matter' (GA 202, lecture of 5 December 1920). And see also: 'What comes towards us through the senses is something in which matter is not present ... these are only appearances ... What bubbles and is cooked in [our] metabolism, also when so refined [is matter]. Inside the human skin we find the real material matter, not in the outer world that impresses us. We discover matter when we let that which is kindled in the metabolism arise in us.' (GA 197, lecture of 25 July 1920.)

96 GA 1, Chapter 16. 'The world-picture which is prone to the senses is the sum of perception-content, that metamorphoses itself without any matter lying there as its basis.'

97 'With this [sense of touch] there comes nothing from an object of the external world into the experiences of the "I". The "I" radiates its own being up to the point of touch with the external objects, and then lets its own being, according to the measure of the touch, return to itself. The backward radiation of the self-being creates the content of the impression of touch ... the "I" content also comes back with the impression that it receives from outside ... these are really always "I" experiences that only received the mark of the external world.' (GA 45, Chapter 6; and see also K. König, *Sinnesentwicklung und Leiberfarung*, Verlag Freies Geistesleben, 1978.) But we can also ask: what is the objective outer force that works as resistance power over against our sense of touch? Rudolf Steiner described this force as follows: 'We tread on the ground and believe that down there is matter. In reality, what we perceive as [material] power is the same as the rainbow [in its solidity]. That we believe that we tread on solid ground is [caused by] Ahriman, who sends the power *from below* upwards.' (GA 184, lecture of 12 October 1918.)

98 'Also, that which is the foundation of the sensation of touch is not in itself touchable ... out of observation, natural science creates a world picture that, through its own being, cannot be observed' (GA 20). That is, the idea of a purely material, non-qualitative world cannot be a result of a phenomenological judgement of real sense-experience but only an abstract, thoroughly ahrimanized dead concept, which, in the course of the evolution of human consciousness, served as an impulse to free human consciousness from its dependency on direct, vital and sentient sense-perception. But then it must lead into conscious moral-sensible qualitative perception (Goethe) and further to the development of supersensible sight. (About the development of the atomistic-scientific world-picture out of the unconscious incarnation process of man in the bodily ramifications of his nerve-sense system in the age of the consciousness soul, see GA 254, lecture of 16 October 1915.)

99 The unconscious thinking activity holding sway in the perception of the eye is a most subtle process, which strongly influences our world *conception* through the unconscious thinking that shapes unknowingly our world *perception*: 'The sentient soul already has in it what comes to consciousness

in the consciousness soul, but the thought in it remains unconscious. It is thinking in the sentient soul that streams through the eye. Here thought substance streams out ... If the impressions that are received by the sentient soul should enter human consciousness, they must be crossed. This occurs in seeing as the result of the fact that the two visual nerves cross in the brain. The crossing of the visual nerves is based on this: that the unconscious thinking process taking place in the sentient soul is lifted to the consciousness soul through this crossing.' (GA 115, lecture of 25 October 1909.)

100 'The experiences of the senses of smell, taste and touch are sedimented as it were on top of what we would have experienced through the senses of balance, movement and life ... through the fact that they [the two groups of senses] are imposed on one another, there arises a solid self-consciousness in man; thereby he feels himself as a real self.' (GA 322, lecture of 3 October 1920, and see also GA 326, lecture of 1 January, 1923.)

101 'When someone has the visual impression "green tree", the content of the judgement "this is a green tree" cannot be found in the directly given physiological or psychological connection between "tree" and "eye" ... the other connection remains in obscure unconsciousness, and appears only in the result that is contained in the affirmation of the "green tree" as an existing beingness. Man has here to do, in every perception that concludes in a judgement, with a double connection of man with objectivity ... When it happens, for example, that an object is seen, and at the same time the sense of balance is activated, so we perceive clearly [only] the experience of sight. The experience of balance remains obscure, but nevertheless it lives on in the judgement: "the seen is" or "this is the seen". (GA 21, Appendix 5, and compare also GA 293, lecture of 29 August 1919.)

The imaginative, rightfully experienced gap between these judgements and mental-sense pictures [*vorsttelungen*] was intensely felt by Franz Brentano who, according to Rudolf Steiner, 'still preserved the last abstract echo from the speaking of the Angels' which was still a living experience of the Aristotelian Scholastics in the late Middle Ages (GA 272, lecture of 19 August 1916). He therefore separated entirely, in his psychology, the faculty of judgement from the mental picture of the ordinary consciousness. Rudolf Steiner says about it that '... through the complete separation of these mental pictures from the concept of judgement by Brentano, ordinary thinking came for him to be only a picture. But as such [as pure picture], the ordinary mental picture exists only in imaginative knowledge.' (GA 21.) (And compare the above with the important study of perception, motor movement and reality experience in Georg von Arnim, 'Die Bedeutung der Bewegung in der Heilpädagogik', printed in Part 2 of *Zür anthroposophischen Heilpädagogik und Sozialtherapie*, Dornach, October 1988. For a systematic epistemological study of the 12 senses, see the fundamental work by H.E. Lauer, *Die zwolf Sinne des Menschen*, Novalis Verlag 1977).

102 What we strive to achieve here is the actual separation of the nerve-sense activity — into which the pure sensible world qualities are streaming — from the bodily blood activity, which receives and materializes them. In such a separation one liberates the pure, living world Imaginations, in which the

true 'I' weaves, from their engravings and entombment in the physical body. (This is the separation of the higher astral-ego organism from its workings in the lower physical-and-etheric organism of man described above from another point of view in the opening of the gates of thinking.) 'When we have a colour impression, which we receive through the eye, it goes in through the visual nerve and draws itself on the tablet of the blood; so we feel what we, for example, bring to expression in the fact: I see red. But let us assume that we made ourselves capable not of continuing down to the blood [with the sense-impression] but only up to the ending of our nerves, and then recoiled back to our inner life before entering the blood. Then we would actually live in our eye up to the visual nerve alone. We recoil from the bodily expression of our blood, live outside of ourselves, are present really in the radiation of the light that streams through our eyes ... There we close off the blood activity, where otherwise normal conscious-ness enters inside man into the blood, and ordinary soul-life feels itself one with the physical man and identifies with it.' (GA 128, lecture of 21 March 1911.)

103 That the intellectual, analytic thinking is a direct metamorphosis of the sense of smell, see GA 180, lecture of 26 December 1917. In the instinctive, auto-matic activity of this analytic, brain-bound intellect of modern man we have the strongest hindrance to the Michaelic spiritualization of the fallen cosmic intelligence.

104 See GA 322, lecture of 3 October 1920. About the great obstacles in Rudolf Steiner's way of research in this domain, in connection with his unfinished study of the 12 senses in the book *Anthroposophy* (GA 45), see his personal remarks in GA 322, lecture of 2 October 1920, and GA 324, lecture of 22 March 1921. The difficulty is the greatest where the reversal of external sense-activity inwards must grasp and cross the inner dynamics of the unconscious will-and-feeling activities of the body, that radiate from within outwards: it is the lemniscatory *Umstülpung* point that must be consciously crossed, which means to undergo the crucifixion experience not only in thinking and sense-perception, as described in this chapter, but *directly* in the will-being itself.

105 'For the investigator in the realm of spiritual life, they [life and death] are getting ever closer ... Man sees how death weaves itself into life, how the dying and the sprouting process merge with one another ... And so man learns in this way of spiritual research to know death already in life, and life in death.' (GA 234, lecture of 22 August 1924.)

106 The achieving of the experience of life and death in the sphere of sense-perception, and the resulting spiritualization of man's experience of space and time, is described by Rudolf Steiner in the lecture of 28 September 1919 (GA 192).

107 GA 130, lecture of 19 September 1911.

108 In the lecture of 29 December 1917 (GA 180) this process is described as the bringing together—now, in the fifth cultural epoch—of the mysteries of birth and of the mysteries of death that formerly were strictly separated: 'The Christian world conception has the mission to unite the two with one another.' This process is deepened and intensified if we continue it to the

human form, as described by Rudolf Steiner in the lecture to doctors of 25 April 1924 (GA 316). And see also the mountain meeting with the spirit child and the meeting with the old man in the earthly depths described in GA 233a, lecture of 5 January 1924, which brings to light the results of the above described meditation: to experience the pre-earthly being of man through the post-earthly, and the post-earthly through the pre-earthly as the real meeting of man with himself in the life-heart of the middle (and see further below).

109 See GA 143, lecture of 7 May 1912.

110 Man learns here to participate in the autumn awakening of the astral body of the plant in the astral world, and its falling asleep in spring (see GA 136, lecture of 11 April 1912, and also GA 219, lecture of 31 December 1922).

111 'What takes place in man at this point . . . is a striving towards a zero or away from the zero . . . We strive for that in which the world does not work any more and in which man does not yet work. Between the two there is a kind of a zero. We have here something in us that is orientated towards a zero. This brings it about that we are free beings, who have responsibility . . . here we have a hypomochlion; there is the origin of man's freedom. There man understands responsibility.' (GA 318, lecture of 11 September 1924.) In the zero point of the macrocosmic evolution of the Earth the Christ is crucified and resurrected. See also the cosmic Easter Imagination written in the Sun, Moon and Earth starry script and Rudolf Steiner's awe-inspiring deciphering of this script given in the Easter lecture of 23 March 1913 (GA 150).

112 This was described by Rudolf Steiner as follows: 'Through such an inner evolution the relation to nature will gradually become again a service of offering [*Opferdienst*] . . . Then in future, to begin with only as a small group, human beings will be allowed to experience the event of Paul before Damascus and perceive the Etheric Christ. But to begin with, man must come to a spiritual conception of nature.' (GA 130, lecture of 28 September 1911.)

113 This is the Michaelic, active and concrete form of meditation, described by Rudolf Steiner as follows: 'You are on the best way if you transform things into devotion. What a lot can become of things! Practising meditation means, really, to turn what one knows into devotion, exactly the individual things.' (GA 217a, lecture of 17 June 1924.)

114 The exact observation of shape and limit strongly activates the bodily senses of life, movement and balance. Then, when we suppress all bodily activity, we will retain their pure spirit dynamics and use them in order to enhance our supersensible sense-perception.

115 In GA 10.

116 About the epistemological importance of realizing this abyss between sense-perception and thinking (a realization that Goethe did not have), see GA 78, lecture of 30 October 1921. This realization is at the same time the starting point for the knowledge drama of Anthroposophy as such. The entrance between thinking and perceiving means opening the gate of pure will in thinking, and of pure world-man activity in perceiving. As we saw above, the will-being, liberated from thinking, leads the soul to its ultimate world-

man abyss. And as we shall see presently, sense-perception will lead us to the creativity of the world-human being.

117 Rudolf Steiner described the relationship of ordinary thinking to sense-perception in the following way: 'How would it be with sense-perception if it could only stream into us from outside — stream as in light and colour into the eye, as warmth into our sense of warmth? What would then happen to us? We must make it clear to ourselves: in our waking state we never let this world only stream into us. When we are even only a little active in developing ideas in our thinking, we bring against the instreaming sounds, colours, smells, tastes ... the world of ideas that arises out of our inwardness ... You see, if we had been simply given to the world of sense-perceptions, then we would have lived as human beings in our etheric body and with the etheric body in the etheric world ... If you were living in an etheric sea as etheric being, you would have never come to that human consistency which you actually have in the world between birth and death. How do you reach this consistency? In that you are organized to suppress and kill this etheric life. And with what do we suppress it? With what do we kill it? Through the counter-thrust of ideas! ... We would have had an etheric world around us if we had not killed it and brought it down to physical form through the world of ideas.' (GA 198, lecture of 10 July 1920.) Immediately thereafter comes the assertion of Rudolf Steiner that in W.J. Stein's Dissertation is to be found the best study of sense-perception that exists in modern scientific literature on the subject. A further important indication concerning the role of the brain and nervous system in killing the living, elemental sense-qualities is given in GA 243, lecture of 15 August 1924. That the killing of the living sense qualities is a Saturn-lead brain process, see GA 232, lecture of 14 December 1923.

118 See Note 102 above.

119 'Beginning in our century, individual people will see the coming again of Christ out of their etheric soul ...' (*Ätherseele*, GA 129, lecture of 19 August 1911).

120 See in GA 129, lecture of 19 August 1911, where the whole Eleusinian drama of Persephone is anthroposophically studied as the dying of the old imaginative perception and its rebirth in the modern Christ experience.

121 GA 168, lecture of 16 February 1916, my italics. That is, when we space out the time difference in sense-perception and open wide its gates we enter the etheric world where, circulating around Hades, the waters of Lethe turbulently stream and stream: we have drunk its waters while still living and entered the land of the dead in search of the lost etheric-soul of imaginative sight. In a similar way, but still before Golgotha, Aeneas looked for and found his father there, i.e. the forces of inheritance that were then still the source of life as well as of initiation and the continuation of consciousness. Today we find there, through our Christ-permeated meeting with the resurrected Persephone, 'the soul element in sense-perception' (Persephone) and the true new 'Christ relation to external nature'. (GA 194, 30 November 1919.)

According to Rudolf Steiner in the lecture of the 26 December 1917 (GA 180), Goethe was the first to spiritualize in this way modern natural science:

'In the field of natural research man begins in this way to turn to the Son if he releases the Mother from the ... atomistic theories of science and turns to the seeing of the pure, virgin-like *Ur*-phenomena.' (And see also Note 138 below.)

122 This birth of light in and through transformed sense perception is an expression of the release of the *light-ether* from its ahrimanic bondage to the physical body: 'Were it possible for the human soul to observe the processes in its own etheric body, it would release itself from the ahrimanic forces that otherwise darken the processes in the light body' (GA 165, lecture of 2 January 1916, and Chapter 1 above).

123 See GA 293, lecture of 23 August 1919, and GA 144, lecture of 3 February 1913.

124 ' ... In that I receive light and its colours, I unite with myself that in nature which it sends into the future ... And that we can receive into our eye what will become in the future out of nature is the result of the fact that we can bring from within ourselves to nature not only our intellect, our thinking, but also that which is also in us of the nature of the will, which is the element of the future.' (GA 293, lecture of 23 August 1919.) Also: 'This is the state of beginning in the external world ... I look outside and see the green plant carpet, the coloured world, red, green, and blue, and I perceive sounds there outside – what are these fleeting shapes that present physiology and psychology consider to be only something subjective? These are the forces out of which the worlds of the future are being created. Red is not something created by matter in the eye or brain; it is the very first seed of future worlds.' (GA 326, lecture of 6 January 1923.)

125 'The human sense-organism does not belong to the human being but is built into him from out of the surrounding world during his earthly life. The perceiving eye is spatially in man, but in its essence it is *in the world*. Man stretches his soul-spirit into that which the world, through his senses, experiences in him.' (GA 26, lecture of 15 March 1925.) This process of the eye could still be livingly experienced in the Christian Platonic traditions up to the twelfth century. It is described as follows by Bernardus Silvestris:

> Every nerve that illuminates the eye with its light
> receives from the brain its luminous power.
> Because an inner light out of the soul
> meets the fiery radiation of the Sun's light
> and its light-ether brilliance.
> From this meeting the power and nature of sight
> takes the substance and origin of its existence.
> [...]
> Because in the eye alone is already the whole man.

(after Wilhelm Rath's translation of Bernardus Silvestris: *Uber der allumfassende Einheit der Welt – Macrocosmos und Microcosmos*, J.Ch. Mellinger Verlag, [no date].) And see also the excellent English commentary and translation by W. Wetherbee, *The Cosmographia of Bernardus Silvestris*, Columbia University Press (New York and London, 1973).

126 The problem of time difference has already been referred to above (see Note

66). Now another aspect may be mentioned. The experience of a gap in space — a distance between self and object — is the result of the devitalization of living time in every act of conscious perception and thinking, which creates a memory picture (mental image) in self-consciousness. Now the power of physical memory is created out of a special condensation of the soul experience of the time element (that is, it is a matter of the events between the astral and etheric bodies). According to Rudolf Steiner, the incarnation of the astral body every morning brings about this process: '[In the night experience] you are going backwards in your astral body and "I" up to the morning of the 22 December and then, on awakening, you rapidly return to the morning of 23 December. You push your soul being forward in time. This is a condensation of time or, more precisely formulated, of that which lives in time. And through this process our soul, our astral body, is so condensed in time that it can carry the impressions of the external world not only for a brief time but as a permanent memory. In the same way that a condensed gas displays a stronger pressure capacity, that is, has more power inside, so your astral body acquires a strong power of memory ... through this compressing together of time.' (GA 219, lecture of 22 December 1922.) When we release our etheric body in sense-perception from its bondage to the brain, we also release this compression of the astral. We undo this condensation and travel forward in time, as in any moment of falling asleep (GA 207, lecture of 30 September 1921). And at the same time the object loses its distant space location and time difference and moves into its real supersensible time element, and this movement is experienced as the flow from the future towards the past. It is, therefore, the crossing out of the abyss of space and beyond the gap of objective time into the real present, or duration, which is experienced in etheric sense perception described here. (On the question of the time difference in regard to ahrimanic influences in the external world, see GA 183, lecture of 2 September 1919.)

127 See GA 18, last chapter, and also GA 35, *The Psychological Foundations of Anthroposophy*. And see also GA 208, lecture of 4 November 1921, and GA 187, lecture of 27 January 1918.

128 'We have in the sight process ... nothing other than a metamorphosis of a fertilization process, and vice versa' (GA 323, lecture of 7 January 1921).

129 'When we see, we hold an etheric conversation with our own being. It is a self-conversation which the eye makes.' (GA 320, lecture of 31 December 1919. The whole lecture is of the greatest importance for our study here; and see also the earlier lecture of 25 December.) The *astral* process, on the other hand, is as follows: 'Here it is so that what the etheric body works through and flows into is the sentient soul. The event here is of thoughtlike nature. A thought principle holds sway here. The sentient soul already has in it what is conscious in the consciousness soul, but the thought in it is unconscious. It is a thinking in the sentient soul that flows out through the eye ... it lets stream out to the object an astral element as thought substance and it reaches so far until it encounters somewhere in the distance a resistance, and another astral element opposes it. This mutual fight between the two astral elements that takes place there outside creates the colour that we sense on the things. The colour appears at the limits of things where the astral

element that streams out of man mingles with the astral of things. *On the border of the external and inner astral the colour appears.'* (GA 115, lecture of 25 October 1909.)

Some valuable studies that can substantiate our description here, which to be complete ought to include a thorough study of the physical, etheric, astral and ego activity of the eye—a study which we cannot enter here in a systematic way—are to be found in the following titles:

E. Lehrs, *Man or Matter* (third edition, revised and enlarged, Rudolf Steiner Press, 1985), especially Chapters 14–17.

E. Lehrs, *Vom Geist der Sinne* (Vittorio Klosterman, 1982), Chapter 8.

F.H. Julius, *Entwurf einer Optik* (Verlag Freies Geistesleben, 1984), Chapter 10.

H.J. Scheurle, *Die Gesamtsinnesorganisation, Überwindung der Subject-Object Spaltung in der Sinnesleher* (Georg Thieme Verlag, 1984), second part, 6–7.

V. von Weizsacker, *Der Gestaltkreis* (Georg Thieme Verlag, 1986), Chapters 3–5.

H.E. Lauer, *Die Zwolf Sinne des Menschen* (Novalis Verlag, 1977), Chapter 4.

W.J. Stein/Rudolf Steiner, *Dokumentation eines Wegweisenden zusammenwirkens* (Verlag am Goetheanum, 1985), Chapter 4, sections 7 and 12.

G. Adams and O. Whicher, *The Plant between Sun and Earth* (Rudolf Steiner Press, 1980), the whole book.

K. König, *Earth and Man* (Bio-dynamic Literature, 1982), lectures 1 and 2.

T. Gobel, 'Über den Nerven-sinnes-prozess' (in: *Der Heilmittelbegriff bei Rudolf Steiner, Referat der Tagung*, 1980, Verlag Freis Geistesleben, 1981).

130 GA 2, Note 1 to the 1924 edition. (Here we come again to the place where, out of enlivened, resurrected Christ knowledge, we begin the conscious creation process of the new earthly-human Sun.)

131 To this 'situation of perception', the life-long phenomenological research and struggle of the French philosopher Merleau-Ponty was directed. What was presented above (Note 124) as the future will-element in sense-perception was his life's element and experience: 'Our own body is in the world as the heart is in the organism. It keeps the visible spectacle constantly alive, it breathes life into it and sustains it inwardly, and with it forms a wholeness... The relations of sentient to sensible are comparable with those of the sleeper to his slumber: sleep comes when a certain voluntary attitude suddenly receives from outside the confirmation for which it was waiting. I am breathing deeply and slowly in order to summon sleep, and suddenly it is as if my mouth were connected to some great lung outside myself that alternately calls forth and forces back my breath. A certain rhythm of respiration, which a moment ago I voluntarily maintained, now becomes my very being, and sleep, until now aimed at as a significance, suddenly becomes a situation. In the same way I give ear, or look, in the expectation of a sensation, and suddenly the sensible takes possession of my ear or my gaze, and I surrender a part of my body, even my whole body, to this particular manner of vibrating and filling of space known as blue or red. Just as the sacrament not only symbolizes, in sensible species, an operation of Grace but is also the real presence of God, which it causes to occupy a

fragment of space and communicates to those who eat of the consecrated bread, provided that they are inwardly prepared, in the same way the sensible has not only a motor and vital significance but is nothing other than a certain way of being in the world suggested to us from some point in space, and seized and acted upon by our body, provided that it is capable of doing so, so that *sensation is literally a form of communion*. ... The sensible gives back to me what I lent to it, but this is only what I took from it in the first place. As I contemplate the blue of the sky I am not set over against it as a non-cosmic subject; I do not possess it in thought, or spread out towards it some idea of blue such as might reveal the secret of it; I abandon myself to it and plunge into its mystery, it "thinks itself within me" ... I am the sky itself as it is drawn together and unified, and as it begins to exist for itself: my consciousness is saturated with this limitless blue.' (Merleau-Ponty: *The Phenomenology of Perception*, Routledge & Kegan Paul, NY, 1962.) On Rudolf Steiner's description of sense-perception as a sleeplike process, see GA 219, lecture of 22 December 1922; on the meditative, pure perception of the blue of the sky, the etheric quality in sense-perception as a whole, and its enhancement up to the intensity of a religious-moral experience, see GA 136, lecture of 3 October 1912.

132 According to Rudolf Steiner's description in the lecture of 6 July 1915 (GA 157), sense-perception, imaginatively seen, is a living infilling of space with etheric light, and in living thinking man becomes 'a time being' (that is, moving back and forth in the stream of time). The point where the light-filled space of perception is transformed into flowing time experience is the senses' gate of entrance into the world's creating thought pictures (or Imaginations) that continuously stream in through every sense-impression (GA 322, lecture of 3 October 1920).

133 To the fact that every crossing and reversal (*Umstülpung*) point—when consciously grasped—is an openness, gate or 'eye', we have already referred in the Introduction, when we described our Pauline Yoga method of soul-spirit breathing. Quoted there is Rudolf Steiner's characterization of this method as it was practised by Paul's great pupil, Dionysius the Areo-pagite: at the crossing point of his positive and negative 'theology' (i.e. meditative practice), the *living* divine being was to be found. And so it was in the above-described crossing of thinking with, in and through the will. And so it is also in sense-perception, where the outstreaming will element of our perception's ray is crossed by the etheric will element of the external object. Physiologically, Rudolf Steiner speaks about this crossing abyss as the space between the so called 'sensory' and 'motor' nerves. This is the place of time where the streams of perception and volition are separated and reunited in a lightning, flashing, 'twinkling *of an eye*' moment that divides and unites itself continuously in every incarnation-excarnation pulse of the ego and astral body when they enter, exit and re-enter the physical and etheric bodies in order to perceive and act in the physical world (GA 179, lecture of 2 December 1917, and GA 194, lecture of 7 December 1919). Rudolf Steiner refers to three such points of springing over and touching of sym-pathy and antipathy (which are the form that will and thinking, respec-tively, assume in the middle, rhythmic system), along the nervous system in

the head, chest and lower body (GA 293, lecture of 22 August 1919). Such an 'eye point' is clearly distinguished because of its special light radiance in contradistinction to other parts of the etheric body that are active in the same time-place, for example, those that serve the nutritive and vegetative life of the sense-organs themselves. (GA 171, lecture of 2 October 1916: 'The etheric body breathes in light, transforms the light in itself to darkness, and in this darkness it can receive its nutrition as world sound that lives in the harmony of the spheres, and can receive the life impulse.')

134 The formative spaces of creative world time belong to the spirit Being of the Sun who, since the Mystery of Golgotha, lives in creative and formative *earthly*-Sun time: 'Since the founding of Christianity *Time* takes the place of space ... What man had to look for previously outside the Earth he can now find in the Earth happenings. The ancient Mysteries lost their Sun brightness in face of the radiating star of Golgotha. They find in it their fulfilment.' (GA 260a, lecture of 4 May 1924, and see also GA 8 on the Mystery of Golgotha as the fulfilment and rebirth of the old Mysteries.) The inner, meditative-esoteric meaning of this time-reversal and rebirth, which is one of the deep secrets of Christ's being, is given by Rudolf Steiner in his commentary on Mabel Collins' *Light on the Path*, GA 245.

135 See GA 236, lecture of 4 June 1924. In sense-perception, the recapitulation of the modern Christ experience leads to the actual perception of the birth of living time out of space, and its dying as space in every single act of perceiving. The etheric, living Christ-light of sense-perception appears when the objectified, devitalized physical space collapses. This is the actual resurrection moment of the etherically-crucified Christ in every sense impression. It is everywhere and always potentially happening around us. In human, imaginative sense-perception, it is actualized. It is the very foundations of the ordinary, but today thoroughly Christ-permeated, space of living time: '... In the moment when the lightning appears, space is rent asunder, and that which fills space intensively, undimensionally, comes forth, as the blood would do if I cut myself. This is the case every time light appears together with warmth: space is rent asunder, space discloses its inwardness.' (GA 321, lecture of 14 March 1920.) It belongs to the essential characteristics of the etheric appearance of the Christ that, as we tried to show in Chapter 4, He takes on its body cross of visibility, or incorporates Himself, precisely at the limit of the physical-etheric world, in man's deadened etheric elements. And His resurrection, therefore, takes its time in and through these forces of death, so that one cannot find a better expression than the above, quoted from Rudolf Steiner's second natural-scientific lecture cycle: '... Space is rent asunder, space discloses its inwardness.' But today the inwardness of space is the Christ as the living warmth, light and life of the new earthly-human Sun; and in every sense-perception this Sun lights up as His etheric resurrection from His etheric death.

136 GA 176, lecture of 14 August 1917. On the universal, true 'I' of man streaming into him from outside through the gates of the senses, see also GA 206, lecture of 13 August 1921. A further indication concerning the light breathing of the senses is to be found in the pastoral-medical course, GA 318, lecture of 15 September 1924: 'When a light ray streams into your eye,

the spirit of the Sun is the substance of this delicate breathing. We breathe in the manifold ingredients of the Sun spirit with our sense impressions.'

137 GA 152, lecture of 2 May 1913, and see Part 3 of this chapter, below.

138 'When we learn to receive in nature *the soul element in sense-perception*, then we will have the Christ-relation to external nature. Then *this Christ-relation to external nature* will be something like a spiritual breathing process.' (GA 194, lecture of 30 November 1919, my italics.) This is the etheric 'light breathing' in which the crossing, reversal and mutual fertilization of man-world, world-man can be experienced imaginatively, already in sense-perception, as Christ's living rhythm in the new life and light spheres of the earthly-human Sun.

139 GA 66, lecture of 17 March 1917.

140 'We only have dead light today. However, the Christ once drew in on the rays of this dead light and fulfilled the Mystery of Golgotha. This is the great cosmic secret of our modern time. Albeit we have dead light. Dead light cannot make us happy. The Christ drew in upon Earth on the rays of dead light and fulfilled the Mystery of Golgotha. If we have dead light outside ourselves today, then we can enliven the Christ in ourselves. With the Christ in ourselves in the right way, we enliven all light on the Earth around, carry life into the dead light and have ourselves an enlivening effect on the light.' (GA 218, lecture of 23 October 1922.)

141 See GA 253, lecture of 14 September 1915.

142 GA 22, and see also Note 55 to Chapter 4.

143 GA 17. And see also lectures in GA 73 (5 November 1917), GA 72 (23 November 1917) and GA 162 (29 May 1915).

144 '... the content of spiritual perception can be transported into ordinary consciousness. There it becomes an abstract [deadened] mental picture. And *this* can be remembered in the usual way.' (GA 21, Appendix 4.)

145 About the etheric and astral remembrance and forgetfulness in the life between birth and death and in Kamaloka, see GA 107, lecture of 2 November 1908.

146 The thief on the cross on Christ's left did recognize Him and was promised 'today thou shalt be with me in paradise'. This is the inner, luciferic cross, obscuring and limiting man's knowledge and control of his soul forces. Lucifer is redeemed from his inner bondage when the three soul forces are purified from his influence and are separated from one another, obeying no more him but the free, Christed 'I' of man. Then, from being an inner god, he is liberated through Christ in man, and becomes again an outer, planetary god who 'lights up in the external world' (GA 113, lectures of 28 and 29 August 1909). And it is Ahriman's cross on the outer boundary of consciousness, which limits man's cognition only to what he causes to appear physically heavy and opaque. (The overcoming of Lucifer in the inner world leads to the ability to use his forces for the illuminating of the new Heaven. The forces redeemed from Ahriman in the external world are used in the inner work of the building of the new Earth, in the sense of Rudolf Steiner's saying that, as a continuation and resurrection of the impulse of St Paul and the old Hebrew prophets, 'geology should be Christ-permeated' [GA 149, lecture of 31 December 1913]. And see next chapter.)

147 See Note 89 above. The crossing is of the imaginative world thoughts, streaming inwardly through the senses, and the inspired, freed will-being, streaming from within outwards, seeking to merge with the source of these world-Imaginations at the farthest reaches of the cosmos. At the point of crossing, the real being of world-man, Anthropos, is intuited, as described by Rudolf Steiner at the end of the lecture of 21 October 1923 (GA 84). In the old Mysteries this process was regulated through the will-outbreathing on the wings of human questioning sent in the direction of the morning instreaming of the Sun's rays at sunrise, and the receiving of the world answers as cosmic thoughts inbreathing at every full Moon. See GA 213, lecture of 25 June 1922.

148 That is, through the overcoming of the two side crosses of inner and outer — luciferic and ahrimanic — limitation of cognition, we reach the central, etheric cross of Christ, where the riddle of human cognition as such is illuminated by his etheric death and resurrection.

149 The phoenix mystery of the 'I' is an expression of the Grail Mystery of the 'I': 'a phoenix "I"' is an 'I' that receives the intuited and inspired Imagination of Christ's 'I' that lets stream its resurrection power into the depth of the human soul and spirit.

150 GA 194, lecture of 30 November 1919, my italics. And see also GA 211, lecture of 1 April 1922 where the inbreathing of world thoughts and its crossing with the outbreathing of the human will is described as the crossing of world light with the inner human sound: 'The world of sound in us is really a touch organ for the [world's] light ... [this is] the touching of world thought through human will.' A further important aspect of the above indicated 'light breathing' is to be found in the first medical course, GA 312, lecture of 21 February 1920, where the creating of the 'inner light' in the organism of man is described in relation to the light process of the earthly atmosphere.

151 See the picture of the ahrimanic and luciferic influences in man's etheric body in GA 158, lecture of 22 November 1914.

152 Freezing the etheric life-body voluntarily means, esoterically, to lead consciously and directly the death-cold and black stream of time's and life's annihilation into the etherically radiant human heart aglow with Christ's fire and to let it thereafter be raised back to the head as etheric self-consciousness in which a living conscious Imagination the Ahriman's being and influences can come to light. Through this process the ahrimanic being which 'sits with the Twelve around the Christ in the human heart' is forced 'out into the night', that is, into a direct, face-to-face confrontation in which he is clearly recognized for what he is and *what he can become*: the being whose forces — when overcome and transformed — make possible a clear *supersensible* sight, as on the Earth they allow for the development of clear earthly thinking. But this is to say that the etheric bridge-work is accomplished. (See also Note 167, below.)

153 The etheric 'sedimentation' of the bridge is in reality a most subtle *healing* process, the building of luminous, pearl-like etheric 'scar formations' around the points and lines of etheric heart bleeding (see also Notes 155 and 167 below). It takes place of its own accord along the twelvefold lines of

force engraved between the physical and etheric bodies out of the intensive battle between love and hatred, life and death, in the heart region. This process can be *experienced* only through mastering the secret of the One, the Three, the Seven and the Twelve from a certain point of view. Firstly, man contemplates repeatedly and from many different points of view (12 at least) the psycho-physical process that supports and balances the *threefold* soul activity of thinking, feeling and willing in normal and then supersensible self-consciousness. One important detail is to be found, for example, in GA 209, lecture of 23 December 1921. Another important indication—about the threefold soul activity in the blood, that is, in the physical ego foundations—is found in GA 128, lecture of 27 March 1911. This is the *scientific Sun* basis of the bridge. And secondly, when the *twelvefold* sense process (GA 45) and its ahrimanic-luciferic corruption (GA 170, lecture of 12 August 1916) is thoroughly assimilated into the *sevenfold* life processes (GA 170, lecture of 12 August 1916) and its ahrimanic-luciferic corruption (GA 170, lecture of 3 September 1916), as indicated in the lecture of 15 August 1916 (GA 170), 'The real aesthetic condition of man is to be found in that the sense-organs, in a certain way, would be made alive, and that the life-processes will be ensouled.' This creates the metamorphosed *artistic Moon* basis of the bridge. Thirdly, the moral-religious basis is sedimented when the Last Supper experience, as described in John 13–17, is livingly engraved into the etheric body in the sense of Rudolf Steiner's lecture of 13 February 1906 (GA 97), when Judas—the personification of Ahriman among the twelve—is described as a martyr as well as a betrayer: 'The deed of Judas is woven completely organically into the mission of Christ. Judas goes through a kind of martyrdom. He is the betrayer and also, in a certain sense, a martyr. He brings about the sacrifice of Christ.' Here the quintessence of the heart's blood itself becomes the basic substance of the bridge through the most profound spiritual-bodily alchemy. It is the force of *Saturn* that is active here, because 'Parsival comes [at the first time] with Saturn's power and the wound burns as it never burnt before'. (GA 149, lecture of 2 January 1914.) At the second time he can transform the death-and-illness-bringing of Saturn into Saturn's highest healing power.

154 This highly significant moment of time marks the consolidation of the crystal foundation stone of Goethe's bridge. In the second stage of the modern Christ experience it was demonstrated as a spoken, gestured 'teaching' by the Christ inside man's being, as described in Chapter 4. There it was described as the interaction of the consciousness soul as imaginative soul, with Christ's archangelic Life Spirit nature, which resulted in the fully conscious deconstruction and living reconstruction of the human 'I' identity in the astral world. In the new yoga teaching of the Nathanic-Krishna (Pauline) method, this moment can be 'recapitulated', that is, grasped in full consciousness through purely individual spiritual effort. It is then understood as a specific stage in the transformation of the etheric body through the spiritualization of thinking and sense-perception. Imaginatively expressed, this stage is the sacrificial metamorphosis of the Green Snake (the imaginative picture of the etheric body) into the shining, crystalline, living-mineral resurrected bridge that will connect the new Heaven with the new

Earth in the being of the new earthly-human Sun. In the lecture of 31 December 1912 (GA 142) Rudolf Steiner described in detail the history of this bridge-building process, from the time of the Fall from Paradise up to Krishna, and through Golgotha to Paul. Krishna had the following twofold task. First, in order to prepare man's earthly self-consciousness for the Mystery of Golgotha, he had to kill the atavistic etheric supersensible snake being and consciousness of humanity. And second, already in his appearance as the light-aura (the Nathanic being) of the Etheric Christ before Paul in Damascus, he could prepare the present, universal reawakening of supersensible etheric perception in the mature self-consciousness of the consciousness soul. The first 'drop' of this new water of life, still in the stage of supersensible preparation in the Michael school in the Sun-sphere, could be received by Goethe, and was composed by him in the form of the 'Legend' (GA 237, lecture of 8 July 1924, and GA 238, lecture of 16 September 1924). In the legend is to be found, therefore, the first intimation of what must, through anthroposophical spiritual science at the end of the twentieth century, be consciously achieved on the Earth, namely, the conscious building of the bridge of consciousness continuation, according to the eternal model of Christ's etheric body, seen and understood through the life of Rudolf Steiner, and through the united work of the whole community of Michael's pupils on the Earth.

155 Emil Bock described the archetypal bridge element of Christ's resurrected body in the following words: 'The draught of Lethe which man swallows when he reaches the far shore of his flowing ether body, and exchanges the sum of his memories for the great oblivion, can be a miserable drop which is consumed by the fires of the zone of trial. But it can also resemble a shining crystal, which draws to itself a permanent spiritual component, not only from the etheric forces of the cosmos but also from the creative plane of corporeal potentiality which lies between the etheric and the physical. Christ's power over matter and death was so great that He was able to wrest from death the whole of the etheric body in which He had dwelt for three years. After three days of spiritual struggle, the victory of Easter morning lay in the fact that the Christ, instead of being made to vanish by death into another world, remained on Earth in His etheric body, which had become entirely a crystal of light.' (E. Bock, *The Three Years*, Floris Books, 1980.)

156 GA 302a, lecture of 16 October 1923.

157 GA 104, lecture of 30 June 1908.

158 For the thinking of the twentieth century we would have to be able to clearly differentiate between luciferic and ahrimanic influences when they occur *intermixed* together in the most varied and bewildering ways. Nietzsche would be the best teacher and forerunner, and Heidegger, Foucault and Derrida somewhat his modern followers. However, this training—invaluable as it is in other connections—does not belong directly to this aspect of the construction of the bridge.

159 GA 199, lecture of 27 August 1920; and see also GA 157, lecture of 19 January 1915.

160 This means to enter consciously into the sub-earthly kingdom of Ahriman, where, since the new Michael age, he has established his anti-Michael

school, whose function is to teach humanity the art of mechanization and materialization of cosmic intelligence in and through man (GA 240, lecture of 20 July 1924). (On the power needed for meditation in a train or steamship, and the etheric fight with Ahriman from this perspective, see GA 275, lecture of 28 December 1914.)

161 This fully conscious and self-willed *spiritual* materialization process is necessary, because Ahriman gets hold of human thinking at the moment he succeeds to conserve the brain- and sense-bound thinking intact in the stream of death. This is the reversed, anti-Michaelic 'immortalization' of thinking referred to in Note 30 above. In order to retrieve this fallen Michaelic intelligence for the formative and creative universal forces, man has to be present also at this very moment, that is, when it is firmly materialized in time's annihilation stream and separated from its living universal life-blood.

As was mentioned above, the book *Von Seelenrätseln* ('The Riddle of the Soul') (GA 21, 1917), whose writing Rudolf Steiner compared to breaking through the tightly blocked wall of the scientific limits of knowledge 'as if with sledgehammers', provides one with the best help in the training required here. Together with the dissertation of W.J. Stein, it opens the way for the deepest Aristotelian grasp of the intellect in the last 2,500 years, that is, from Michael's last pre-Golgotha rule of the still cosmic intelligence, through its purely human individuation as well as non-human ahrimanization process in the last centuries, up to his first post-Golgotha reuniting with the fallen and redeemed cosmic intelligence in the reascending self-consciousness of man.

162 See GA 233a, lecture of 12 January 1924.

163 Such a hollowing of the brain is the result of the activation of the Mercury-Raphael process in the head, which transforms the pure thought activity of Michael into actual imaginative perception. (See GA 243, lecture of 15 August 1924.)

164 Man achieves consciously, through his own effort, that which enters more and more into the natural evolution of our time, namely, the release of the etheric body from the hardening physical body through the growing intellectualism of our times: 'One and a half millennia ago the physical body was considerably more soft and pliable. The physical body has become ever harder. On the other hand something quite different has occurred in the etheric body too, something that the human being has less experience of because the etheric body has passed through an upward development ... this is an event that will take place just in the twentieth century. While on the one hand an intensification of the intellectual element is making itself felt, on the other hand the etheric body will become so much more independent that human beings are bound to become aware of it ... Strengthening the intellectual element causes the etheric body to become more and more independent, so that it can also be used as an independent instrument. And during this process it can be seen to have gone through a hidden development that makes possible the perception of the Christ in the etheric body.' (GA 130, lecture of 17 September 1911.) Here lies a deep secret of the Semitic-Abrahamic mission that once led into Kali-Yuga and to the loss of

the last vestiges of the old supersensible sight as the preparation for the purely physical perception of the physically incarnating Christ, and that opens today the way for the regaining of new, self-conscious imaginative faculties through the etheric Second Coming of Christ. So, according to Rudolf Steiner, Moses, Abraham and the prophets are today once again leading the way to the Christ, only now on the etheric plane. (See GA 118, lecture of 25 January 1910.)

165 See GA 10 regarding the larynx centre that perceives the *forms* of imaginative sight, and the heart centre that perceives the inner *warmth* radiations. Also: 'The head thinks the thoughts, but the heart begins to feel the thought's brightness or shade.' (GA 26, lecture of 16 November 1924.)

166 'But what we let stream into ourselves as a dying element we pour into the being of Christ ... Down into the Christ in us we pour the death that is present in each perception. And we pour down into the Christ Being the darkening of thinking. Into the light, into the spiritual Sunlight of Christ we send our darkened thoughts ... if we understand this development rightly, we say of it: We die into Christ. *In Christo morimur.*' (GA 153, lecture of 11 April 1914.)

167 A more traditional way is given in the Theosophical Rosicrucian treatise *Light on the Path* by Mabel Collins. Through eyes, ears and larynx man is guided to the place where 'Before the soul can stand in the presence of the Masters, its feet must be washed in the blood of the heart.' (And see also GA 8.) This is the actual inner process by means of which man individualizes in his etheric heart consciousness the cosmic fight of Michael with the ahrimanic dragon, described by Rudolf Steiner as follows: 'Externally [we can see] the human form, in the lower animal parts the dragon winding itself, and winding itself also even around the heart. But then, behind the human being — because man sees the higher with the back of the head — we see the external cosmic form of Michael, towering, luminous, giving form to his cosmic being but reflecting his being in the inwardness of the higher nature of man, so that man shows in his etheric body a mirror picture of the form of Michael. And then there becomes visible in this human head, but working down to the heart, the power of Michael crushing the dragon *so that his blood flows down from the heart into the limbs of man.*' (GA 223, lecture of 27 September 1923.) The same is described again from another point of view in GA 26, lecture of 16 November 1924, as 'the world thoughts in the working of Michael and in the working of Ahriman', and again in the same book as follows: 'But Christ will be there; He will live through His great sacrifice *in the same* sphere in which Ahriman is also living. And man will be able to choose between Christ and Ahriman.' (GA 26, lecture of 26 November 1924.)

168 The final, *permanent* consolidation of the bridge, referred to here, on which 'Horses and carriage and travellers of all sorts would travel at the same time back and forth', is described further by Goethe thus: 'These swimming and shining precious stones, the remnants of [the Snake's] sacrificial body [that the Old Man with the Lamp threw into the river of forgetfulness, Lethe], are the ground pillars of this wonderful bridge, on which she shaped herself and *on which she will preserve and hold herself.*'

169 See Rudolf Steiner's reference in the lecture of 29 June to his lecture to youth

at Köberwitz on the morning of 17 June (in GA 217a). There he speaks about the future task of the steeling of Michael's sword in the fire of the subterranian altar.

170 GA 217a, lecture of 20 July 1924. And compare also the fiery words of Rudolf Steiner concerning the sword of Michael, fighting Ahriman's intelligence in the human heart: '... The first penetration of earthly intelligence with Michael's spiritual sword is to be seen in this, that now this spiritual sword of Michael's will be used by the hearts into which the Michael wisdom has entered ... the hearts must become the helpers of Michael in the conquering of the intelligence that fell down to the Earth.' (GA 240, lecture of 20 July 1924.)

171 See the full quotation of this passage at the beginning of this section, pp.94–95.

172 This mystery of Christ's sevenfold nature is revealed only at the higher stages of the anthroposophical modern Christ experience. An indication is given in GA 13, when Rudolf Steiner describes the conscious sevenfolding of the human soul forces in the course of anthroposophical esoteric development. After the separation of the three soul forces is accomplished, 'the development continues. Thinking that has become independent stimulates the emergence of a special fourth soul-spirit being that may be described as a direct influx of currents into man, similar to thoughts. The entire cosmos then appears as a thought structure ... Likewise, feeling and willing that have become independent stimulate two forces in the soul that act in it like independent beings. Still another seventh power and being appears that is similar to one's ego itself.' A further indication, concerning the perception of the being of Jesus Christ by a representative of the Slavic people is to be found in the lecture of 16 June 1910 (GA 121).

173 GA 265, lecture of 8 February 1913, my italics. And see also GA 152, lecture of 2 May 1913. Since in the English translation of this lecture an essential passage was omitted, we give it here: 'This black sphere [of materialistic thinking, brought to the spiritual world with the dying souls of the nineteenth century], was taken by the Christ, *in accordance with the Manichaean principle*, into his being, in order to transform it. It caused, for the angelic being in which the Christ has revealed Himself since the Mystery of Golgotha, 'the death of suffocation'. This sacrifice of Christ in the nineteenth century is comparable to the sacrifice on the physical plan in the Mystery of Golgotha, and can be termed the second crucifixion of Christ on the etheric plane. This spiritual suffocation death that caused the annihilation of consciousness of an angelic being is a recapitulation of the Mystery of Golgotha in the worlds immediately above our own, in order to make possible an enlivening of the formerly hidden Christ consciousness in human souls on the Earth. This enlivening will become clairvoyant sight in humanity in the twentieth century ... the dying of Christ's consciousness in the angelic sphere in the nineteenth century will lead to the resurrection of direct Christ consciousness in the earthly sphere.'

174 This second stage can be prepared in the sense of Rudolf Steiner's lecture of 29 December 1918 (GA 187) in which he described Brunetto Latini's initiation. We take with us—so it is described in this lecture—as we enter the

spirit ocean the most decisive life and destiny event as our 'soul-compass' of navigation and orientation. In our case it is the spiritualized form of the modern Christ experience described in Chapter 4.

175 This is the esoteric meaning of the words: 'And he that taketh not his cross, and followeth after me, is not worthy of me. He that findeth his life shall lose it: and he that loseth his life for my sake shall find it.' (Matthew 10:38–39.)

176 The sending of a ray—or a seed-centre—of the self on the wings of the liberated will-being into a higher spiritual world means, occultly, to *sleep into* the higher Being to which man directs his supersensible attention, and to reawaken with this ray of self as a part of this Being's consciousness in the higher world as one's own extended self-consciousness: 'This is what it means to know a higher Being: to surrender our consciousness as we do in sleep, but to surrender it in such a way that, thanks to the higher forces awakened in us, this consciousness reawakens and radiates towards us as the consciousness of this higher Being.' (GA 145, lecture of 29 March 1913.) When man has internalized and individualized fully, through the modern Christ experience and the knowledge drama of the Second Coming, Christ's 'I' Imagination into his own 'I', he can independently send this inner, imaginative Christ-permeated 'I' aspect upwards, in order to look for and unite with the higher, Christlike self of man, which is always one with the cosmic Christ.

177 The sending of a ray of the self over the abyss of the soul world into a still higher world represents an advanced stage of co-operation between the sixth and seventh independent beings of the human soul (the will-being and the selflike being). The selflike being of man, becoming independent, now stands as an obstacle in the way of further development of the building process. This is also experienced in the fact that he refuses, to begin with, to admit and take in the world-thoughts as objective world content and let them crystallize in the centre of man's evolving world-individuality. The reason for this refusal is to be found in the self's proud conviction that he has no need of such an objective world content as a new self-centre. A battle then develops between the will-being and the self-being. Rudolf Steiner describes this process in *Occult Science* as follows: 'First [the student of spiritual science] will note that an inner relationship exists between this "Guardian of the Threshold" and the soul power that, in the above description [see Note 172 above], has resulted as the *seventh*, and shaped itself into an independent principle. Indeed, the seventh principle is in a certain regard nothing other than the *Doppelgänger*, the "Guardian of the Threshold" himself, and this principle sets the student a special task ... A sort of battle against the *Doppelgänger* will result. The latter will strive for supremacy ... We must observe what appears in the *Doppelgänger*, the "Guardian of the Threshold", and place it before the "higher self" in order to note the contrast between what we are and what we are to become. Through this observation the "Guardian of the Threshold" begins to take on quite a different form. He presents himself as an Image of all the *hindrances* that the development of the higher self must encounter. The student will perceive what a load he must drag about in the form of his ordinary self.' It is this experience that causes the great crisis, shortly to be described below.

In such a threshold experience it becomes, for example, especially evident how important the transformation of sense-perception is in addition to the transformation of the three soul forces. Precisely in the moment of battle with the Guardian and then in the comparison of the lower and higher selves, it becomes clear that the inbreathing of world-thoughts into the emptied centre of the earthly self that is forsaken by his higher being—and its crystallization there as a new earthly-orientated self—would not be 'earthly' enough without the possibility to find in the (spiritualized, etherized) senses such a magnetic point of attraction that can gather around it *firmly* these flitting world-thoughts and densify them into coherent etheric-earthly self-identity.

178 The first (physical) and the second (etheric) Mysteries of Golgotha are, supersensibly speaking, the basis of all self-consciousness and memory in the higher worlds. They constitute the united earthly-cosmic engraving, or 'sign', which alone can bring man safely home to his etheric and earthly selves through the abyss of Lethe when he advances ever deeper into the soul and spirit worlds. It is the only guarantee of free human identity in the cosmos: '... this Christ Impulse is today the only help that enables us to forget the "I"-thought in Earth evolution.' (GA 137, 10 June 1912.)

179 Rudolf Steiner describes this situation as follows: 'Hence the man of our time, when he has thus mounted to the higher worlds, feels it to be above all painful that in spite of all the splendour, in spite of his meeting with those glorious beings, he has an immense emptiness in his inner life. And if nothing else were to happen, a protracted experience of his loneliness, this forlorn condition in the higher worlds, would finally bring about something like despair in his soul ... Then, however, there arises a great longing, a longing that becomes terrible for a man of the present time. It is the longing to know something of how the astral body and ego are born out of the cosmos, how they come into existence ... In deepest darkness and secrecy is veiled everything that has to do with the astral body and ego. Thus the feeling grows: what you are in your innermost nature, what you yourself really are, is veiled from your spiritual sight ...' (GA 144, lecture of 5 February 1913.) Today, after the experience of the world's abyss of evil in the second third of the century, the mystery of the origin of man's higher nature is inseparable from the mystery of evil and is, from a certain point of view, the *same* question, that is, that the Christ alone can provide the answer to this double mystery.

180 This is, of course, the exact opposite of the common, daily soul experience. In the physical world, the basic unity and more or less harmonious inter-weavings of the soul forces and beings give man an instinctive confidence and assurance in his mental and practical life. His questions and doubts, when they appear, are firmly grounded in this basic confidence. In the transition to the soul and spirit worlds, precisely the opposite is true. Here the abyss is the 'ground' under man's moral and cognitive feet, and the helpless dividedness of the soul forces is the usual, 'daily', soul condition. Doubt and questioning here are, therefore, the essential substance and anchorage, the only true (i.e. not luciferic-ahrimanic) world and man reality. (Ultimate assurance and confidence here are a sure sign of luciferic-

ahrimanic possession; the consciously formed question is the only Christed, safeguarded soul and world existence.) But man achieves the moral and cognitive strength required in order to mould himself into the form of a man-world question only when the riddle of evil becomes the substance of his own supersensible existence (see also GA 275, lecture of 30 December 1914). The sought-for 'solution' of this world-man question can, therefore, only be a complete self-transformation, the forces of which are, to begin with – and for a very long time still to come – altogether beyond the practical moral capability of modern man. (This uncomfortable truth is drastically conveyed to man by both the lower and higher aspects of the Guardian of the Threshold when the threefolding of his astral, etheric and physical bodies has advanced so far, as is described by Rudolf Steiner in GA 10.)

181 About the creative spiritual force inherent in spiritual renunciation, see GA 132, lecture of 14 November 1911.

182 'The man of the modern age carries this double nature in him: striving Parsival and wounded Amfortas. So he has to feel himself in his self-knowledge ... in order to generate in man the forces of Parsival, the Amfortas nature in man must be known.' (GA 144, lecture of 6 February 1913.)

183 About the role of questioning in the supersensible Christ experience, Rudolf Steiner says the following: 'Therefore Parsival should not be one of those who have learnt in an external way what was once sacrificed on Golgotha, which the Apostolic Fathers and Doctors of the Church afterwards taught. He should not know how the knights with their virtues put themselves into the service of the Christ. He should singly and alone come into connection with the Christ-impulse in the substratum of the soul, into which he could come according to the criterion of his time ... Not what people did or said, but what the soul experienced, when it is devoted only to what happened supersensibly in the onward process of the Christ-impulse. Outer doctrine always also belongs to the material world. But the Christ-impulse was active supersensibly and should work supersensibly into the soul of Parsival. To nothing else should his soul be driven than to ask there, where the significance of the Christ-impulse could come to meet him at the Holy Grail. He should ask ... singly and alone through what is virginal, but in the sense of the living soul in its time epoch. He should be stimulated to ask what the Holy Grail could disclose, and what exactly the Christ Event could be. He should ask!' (GA 148, lecture of 6 January 1914.) This purely virgin (that is, supersensible) act of asking must be understood as the complete metamorphosis of the soul into its Amfortas-Parsival dualistic nature, shaping itself thereby, through the highest act of spirit freedom, into a world-man riddle that can be raised to the higher worlds and offered to man's higher archetype, that is, his higher, Christ-self, which can then, descending, cross the self-conscious astral-etheric bridge of remembrance, unite itself with man's offered, transformed lower being, and etherically-physically penetrate him and the Earth. (About the connection of this 'Parsival's question' with the receiving of the 'I' copy of Christ's 'I' through the continuation of Rosicrucianism in Anthroposophy, see GA 104a, lecture of 16 May 1909.)

184 Anthroposophically speaking, what we have described here is an important aspect of that which is experienced at the moment of the crossing of the soul world into the spirit world. In its higher archetypal form, Rudolf Steiner described it the following way: 'At first we are like nothing at all, but then, even as a nothing, we are born through listening to our own past converse with the spiritual beings of the spiritual realm [through which man's future, highest being speaks to him] ... In this process in the spiritual world we find ourselves within a triad. One member of this triad is our own past being, which we have carried up into the spiritual world ... the second is the whole spiritual environment, and the third member is ourself. This is the three-foldness of the spiritual world; within the triad through the antithesis of past life and living spiritual being, the third, the middle part, the mere pointlike past, develops itself and becomes—listening to the spirit conversation of the other two—more and more filled out: a being that is developing itself within the spiritual world. In that world we thus "become" ourselves through clairvoyant consciousness.' (GA 147, lecture of 29 August 1913.)

185 This questioning process—taking place every night unconsciously—was described by Rudolf Steiner in the following way: 'Every night in his sleep, man puts before another world, the spiritual-soul world, a wholly unique question ... He puts the question before the spiritual world: how does the being of the spiritual world receive my moral soul constitution? And he is given an answer. It is given to him so that he, according to his moral soul form, receives the [appropriate soul] colouring and formation ... In waking life, this answer that man receives through the [soul] colouring and shaping, is transformed into the voice of conscience.' (GA 208, lecture of 12 November 1921.)

186 That is, a real spiritual meeting with the Christ on the border of the astral world is consciously achieved as the final anchorage of the bridge of consciousness continuation, in the knowledge drama of the Second Coming. This is a true, inspired and intuited Imagination that reflects, on *this* level, the higher stages of initiation. According to Rudolf Steiner, what happens in every unconscious ordinary sleep is raised for the initiate to full self-consciousness in the astral world: 'If a person—in that he exists here with his astral body—could penetrate into the consciousness of his Life Spirit, then he would be able to speak about what happens with his astral body ... Who would speak if a person suddenly while asleep attained the consciousness of his Life Spirit? You cannot say anything other than: "There would speak the astral body of a person as judge of good and evil in man. While asleep the astral body will be the judge of the soul."' (GA 208, lecture of 13 November 1921.) And when the ego experiences his earthly, lower form in the same night soul-spiritual world in his conscious meeting with the spiritual forces that shape and penetrate the physical body during sleep, namely, the forces of Spirit Man, then, so continues Rudolf Steiner, 'I can find no other expression for this fact, if I want to coin it in a sentence, than when I say: The "I" becomes the sacrifice of itself, the sacrifice of the spirit active in the body ... And again—if we look at what comes to meet us as a so tremendously gripping image of the Lamb of God, of the Christ, that Christ *who is bound*

215

with the human "I" who permeates this human "I" — then the thought will be in motion in our soul (just if we look at the Lamb offering itself) of the sacrifice that will be the "I", in that it goes over to the condition of sleep, and we find how aptly through the image of the Lamb of God this sacrificial nature of man is experienced through sleep.' (My italics.)

187 GA 145, lecture of 27 March 1913.

Chapter 6

1 That is, through the building of the 'etheric ring' around the Earth out of the Christ-permeated remains of human etheric bodies. (See Chapter 1, and the relevant quotations in Notes 29 and 30 there; and further below, in this chapter.)

2 'What the Scholastics could not answer was the question: how does the Christ enter into human thinking? how will human thinking be Christed? ... With his Christology man was not yet able to continue the redemption of man from sin into human thinking ... How can man carry Christology into thinking? How shall thinking be made Christian? This question stands there in world history in the moment in which Thomas Aquinas died in 1274. Up to this moment he could only advance to this question, which stands there with all heartfelt inwardness in European spiritual culture.' (GA 74, lecture of 23 May 1920.) About the same question in the thought of Alanus ab Insulis, see his *Rhythmus über die Inkarnation Christi*, translated from the Latin with commentary by Wilhelm Rath (*Die Drei*, 1951/3).

3 Compare also Wilhelm Hoerner, *Zeit und Rhythmus* (Urachhaus, 1978). Another important time-process is the expression of the convergent evolution of the being Philosophy together with the Christ-impulse (or the streaming together of the Old Sun evolution within the Earth with the impulse of its new, Christed, Sun-becoming, according to GA 161, lecture of 19 January 1915). The forces of consciousness necessary to understand the Christ-impulse descend to the Earth in great periods of 700–800 years. First, through the still divine forces of inspiration that descended through the Grecian culture (800 BC–AD 0), then, in the first period of eight hundred years after Golgotha (AD 0–800), the Christ-impulse was still working down to the Earth from higher Devachan. In the second period (AD 800–1600), He worked from lower Devachan. In the fourth period (our own, AD 1600–2400), He works from the astral world. But already in this period the direct human earthly knowledge drama of the Second Coming must begin: 'After the year 2400 there will come the epoch where the forces to understand the Christ will come from the Earth alone, when the Christ works on human beings from out of the physical plane. But in our time there is already beginning what after 2400 will be essential: the Christ will appear on the physical plane in etheric form ... in my book *Die Rätsel der Philosophie* ['The Riddles of Philosophy'] man can follow up the development of human consciousness in these periods ... The plant seed must be planted according to its essence in the living world to which it belongs if it would sprout to new life. In the same way the thought seeds of Hegel can be planted in the soil of spiritual

science; there they can grow up and bear the living fruits of Imagination, Inspiration and Intuition ... then it will be possible to understand the coming Christ-impulse through earthly forces. This is the connection between the world of thinking in *The Philosophy of Freedom* and the higher forces of knowledge that develop in our souls ...' (GA 152, lecture of 5 March 1913.)

4 See GA 130, lecture of 1 October 1911. Out of the conscious uniting of the sleeping moral will with the awakened earthly thinking (through the etherization of the blood brought about by the anthroposophical Christ experience), the shaping and condensing of 'a moral fiery atmosphere' around the Earth is gradually created (the new Heaven of the earthly-human Sun).

5 GA 214, lecture of 30 August 1922. From another aspect, the earthly-human Sun as the foundation of this new initiation of world-man rhythm is the rebirth of the ancient — now thoroughly Christ-transformed — Tao breathing and pulsating between Heaven and Earth, described by Rudolf Steiner in his lecture of 22 May 1923 (GA 325).

6 GA 132, lecture of 7 November 1911. This process is, at the same time, the beginning of the birth of space out of time: 'The earlier and later transforms itself, so that it is changed into inner and outer. "Space" is born! Through the offered virtue of the Spirits of Wisdom [reflected back later through the Archangels], space is created on the Old Sun.' (Compare our study of the problem of space and time in the transformation of sense-perception in Chapter 5.)

7 Ibid. That the Christ Being could have brought with Him 'the extract' of the old Sun to the Earth is the result of His special evolution on the Old Sun itself. This is described by Rudolf Steiner as follows: 'But the Christ received on Old Sun the World Word; and this World Word has the property that it kindles itself anew in the soul that receives it, so from the time of the Old Sun onwards the World Word became light in Christ.' (GA 137, lecture of 12 June 1912.)

8 The differentiated sevenfold soul being of man was referred to earlier. According to GA 13, the separated soul forces divide themselves into a sixfold organism of three earthly-cosmic pairs of soul forces. And the ego — as the double in some respects — is the seventh being (see Chapter 5, Notes 172 and 177). According to Rudolf Steiner in the lecture of 8 January 1911 (GA 127), this process involves the transformation of the three soul forces together with the transformation of the three soul members, through which man begins to perceive and work consciously with the individual beings of the Third Hierarchy who are his closest associates in the creation process of the new earthly-human Sun.

9 GA 217a, lecture of 17 June 1924. These words, which must have had a prophetic meaning for those who listened to them at the beginning of the century, must become at its end an actual, living, anthroposophical *experience* of the new Earth being of the earthly-human Sun.

10 'The God who dwells within man speaks when the soul becomes aware of itself as "I" ... Man can find the Divine within himself because his innermost being is drawn from the Divine ... The true nature of the "I" reveals

itself only in the consciousness soul ... But if the "I" is to observe itself, it cannot simply surrender itself; it must, through inner activity, first lift its being out of its own depths in order to have a consciousness of itself ... The force that discloses the "I" within the consciousness soul is indeed the same force that manifests in all the rest of the world ... In what fills the consciousness soul, the hidden enters unveiled into the innermost temple of the soul ... Thus the consciousness soul is united with the spirit which is hidden in all that is manifest. If man wishes to take hold of the spirit in all manifestation, he must do it in the same way he takes hold of the ego in the consciousness soul.' (GA 13, Chapter 'The Nature of Humanity'.) And see also Helmut Kiene: *Grundlinien einer Essentialen Wissenschaftstheorie*, Urachhaus, 1984, p.203, expressed in Heideggerian terms: 'It is the spiritual *essence* of the thing in question that is released from its concealment, and *it is the "I" of man that is the place of truth*.'

11 See the lectures of 19 December 1920 (GA 202) and 6 September 1921 (GA 78) for a detailed study of the development of this world creative will-love being in man, which is shaped through the transformation of thinking.

12 'You have in man, *especially in the lower man*, the origin of nature in all reality. This means that you must look for the origin of nature in the physical and etheric bodies, in the physical and etheric organization, of man.' (GA 326, lecture of 6 January 1923.)

13 This world-man, embryonic will-being as future enlivened seed of the new Christ-permeated Earth is from another point of view what was referred to by Rudolf Steiner in a lecture of 17 June 1924 (GA 217a) as the place where the subterranean altar is to be found in whose fire alone the Michael sword is forged. This altar can be thus experienced as the will-being of the human heart (see Note 169 to Chapter 5, where the construction process of the bridge of consciousness continuation and Michael's sword was described). In planetary terms Rudolf Steiner shaped it into the following Imagination: 'To learn to know nature forces under the earth leads to the understanding that Michael's sword must be carried in order to be forged on an altar that is under the earth. There it must be found by receptive souls.' (GA 217a.) In the *mémoires* of Johanna Keyserlingk we also find the following formulation: 'Spiritual light comes in this century only when Michael succeeds, in the astral light, to find the way to the altar where the fire burns that Ahriman fears' (*Köberwitz 1924, Geburtsstunde einer neuen Landwirtschaft* (Verlag Hilfswerk Elisabeth, Stuttgart 1974, p.71).

14 GA 113, lecture of 25 August 1909, my italics.

15 See GA 265.

16 The above can be compared also to the following words of Rudolf Steiner: 'Spiritual science shows us how we could feel ourselves as members of the whole Earth life; spiritual science shows us that the Christ is the Spirit of the Earth! Our fingers, our teeth, our nose, all our organs are supplied with blood from the heart. Without a central organ they would not exist, because without a heart their existence is impossible. And Theosophy [Anthroposophy] shows man that in the future of Earth evolution it will be a folly not to accept the idea of Christ, because *what the heart is for the organism the Christ is for the Earth body*. And just as the blood supplies the whole body

with life and power through the heart, so must the being of the Christ flow through all single human beings so that for them the words of Paul must come true: not I, but the Christ in me! The Christ must stream forth into all human hearts.' (GA 127, lecture of 6 March 1911.)

17 'When the Sun separated itself from the Earth, the Word was buried in the Earth. It will be resurrected when the Earth advances to the sixth root-race. Man will reawaken this Word out of the Earth, but beforehand the spirit must live in him, so that the Word resounds in himself ... The great initiator Jesus Christ went ahead. The Holy Spirit followed and fertilized the astral bodies, so that they will be ripe enough to make their etheric bodies immortal ... every human being must arrive at this point in the middle of the sixth root-race. Today he is still under the influence of death, because his etheric body has not yet achieved immortality. In Christianity the secret is contained of how man can gradually develop himself towards the resurrection of the etheric body.' (GA 93, lecture of 5 June 1905, and see also Chapter 1 above.)

18 In the past, man was the son of the Earth. From our time on, the Earth becomes the daughter of man. According to GA 104, lecture of 26 July 1908, man was then part of Mother Earth, formed out of her body as the embryo is formed in the mother's womb, nourished through her blood vessels (the Hebrew language still retains this mystery: *A'da'ma* = Earth; *Da'm* = blood: *A'da'm* = man). What begins today is the reversal of this ancient process. Man is beginning to create the new Earth out of his (spiritualized) blood; the future Earth is humanity's child and will be made in the Christed image of man himself. Today it appears before supersensible anthroposophical imaginative sight in the Imagination of the earthly-human Sun.

19 Man can compare this expression with what is said, from another point of view, about the Christ-infilled metabolic system of the Earth in *Köberwitz, 1924* (op.cit.), p.80.

20 'Human evolution thus implies a transformation of the Earth's interior. In the beginning the nature of the Earth's body was such as to hold subsequent developments in check. In the end, when human powers will have transformed the Earth, it will be a spiritualized Earth. In this way man imparts his own being to the Earth ... Man transforms his dwelling place and himself at the same time, and when he spiritualizes himself he spiritualizes the Earth also ... Every moment when we think and feel, we are working on the great structure of the Earth. The Leaders of mankind have insight into such relationships and seek to impart to men the forces that will work in the true direction of evolution ...' (GA 95, lecture of 4 September 1906.)

21 Felix Balde draws attention to this fact in his words uttered in the *subterranean Sun-temple* (*The Portal of Initiation*, Scene 5):

The light that shines in men
and is the fruit of knowledge
has to become the nourishment
for powers who in earthly darkness
do service to the cosmic course.

But now for long they have been forced
to lack such sustenance.
For what evolves today
within the brains of men
can serve the surface of the Earth,
but does not penetrate the depths.

[...]

As long on Earth
those men alone find hearing
who are unwilling to recall
their own true spirit source,
so long the lords of metal ores
will hunger in the depths of earth.

22 GA 3, my italics. This passage expresses in philosophical terms the heart
activity that marks the essence of the earthly-human Sun creation process.
23 The living light of thinking that man produces in this way becomes the
substance by means of which the Cherubim work in world becoming: 'We
are all light-givers appointed in the world order. In that we think, perceive
and form mental pictures, we are the light-givers of the Cherubim in the
world order ... in that we think, the light of thinking radiates out and
illuminates the world in which the Cherubim live.' And when man exerts
his will in moral action, he creates the warmth needed for the work of the
Seraphim in the cosmos: 'Under the influence of moral acts the Seraphim
achieve the forces by means of which the cosmic world order is supported as
the physical world is supported by physical warmth ... when you think,
make mental pictures, you are the kindled light of the Cherubim; when you
work, when you do something out of your will, then you are the warmth
source, the fiery source of the Seraphim.' (GA 156, lecture of 19 December
1914; and see also GA 202, lecture of 18 December 1920 on the moral cognitive radiance of humanity as the light and life-giving source of the visible,
old cosmic Sun.) When we bear in mind that it is the beings of the First
Hierarchy (including the Thrones) that give substance to and form the
physical Earth (GA 121, lecture of 11 June 1910) and, since the fifteenth
century, also implant the cosmic Intelligence in the human nerve-sense
system (GA 237, lecture of 28 July 1924), we can understand why, through
the transformation of thinking into the creative will being, man becomes
directly aware of his participation in this planetary work in the depths of his
own being and in the depths of the new forces of the earthly Sun.
24 That is, the new earthly-human Sun is created according to the image of the
threefold, Christ-permeated being of man: a limb metabolic planetary will
system in the depths, a headlike organ, with a planetary reflecting nerve-
sense system in the etheric-astral atmosphere above, and a heart-lung
system that unites the two in the middle, human-social zone of the Earth.
(As we shall presently see, the two poles—the Earth and Heaven—of the
new earthly-human Sun can be created out of the individual knowledge
drama of the Second Coming. However, they remain in a certain way dis-

connected and, in a sense, paralysed, so long as the social, mutual co-working of human beings in society does not reach the same level of creativity.)

25 About the Grail Mysteries of the planetary *pietà* Imagination, the Earth Mother who through her penetration by the Christ-impulse regained her cosmic virginity and creativity, and the description of this process as the resurrection of the old Hebrew Geo-logia of the Prophets and St Paul, see GA 149, lecture of 2 January 1914.

26 Rudolf Steiner pointed out in the lecture of 29 March 1913 (GA 145) that the forms of animals and, to a lesser degree, plants and minerals in the physical world are ahrimanic Imaginations. That it is Lucifer who destroys the colourful radiance of the starry worlds of the cosmic Sophia, see GA 202, lecture of 24 December 1920.

27 Man lives and works through his liberated sense-and-thinking being in this living light world of the earthly 'Heaven' together with the beings of the Second Hierarchy who weave in the warmth, light and life elements of the earthly atmosphere (GA 121, lecture of 11 June 1910), as with his liberated will being he works in the earthly depth with the beings of the First Hierarchy (see Note 15 above). In the middle zone of the new Sun, where he meets his fellow human beings in his daily activity and karma, he works intimately with the Christ as the leader of humanity and the beings of the Third Hierarchy.

28 'This is precisely the meaning of higher development at a certain stage, that to the streams and movements of the etheric body, which are independent of consciousness, such streams are added that man himself creates in a conscious way.' (GA 10, 'Some Effects of Initiation'.)

29 Such an organism has actually *two* sides. It can reflect and bring together—on both sides of its mirroring surface—that which happens 'above' (in the cosmic starry worlds) and 'below' (in the embryonic will-centre of the new Earth). And this creative, united impression from above and from below constitutes—through man's active sensing—the new Heaven, in so far as it comes within the limits of perception of the new imaginative faculties of man in our time.

30 In the article 'What is the Earth in reality within the macrocosm?' (GA 26), Rudolf Steiner describes the way in which the living forces of the mineral and animal kingdoms gather the future seed-power of the plant kingdom into a cosmic sphere Imagination of an evolving seed macrocosm: 'It is thus that the spirit-seeing consciousness beholds the essence of the earthly realm. *It stands as a new, life-kindling element within the dead and dying macrocosm* ... It is a true contemplation of the Earth-nature, which sees in it everywhere a germinating universe. We only learn to understand the kingdoms of nature around us when we feel the presence of this germinating life.'

31 Ibid.

32 GA 130, lecture of 27 November 1911. The power that in the past was received by this etheric body can be received nowadays—with the help of this etheric body—directly from the etheric body of the Christ himself.

33 GA 148, lecture of 10 February 1914, and see also Chapter 4 about the first part of the first stage of the modern Christ experience.

34 GA 181, lecture of 1 April 1918, my italics. According to GA 291a an astral, starlike crystal formation signifies the pre-formation (in the third elemental kingdom) of a future mineral kingdom, which, in this case, is the future Jupiter existence form of the Earth which now appears in the imaginative form of the Heavenly Jerusalem into which the dead depart. The essential thing here is to note that this form *enlivens itself* when the dead gaze upon it, indicating the fertilizing, awakening power of this kind of human gaze after death. But this is precisely the essence of the spiritualized gaze developed through the transformation of sense-perception during the knowledge drama of the Second Coming, that it becomes a direct creative power in the construction of the new Heaven of the earthly-human Sun, which is the Heavenly Jerusalem or the elemental pre-formation of Jupiter to come.

35 Rudolf Steiner describes the etheric preservation and resurrection of Goethe's etheric (thinking) body in the Christ-permeated etheric Heaven of the new Earth in the following way: 'The spiritual is around us now in a way that it was not around the human beings of past times. The etheric body is separated from the soul as a second corpse, but is in a certain way preserved through the Christ-impulse which remained from the Mystery of Golgotha ... When man has the faith that Goethe is resurrected as an ether-body, and then studies his work, then his concepts and mental pictures begin to be living, and man describes him not as he was but as he is today. Then the concept of resurrection is brought into life. Then man believes in the resurrection ... because this belongs to a deep mystery of the new age ... So long as we are in a physical body, it is an obstacle to the right development of thinking. As great as Goethe was, his mental pictures are greater still ... In the moment when they are received by someone who accepts them with love and thinks them further, they become something else, they gain new life. Do not believe that the first form in which mental pictures appear in someone is in any way the finished form of this thinking; believe in the resurrection of thinking!' (GA 175, lecture of 24 April 1917). Again, one must pay careful attention to the context and content of this lecture as a whole: it contains a veiled open secret concerning the relationships between the individualities of Aristotle and Goethe.

36 This esoteric knowledge ideal aims at the fully conscious co-working of free human beings in the building process of the earthly-human Sun through the spiritualization of the modern Christ experience by means of the resurrected life body of Rudolf Steiner. Sergei O. Prokofieff described it as follows: 'One of the most important tasks of anthroposophists at the end of the century is to give to the ether-body of Rudolf Steiner — thanks to their spiritual work carried on in faithfulness to the fundamental anthroposophical impulse — such a power that his pupils who are overshadowed by this ether-body will be able to experience the Christ Himself directly or, in other words, the Christ Himself, from the end of the century onwards, will be able to work through the ether-body of Rudolf Steiner into his pupils. This can happen, however, only when the Holy Spirit [the spirit of awakened Christ consciousness, working through the planetary etheric ring or new Heaven], after it united itself with the Christ-light that is reflected from this ether-body, can enter into the consciousness of the pupils and so awaken in them

the experience of the Christ. (Sergei O. Prokofieff, *The Cycle of the Year as a Path of Initiation*, Temple Lodge Publishing, 1986, Chapter 9, p.259.)

37 An important Imagination in this connection is the transfiguration scene on Mount Tabor, where Elijah and Moses (Might and Wisdom respectively, according to GA 104, lecture of 26 August 1908) appear on either side of the Christ when Jesus's etheric body was transformed into Life Spirit and the ahrimanic-luciferic forces were thereby cast out of his physical body (GA 112, lecture of 5 July 1909). Through anthroposophical meditation on this Imagination, deepened through the modern Christ experience and the knowledge drama of the Second Coming, we experience how, superimposed on the pre-Golgothean transfiguration picture, a modern post-Golgothean Imagination appears through which important mysteries of the new Christ-impulse are revealed. *We mean the picture of Novalis and Goethe on the right and left sides of the etheric, planetary Christ.* This appearance can be understood if we consider Rudolf Steiner's lecture of 9 April 1921 (GA 271), where he described how the art of eurythmy is created out of the dynamic metamorphosis of the formative forces of Goethe (which penetrate and spiritualize time and space up to the sense organs and through them also external nature) and the musical forces of Novalis (which spiritualize the poetic-musical element beyond time and space). When we bear further in mind that the art of eurythmy comes about when the Spirit Self begins to develop the Life Spirit (GA 275, lecture of 29 December 1914) or, in other words — if we keep to the artistic way of expression — when the spiritualized astral body (music and poetry, Novalis' impulse) advances so far that a spiritualization of the etheric body (plastic arts, Goethe's impulse) is made possible, then we can receive an inspired Imagination of the new transfiguration scene of our time. But this is now not only of the personal, microcosmic etheric body of Jesus (as was the case on Mount Tabor before Golgotha) but of the planetary etheric ring, the Heaven of the new earthly-human Sun, uniting itself with Christ's macrocosmic Life Spirit (which in the ninth century united with Christ's planetary Self and Spirit Self (see GA 240, lecture of 27 August 1924). Through the etheric ring of the new Heaven — the creation of humanity's Christ-permeated life forces — streams forth Christ's cosmic spirit of life; and the entelechy of Novalis and that of Goethe are its two great, eternal guardian spirits, opening the gates to that sphere where 'Man sees as an Archangel' and inscribes his Imaginations as world Imaginations in the new planetary script of his future.

38 About the weaving of Christ's bodies of planetary resurrection out of the forces of wonder (astral body), love and compassion (etheric body) and conscience (physical body), see GA 143, lecture of 8 May 1912. It is of value to note that in the opening of this lecture — which was dedicated to the death-day of H.P. Blavatsky — Marie Steiner von Sivers recited the poem 'Eleusis' written by Hegel to his beloved young friend, Hölderlin. Then comes the study of the repeated earthly lives of Elijah-John the Baptist-Raphael-Novalis in its relation to the Mystery of Golgotha and the further working through of the Christ-impulse. When we assimilate this content in this unique context and let it work especially on the feeling element of our soul, deep secrets of *one* aspect of the Platonic stream are revealed to us, namely, its special dedication to the redemption and transformation of the

Earth as the body of the Christ. Since a lengthy study of the connection between Novalis, Hegel and Hölderlin from this aspect is beyond our scope here, we shall mention some related facts concerning the last only.

Hölderlin was a personal, enthusiastic and one-sided idealistic pupil of Plato (see GA 236, lecture of 26 April 1924), as he himself almost fully consciously described it in his letter to his friend Neuffer (see the important study of Hölderlin by Rudolf Treichler, in: W. Schuchhardt [ed], *Schicksal in Widerholten Erdenleben*, Vol 3, Verlag am Goetheanum, 1983). But precisely this one-sidedness created in him the strongest desire to penetrate in the future ever deeper into the mysteries of the Christed Earth: 'The old pupil of Plato wishes to transform the spiritual revelation, which once lifted him away from the Earth, and make it fruitful for the Earth' (Treichler, ibid. p.146). Johanna Keyserlingk described how Hölderlin's soul became her spirit guide to the Sun-mysteries of the Earth's inner core: 'He himself, who left the Earth in order to look for the Gods ... he knows the Christ in the depths ... in the depths he strives to penetrate to the leader of the Sun-kingdom of the Earth's interior' (*Köberwitz, 1924* (op.cit.), p.77). Goethe himself could testify to this aspect of Plato's unique spirit being from a direct personal, but balanced, experience (GA 144, lecture of 6 February 1914, and GA 238, lecture of 3 September 1924): 'Plato stands in relation to the world as a spirit pleased to dwell here for a while. He is not so much concerned with learning about it — for he has always accepted its existence — as he is with imparting to it in a friendly way what it so sorely needs. *So he penetrates to the depths more to fill them with his being than to investigate them ... It is to the heights that he ascends with longing, to participate again in his origin ...* All that he says refers to an eternal unity of the Good, the True and the Beautiful, and he strives to kindle every human heart with love for it while the details of earthly knowledge melt, we could even say vaporize, in his method ...' ('Geschichte der Farbenlehre' [Theory of Colour], in: *Goethes Naturwissenschaftliche Schriften*, Vol. 3, p.27; and also see there Rudolf Steiner's commentary concerning Plato's philosophy [GA 1 a–e]).

39 About the way in which the Earth Spirit, through its transformation by the Christ-impulse, becomes the spirit teacher of the macrocosmic secrets of Anthroposophy, see GA 221, lecture of 9 February 1923: '... now man must look at his relation with the Earth, that is, ask himself if the genius of the Earth speaks within him ... Previously, Heaven revealed to man what he had to know for his life on the Earth; now man turns to the Earth ... We cannot but turn, in the modern age, to the genius of the Earth that lives in ourselves.' (It is further mentioned that the achievement of this 'world consciousness' in the age of the consciousness soul is possible only through the transformation of the mode of thinking of natural science.)

40 Goethe, *Faust*, Part 1, Night.

The power that enables man to imprint and preserve his self-created Imagination in the Heaven of the earthly-human Sun was described by Rudolf Steiner as follows: 'Man does not keep the Imaginations within him. They are drawn as cosmic pictures into cosmic existence and thence he is able to copy them, painting them again and again in his own life of picture-ideation.

'Thus what Michael preserves from crystallization in the inner being of man is received by the spiritual world. What man experiences of the force of conscious Imagination becomes a part of world-contents. That this can be so is an outcome of the Mystery of Golgotha. *The Christ-force impresses the spiritual Imaginations of man into the cosmos*. It is the Christ-force united with the Earth ... since the Christ-impulse has been living with the Earth, man in his self-conscious being is given back again to the cosmos.' (GA 26, January 1925.)

41 Some results gained through the *reading* of these Christ-permeated imprints of human Imaginations in the earthly Heaven of the twentieth century are described in my book: *The Spiritual Event of the Twentieth Century* (op.cit.).

42 GA 112, 6 July 1909. This creative power of the Earth—building around itself the sphere of the Holy Spirit—is actually the creative power of humanity, who will also increasingly participate in this building process through its awakened anthroposophical consciousness.

43 Before the separation of the Earth from the Sun—before the opening of the senses to the external Sun light (GA 102, lecture of 16 February 1908)—man was a primitive, pre-individual, but beautifully-radiating Sun being: 'Man can imagine how that same power which the eye receives from outside in the light ether streams from within outwards, in the opposite direction, from the eye outwards. If this were so, this being would illuminate the other beings around it ... Man illuminated then—as some marine animals do today—the objects around and also his own body. In those times the human being did not yet have a consciousness of himself, but rather he was only a tool in the hands of the Divinity concerned in order to illuminate the world for it. *Divinity had no other way to illuminate the objects around than the eyes of the human being.*' (GA 93a, lecture of 31 October 1905.) That we have lived since the Mystery of Golgotha in a process of evolutionary reversal of this ancient Hyperborean situation can be made clear through the following words of Rudolf Steiner: 'In the time prior to the Mystery of Golgotha, the Earth had an atmosphere which contained the soul element that belongs to the soul of man. Today the Earth has an atmosphere that is devoid of this soul element. Instead, this soul element, which was previously in the air, has now entered into the light that surrounds us from morning till evening. This was made possible through the fact that the Christ has united Himself with the Earth. Air and light have changed inwardly. We live in an atmosphere and in a light sphere that are different from those in which our souls lived in previous earthly lives ... We must strive to become conscious of a much more subtle relation of man to the external world, so that in regard to our ether-body something takes place which must enter our consciousness more and more, similar to the breathing process. In the breathing process we inhale fresh oxygen and exhale unusable carbon. A similar process takes place in all our sense-perceptions [this Goethe experienced in the formation of coloured after-images in the etheric body] ... *Jahve revealed himself through the night dreams of his prophets ... It must become a certainty for us that with every ray of light, with every tone, with every sensation of heat and its dying down we enter into a soul-intercourse world ...*' (GA 194, lecture of 30 November 1919.)

And in another place: 'And when another being ... looked down upon the

Earth, and saw the Earth radiating with light, he would have said to himself: this Earth radiates light, not because the Sun-rays are reflected back but rather because on the Earth human beings are present that perceive through their eyes. This process of sight does not mean something only for our consciousness, but it radiates out into the whole world space and what human beings are doing when they see is the light of their planetary body . . . Man is, through his sense-perception, a world being.' (GA 157, lecture of 6 July 1915.)

44 See, for example, GA 183, lecture of 24 August 1918, and GA 162, lecture of 3 June 1915.

45 About the future forces inherent in the pure sense-qualities of perception, see the relevant quotations in Note 124 to Chapter 5.

46 This is what Rudolf Steiner also termed the 'holding sway of the Holy Spirit in the world ... the holding sway of world-thought in the world', which, independent of any historical-external knowledge of Golgotha, without any knowledge of the written Gospels, is possible 'because something came into the world through the Mystery of Golgotha that enables a man to under-stand the impressions of the spiritual world directly through his own impressions'. (GA 132, lecture of 31 October 1911. And see also GA 221, lecture of 18 February 1923.)

Chapter 7

1 Imaginatively observed, one can speak quite concretely about three adver-sary appearances that strive unceasingly to obscure and destroy the Christ-permeated light and life of the new earthly-human Sun. First, we can observe the astral cloud formations that darken and disperse—also twist and caricature—the astral light atmosphere of the earthly-human Sun. Here are gathered together all the evil luciferic forces that emanate from the distorted cultural and social life on the Earth. Second, there are real Sun spots or black holes that, as ahrimanic parasites, attack the life-giving etheric ring of the new earthly-human Sun. These sucking, annihilating beings grow and develop through the evil deeds of human beings in human and social life on the Earth, especially when ahrimanic thinking and action is practised on a mass scale. These two—the cloud and spot formations— emerge from the middle social zone of the new earthy-human Sun and prevent the conscious and therefore harmonious and rhythmical mutual penetration, in human hearts and mind, of the new Earth below (Christ-man will activity in the depths) and of the new Heaven above (human-Christ world-shaping perception and Imagination in the heights). The third force attacks the will-being—the Christ-permeated 'I' seed—directly in the earthly depths. From there it controls the other two adversaries. This is the destructive force of evil whose influence in our century is described in my book *The Spiritual Event of the Twentieth Century* (op. cit.). (On the interior of the Earth as the stronghold of evil and black magic, see GA 95, lecture of 4 September 1905, and GA 97, lecture of 21 April 1906.) According to precise astral climatic and weather rules, such evil masses must, after reaching a

certain stage of accumulated tension, explode in astral-elemental storms that create the human and natural catastrophes of our century. (Such 'astral synoptic maps' have always existed and are made use of in occult connections in order to direct and control, for good or ill, the social and geopolitical evolution of humanity. About the astral cloud formations over Europe, see GA 225, lecture of 15 July 1923.) This process was described by Rudolf Steiner at the time of the First World War (1917). In an interview with the French journalist Jules Sauerwein, he described the war as 'an explosion of forces that were pressed together in a wrong way ... It is a healing process brought about through violent means by the spiritual organism of our planet. As the physical organism reacts through fever ... to unbearable poisonings, as the fire that smoulders under the Earth comes suddenly to volcanic eruption, so the unhealthy and abnormal use of energy leads to wars. Under a pressure they cannot understand, governments and nations then lose their reason.' (In: C. Lindenberg, *Rudolf Steiner, eine Chronic*, Verlag Freies Geistesleben, 1988, p.381.)

2 Wrong social structures and relationships have, in our time, a powerfully destructive planetary force, not only on the observable ecological conditions but even more acutely when used as a means of occult attack on the embryonic earthly-human Sun. From this perspective we can understand why the Threefold Social Order has a planetary-cosmic justification and significance: it alone can create a social formation that is in accord with the threefold Christ-permeated formation of the new earthly-human Sun, described above, and hold the opposing forces within controllable limits. (On the metamorphosis of the rights — middle — sphere of social life into the future formative forces of natural, climatic and atmospheric planetary forces, see GA 199, lecture of 4 September 1920.)

3 The direct transition from sense-perception to moral intuition is the main characteristic of the cognitive side of the moral social life: 'Already in the first stage [sense-perception] man achieves what [in the experience of nature] is first achieved in the third stage. In the moral world the Intuition comes immediately after external perception. In nature, two other stages come between [Imagination and Inspiration].' (GA 217, lecture of 7 October 1922.) In this light man should study the descriptions of the human meeting, given below: Inspiration comes last, when the imaginative (perceptive) and intuitive elements are brought to a true social dynamic.

4 Free spiritual relationships between human beings, steeped in true human love and based on communal study and research of anthroposophical spiritual science, create in the soul and spirit of the participators in an enhanced measure the organs for perception and experience of the higher spiritual world (GA 93a, lecture of 9 October 1905). And when we bear in mind that today the new higher spiritual world is already here, in the new Earth and Heaven of the earthly-human Sun, and further that a growing number of people will be able to work consciously with one another on the development of this earthly-Sun process, then we can realize quite new perspectives and goals for social life on the Earth in the not too distant future.

This new earthly-Sun sphere is the true sphere of human soul *freedom* in

227

social life – the freedom that is based on true human love: 'Man shall be free when the relation between soul and soul is such that one soul can follow the other with ever greater and greater understanding and ever greater love ... [through] the forming of that gentle union that develops itself from soul to soul ... Because only in this way can souls be free, *and only souls can be free.*' (Brotherhood is the economic, and equality the spiritual social aspect from this perspective; see GA 171, lecture of 2 October 1916.)

5 'What will be achieved through this advance of humanity is that the two poles ... the intellectual and moral poles, will become increasingly one, will merge into oneness ... You will be more and more penetrated, also in the day, by the direct influence of the Good from the spiritual world ... the moral fire [that] streams out of this Christ figure ... And so man transforms the Earth if he can feel that morality belongs to the Earth ... Then will come that time to the Earth ... when this moral atmosphere will be strengthened to a high degree ... when the Earth will be penetrated by a moral-ether sphere.' (GA 130, lecture of 1 October 1911.)

6 'The human being must become much more [for his fellow human being] than he has been hitherto. He must become his awakener. Human beings must approach one another more closely than they have done until recently: every man must become an awakening being to everyone he meets. For modern human beings have accumulated so much karma that they cannot but feel themselves karmically connected with everyone they meet in life. When man goes back to earlier times, souls were younger and had fewer karmic relationships. Now it becomes necessary that man is awakened not only through nature but through human beings who are karmically connected with him.' (GA 257, lecture of 3 March 1923.) About the concrete moral-social experiences that man will have to develop in the future in meeting his fellow human beings through the modern Christ experience, see GA 185, lecture of 26 October 1918, and see further below.

7 GA 54, lecture of 7 December 1905.

8 We refer here above all to the descriptions of the '*Ur*-phenomena' of social life, that is, to the largely unconscious supersensible process taking place in the actual moment of human meeting. See GA 186, lectures of 6 and 12 December 1918, and GA 191, lecture of 19 October 1919 to which also GA 271, lecture of 6 May and 1 June 1918 is related, and the description of the ego-sense in GA 293 which is quoted below. And see also the relevant chapter in Dieter Brüll's book: *Der Anthroposophische Sozialimpulse*, Novalis Verlag, 1984.

9 'The astral body is, according to its innermost nature, the greatest egoist. The ego is more than a great egoist; it wants not only itself but wants himself in the other, wants to go over into the other. And the knowledge that we gain on the Earth is but this mitigated drive, to take over the other, to expand and extend everything that man is beyond oneself into the other.' (GA 145, lecture of 27 March 1913.)

The luciferic-ahrimanic extremes of this rhythm are obvious. Because today man increasingly but unconsciously passes the threshold of the spiritual world, he loses the natural-neutral balance and therefore healthy middle state of normal earthly consciousness and is pulled, according to his constitution, in one direction or the other, or in both. This means that a growing ahrimanic-luciferic possession is experienced in the so-called 'normal' or 'usual' daily intercourse of people in the social life of our time. A balanced and healthy, rhythmical equilibrium in human meetings will be possible in the future only when a conscious imaginative perception of this rhythm is developed out of the gradually emerging Christ consciousness of humanity, through which the interest of people for one another will be strengthened to such a degree that the Christ Himself can be seen as the active spirit of balance bearing the destiny-cross of every human encounter. Rudolf Steiner described the conditions for this vision as follows: 'You may look at such a sculptural form as that of our Group: the Representative of Humanity, Lucifer and Ahriman. There you confront for the first time what works in the whole man, for man is the state of balance between the luciferic and ahrimanic. If you permeate yourself in actual life with the impulse to confront every human being in such a way that you see this trinity in him, that you see it concretely in him, then do you begin to understand him ... in the intercourse of man with man we have nothing but a bundle of abstract concepts. This is the essential element which has entered into humanity out of the Old Testament form of life: ''Make unto thyself no image'', and which must inevitably lead in a pre-eminent degree to antisocial life if we should continue it further. What radiates outwards from the innermost nature of man, striving towards realization, is that when one human being confronts another a picture will stream forth in a certain way from the other person, *a picture of that special form of balance* manifested individually in every human being ... This capacity to be mystically stimulated in a certain way as we confront the other person will come to realization.' (GA 186, lecture of 7 December 1918.) In a later lecture of the same cycle (12 December 1918), Rudolf Steiner described this capacity as the ability '... to let other human beings be resurrected in one's soul ... This capacity to develop imaginative forces through other human beings.' (And compare also the lectures of 30 January 1921 [GA 203] and of 28 November 1911 [GA 194].)

10 GA 293, lecture of 28 August 1919. This rapid oscillation between the unconscious, sleeping blood-will process and the self-conscious, awakened brain-thinking process was described in detail in the study of the knowledge drama of the Second Coming in Chapter 5 (see, for example, the references given in Note 133 of that chapter). The same spiritually saturated imaginative faculty, developed through this knowledge drama, will serve us here in the further investigation of the supersensible aspects of human encounters.

A penetrating philosophical investigation of the meaning of human encounters and the activity of the ego-sense is to be found in Jean-Paul Sartre's book *L'Etre et le Néant* ('Being and Nothingness'), from which we can give here only a small, fragmentary example: 'First, the *Other's look* as the necessary condition of my objectivity is the destruction of all objectivity for me. The Other's look touches me across the world and is not only a transformation of myself but a total metamorphosis of the *world*. I am looked at in a world which is looked at. In particular the Other's look, which is a look looking and not a look looked at, denies my distances from objects and unfolds its own distances. This look of the Other is given immediately as that by which distance comes to the world at the heart of a presence without distance. ... In other words, in so far as I experience myself as looked at there is realized for me a trans-mundane presence of the Other. The Other looks at me not as he is "in the midst of" *my* world but as he comes towards the world and towards me from all his transcendence; when he looks at me, he is separated from me by no distance, by no object of the world — whether real or ideal — by no body in the world, but by the sole fact of his nature as Other. Thus the appearance of the Other's look is not an appearance *in the world* — neither in "mine" nor in the "Other's" — and the relation that unites me to the Other cannot be a relation of exteriority inside the world. By the Other's look I effect the concrete proof that there is a "beyond the world". ... such is the Other's look when first I experience it as a look.' (Jean-Paul Sartre, *Being and Nothingness, An Essay on Phenomenological Ontology*, NY, Philosophical Library, 1956.)

11 'But while in ideation man becomes free from the cosmos, in his unconscious life of soul he is still organically connected with his former earthly
lives and his lives between death and a new birth ... He experiences freedom in his *present* ego, while his past ego preserves him in the element of
real being. We are here pointing to the abyss of nothingness in human
evolution which man must cross when he becomes a free being. It is the
working of Michael and the Christ-impulse which makes it possible for him
to leap across the gulf' (GA 26, January 1925). This abyss is, therefore, also
the abyss of karmic disconnectedness, forgetfulness and disorder, which
must be bridged today in the human meeting itself. This is, again, one of the
deepest tasks of Anthroposophy: 'It would almost shatter one to pieces if
one held oneself entirely upright with the true sense of the cosmic intelligence, face to face with such overpowering relationships. It is a thing of
untold significance that has already happened and is happening more and
more. The Angel of the one human soul who was karmically connected with
another human soul did not go on with the Angel of that other soul. The one
Angel of the two karmically connected human souls remained with Michael
while the other went down to Earth ... Thus we may say: what is it in the last
resort that unites the members of the Anthroposophical Society? It is that
they are to bring order again into their karma. This unites them ... This is the
cosmic ray that pours through the anthroposophical movement, clearly
perceptible to him who knows. It is the restoration of the truth in karma.'
(GA 237, lecture of 8 August 1924.)

12 This is the situation that was repeatedly described by Rudolf Steiner in his
lectures on the esoteric aspects of the social question: if the forces of blood
relationships, which are now rightly dwindling, are not replaced by conscious human *Wahlverwandschaft* (affinity), then what results is a mutual
lack of interest, the bypassing and ignoring of human beings by each other.
Formerly, in ancient cultural epochs (for example, under the leadership of
the Moon god Jehovah), human beings were instinctively related and
therefore 'interested' in one another. But this interest was preserved only for
the members of the family, tribe or nation, in the veins of which flowed the
same blood. And it was, therefore, not an individualized interest but a

group interest—that is, man felt himself attracted to the other person because in the other he felt his collective self, i.e. his own blood element, while those who belonged to other blood communities were very often not even considered as human beings at all. But modern man has internalized the group-egoism, which used to be mitigated through religious and social commandments, and made it an unlimited personal egoism. And on the other hand the separative element that once prevailed mainly between tribes and nations has been universalized, making it a general non-relation to every other human being. (GA 186, lectures of 7 and 21 December 1918.)

13 '... really for the first time in this [modern] age one human self stands in a soul relation to another human self—I would say—uncovered [hüllenlos]' (GA 217, lecture of 14 October 1922).

14 'We have to meet the human being so that we shall feel him as the world riddle itself, as a living world riddle.' (GA 217, lecture of 8 August 1922.)

15 GA 207, lecture of 30 September 1921.

16 This physiognomy is the expression of the fact that the soul is always unconsciously 'judged' (i.e. formed) according to its true moral value in the cosmos by its own higher self. (See GA 207, lecture of 12 November 1921, out of which the quotation in Note 185 to Chapter 5 is taken.)

17 This is the picture of the self as an offering of itself (see the reference in Note 16, above), in which the impulse is contained for the unfoldment of conscience in daily life. In the imaginative experience of the human encounter, however, the unfoldment of conscience must be consciously carried through. (Rudolf Steiner speaks about the threefold time-configuration of man, externalized before the imaginative gaze, in the lecture of 23 July 1918 [GA 181]).

18 Here we have the motivating power for the rapid hiding of the truth from oneself through awakening back in the physical world. Man does not at all like what he sees! His *shame* drives him to conceal himself from himself in the physical body, and his *fear* leads him to attack what he considers to be the source of his trouble in the other human being. Therefore he hurriedly and aggressively plunges with a feeling of release into his body, seeking to devour the other, to whom, so he all too clearly knows now, he owes so much karmic adjustment. (Of course, the full outworking of the results of ordinary encounters can only be *suppressed* in waking daily life, not cancelled; in the night the whole process of objective moral evaluation takes place as a preparation for the karma built up during the life between the next death and rebirth. And yet, we must carefully note that the times are rapidly changing, and more and more it will be the case that this 'night work'—the unconscious development of conscience and moral-karmic adjustment—will have to be practised during wakeful, imaginative earthly life, and that the work during sleep will be increasingly dependent on the imaginative day process. If the latter did not happen, then the true unconscious night process would gradually cease and an increasing ahrimanic-luciferic possession of the process of karma regulation would take its place.) These truths belong together with the crossing of the threshold and the developing of the new imaginative faculties that enable man to share in the new role of the Christ as the regulator of human karma, as will be described

below. (About Christ as the new lord of karma and about the developing of karmic moral sight into the past and future out of the spiritualized force of conscience, see, for example, GA 130, lecture of 2 December 1911: 'The judgement begins from our twentieth century on, that is, the ordering of karma'; that is, the self-judgement and self-offering of the usually unconscious night process is raised through the Christ into the daily imaginative consciousness and moral responsibility of man. And see further GA 116, lecture of 8 May 1910, GA 143, lecture of 3 February 1912 on the metamorphosis of conscience to conscious karmic sight of the future results of one's deeds, and GA 131, lecture of 14 October 1911 where there is a conclusive summary and deepening of the different elements mentioned here.)

19 Here we may have, to begin with, only a *general* moral guidance in relation to the other, which distinguishes itself, however, from the ordinary voice of conscience not only in its intensity but in the much higher degree of self-consciousness and self-knowledge. The moral social responsibility awakened is specific, and points towards a *concrete* personality or connection of events; it stands, therefore, between the usual conscience, which speaks from the completely unconscious night process, and the new, fully developed imaginative perception of the forces that form and transform this conscience into an independent and consciously grasped *being* of moral-karmic reality.

20 Thus the supersensible reality of the meeting with the other is archetypally given in the occult meeting of the lower and higher selves of man, described in the biblical story of Cain and Abel. The process as a whole is described by Rudolf Steiner as follows: 'We have the feeling of a Self that dwells within us when we look downwards [into one's own abyss, from which the moral form of one's karmic obligation to the other springs forth], and we have this terrible impression: a determination is slowly maturing within you, a dreadful resolve, to kill the other who is superior to yourself ... And now we hear again the voice that previously had inspired him, but now it is like a voice fraught with dire revenge and asks: "Where is thy brother?" ... Previously, the Inspiration was as follows: "Because you have united yourself with the beneficent powers of the other being you will pour your beneficent powers Earthwards, and I will make you guardian of the other being [on the Earth]." Now from this being, which one recognizes as one's Self, comes the retort: "I will not be my brother's keeper."' (GA 145, lecture of 27 March 1913.) This is the social reciprocal crucifixion of oneself in and through the other, and of the other in and through oneself, which is the usual form of the human encounter seen from beyond the threshold.

21 See John 21: 15–17. That such a temptation should not be taken by the student of anthroposophical spiritual science in a theoretical sense, believing it to be something that can be easily solved and done away with, has been pointed out through the whole way of presentation of the problem of evil in Chapters 4 and 5. It is, after all, a spiritual scientific fact of human evolution that the problem of evil in man is today only in its first stages of inner formation, and therefore cannot be completely externalized and satisfactorily penetrated with pure spiritual Intuition. That is: 'Evil will be developed in the inner life of man in the fifth post-Atlantean epoch, and

must stream out and be experienced externally in the sixth [post-Atlantean] epoch ...' (GA 185, lecture of 25 October 1918; and see also GA 271, lecture of 3 November 1917.) But does this mean that the man who finds himself inwardly deeply confronted with this problem today must give up his further anthroposophical efforts in this direction and lose the comforting and hope-sustaining power of spiritual endurance and far-seeing evolutionary perspective? It seems that this was *one* cliff on which the—in many respects strong and beautiful—anthroposophical ship of Valentin Tomberg disastrously foundered: 'There must be no Intuition of evil. For Intuition becomes Identification and Identification Communion ... One can only intuitively grasp what one loves ... But one cannot love Evil. Evil is *unknowable in its essential nature.*' (In Thomas Meyer, *The Bodhisattva Question*, Temple Lodge Publishing, 1993, p.89.) In these words of Tomberg we find a tragic denial of the deeper being of Christ, and the meaning of His five great sacrifices in human evolution up to the twentieth century. (Precisely the present, second Mystery of Golgotha reveals the Christ as the source of the true Manichaean impulse, in which *essentially*—though its human fulfilment in the course of time is still far in the future—the knowledge of evil and the secret of its redemption is livingly demonstrated, as described in the above-mentioned book *The Spiritual Event of the Twentieth Century*; and see Note 173 to Chapter 5.)

22 Until now, but in a rapidly diminishing way, the aggressive incarnation in the physical and etheric bodies protected man from this elemental hatred and destructive drive. But as humanity increasingly advances unconsciously across the threshold, a proper, instinctively balanced incarnation becomes more and more impossible, so that this protection gives way and those forces that were until now rightfully suppressed break into physical life. (Also the forces generated by man in his science and technology, which are as Rudolf Steiner pointed out [GA 145] the weakened and sublimated destructive forces of Cain, are becoming in the twentieth century rapidly uncontrollable and openly show on the physical plane their true evil nature.)

23 'If, because of incorrect spiritual training a person was to enter upon this experience unprepared [and, to some extent, at the end of the twentieth century, many unconscious crossings of the threshold belong to this category], then, in the encounter with the Greater Guardian of the Threshold, something would pour into his soul that can only be compared to a "feeling of immeasurable horror", of "boundless fear".' (GA 13, 'Knowledge of the Higher Worlds [Concerning Initiation]'.)

24 This is, therefore, another related aspect of the situation of humanity as a whole—and of anthroposophists—before the Guardian of the Threshold, described by Rudolf Steiner in the lecture of 1 January 1924 (GA 233).

25 This fact must today be openly admitted and described, if man wishes to be awakened through the truth to free, truly human social life: 'This means: the Christ is crucified and is further crucified in human deeds. The crucifixion is not a mere single deed; the crucifixion is a continuous deed. So long as we do not expel the demons through what lives in our soul by changing external mechanical actions into holy actions, we will continue to crucify Christ.' (GA 172, lecture of 27 November 1916.)

26 GA 123, lecture of 11 September 1910, and see below. About the 'atmosphere of trust' that must become the heart-blood of social life in the future, and the bitter experience of mistrust, see GA 217, lecture of 8 October 1922.

27 GA 257, lectures of 27 February and 3 March 1923.

28 The modern Christ experience reveals, when experienced not only individually but *between* people, the inner work of the Christ in his role as the new lord of karma, which strives to transform the karma of the individual in such a way that the greatest good will result for the whole, that is, for the social body or karmic group of the individuals concerned (see Note 19, above). This important aspect of the new Christ experience was described by Rudolf Steiner as follows: '... sometimes, when people sit together without knowing what to do, and also when greater numbers of human beings are sitting together and waiting, then they shall see the etheric Christ! There He will be Himself, will give counsel, will throw His word into such gatherings. We are surely advancing to such times.' (GA 130, lecture of 1 October 1911.)

29 This weaving of the common web of destiny is, at the same time, the substance of Christ's new etheric body, created out of human love: '... the forces streaming from man to man are the units integrating the etheric body of Christ ...' (GA 133, lecture of 14 May 1912.) As was indicated in Chapter 6, this is the sensing, harmonizing middle organ, the social heart-and-lung system (whose blood and air are true human love and true human relationships), of the earthly-human Sun.

30 Chapter 4, pp.58–59.

31 Op cit. p.59.

32 About this comparison experience between the lower and higher self, see Note 177 to Chapter 5.

33 This 'I archetype' can also be compared to the child's inherited physical body model (GA 311, lecture of 12 August 1924). Here it is the Christ-child just born that receives his 'I' archetype through the appearance, words and acts of the Christ, in order to create around it its own future spirit 'I' identity. That the higher self, when first externalized in the supersensible experience out of the lower self, is a real spirit-child is described by Rudolf Steiner as follows: 'It must be remembered that the "higher self", which existed in man as an embryo in a sleeping, unconscious state, is now born into conscious existence. It is not just a phrase, a picture, when we speak about a birth; it is a real *birth* in the spirit world.' (GA 10, chapter 'Some Effects of Initiation'.) Further, Rudolf Steiner says that the healthy and energetic development of the cognitive and moral forces *on the physical plane* supplies the new-born being with the necessary spirit-organs for its conscious life in the spiritual worlds. As we saw above, Christ's appearance, words and acts are taking place not only in the greatest harmony with such a development but, what is more, the Christ *demonstrates* the actual practical use and value of these qualities in supersensible experience; and this demonstration is the spirit archetype of right 'I'-beingness in supersensible reality.

34 With the term 'moral form' we mean here the self-judgement of the astral body (through the Life Spirit) and the self-offering of the ego (through Spirit Man), described in Chapter 5 (and see Note 185 there).

35 In this rhythmical dance of the human encounter, the one excarnates while retaining self-consciousness in his sleep and the other incarnates and retains the spirit-memory of the etheric body when awakening in physical reality, and vice versa. The one above is the higher self, the brother; the one below is the lower self, his brother's keeper on the Earth. So both sides experience in their turn the drama of mutual temptation, betrayal and overcoming, described above in the case of the single person and his betrayal of his — and the other's — higher self. The excarnating partner (the awakened sleeper) can receive the strongest ego Intuitions of the common karmic goals and duties of this concrete relationship, while the incarnating partner (the sleep inducer) perceives in etheric imaginative pictures the past causes of the karma involved. When these first gentle and delicate spiritual intimations are individually developed further by the persons concerned, according to the meditative indication given by Rudolf Steiner in the lecture of 9 May 1924 (GA 236), a mutual spiritualization takes place between the modern Christ experience, with the new supersensible faculties that it offers to man, and the fully self-conscious and self-regulated karma practice in the spirit of the new Michael Age.

36 Gradually man learns to feel the reality of this mutually created 'third being', which is present in every human encounter, as a helping, warning, spiritually embodied and ensouled being of conscience, through whose word-gestures and physiognomy the partners in the meeting can learn instantaneously to experience the moral value of their *present* deeds and therefore direct their earthly relationships in accord with the true moral form of their destiny — that is, begin practically to transfer the unconscious moral night work into incarnated earthly life. This mutual moral-karmic Christ-permeated being is the hidden source of the new, prophetic karmic vision that will more and more develop in humanity during the next three thousand years as the metamorphosed force of conscience, described by Rudolf Steiner.

37 One of the greatest mysteries of the Guardian is his extremely complicated and multi-faceted *time-formation and complexion*, i.e. his overall etheric gesture, of facial formation and expression. His *seeming* aggressiveness (first when he blocks one's way of entrance and then, later, when he wishes to be man's *only* guide and master in the astral world) should not be used as an abstract, general characteristic of his being, and neither should his frightful imaginative appearance. He is a speaking, teaching being whose most fundamental life and soul element is morally motivated. He strives — most of the time he must patiently fight man's own resistance — to be *timely*; he is always seen fighting to be 'on time', to fulfil his mission at the right time in man's destiny — that is, to mould himself and externalize the aspect of man's lower nature that will be the exact karmic counterpart of the present daily moral content of man's being and action. And because man is, as we saw above (Note 11), completely outside his karmic reality in his awakened daily modern self-consciousness, it obliges the Guardian — and this becomes ever more difficult for him the more man remains unconscious beyond the threshold — to keep him 'in touch' with his true karmic-moral form, *in order not to let his conscience die entirely* in his earthly life. But in the twentieth century the first signs of the losing of the Guardian's control (and the

235

resulting death of human conscience) are more and more apparent; and this has to do also with the tragic disorder of karma mentioned above (Note 11). In the human encounter discussed here it shows itself in his increasing difficulty — this is seen as soon as the meeting is raised to the imaginative level — in co-ordinating the times rightly: to hold together the karmic pasts (that must be brought continually to expression in the physiognomy of the Lower Guardian), in accordance with the presently living time flow, with physical happenings between human beings. In other words this means that today it is not at all rare to experience that, when human beings meet each other on the Earth, behind them appears not the *relevant* past karmic counterpart but another, non-relevant karmic moral aspect that creates a tremendous moral havoc in the *present* meeting. And the Guardian then appears to be helpless, *disconnected from his rightful stream of time*. And this causes him to assume — in his anxiety — the most evil and destructive form in the face of man's continuous sleep beyond the threshold. Only when we bear all this in mind can we begin to comprehend some of the inner aspects involved in the fact that Christ assumes today the role of the regulator of human karma, and this helps us to orient ourselves towards the only source of hope in these matters: to the *future karmic time-stream*, which is the power flowing directly from Christ's Life Spirit through His etheric body. This stream enables man to act out of his moral freedom in the *present* in such a way that, in the *future*, that which he did wrongly because of the disordered *past* karma will be put in order again, on a much higher level. (About the Christ as the always-living cosmic present on the Earth and as the 're-timer' of earthly and human evolution, see Chapter 1.)

38 We can begin to see here the practical, social realization of the Cain and Abel legend and the motif of *The Temple Legend* of Cain and Abel's reunion and mutual healing and redemption through Christ as the first, still clearly rudimentary and humble but yet most important *exoteric* practice of that which was regarded, up to our time, as the esoteric core of Rosicrucianism. It belongs to the increasingly stronger exoteric influence of the etheric body of Christian Rosenkreutz (GA 130, lecture of 27 September 1911), which makes possible in our time the modern Christ experience and the new soul faculties related to it. This is, streaming from the same source, also the first rudiments of the 'kingly art' of the future, described by Rudolf Steiner as follows: 'For the great evil existing in the world today, the tremendous misery that expresses itself with such frightful force in what is called the social question, can no longer be controlled by the inanimate. A royal art is needed for that; and it is this royal art which was inaugurated in the symbol of the Holy Grail. Through this royal art, man must acquire control of something similar to the force that sprouts in the plant, the same force that the occultist uses when he accelerates the growth of a plant in front of him. In a similar way, a part of this force must be used for social healing ... the royal art will in the future be a social art.' (GA 93, lecture of 2 January 1906.) The germinal power which will be used by the 'social magicians' of the future in the work of social healing is none other than the future life-stream of Christ's Life Spirit, in which the deepest absorption and healing of evil is *always* taking place.

39 GA 123, lecture of 11 September 1910.

40 In this experience we find the first conscious seed of that karmic will of sacrifice that must from now on penetrate more and more into human hearts through the power of Michael-Christ, which works in the strengthened moral fiery atmosphere of the new earthly-human Sun. Rudolf Steiner described this future will of karmic sacrifice as the ability that human beings will have, before birth, to take over another human body, exchanging their karma with the other's (see the lecture of 19 November 1922 GA 218). Rudolf Steiner further said that this sacrificial act before birth is in itself a preparation for the much greater act of sacrifice – which he calls the 'white magic' of the future (in the sixth great epoch) – that will come about through the moral ability of human beings to exchange their bodies *in full earthly consciousness* with the body of another human being. The consciously transformed human encounter described here can be seen, therefore, as a first Manichaean seed for the development of much stronger moral social forces of the future.

41 GA 218, lecture of 18 November 1922.

42 This is the true spirit essence of the future, world-transparent and world-enlivening Anthroposophical Society, 'Community above us, Christ in us', that Rudolf Steiner described in the lecture of 15 June 1915 (GA 160/159).

43 About this communal crossing of the threshold and the fully conscious unity of earthly anthroposophical work with the supersensible being of Anthroposophy through the spiritual work of anthroposophists, see Rudolf Steiner's lecture of 3 March 1923 (GA 257).

44 'The most divergent, the most opposite conceptions work together in the world, weaving a living whole' (GA 237, lecture of 13 August 1924).

45 The ability to experience and understand the inner, Christ-permeated speaking of the new Earth (which, at the time of the birth of Jesus, was the unique earthly spirit faculty of the shepherds), together with the speaking of the stellar script of the new Heaven (which was then understood only through the cosmic eastern wisdom of the Magi kings), can only be developed through the true anthroposophical development of the social sphere. In the fully conscious and individualized heart organ created in anthroposophical social life, the two streams can meet, blend and grasp each other today in every human soul. In the lecture of 25 December 1920 (GA 202), Rudolf Steiner describes how in the past this was only possible for the unique spiritual development of the old Hebrew prophets. By means of their special, inherited constitution, they could bring about a mutual fertilization of the forces of the pre-earthly (past) and post-earthly (future) life-streams of the kings and shepherds respectively, and so develop those faculties of prophecy of the coming Christ event in its fullness. So we find, for example, especially in the prophecies of Isaiah, not only an exact description – one could almost say a face to face encounter – of the *personal*, human aspect of Christ Jesus (Isaiah 53) but also a clear perception of the future *planetary-cosmic* apocalyptic transformation of the Earth into a new Heaven and Earth (Isaiah 65:17). Two further aspects of this special prophetic power can be briefly mentioned here. The first has to do with the specific nature of the work of the servants of Jehovah, the Elohim: 'You see

237

how the Elohim stand in the middle. The Elohim would like to connect the beginning with the end [of the evolution of the Earth].' (GA 203, lecture of 11 March 1921.) The second aspect belongs to the special future orientation of the heart organism in the middle system of the human being, where, as was already shown in detail in Chapter 5, the time-streams of past and future, life and death are transformed, and the Christed time-stream is born: '... when you look into the inwardness of your heart, you would see what you will strive for in your next life'. (GA 205, lecture of 2 July 1921.)

List of Works by Rudolf Steiner Referred to in the Present Book

The English title is given only in cases where a similar (though not always identical) volume to the original German edition from the collected works—the *Gesamtausgabe* (abbreviated as 'GA')—has been published in English translation. In many cases, lectures are available in typescript or in print as single lectures or compilations from the collected works. For information on these contact Rudolf Steiner House Library, 35 Park Road, London NW1 6XT, or similar anthroposophical libraries around the world.

Publishers:

AP: Anthroposophic Press (New York)
APC: Anthroposophical Publishing Company (London)
GAR: Garber Communications, Inc. (New York). Imprint: Spiritual Science Library
MER: Mercury Press (Spring Valley, New York)
RSP: Rudolf Steiner Press (Sussex)

GA

1	*Goethean Science* (MER, 1988)
1a–e	*J.W. Goethe: Naturwissenschaftliche Schriften*
2	*The Science of Knowing* (MER, 1988)
3	*Truth and Knowledge* (Steiner Books, Blauvelt, 1981)
4	*The Philosophy of Freedom* (RSP, 1988)
6	*Goethe's World View* (MER, 1985)
7	*Mysticism at the Dawn of the Modern Age* (GAR, 1980)
8	*Christianity as Mystical Fact* (RSP, 1972)
9	*Theosophy* (RSP, 1989)
10	*Knowledge of the Higher Worlds* (RSP, 1989)
12	*The Stages of Higher Knowledge* (AP, 1990)
13	*Occult Science* (RSP, 1962)
14	*The Four Mystery Plays* (RSP, 1983)
15	*The Spiritual Guidance of Humanity* (AP, 1992)
16	*A Road to Self-knowledge* (RSP, 1975)
17	*The Threshold of the Spiritual World* (RSP, 1975)
18	*The Riddles of Philosophy* (AP, 1973)
20	*The Riddle of Man* (MER, 1990)
21	*Von Seelenrätseln.* Some articles appear in *The Case for Anthroposophy* (RSP, 1970)
22	*Goethe's Standard of the Soul* (APC, 1925)
25	*Cosmology, Religion and Philosophy* (RSPCo., no date)
26	*Anthroposophical Leading Thoughts* (RSP, 1985)
35	*Philosophie und Anthroposophie*
36	*Der Goetheanumgedanke inmetten der Kulturkrisis der Gegenwart*
39	*Brief Band II: 1890–1925*
40	*Wahrspruchworte*

127   *Die Mission der neuen Geistoffenbarung. Das Christus-Ereignis als Mittel-punktsgeschehen der Erdenevolution*

128   *Occult Physiology* (RSP, 1983)

129   *Wonders of the World, Ordeals of the Soul, Revelations of the Spirit* (RSP, 1983)

130   *Das esoterische Christentum und die geistige Führung der Menschheit.* Some lectures appear in *Esoteric Christianity and the Mission of Christian Rosenkreutz* (RSP, 1984)

131   *From Jesus to Christ* (RSP, 1991)

132   *The Inner Realities of Evolution* (RSP, 1953)

133   *Earthly and Cosmic Man* (GAR, 1986)

134   *The World of the Senses and the World of the Spirit* (Steiner Book Centre, N. Vancouver, 1979)

136   *The Spiritual Beings in the Heavenly Bodies and in the Kingdoms of Nature* (AP, 1992)

137   *Man in the Light of Occultism, Theosophy and Philosophy* (GAR, 1989)

141   *Between Death and Rebirth* (RSP, 1975)

142   *The Bhagavad Gita and the Epistles of St Paul* (AP, 1971)

143   *Erfahrungen des übersinnlichen. Die Wege der Seele zu Christus*

144   *The Mystery of the East and of Christianity* (RSP, 1972)

145   *The Effects of Spiritual Development* (RSP, 1978)

146   *The Occult Significance of the Bhagavad Gita* (AP, 1968)

147   *Secrets of the Threshold* (AP, 1987)

148   *Aus der Akasha-Forschung. Das Fünfte Evangelium.* Some lectures appear in *The Fifth Gospel* (RSP, 1985)

149   *Christ and the Spiritual World and the Search for the Holy Grail* (RSP, 1963)

150   *Die Welt des Geistes und ihr Hereinragen in das physische Dasein*

151   *Human and Cosmic Thought* (RSP, 1967)

152   *Vorstufen zum Mysterium von Golgotha*

153   *The Inner Nature of Man and the Life Between Death and Rebirth* (APC, 1959)

154   *The Presence of the Dead on the Spiritual Path* (AP, 1990)

155   *Christus und die menschliche Seele*

156   *Occult Reading and Occult Hearing* (RSP, 1975)

157   *The Destinies of Individuals and of Nations* (RSP, 1987)

157a   *The Forming of Destiny and Life After Death* (APCo., 1927)

158   *Der Zusammenhang des Menschen mit der elementarischen Welt*

159/160 *Die Geheimnis des Todes. Wesen und Bedeutung Mitteleuropas und die europäischen Volksgeister*

161   *Wege der geistigen Erkenntnis und der Erneuerung künstlerischer Wel-tanschauung*

162   *Kunst und Lebensfragen im Lichte der Geisteswissenschaft*

163   *Chance, Providence, Necessity* (AP/RSP, 1988)

164   *Der wert des Denkens für eine den Menschen befriedigende Erkenntnis*

165   *Die geistige Vereinigung der Menschheit durch den Christus-Impuls.* Some lectures appear in *The Christmas Thought and the Mystery of the Ego* (MER, 1986)

168   *Die Verbindung zwischen Lebenden und Toten*

169   *Towards Imagination* (AP, 1990)

243

264   *Zur Geschichte und aus den Inhalten der ersten Abteilung der Esoterischen Schule von 1904 bis 1914*

265   *Zur Geschichte und aus den inhalten der erkenntniskultischen Abteilung der Esoterischen Schule von 1904 bis 1914*

271   *Kunst und Kunsterkenntnis*

272   *Geisteswissenschaftliche Erläuterungen zu Goethes 'Faust', Band I*

273   *Geisteswissenschaftliche Erläuterungen zu Goethes 'Faust', Band II*

275   *Kunst im Lichte der Mysterienweisheit.* Some lectures appear in *Art as seen in the Light of Mystery Wisdom* (RSP, 1984)

284   *Bilder okkulter Siegel und Säulen*

291a   *Farbenerkenntnis*

293   *Study of Man* (RSP, 1990)

295   *Discussions with Teachers* (RSP, 1983)

302a   *Erziehung und Unterricht aus Menschenerkenntnis.* Some lectures appear in *Balance in Teaching* (MER, 1982)

311   *The Kingdom of Childhood* (RSP, 1974)

312   *Spiritual Science and Medicine* (RSP, 1975)

316   *Meditative Betrachtungen und Anleitungen zur Vertiefung der Heilkunst*

317   *Curative Education* (RSP, 1972)

318   *Pastoral Medicine* (AP, 1987)

320   *First Scientific Course: Light* (Steiner Schools Fellowship, 1977)

321   *Warmth Course (Second Scientific Lecture Course)* (MER, 1988)

322   *Boundaries of Natural Science* (AP, 1983)

323   *The Relationship of the Diverse Branches of Natural Science to Astronomy* (Rudolf Steiner Research Foundation, no date)

324   *Naturbeobachtung, Experiment, Mathematik und die Erkenntnisstufen der Geistesforschung*

325   *Die Naturwissenschaft und die weltgeschichtliche Entwickelung der Menschheit seit dem Altertum*

326   *The Origins of Natural Science* (AP, 1985)

327   *Agriculture* (B.D. Farming & Gardening Assoc. Inc., Kimberton, 1993)

333   *Gedankenfreiheit und soziale Kräfte*

334   *Spiritual Approach to Social Issues* (AP, 1992)

347   *The Human Being in Body, Soul and Spirit* (AP/RSP, 1989)